D1556421

From St. Vith
to Victory

*For Wing Commander Don Saville DSO DFC and crew and
all those who served with 218 (Gold Coast) Squadron.*

Also Jill, for showing me what bravery really is.

From St. Vith to Victory

218 (Gold Coast) Squadron and the Campaign Against Nazi Germany

Stephen C. Smith

Pen & Sword
AVIATION

First published in Great Britain in 2015 by
Pen & Sword Aviation
an imprint of
Pen & Sword Books Ltd
47 Church Street
Barnsley
South Yorkshire
S70 2AS

ISBN 978 1 47383 505 4

Typeset in Ehrhardt by
Mac Style Ltd, Bridlington, East Yorkshire
Printed and bound in the UK by CPI Group (UK) Ltd,
Croydon, CRO 4YY

Pen & Sword Books Ltd incorporates the imprints of Pen & Sword
Archaeology, Atlas, Aviation, Battleground, Discovery, Family History,
History, Maritime, Military, Naval, Politics, Railways, Select, Transport,
True Crime, and Fiction, Frontline Books, Leo Cooper, Praetorian Press,
Seaforth Publishing and Wharncliffe.

For a complete list of Pen & Sword titles please contact
PEN & SWORD BOOKS LIMITED
47 Church Street, Barnsley, South Yorkshire, S70 2AS, England
E-mail: enquiries@pen-and-sword.co.uk
Website: www.pen-and-sword.co.uk

Contents

Acknowledgements

This book owes its existence to the men and women who served with 218 (Gold Coast) Squadron, who over the years provided me with a great deal of information. It was also made possible by the enthusiastic support of a number of individuals some of whom have, sadly, passed away in the recent years.

I would like to acknowledge in particular the help of Margery Griffiths, Secretary of the 218 (Gold Coast) Squadron Association, Squadron Leader Geoff Rothwell DFC & Bar and my good friend and Bomber Command historian Chris Ward. I would also like to thank the following for their unstinting assistance and support. If I have omitted anyone I do apologize.

Dr Theo Boiton, Errol Martin, Kelvin Youngs, David Duxbury, Greg Harrison, Joss Leclercq, Andy Bullock, Thomas Cocker, Hans Nauta, John William, Martin Bowman, Pavel Vancata, Max Lambert, Sara O,Brien, Richard Perry, Richard Allardyce, Andrea Birkett, Bob Collis, Bod Boby, John Tales, Linzee Druce, Soren Flensted, Ron Hiles, John Reid, Rod MacKenzie, S/Ldr Ian Ryall DFC & bar, Don Moore, Harry Fisher, Johnnie Wortley, S/Ldr Jell DFC, the family of S/Ldr John Overton DFC, Roger Smith, Melinda Evans, Steve Furst, Bernard Ives, Richard & Patricia Purves, Ron Warburton, Hugh Haliday, Frank Haslam, Jock Whitehouse, Nigel Wright, S/Ldr Phil Brentnall DFC and family, Dave Richardson, Ian Connell, John Marsh, Paula McDermott, Michiels Vanhorensbeek, Stephen Saville, Nick Price, Volker Krappen and Alan Fraser.

I would also like to thank Peter Elliott, head of archives at the RAF Museum Hendon.

Foreword

By Squadron Leader Geoff Rothwell DFC & Bar, Order of Leopold II & Palme, Croix de Guerre 1940 & Palme

Aviation history requires authentic recording of events continually, particularly those which occur in wartime and Stephen Smith is to be complimented on compiling a book which achieves this. Through exhaustive, meticulous research and interviewing survivors, many of the hair-raising incidents which took place in 218 (Gold Coast) Squadron during the 1939–1945 World War II are described in great detail.

Plagued by unpreparedness and inadequate equipment in the early days 218 became one of Bomber Command's most effective squadrons having been equipped with a succession of aircraft from Fairey Battles, Bristol Blenheims, Vickers Wellingtons and Short Stirlings to the most successful famous Avro Lancasters.

The movements of the squadron to numerous bases are covered along with the reporting of the operations in which the squadron took part. These lead us, month by month, throughout the war and in some cases the reports are in the actual words of those who were engaged in the sorties. This adds to the authenticity of the narrative.

The impressive list of decorations, including a Victoria Cross to Flight Sgt Arthur Louis Aaron DFM, the horrific circumstances of which are described in full, a list of Commanding Officers, aircraft details, etc., pay tribute to the intensive research undertaken by the author into the hazardous operations of the flying crews. The detailed reporting brings home to the reader the enormous workload which was carried out by the personnel in Bomber Command squadrons. The skill which operations demanded is highlighted by the special sorties which were undertaken in the opening of the Second Front in 1944. The fortunes and misfortunes of 218 Squadron are well-written making this book a welcome addition to the literature of the air war in WWII and determining it as an essential to all aviation libraries.

G.M. Rothwell
Murrays Bay, Auckland, New Zealand. April 2014

Preface

Only a handful of squadrons serving within RAF Bomber Command can claim an existence as diverse as that of 218 Squadron during the course of the bombing offensive of WWII. The squadron's activities cover almost every facet of Bomber Command operations from the "Phoney" war of 1939 to the massed attacks on Germany's industry, communications and oil during the final two years. In between came the bloody annihilation of the Advanced Air Striking Force during the French campaign of May 1940 and the suicidal daylight operations with 2 Group while the Battle of Britain raged overhead. Transferred to 3 Group in 1941 it entered the strategic bombing war, serving on Wellingtons and later Stirlings, until the latter type's vulnerability to enemy defenses saw it withdrawn from main force operations. By then 218 Squadron had been adopted by the Government and peoples of the Gold Coast, but in the United Kingdom it was known as "Weston-super-Mare's Own." The squadron's battle honors include the Thousand Bomber raids in the summer of 1942, the campaigns against the U-Boat bases along the Atlantic Coast, the 1943 Ruhr offensive, Operation Gomorrah against Hamburg and the summer attacks on Berlin. It also participated in the raids on Italy and the attack on the V1 Rocket research and construction site at Peenemünde.

The inadequacies of the Short Stirling removed the squadron from the front line for the winter campaign of 1943/44, which included the ineffective sixteen-raid series against Berlin. However, 218 Squadron did not stand idle, committing extra effort instead to mining operations and selective raids on key industrial and transportation targets in France and Belgium. It also played its part in the secret war, by supplementing the efforts of the "moon" squadrons at Tempsford in their SOE and SIS operations to deliver arms and equipment to the resistance organizations in the occupied countries, and to drop agents. On D–Day Eve two squadrons carried out meticulously planned and executed spoof operations to deceive the enemy concerning the true location of the landings. One of the squadrons was 617, the other was 218 Squadron, and history can confirm the success of these unsung but vital contributions to the successes on that monumental day. The squadron was chosen to re-introduce the G-H blind bombing aid in early 1944, and its success with the device led to it marking some important targets for 3 Group. When the second Ruhr campaign began in October 1944, the success of G-H in 218 Squadron hands enabled 3 Group, when required, to operate independently of the main force and Pathfinders.

Away from the battles over Germany, the squadron's ground crews were also active. Few are aware that they were instrumental in resolving a serious problem with the Mk XIV bombsight, the equipment employed by all front-line units. The squadron took great pride in the posthumously awarded VICTORIA CROSS earned by Flight Sergeant Arthur Aaron, DFM. Other awards gained by the squadron members include four DSOs, two bars to the DSO, 109 DFCs, 46 DFMs, two CGMs, twenty-five Mentioned in Dispatches, one Military Medal and finally one BEM. The squadrons of 3 Group went about their business without fuss, and generally attracted less publicity than other groups. Although veterans are fiercely loyal to the Stirling, there is no question that it restricted the ability of 3 Group to play a full part in some campaigns. The legendary Lancaster came late in the war to 218 Squadron, and thus without fanfare, but once on charge it allowed the squadron to operate in the vanguard for the final eight months of hostilities. There was no Gibson and no Cheshire serving within the ranks of 3 Group, but there were many of equal stature, whose names never became familiar to the general public. 218 Squadron boasted some of the finest airmen to grace the Command, and the names of many are contained within these pages. This book is humbly dedicated to them all.

No 218 Squadron bases 1937–1945

Chapter One

The End of the Slaughter:
Inter War Years

With the defeat of the Kaiser's Germany the bloody slaughter of the Great War was finally over, 218 Squadron continued to occupy its wartime aerodrome of Reumont, although it would prove to be for only a matter of a few more days. By November 16th, just five days after the armistice, the squadron had successfully de-camped and moved to occupy Ver Galand aerodrome, where it quickly settled into its new peace-time routine. This was soon interrupted, however, in a way that no-one could have expected. A signal was received from Command HQ informing the squadron that there was to be an immediate change in leadership. The popular and highly respected Major Burt Stirling Wemp, DFC, was to be replaced, and this was a bitter blow to all squadron personnel, who, over the previous months, had taken to their hearts this rather strict and forthright Canadian. Bert Wemp was born near Tweed, twenty miles north of Belleville, Ontario, and graduated from the Curtiss Flying School in Toronto in 1915, from where he sailed to England and joined the Royal Naval Air Service. On January 10th, soon after relinquishing his command, Wemp was invalided back to England for a well earned rest, and for the next five months he convalesced at a rehabilitation 'Camp before returning to his native Canada. In February 1919 he was awarded the Belgian Chevalier, Order of Leopold. Post war returned to journalism and became mayor of Toronto.

On December 29th Captain Adrian William Edmunds Reeves DFC assumed command of the squadron. Reeves was a distinguished pilot, who had flown on sixty-four bombing raids and had been credited with the destruction of four enemy scouts. Reeve's command was brief and he was replaced on January 9th 1919 by Major W E Collison. Collison's command like that of his predecessor was equally brief, and within three weeks he had been replaced by the squadron's final commanding officer, Major Cecil Hugh Hayward, who took up his post on January 30th. On February 7th 218 Squadron's long awaited return to England finally took place. Its new home was at Hucknall Aerodrome, located some six miles north-east of Nottingham. Safely back in Blighty the squadron continued to operate its D.H.9 bombers, but now in a less demanding and hostile climate. Throughout the spring of 1919 the squadron occupied itself with training, with an emphasis on formation exercises.

How it all began, an Airco De Havilland DH9 of 218 (Bomber) Squadron France 1918. The "Ninak" as it was known served the squadron well over the bloodbath of Belgium and France during 1918. Underpowered until the introduction of the DH9A 218 Squadron pilots notched up a number of kills over the more nimble and heavily armed German scouts.

It was soon apparent that a massive scaling down of the new Royal Air Force was required, and with systematic and ruthless determination over 380 squadrons were disbanded, putting more than 300,000 officers and men back into "Civvy" Street. On June 24th 218 (Bomber) Squadron was given the order to disband, and for the next nineteen years it existed only on paper.

The catalyst for the reformation of 218 Squadron in 1936 was an evil force spreading across Germany in the shape of the National Socialist Party under the leadership of German Chancellor Adolf Hitler. Hitler's expansionist policies finally persuaded the British Government of the necessity to rebuild its armed forces, and this meant the resurrection of many of the Great War squadrons. On Sunday March 16th 1936, 218 (Light Bomber) Squadron was reformed from C Flight of 57 (B) Squadron at Upper Heyford in Oxfordshire. At the time 57 Squadron was part of 1 Group and was equipped with the Rolls Royce Kestrel X-powered Hawker Hart day bomber. With the detachment of C Flight under the initial command of F/L Aldan Carey, 218 Squadron was officially reborn. Joining F/L Carey on the new squadron were other 57 Squadron transferees, P/O Alexander Olney, along with one flight sergeant, two sergeants, five corporals and nine aircraftsmen. Unlike its parent unit 218 Squadron was to be equipped with the new Hawker Hind biplane which was powered by a single Rolls Royce Kestrel V.

Initially 218 Squadron fell under the command of 57 Squadron's commanding officer, thirty-nine-year-old S/Ldr F Reeve, and effectively served as a third flight to this unit. On March 27th, eleven days after its formation, 218 Squadron departed Upper Heyford and joined 57 Squadron at 2 Armament Training Camp at North Coates in Lincolnshire. This was one of a number of Armament Training Camps set up around the British Isles for the purpose of bombing and gunnery training. The course continued until April 25th by which time the two squadrons had dropped a total of 724 practise bombs and fired over 20,000 rounds of ammunition. The prestigious Armament Officers Trophy, known as 'The Cock', was an annual competition held between air gunners and air bombers drawn from all day-bombing squadrons. This year it was awarded to 57 squadron for the achievement of an average bombing error of only 67.3 yards during the long range bombing tests. Upper Heyford was opened to the public on Empire Day on May 23rd, when, among the dignitaries attending were A.D Cunningham CBE, a senior staff officer in the Air Defence of Great Britain, and the Air Officer Commanding (AOC) 1 (Bomber) Group, Air Commodore Boyd MC OBE. The BBC was also present and conducted a broadcast during the afternoon.

At the end of May both squadrons were affiliated to the Air Fighting Development Establishment based at Northolt. The purpose of this affiliation was to find the best method of formation flying for day bombers. With the dramatic increase in performance of both bomber and fighter aircraft at the time, a radical overhaul of formation flying techniques was required. Experimental formation exercises were carried out in conjunction with the Gloster Gauntlet biplane fighters of 111 (F) Squadron, and after a number of flights, a system known as the 'Up and Down' formation was devised. The five-aircraft formation would fly in an asymmetrical V at various heights, which, it was hoped, would give them "the maximum flexibility, manoeuvrability and defence".

Over the ensuing months the squadron gradually built up its pilot strength. On July 13th two arrived from 7 Flying Training School while three more joined on August 24th from 11 FTS at Wittering. Within a week these officers were joined by others and September saw the arrival of F/O Terence Morton from 7 (B) Squadron at Finningley to assume the role of squadron adjutant. Pilot Officer Harry Daish was posted in from 3 FTS at Grantham on the last day of September to ultimately and successfully fill the role of A Flight commander. Harry Daish was a native of Sydney, Australia, and graduated from RAAF Point Cook Flying Training School as a pilot officer in June 1935. He was selected along with six other graduates for transfer to the RAF (UK) for a five year short service commission, travelling first class on the luxury liner Strathnaver. Harry would have a long and distinguished career in the RAF, rising through the ranks to reach wing commander by the 18th of June 1945. Harry was the first commander of 27 Squadron in India, which was equipped with the Bristol Beaufighter. He had a reputation for thoroughness and professionalism, and would survive the war. On the 4th of October F/L Cary relinquished command of 218 Squadron on posting to Calshott in Hampshire. On the same day 218 and 57 Squadrons returned to 2 Armament Training Camp at North Coates.

Within two days of the squadron's arrival and while performing a number of dive bombing exercises, tragedy struck Hawker Hind K5516. As the pilot attempted to recover from a dive-bombing simulation, both upper wings folded over Theddlethorpe bombing range in Lincolnshire. The ensuing crash killed both occupants, twenty-five year-old Sgt George Dodsworth and his observer, acting Sgt Walter Devoil. These were the squadron's first fatalities since the Great War, and the loss of both airmen was keenly felt.

Following the accident training continued under restrictions that imposed limited dive-bombing practice on the Hinds. With the weather turning and high winds forecast both squadrons returned to Upper Heyford four days earlier than planned. Following F/L Cary's departure, temporary command of 218 Squadron was given to F/L Arnold Louis Christian, who was posted in from Uxbridge. Arnold Christian was reputedly a descendant of Fletcher Christian, of 'Mutiny on the Bounty' fame, and had joined the RAF in 1930. Commissioned as a pilot officer on October 10th 1930, he spent the first four years of his career as a fighter pilot with the famous 54 Squadron. In 1935 he transferred to 207 Squadron, a bomber unit with which he spent a spell in the Sudan during the Abyssinian crisis.

Four days after Christian's arrival 218 Squadron finally became independent of 57 Squadron, and from this date on all day to day training, administrative duties and activities would be undertaken solely by 218 Squadron staff. The squadron would, however, continue to share Upper Heyford with 57 Squadron. Flight Lieutenant Christian's brief tenure as squadron commander came to an end on November 2nd 1936, when S/Ldr Francis Harbroe Shales arrived from 40 (B) Squadron at Abingdon. As for Christian, a period as an instructor with 5 EFTS and 13 OTU resulted in promotion to squadron leader and the award of a Mentioned in Dispatches. He would be killed while serving as the commanding officer of 105 Squadron on May 8th 1941 during an attack on shipping off Stavanger. At the time of his death he was one of 2 Group's most respected squadron commanders.

With 218 Squadron's independence came the inevitable official inspections. The first of these came on November 27th, when ACM Sir John Steel carried out a formal inspection. He was followed on December 1st by the A-O-C 1 Group, Air Commodore Owen Tudor Boyd, MC, AFC. Finally, to the relief of all, the round of inspections ended with a visit by Air Chief Marshal Sir Robert Brooke-Popham on December 7th.

The start of 1937 brought the arrival of new pilots, among them acting P/Os Charles Crews and Stewart Coutes-Woods and P/O Eric Arthur Hunt, all from 8 FTS, and P/Os William George Warren, William Newton-Howes, Anthony Beck who will feature in the squadrons subsequent history and Russell John Oxley from 18 (B) Squadron. February and March 1937 witnessed a considerable amount of activity in the form of training and postings, and a number of aircraft sustained minor damage in landing accidents. On April 24th the squadron proceeded north to West Freugh in Scotland to carry out a month's training at 4 Armament Training

Camp. West Freugh was a new camp situated five miles south-east of Stranraer. May's highlights included the coronation of King George VI on the 12th, when P/O Daish represented the squadron in London, while the remainder turned out in best blues to parade at West Freugh. A month to the day after leaving Upper Heyford for Scotland, the squadron returned, and S/Ldr Shales was informed that his brief period in command was soon to end.

A flying display by the squadron over the aerodrome attracted thousands to Upper Heyford on Empire Day on May 29th. The squadron performed a series of bombing runs and formation flying passes over the enthralled crowds, the day went off without incident in fine weather conditions. On June 1st F/L Cunningham arrived as commanding officer elect, and was immediately promoted to the rank of squadron leader. Thirteen days later S/Ldr Shales officially handed over to him, and departed to take up administrative duties at 1 School of Technical Training (Apprentices) at Halton. Flight Lieutenant James Charles Cunningham already had command experience, having been at the helm of 49 (B) Squadron between February and July 1936. On June 8th P/O Russell Oxley was posted to XV (B) Squadron to continue a career that would take him to the command of 50 Squadron in 5 Group. Here he would be awarded a DFC in 1941 and a DSO in 1942, before ending his career as a group captain. To compensate for the departure of such a fine officer, five new pilot officers arrived during the last week of June. They were Thomas Brock, John Mahoney, David Devoil, Arthur Imrie and John Crump. These additions to the squadron were augmented by the arrival also of F/O Richard Seys, DFC on July 13th. This officer had been awarded the DFC while operating in Palestine during 1936.

An accident occurred on July 15th, when Sgt Pays was engaged in an Observer Corps calibration exercise in Hind K6630. He became separated from the remainder of the squadron in thick rain cloud over Leicestershire, and either while attempting to establish his position or make a forced landing, he collided with a tree in zero visibility near the village of Kirby Bellars. The aircraft was destroyed, but Sgt Pays and his unnamed observer survived with minor injuries. A more serious accident on September 16th resulted in acting P/O John Mahoney and his observer sustaining serious injuries. They had become lost during a tactical exercise, and in attempting a landing at Barnard Castle near Catterick, overshot and crashed into a stone wall writing off the Hind.

More new pilots arrived in the autumn and early winter, and the role of squadron adjutant was taken over on October 4th by the recently arrived F/O J Hughes. To date the squadron had fared relatively well in terms of accidents, sustaining just the two fatalities on October 6th 1936. Sadly, this was to change on November 26th, when P/O Eric Hunt and his observer, AC1 Joseph Thomas were scheduled to carry out a routine cross country flight. Emerging from clouds just off the Cambrian coast, Hunt turned towards the coastline at low level. With land only a matter of a few miles distant the aircraft's Kestrel Mk V engine cut, causing a rapid loss of altitude. Eye witnesses reported that the aircraft turned steeply to starboard whereupon the lower wing touched the surface of the freezing waters of Moss Bay. The bomber cartwheeled into the sea near Wokingham and both crewmen drowned.

The remainder of the year was spent carrying out various training exercises, and there were no further accidents to report. Squadron Leader Lewin Bowring Duggan was appointed as the new commanding officer on January 4th 1938, succeeding S/Ldr Cunningham, who was posted to the Staff College at Andover. Duggan was originally an Army man, who had served later with some distinction in the Royal Flying Corps and Royal Air Force during the Great War. He finished the war as a 2nd Lt with 99 Squadron flying DH9s. The start of the New Year also brought the long awaited conversion from the biplane Hind to the monoplane Fairey Battle light bomber. The first Battle, Stockport-built K7647, arrived on squadron charge on January 17th, and over the ensuing three weeks a further fifteen aircraft arrived from the Fairey Aviation Company. This brought the unit's total strength to sixteen Battles, allowing two flights of six aircraft each plus four in reserve.

The single engine Battle light bomber was designed to specification P27/32 as a replacement for the Hawker Hart and Hind biplanes. When production of the Mk 1 began in mid 1937, the stressed skin monoplane epitomised the latest in aircraft design. The Battle was the first production aircraft to have the Rolls Royce Merlin as its power plant, and it also had an internal bomb load of 1000lb, which was carried in enclosed bomb bays located in the wings. On April 22nd 1938, 218 Squadron departed Upper Heyford and took up residence at Boscombe

The peace before the storm. A flight of Hawker Hinds are captured in the sunlight during the summer of 1937.

Down in Wiltshire. This airfield had opened in 1917, initially as a training school for RFC pilots, but with the mass scaling-down of the RAF after the Great War, the aerodrome, which, by this time had acquired over fifty buildings, was closed in 1920 and returned to agricultural use. However, the need for a peacetime air force resulted in Boscombe Down being purchased in 1926 as part of the expansion programme. The airfield re-opened in 1930 as a bomber station in the Air Defence of Great Britain, the forerunner of Bomber Command.

The squadron carried out a number of local familiarisation flights over the next week, including a tactical exercise with 11 (F) Group on May 10th, when the squadron participants were intercepted by four Hawker Furies. Flying as deputy leader on this occasion was New Zealander P/O Ian Richmond in Battle K7654, over the ensuring years he would become one of the squadron's most experienced and accomplished pilots. On May 23rd the squadron carried out a mass formation demonstration along with 105 and 226 squadrons, when twenty-four Battles were routed over Harwell, Cheltenham, Gloucester, Monmouth, Hereford, Worcester, Kidderminster, Leamington and finally Banbury. The squadron was once again detached to 4 Armament Training Station at West Freugh in Scotland for the month of June. July saw a continuation of the daily training flights, the only departures from this routine coming on the 16th, when the squadron gave a flying display at the opening of Luton Airport, and on the 18th, when the squadron participated in a two-day Observer Corps exercise. In August a major air exercise was undertaken between the 5th and 7th in conjunction with 88 (B) Squadron, the other Battle unit sharing Boscombe Down. These sorties were under the auspices of the Air Defence of Great Britain. The ADGB was created in 1925 following a recommendation that the RAF should take full responsibility for homeland air defence, and the above-mentioned sorties simulated attacks on strategic and military targets, giving all commands the opportunity to test peace-time training under operational conditions.

New Zealander Ian Richmond was one of the squadron's most able and courageous pilots. He served on the squadron between 1938 and 1941 operating almost continuously. He had reached the rank of squadron leader and was awarded the DFC by the time of his posting.

The growing international crisis in the Czechoslovakian Sudetenland during late August finally galvanised the Air Ministry and senior Air Staff to implement the partial mobilisation of a number of front line squadrons. This had an immediate effect on both 218 and 88 Squadrons, which would form 75 (B) Wing under the command of Boscombe Down's Station Commander, Wing Commander Gerard Oddie, DFC, AFC. Oddie had won his DFC with 31 Squadron in Afghanistan flying Bristol Fighters in 1920. During early September orders from 1 Group HQ instructed 75 (B) Wing to proceed overseas and be ready for immediate active service as a component of the Advanced Air Striking Force. Up until this time the squadron had been allowing its personnel to take scheduled leave, but in the face of the worsening political climate this was cancelled on Saturday September 17th. On that day 1 Group officially ordered the immediate recall of all personnel and the cancellation of all leave. Further orders required ground crew to collect forty additional vehicles in preparation for the wing's departure for France. All sixteen 218 Squadron Battles were re-painted during late September, and the peace-time practice of painting squadrons' numbers on the fuselage and serials on the underside of the wing was ended when the new squadron code of SV was added. With the squadron now on a war footing, the families of the married officers and men were ordered to make ready for their evacuation. To the relief of all the period of crisis ended on September 29th, when Prime Minister Chamberlain and Frances Edouard Daladier signed the Munich Agreement with Herr Hitler, which, in effect, transferred the Sudetenland over to Nazi Germany.

With the threat of war now apparently replaced by a promise of peace, the recent lessons learned were, for once, not wasted on the Air Ministry and Air Staff. It was obvious to all that the RAF would have been in no position to go to war with

A rare bird, pre Munich Crisis. Fairey Battle Mk.I adorned with 218 along the fuselage. Few photos remain of the Battles marked in this way, this poor quality photo was taken at Boscombe Down in May 1938.

Germany in the summer of 1938. Most importantly, the signing of the Munich Agreement allowed time for the RAF to rethink, re-equip and prepare. A new 218 Squadron adjutant was appointed on October 1st, when F/O Crews assumed responsibility for the role. 218 Squadron's strength was increased on October 9th, when the total number of allotted aircraft per squadron was increased from twelve to sixteen with five in reserve. With this increase in aircraft numbers came a change in power plant, between October 10th and 13th all of the squadron's Merlin I powered Battles were transferred to 105 Squadron. During the preceding weeks the squadron had gradually re-equipped with the Merlin Mk II powered Battle, which had been collected directly from Fairey Aviation at Ringway Aerodrome, Stockbridge, and from 185 (B) Squadron at Abingdon in Oxfordshire. October witnessed the departure of W/Cdr Oddie, DFC, AFC, the station commander at Boscombe Down, who was posted to HMS Nelson as Fleet Aviation Officer. He was replaced temporarily by 218 Squadron's commanding officer S/Ldr Duggan.

Two important visits were received on the station during November. On the 1st the Inspector General, Sir Edward Ellington, GCB, CBE viewed the squadron, he was followed two weeks later by the arrival of the Commander-in-Chief of Bomber Command, Air Chief Marshal Sir Edgar Ludlow Hewitt, KCB, CMG, DSO, MC, who spent the day with the crews of 88, 218 and 150 Squadrons. On December 6th the A-O-C of 1 Bomber Group, Air Vice Marshal P.N.L Playfair, CB, CVO, and MC, officially presented the squadron with the squadron crest, signed and approved by the King. The crest was in the design of an hourglass with the sand running out, and included the squadron motto *IN-TIME*. The significance of the design and legend was the squadron's original formation in time to take an active part in the operations of the Great War.

A new Air Ministry policy at the start of 1939 allowed for all squadron commanders of medium bomber squadrons to be promoted immediately to the rank of wing commander. On January 8th the squadron proceed to 5 Armament Training Station at Penrhose in Caernarvonshire for a month's air firing and bombing training. High and low level bombing exercises were undertaken almost daily, interspersed with both air to air and air to ground gunnery flights. On January 27th the squadron returned to Boscombe Down in formation, routed over St David's Head and Cardiff. A series of wing exercises were undertaken during February, the one on the 6th, conducted in concert with 88 and 150 Squadrons, simulated an attack on Leicester with 218 Squadron in the lead. The three squadrons had assembled over Swindon before carrying out the raid on the city from 10,000 feet. A similar exercise on the 9th was thwarted by poor weather conditions when Falmouth was the intended target and 218 Squadron was again selected to lead. On the 16th a mass group formation exercise was carried out taking in Weston-super-Mare, Bristol and Guildford with 218 Squadron once more at the head. This was followed on the 24th by a further exercise, in which the three Battle units visited Bristol, Halton and Tonbridge Wells. Once again

Ron Gill stands on the port wing of Fairey Battle K9260 after it overshot its landing at Boscombe Down on the night of April 11th 1939 with Pilot Officer R Balls at the controls. Ron Gill joined the squadron in 1938 after training at RAF Cranwell as a radio operator. He survived the bloodbath of May 1940 to convert to the Blenheim's and then the Wellingtons. He completed over 30 operations before being screened in late 1941.

218 Squadron was given the task of leading, a great honour of which the members were justly proud.

As a part of the Municipal Liaison Scheme the town of Weston-super-Mare was chosen to be affiliated with the squadron on March 1st 1939. The scheme was intended as a means of promoting regional affiliations between squadrons and towns and cities. This would provide the unit with a territorial 'home' and give towns and cities a more personal interest in the welfare of the squadron and the war in general, if and when it came. The reason for the choice of Weston-super-Mare is unclear, but a close bond quickly developed between the residents of this small Somerset town and the squadron.

The dark shadow of war once again loomed over the country and on April 3rd orders were received to prepare to mobilize. With the possibility of another world war looming ever closer the squadron continued its day-to-day activities, but now in a more urgent manner. May 5th was Empire Air Day, and the entire squadron carried out a series of flying demonstrations over a number of towns including Stockbridge, Winchester, Guilford and Kenley. Each town was visited in turn with the squadron flying in a twelve-aircraft diamond formation. With the continuing unrest the squadron was ordered to increase its existing two flights to three. Between July 3rd and 17th a further eleven new Battles were collected directly from the Austin Works in Birmingham, and the new flight raised the squadron strength to twenty-four front line aircraft with eight in reserve. A regional air exercise was undertaken on July 8th by both 88 and 218 Squadrons, and this took the formation to within three miles of the French coast.

July 11th saw the aircraft of 218 Squadron actually flying above the fields of France. A series of low-level flights over French towns and cities had been organised to try and put to rest growing fears in France that a war with Germany was imminent. These flights were arranged to show the French people that the RAF was ready to meet any potential threat, but in truth, it was little more than sabre rattling. Boscombe Down's two squadrons were joined by aircraft of 103 Squadron from Benson, and thus a total of eighteen aircraft flew over the towns of le Treport, Orleans and le Mans and finally Barfleur, before returning to Boscombe Down after a flight of over five hours. A similar exercise was carried out on July 25th.

A number of Home Air Defence exercises started on August 8th and continued until August 11th. At around noon on Friday August 11th 218 Squadron suffered a fatal flying accident. It happened on the final day of a major low-level Home Defence Air Exercise, when the squadron was employed as part of the attacking force. Two Battles, flown by F/O William Kinane and P/O Max Freeman, were operating at low level and heading towards Carlton in Bedfordshire from the north. Approaching Carlton K9328's port wing hit the top of an eighty-seven foot high electricity pylon, breaking off the topmost steel girder and bringing down two cables. With its wing ablaze the stricken aircraft hurtled towards the ground with flames trailing behind, colliding with an elm tree close to a cricket pavilion before somersaulting on in a manner which precluded any chance of survival. Two local residents, a Mr Bevington and his son, were the first on the scene, and they courageously pulled clear the injured wireless operator, AC1 Ivor Roberts. A further attempt was made by the Bevingtons to extricate the remaining trapped crew members, and they were assisted on this occasion by a local farm labourer. Unfortunately, however, the starboard fuel tank exploded, and the ensuring fire made any further attempt impossible. Circling less than 150 feet above, P/O Max Freeman saw the tragedy unfold below him. His subsequent report stated:

"I was flying in a formation behind the other aircraft, and slightly higher. We were carrying out exercises in connection with the home air defence. At mid day we came over Carlton Training School and I saw a high tension wire and pylon a second before I saw the other plane fly into them. There was a blue flash and the machine immediately burst into flames and crashed. I circled around and later landed at Cranfield aerodrome, where I reported I had noticed nothing wrong with the other machine and it seemed to be flying normally. But as I was flying slightly higher I could not see exactly what he (Kinane) was doing."

Another witness was fourteen-year-old Ray Holmes:

"I was walking up the school lane when I saw two aircraft coming towards me about ¼ mile away, both were flying very low. Both aircraft were flying from an east to west direction one behind the other. The rear aircraft was slightly higher than the other, the next thing I saw was a mass of flames falling earthwards straight into a row of mature elm trees directly in front of the school farm house. Both wings had sheered off due to the impact with the trees. The other aircraft circled low over the crash site, I have often wondered how this crew must have felt. Some time after the bodies had been removed we were allowed to see the wreckage of the bomber. The wreckage was in two halves, the front of which was facing in the direction from which it came. The rear section was most effected by the fire, and in a field near the pylon I found the windscreen with the ring sight still attached. I gave it to a RAF guard."

William "Bill" Kinane was 18 when he and two other young Aussies were selected from over 700 candidates to join the RAAF in 1936. A champion athlete he held a number of records while attending the Christian Brother College, Perth. He was just 21 when killed in the tragic but avoidable collision.

Aircraftsman Roberts was rushed to a hospital at nearby Cranfield Camp, where the doctor in charge, Dr Thomas, a flight lieutenant serving in the RAF, was initially hopeful that Ivor might recover despite his extensive burns. However, around midnight on the Saturday his condition worsened, and Roberts died of his injuries at 04.30hrs, thirty-six hours after the crash. The body of the observer Sgt Peter Aitkin, a twenty-eight-year-old married Scotsman from Farnborough in Kent, was buried with full military honours on Wednesday 16th at Farnborough Churchyard. His body was carried on the back of an RAF lorry to the churchyard, where his coffin bearers were drawn from fellow sergeants from 218 Squadron. Alan had served in the RAF for ten years and had recently been stationed at Biggin Hill, also in Kent, where he had met and married Lily Parker. In a sombre twist to this tragic incident, the day of the crash was the very one on which Peter was to return home to Farnborough to collect his wife and eight-month-old baby to move them to the married quarters at Boscombe Down. As for the pilot, F/O William 'Bill' Kinane, a twenty-one year-old Australian, the official post crash investigation report records in a rather impassionate style that he was *"flying below minimum authorised height, not culpable, excess zeal on the part of the pilot"*.

At precisely 23.59hrs on August 23rd 1939 orders were once more received from the Air Ministry that 75 Wing of the Advanced Air Striking Force was to form at Boscombe Down. All 218 Squadron and station personnel were ordered to return immediately, while Boscombe Down's defence posts were manned. In addition 250 class 'E' Reservists were called upon to report to Boscombe for duty with the squadron on its departure to France as a part of the AASF. On August 24th, W/Cdr Duggan instructed S/Ldr G Warrington, second in command, to oversee the re-painting of the Battles, this time with their wartime code of **HA**.

Mobilization continued throughout the next three days, on August 28th the 3 Group A-O-C, Air Commodore Arthur Thomson, MC, AFC, made an unscheduled landing at Boscombe Down in a Wellington of 115 Squadron. It was the culmination of an unsuccessful test flight to evaluate a special type of live bomb at Larkhill range. Faulty bomb release gear had brought an end to the test, and once on the ground the air commodore clambered out of the Wellington to inspect the offending device. It was while he was under the bomb-bay that a bomb accidentally released causing Thompson instinctively to step backwards and come into contact with the rotating propeller. He received severe injuries, including a compound skull fracture and fatal brain injuries. He was immediately rushed to the Tidworth Military Hospital, but so great were his injuries that he died in the ambulance on the way.

The squadron strength on August 28th 1939 stood at twenty-five pilots spread among A, B and C Flights, and on this day the squadron records show the following pilots under the command of W/Cdr L B Duggan.

F/L Daish	P/O Richmond	S/Ldr Warrington
F/L Rogers	P/O Imrie	F/O Hulbert
P/O Givens	P/O Crane	P/O Rhind
P/O Shaw	Sgt Horner	Sgt Dockerill
F/O Balls	P/O Freeman	P/O Robin
Sgt Jupp	F/Sgt Fleet	F/O Crews
Sgt Herring	P/O Thynne	F/O Hughes
P/O Waring	P/O Forth	P/O Harris
Sgt Owen		

On September 1st, with the European situation at a critical point, 1 Group issued instructions for the immediate departure of the forward air and ground parties of the AASF to the continent. On September 2nd, Group Captain Archibald Wann, commanding officer of Boscombe Down, addressed all ranks of 75 Wing prior to their departure. The following day G/C Wann and a number of NCOs embarked on an Imperial Airways Ensign to France, the same day that the forward sea party of Wing HQ personnel proceeded to their embarkation points on the south coast.

At 11.10hrs on the 3rd the squadron operational records book records that Great Britain declared war on Germany. At 1600hrs aircraft from the Aeroplane and Armament Experimental Establishment (A&AEE) aircraft began to arrive at Boscombe, and in all, thirty-five aircraft were dispersed around the airfield that night. A number of civil aircraft were employed to carry key squadron personnel and equipment to France over the coming days. A total of sixty-five tons of essential parts, including replacement Merlin Mk II engines, were crated up and loaded onto sixty-five vehicles ready for departure on the 11th, this party comprising two officers and 122 other ranks. On the 16th the main party of twelve officers and 150 airmen left by train for France under the command of S/Ldr E Routh. The squadron had acquitted itself well in undertaking such an enormous move at relatively short notice and all those involved could be justly proud that, despite the complexities and logistical problems, all had gone well.

For the squadrons charged with going to war in the Fairey Battle, the coming months would test their courage and professionalism to breaking point. The air crews of 218 Squadron, although supremely confident in their own ability, were aware that their Battles were woefully under-armed and vulnerable, but these shortcomings were shrugged off with an unflagging optimism. The crews carried out flight tests in an atmosphere of anticipation and excitement, for now it was time to put their training into practice. With the departure of the squadrons to France the base adjutant recorded the simple entry "The End" on the last page of Boscombe Down's record book. 218 (Light) Bomber Squadron's association with its last peace-time base was over. These "golden" years would prove to be formative in producing extremely well-trained and courageous airman for the impending conflict, and their character, especially of those destined for the Battle squadrons, would be tested to breaking point in the coming months.

Chapter Two

The End of a Dream:
September 1939 to June 1940

On the afternoon of the 2nd, 88 and 218 Squadrons departed Boscombe Down for their new base at Auberive-sur-Suippes. Under the command of W/Cdr Duggan, sixteen Battles took off in two formations of eight for the flight to France, while the squadron's remaining aircraft were dispersed to other units. The aircraft were; K9251, K9252, K9254, K9255, K9256, K9273, K9323, K9324, K9325, K9326, K9327, K9329, K9353, K9355, K9356 and K9357. The two squadrons formed 75 Wing under G/C Wann, whose HQ was at Auberive, with Mourmelon-le-Grand as a satellite, and 88 Squadron moved there on the 12th.

The squadron conducted its first operation on the 10th, when Duggan led a section of three aircraft to carry out a reconnaissance of the Reims, Nancy, Bitche and Sierck areas to enable the crews to familiarize themselves with the lay of the land. Pilot Officer Freeman led a further reconnaissance outing by two aircraft on the 15th, and on the 17th, F/L Daish and two others reconnoitred the Franco-German frontier as far as Lauterbourg, and became the first 218 Squadron crews to enter enemy air space. Wing Commander Duggan led a further six aircraft on the 20th in what was supposed to be an escorted incursion pushing ten miles into German air space at 23,000 feet. In the event, the seven French Morane Saulnier MS406 fighters of the Coupe de Chassde did not appear, and complete cloud cover invalidated the reconnaissance aspect of the operation. Despite these setbacks, the squadron continued as planned, encountering no opposition before eventually putting down at the aero-club at Gray due to failing weather conditions. The squadron returned home on the following morning. Two sections of three aircraft carried out separate reconnaissance flights over the frontier on the 22nd, and on the 28th F/L Daish led six aircraft twenty miles into Germany for high level unescorted reconnaissance at 23,000 feet. Pilot Officer Freeman had to return early when the oxygen system failed in K9355, but the others pressed on and encountered no opposition.

What the Americans dubbed the "Phoney War" provided a gentle introduction to hostilities for most squadrons of the AASF, but two incidents served to banish any complacency, and ultimately to restrict daylight operational activity for the remainder of the year. On the 20th 88 Squadron lost two out of three aircraft to Bf109s, and on the 30th 150 Squadron had four out of five Battles shot down in

A section of Fairey Battle Mk.I's of "A"Flight over the French countryside January 1940. Battle K9325 D was shot down on May 11th 1940 with F/O Hudson at the controls. K9324 K survived the French campaign and was transferred to the RAAF in September 1940. Battle K9353 HA-J was shot down by light flak on May 12th with the crew of F/Sgt Horner.

identical circumstances. From this point on the crews were involved in a boring round of training flights and exercises with the army, and it was during this period, that the squadron suffered its first loss of an aircraft and crew. Pilot Officer Thynne and his crew were engaged in a high level dive bombing practice over the airfield in K9356 on the 13th of November. The Battle appeared to commence the dive with something more like a half roll than a stall turn, and it was witnessed to go well over the vertical and begin to descend from 6,000 feet. With engine at half throttle the Battle gradually reached the near vertical dive, when, at 1,500 feet, the port wing ripped off. The aircraft began to disintegrate in mid-air, and at a sickening speed smashed into the ground with its three helpless occupants, exploding on impact. Robert Thynne, Richard Pike and Vivian Richardson became the first to have their names inscribed on the squadron's wartime Roll of Honour. It had been twenty-year-old P/O Thynne's first full dive bombing practice since joining the squadron.

As December progressed, a particularly harsh winter began to set in, and opportunities to fly became even more limited. Meanwhile, the home-based squadrons of Bomber Command had been active over the North Sea in search of enemy warships, and had suffered a number of bruising encounters with enemy

The funeral of Pilot Officer Robert Thynne and his crew who were killed while carrying out a dive bombing exercise on November 13th. The crew received a full military burial on November 15th at the Franco-British Cemetery at Epernay.

single and twin-engine fighters. Unfortunately, lessons were not learned and insufficient account was taken of the threat. This was largely because of the pre-war belief that the self-defending bomber formation would always get through to its target in sufficient numbers by daylight, even against the most determined fighter opposition. Two 3 Group efforts, on the 14th and 18th of December, proved so costly, that the decision makers were forced to re-evaluate the feasibility of daylight operations, and ultimately, to commit the Command, with the exception of 2 Group, to waging war by night.

1940: First Quarter

The winter seemed to deepen as the New Year ground on and it would be towards the end of February before the freezing condition loosened their grip sufficiently to allow unrestricted flying. The squadron sustained its first prang of the year as the result of a training accident, when good airmanship on the part of Sgt Owen resulted in an excellent landing with a dead propeller at Monchy. Unable to return to the squadron, the crew spent a merry night as guests of a local French Transport Section. No 2 Salvage Section was dispatched to Monchy to carry out repairs on K9327, but the engine cut-out several times during the return flight. On the 15th a re-organisation took place, which removed the AASF from Bomber Command control, and made it an independent entity under Air Marshal "Ugly" Barratt. The five Wings were reduced to three, and 103 Squadron joined 88 and 218 Squadrons to make up the new 75 Wing, with HQ at St Hilaire. Landing after a training flight in K9329 on the 23rd, F/O Richmond collided with K9327, badly damaging both machines they would be abandoned during the withdrawal in May. Ian Richmond was injured in the crash, resulting in limited flying over the coming months. On February 22nd, Richmond was posted to the Photographic Development Unit based at Heston airfield, London. Here, he was trained to fly the Supermarine Spitfire. Posted back to France in March he eventually joined 105 Squadron on April 11th as squadron photographic officer. His stay was brief, within a month he was back with 218 Squadron. The Phoney War continued to drag on as both sides did their utmost to avoid civilian casualties and damage to non-military property for fear of reprisals. February passed without incident for 218 Squadron, but on the 1st of March K9252 crashed in bad weather some distance north of Dijon during a cross-country exercise. The pilot, F/O Eric Hulbert, the B Flight commander, survived, albeit with a broken ankle, but his two companions, Sgt Frank Dewar and AC Robert Wiltshire were killed.

The winter of 1939 / 40 was particularly harsh. Two ground crew are seen adjusting the covers over Fairey Battle K9324 HA-B. This photograph clearly illustrates the harsh conditions both the ground crew and aircraft experienced during the winter months.

On the 23/24th F/L Rogers and Sgt Dockrill carried out a reconnaissance of the Rhine and dropped what a future C-in-C would refer to as toilet paper on Mainz, while on the following night, F/O Shaw and P/O Imrie dropped their nickels (leaflets) on Wiesbaden and Frankfurt respectively.

1940: Second Quarter

At dawn on the 9th of April German forces marched unopposed into Denmark, and began landings by sea and air in southern Norway. The British and French responded by launching an expedition to Narvik in the north, and Bomber Command was ordered to slow the enemy advance by attacking shipping on the routes from Germany, and the airfields at Oslo and Stavanger. The AASF took no part in the campaign, which was ill-fated from the start, and occupied itself with further reconnaissance and leafleting sorties. 218 Squadron's few losses to date had all been incurred during training, but its next was the first from an operational sortie. At 20.55hrs on the 20th, P/O Wardle, a tall and rather swarthy Canadian serving in the RAF, took off for southern Germany in P2201, one of four crews briefed to carry out a reconnaissance of the Rhine, and to deliver nickels to the residents of Mainz and Darmstadt. The other Battles and pilots were L5237 Sgt Horner, who was forced to return early, L5235 F/O Newton, and P2192

Sergeants Mess, Auberive 1940. Wing Commander Duggan (six from left front row) looking considerably older than his crews. To his right is Pilot Officer Crane. A remarkable photograph depicting the majority of the NCO aircrew on the squadron at the time, tragically almost all would be killed by the end of the year.

F/L Crews. On his return to England in February 1944 Wardle reported that his engine had suddenly burst into flames, and he had been compelled to order the crew to bail out. Sadly Sgt Edward Davison and AC1 Albert Bailey did not get out in time and both were killed. Recent research can now establish that Wardle had been shot down at around 00.45hrs by a Bf109E flown by Feldwebel Schmale of IV/NJG2. This encounter was one of the earliest known night fighter kills of WWII. On the evening of Sunday 21st, Hamburg Radio broadcast a report on the successful capture of P/O Wardle. The report confirmed that a British bomber had been shot down on the previous evening over Kreilsheim. Within days official confirmation was received from the Red Cross in Geneva.

Whatever the circumstances surrounding the loss of Hank Wardle, he was not destined to return to the squadron. Wardle was captured almost immediately and sent to a local Luftwaffe base near Kreilsheim, where he was initially interrogated by a senior Luftwaffe officer. After receiving medical attention Hank was transferred to Oflag IXA at Spangenberg. While a prisoner at Oflag IXA he succeeded in escaping through the camp gymnasium, but he was recaptured after being on the run for twenty-four hours. As a result of his escape Wardle was moved to Oflag IVC at Colditz Castle in November 1940, where, within a matter of months, he found himself as part of a thirteen man escape team under the leadership of Captain Pat Reid, RASC. Wardle's first escape attempt from Colditz involved a tunnel. The plan was to dig under the canteen into the yard beyond, but, an unknown rival plot by a French team, who planned to file through the canteen's window bars, attracted the attention of the Germans. They were expecting an escape attempt and posted an additional sentry to guard the canteen. Fearing that the sentry would discover the tunnel, the British team tried unsuccessfully to bribe him, and that was the end of the plot.

Wardle's next attempt to escape was made with three other officers. The originators of the plan were Major R.B Littledale, KRRC, and Lieutenant Commander L Stephens (RNVR). Major Little had been captured on May 26th 1940 during

Wing Commander Lewin Duggan officer commanding No.218 (Bomber) Squadron greets the Mayor of Auberive upon the squadrons arrival from England in September 1939. Forty one year old Duggan had served in the trenches in the Great War before joining the RAF. He served with No.99 Squadron during the last months of the war.

the retreat to Dunkirk, when he was serving as a brigade transport officer for the 30th Infantry Brigade. Lieutenant Commander Stephens was the commander of H.M.M.L 192, which took part in the heroic attack on St. Nazaire Docks on March 28th 1942. The fourth member of the team was chosen for his experience in lock picking, and he was the legendary Captain Pat Reid. It was decided that the best chance of escape was to split into two teams, Wardle and Reid forming one. The escape began at 21.10hrs on October 14th, and by sheer good luck and daring the two teams managed to escape Colditz. Once on the outside the teams went their separate ways, and for the next two days Wardle and Reid walked at night and lay up during the day. On the 16th they boarded a train at Penig and headed for Zwickau, where tickets were brought for Munich. To help pass the time before their train's arrival, which incidentally had been held up due to an air raid, both Wardle and Reid spent the evening at the cinema. The pair reached Munich at around 10.30hrs on the 17th, where a meal of soup, potato and vegetables was provided by the local home guard. Two further train journeys were still required before their goal of the Swiss border could be reached, but on October 18th it was finally within their grasp. By sheer determination both Wardle and Reid managed to slip over the border, and they gave themselves up to the Swiss Police at 20.00hrs. Howard Wardle completed his 'home-run' by travelling via Spain to Gibraltar disguised as a hair stylist named Raoul. He left Gibraltar on February 5th 1944, and on his return he was award the Military Cross and promoted to squadron leader. He returned to flying, ferrying aircraft to the Middle and Far East.

Five aircraft were sent to the same region on the 22/23rd to fulfil similar tasks, and this time, all returned safely home. The gallant failure at Narvik demonstrated that the Scandinavian affair had already effectively run its course, and it was at this point that events elsewhere grabbed the attention of the world. At first light on the 10th of May German forces began their advance across the Low Countries, triggering a week of unimaginably furious fighting, in which the AASF would be all but annihilated. Its squadrons, and those of the home-based 2 Group of Bomber Command, would be thrust into the unequal contest against marauding Bf109's, and be required to fly into the teeth of murderous flak defences in prepared positions.

On the afternoon of the 10th the squadron dispatched four aircraft to attack a troop column on the Luxembourg to Dippach road, and all returned showing the scars of battle, L5402 being deemed beyond repair. Flying with F/O Crane in L5232 was LAC Baguley, who on return to base died from chest injuries shortly after 14.30hrs. The injuries were received when his magazine exploded after being hit by enemy cannon shells. At 09.30hrs on the following morning four more aircraft were sent for a low-level attack on a German column on the Dahlem – Olzsheim Road, and not one of them returned. Approaching the target over the densely wooded Ardennes the formation came under intense ground fire, F/O Crews had his instrument panel shatter in front of him. After being

Found within the squadron Records Book this photograph is believed to depict a low-level attack on a German column. This fascinating photograph clearly shows a group of German troops rushing for cover while smoke rises from the transport column further along the road. The photo also gives a vivid idea of the remarkably low level the crews operated.

hit again, flames and smoke entered the cockpit and it was clear that P2326 was finished. They were too low to bail out safely but trees stretched endlessly around them preventing a forced landing. Crews dragged the last inch of altitude out of the failing Battle, and all three men jumped clear. Crews and his observer, F/Sgt Evans finding themselves instantly among the treetops where their parachutes snagged and arrested their descent. Sadly Sgt Cederic Jennings, the gunner, fell between the trees, his parachute only partially deployed, and he was killed. He was buried next to the remains of his aircraft near Amelscheid. The two survivors were unable to evade capture, and were soon in enemy hands. Charles Crews made a number of unsuccessful attempts to escape and ultimately, by feigning illness, he managed to get himself repatriated in September 1944. Twenty-six-year-old Sgt Charles Dockrill, his observer, Sgt Percival Dormer and gunner AC1 Kenneth Gregory were killed when P2203 crashed near Troisvierges, ten kilometres north of Clervaux. Flying Officer Hudson and his crew all survived the demise of K9325 and were taken prisoner, and a similar fate befell New Zealander P/O H Murray and his crew in P2249. The following is an account written by Peter Stubbs, the observer in Murray's crew.

May 11th 1940 was warm and sunny as we climbed in to our vehicles which would take us from the village of Auberive-sur-Suippes to our airfield a mile away. That

*was all it was, a field with a wooden hut set in some trees, the nerve centre of 218
squadron. As we carried our gear into the briefing room German aircraft were flying
a few thousand feet above us on their way to bomb the airbase at Rheims. They did
not notice our small grass field with twelve camouflaged Battles dispersed around
the perimeter. Our target was to be an area near St Vith in Luxembourg, where
the German tanks were massing to support the spearhead thrusting into France. We
were to fly in pairs at very low level to attack with our 4 x 250lb bombs. Important
modifications had been made to the aircraft, in that the bulky bomb aimer's equipment
was found to be useless as we hedge-hopped across the ground, so it was removed, and
replaced by a forward K gun to give us more protection against the intense ground
fire. At 09.30 we were airborne and heading for the front, flying as low as possible
to avoid the enemy fighters. However, long before reaching the front line positions
marked on our maps, we ran into a hail of machine gun and cannon fire, so rapid
had the German advance been. Astonishingly, as we flew further behind the enemy
lines we found the roads packed with horse drawn transport, hauling supplies to the
advancing German columns. The new K gun proved superb against these targets,
and as we swooped over the roads I fired off the pans of ammunition. I could clearly
see the chaos as the drivers fell from their carts and horses crashed into ditches as
they run amok in their death throes. It was then that Adams the w/op reported
that our accompanying aircraft had crashed. The last he saw of it was the face of
AC1 Kenneth Gregory, a gunner in Sgt Charles Dockrill's flaming P2203, which
exploded at thirty feet and hit the trees below. It was obvious that we could not
last much longer. The rattle of bullets hitting the aircraft was continuous now, and
cannon shells were tearing holes in the wings. As I lay on the floor firing at the enemy
below, I felt a couple of shells bend the armour plating beneath me.*

*Soon flames leaped out from the engine and smoke and flames surrounded
P/O Murray, my pilot. All I could see through the hatch was a forest of trees very
close. Then there was a grinding crunch as we hit the ground. We had just missed
the trees and crashed into a field beside a farm house at full speed. My "monkey
chain" snapped with the impact and I shot forward hitting the instrument panel
with my face as earth and stones roared through the hatch. I crawled to the rear
of the aircraft to climb out and found my right hand would not work. It had been
hit by a cannon shell, but in the chaos I had not noticed it. I was wondering how
to climb out went the tanks collapsed, pouring blazing petrol into the cabin. The
heat was unbelievable and a few seconds later I was outside the aircraft standing on
the ground. My chest parachute had come undone and the white silk was covered
in blood. The Germans continued to fire at us as we crouched beside the burning
Battle. About a hundred yards away was a potato field with deep furrows, and
knowing it would not be long before the bombs exploded in the heat of the fire, we
decided our best chance was to make a dash for it. Murray was badly burnt, but
Adams was uninjured. I was rather slower than the others and a bullet hit me in
the elbow as we ducked in the furrow. The enemy continued to fire at us as we lay*

on the ground, then around sixteen Germans walked towards the blazing Battle cheering at their success at shooting us down. Suddenly the bombs exploded and lumps of debris screamed down on the surrounding area. We looked up again and there was no Battle and no Germans, just an enormous hole in the ground.

Early on the 12th the Luftwaffe paid a visit to Auberive, but failed to inflict significant damage. At 16.30hrs that afternoon F/Sgt Horner, P/O Bazalgette and P/O Anstey took off to attack enemy columns near Bouillon, two of them failed to return. Flight Sergeant John Horner's K9353 was hit by flak at a thousand feet and lost its starboard wing tip, before crashing in flames near the Belgian/Luxembourg border with no survivors. Marie Anciaux was living in Bouillon, she witnessed the crash of K9353, *"the aircraft was inflames, it just grazed the village rooftops before crashing near the road. Indifferent to the machine gun firing around her, the wife of Joseph RENAULD was the first on the scene. She seems to hesitate, prays for an instant with a Cross and then starts gathers the scattered human remains all around her. She took off her blue linen apron and lays it on the ground placing the grisly remains on to it. Both Joseph MUCHUROT and I are quickly assisting her, bringing large jute bags. A German officer stops his command-car in front of us, threatening us, we are not affraid.*

The ranking soldier then tries to reason with us in broken French, saying that we should go home because the battle has not ended and then threatens us saying that civilians do not have to get involved in these things. Joseph MUCHUROT who has known the horrors of WW1 returns to the village. We, the women, are made of stronger stuff, we persist and continue our macabre task. After a while, Joseph MUCHUROT returns to the scene with a shovel and helped by Joseph PONCELET we dig temporary graves while we are praying. German soldiers start descending en masse to Bouillon, all are looking at the scene with indifference. Little after, villagers put wooden crosses and flowers on the graves. You know, it still makes me sad. Poor young guys".

This touching gesture on the part of the villagers in the midst of a frantic battle is perhaps one of the more poignant actions during an otherwise savage day. Pilot Officer Frederick Bazalgette successfully bombed the target, but P2183 picked up sufficient damage to necessitate a crash-landing close to the village of Donchery, which at the time, was still unoccupied by the Germans. Bazalgette had sustained a severely injured arm and his crew made every effort to save him by carrying him between them towards the front line, but the twenty-two year-old pilot succumbed to his wounds on the night of May 12th. The only survivor from the formation, New Zealander P/O William Anstey, headed back to Auberive-sur-Suippes at 500 feet on completion of his bombing run. In 1947 he recorded his memory of the day.

May 12th 1940, I took off on my first operational trip. The target was a motor convoy moving through Bouillon north-east of Sedan. The payload comprised of 4 x 250lb bombs. We flew as No.2 in a formation of three, and the first indication

The mangled remains of Flight Sergeant John Horners Fairey Battle. A curious German soldier picks over the wreckage of K9353 HA-J.

that we were over enemy territory was the sound of exploding shells. This was followed almost immediately by seeing the roundel of our leader's wing, on which I was formating as closely as possible, suddenly disappear into a large gaping hole. A few seconds later smoke and flames began pouring from the leader's engine, and he passed under me in what appeared to be a shallow controlled dive. His gunner/ wireless operator gave a "thumbs up" sign. A few minutes later the convoy was sighted, and No 3 aircraft dropped his bombs and was last seen still continuing on his course behind enemy lines. We dropped our bombs from about 100 feet, but were unable to observe the results as the machine gun and pom-pom fire was becoming too intense and accurate. On the way back we passed over the burning wreckage of our leader's aircraft. By now we were on our own and receiving the whole undivided attention of the enemy. We were flying at ground level, and as we flew down a valley we could see the tracer bullets coming down from either side. I will remember to my dying day seeing the black and white cows peacefully grazing in the valley as we zigzagged our way out of what seemed to us to be the valley from hell. Right then I would have given anything to be one of those old cows. After getting out of the valley in more or less one piece we found the front line and returned to our base without further incident. Our ground crew greeted us with traditional open arms, and after ascertaining that we had dropped our bombs and fired our guns and that the aircraft had flown alright, they transferred their attention to the aircraft and proudly informed us that we had collected over seventy bullet holes for our fifteen minute joy ride over enemy territory.

The squadron was not called into action on the 13th, but the afternoon of the 14th was to prove disastrous. Seven aircraft departed Auberive to bomb troop columns on the Bouillon-Givonne road while four others were to target the Douzy bridge near Sedan, which was the alternative objective for the first mentioned. It seems that most of the aircraft were carrying a two man crew but the squadron's records were lost during the subsequent withdrawal, and it is not possible to determine either the circumstances of the losses or the names of all those taking part in the operation. What is not in doubt is that five of the eleven Battles were brought down and the following details are known. L5232 was shot down over France with a three man crew, and only the pilot, P/O William Harris survived to return to the squadron in an injured condition. L5235 and L5422 also came down in France, P/O Arthur Imrie surviving in enemy hands from the former, while his gunner was killed, and F/O John Crane in the latter losing his life, while his replacement gunner also became a PoW. Pilot Officer Donald Foster and his gunner survived

Fairey Battle L5235 HA-W guarded by two German soldiers. The Battle was shot down while attacking troop columns near Sedan on May 14th 1940. At the controls was Rhodesian Pilot Officer A Imrie who survived as a PoW while his gunner AC1 T Holloway succumbed to his wounds.

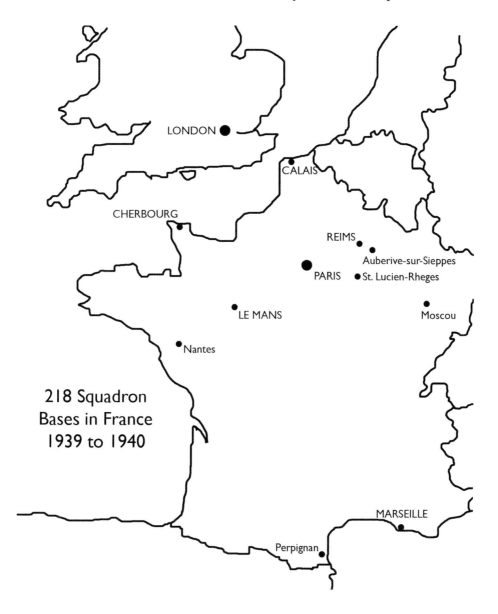

218 Squadron
Bases in France
1939 to 1940

the loss of P2324, and P2360 was lost without trace with the crew of P/O Robert Buttery. Two crews who managed to survive the massacre were those of F/O John Hughes and Sgt Charles Owen. John successfully bombed the target and his gunner, Corporal J A Drummond, managed to shoot down a Bf109. Charles Owen's gunner also claimed a Bf109, and all four men would receive awards for their bravery during this period. John McCulloch Hughes' citation is as follows:

During a period in May 1940, this officer led many successful raids. On one day an attack was made on an enemy column at Dippach. Four days later he successfully pressed home a bombing attack on an enemy position, although attacked by a strong force of Messerschmitt 109's, but by skilfully manoeuvring his aircraft he enable his air gunner to shoot down one enemy fighter. Flight Lieutenant Hughes has shown magnificent leadership as a flight commander and by his coolness and initiative, had maintained the excellent spirit and moral of all his flight personnel.

Fellow pilot, Sgt Charles Owen was recommended for the DFM, his recommendation reading:

On 14th May 1940, whilst carry out a raid on Bouillon, he was attacked by a very heavy formation of enemy fighters. Although his aircraft was badly damaged Sgt Owen pressed home his attack and by his skilful manoeuvring materially assisted his air gunner in shooting down one of the enemy fighters and having completed his mission brought his aircraft safely back to base.

Strangely the DFM was never awarded.

The squadron had effectively been wiped out, and those aircraft and crews that did return were declared non-operational. Within three bloody days seventeen aircraft and twelve brave crews had been lost. The Luftwaffe returned on the 15th, and hit a fully loaded Battle, which was totally destroyed. Later in the day the squadron moved out, and set up temporary lodgings at Moscou Ferme. On the following day a further move was undertaken to St Lucien Ferme, the squadron had already effectively been knocked out of the battle, and would take part in only two more operations. On the 19th the squadron contributed aircraft to attacks on enemy troop columns, and flew some night sorties on the 20th, before its remaining serviceable aircraft were deposited with the now non-operational 105 Squadron on the 24th. Also on the 24th 218 Squadron was transferred from 75 Wing to 71 Wing. All personnel proceeded to 2 Base area at Nantes, where they remained until their evacuation back to England took place. All remaining airworthy Battles belonging to 105 and 218 Squadrons which at this stage was pitifully few were handed over to 98 Squadron, a training unit, on the 4th of June. The dismantling of the original squadron began on the 6th of June, when some of the senior NCOs, together with a number of wireless operators and air-gunners were posted to other squadrons. Wing Commander Duggan had done his best to keep them at 218 by visiting Base Personnel Staff Offices HQ on the 4th, and 2 Base area commander, G/C "Roddy" Carr, a future A-O-C of 4 Group, on the 6th, but his pleas fell upon deaf ears. The remnants of the squadron proceeded to Cherbourg where they would meet the liner Prince Albert, which set sail for Southampton on June 12th. The following day the squadron or what was left of it started to arrive at their new home, RAF Mildenhall.

Chapter Three

A New Role:
Conversion to the Bristol Blenheim

1940: Third Quarter

A new era began for 218 Squadron on the 24th, when it was informed that it would convert to the Bristol Blenheim and join 2 Group. Three days later the first four Mk IV Blenheims were taken on charge, but W/Cdr Duggan unselfishly sent them back as he had no maintenance equipment or qualified ground crews to maintain them. On the 28th W/Cdr Andrew Combe was posted to the squadron to familiarize himself before assuming command two weeks hence. He had been born into a wealthy family of barristers resident in London, and had begun his RAF service in 1930 at Cranwell. While in France he had served with 71 Wing commanded by G/C H Field. By the time he became 218 Squadron's new commanding officer he would have celebrated his twenty-ninth birthday

Working up to operational status would take until mid–August, and in the meantime the inevitable training accidents would cost a number of aircrew lives. Until W/Cdr Combe officially took command, S/Ldr James Gillman filled in and oversaw the arrival of three Blenheims on the 5th. Most of the crews were undergoing conversion training at RAF Upwood, and until the return of F/O Newton and P/Os Turnbull, Smith and Crosse from 17 OTU on the 7th, only ground instruction could take place. On the morning of the 8th all three Blenheims took to the air on cross-country flights, and all remaining unconverted crews were packed off to start their training. Wing Commander Combe looked in on this day to make himself known to the assembled crews and check up on the progress of squadrons conversion before he was installed as commanding officer on the 13th of July, three days after W/Cdr Duggan's posting to Oakington as the temporary station commander. The outgoing C/O had actually been posted to No 3 School of Technical Training at Blackpool, but the unexplained absence of G/C Fields, the intended station commander at Oakington, caused the move to be delayed. It was also on the morning of the 13th, that the squadron registered its first Blenheim casualty, when R3597 was taken by F/O Terrence Newton for a cross-country exercise from Mildenhall to Waddington-Sywell and back to base. Witnesses on the ground watched the aircraft make a low pass over a pig farm in Bedfordshire, some ten miles from the planned route. During one of a series of low-level passes the Blenheim's starboard wing tip struck the top of a 40 foot high ash tree, and the collision sent the Blenheim into a steep turn to starboard from which the pilot had no chance of recovering. The stricken Blenheim smashed into the ground north-east of Harrold and immediately caught fire, killing Terence Newton and two recently posted observers who were carrying out the map reading. The reason for the diversion became apparent after it was discovered that the farm belonged to Newton's uncle, and that Newton himself was well-known in the area. It was an avoidable incident, especially at a time when the squadron was still recovering from its mauling in France. In a moment of high spirits, three young lives were ended.

On the 14th W/Cdr Combe oversaw the squadron's departure from Mildenhall to take up residence at Oakington, and the entire process was completed by the 18th. The squadron now had a full complement of nineteen Blenheims on charge, and spent the remainder of July continuing its march to operational readiness. The experienced S/Ldr Charles House MiD was posted in on the 8th of August as A Flight commander. The first two and a half weeks of August brought a continuation of the working up process, and as this went on, the Battle of Britain was gaining momentum overhead. While Fighter Command was involved in a bitter fight for survival, Bomber Command was committing ever greater resources to eliminating the barges and other marine craft being assembled in the occupied ports in preparation for the intended invasion. The squadron's training period came to an end with a tragic incident on August 18th while B Flight was conducting a formation flying exercise. In almost perfect visibility tragedy struck when L9264 and T1929 collided in the air, both spiralled in flames into the ground. Pilot Officer William Wheelwright in the former and B Flight commander F/L George Newton, who had been with the squadron less than a month, died with the other five occupants, one of whom was a member of ground crew.

On August 19th the squadron was declared operational and would alongside other Group squadrons participate in 2 Group's Operations Order 11, which called for daylight cloud-cover raids on oil and railway targets to maintain the pressure being applied by the night bombers. The ever changing war situation often thwarted the plan, as other considerations became the priority. During August Operational Order 11 was only a small part of the group's remit, as the threat of invasion called for both day and night raids on airfields and long range batteries along the Pas-de-Calais coast, and for North Sea sweeps. 218 Squadron was initially assigned only to the first mentioned, and at 05.30hrs on the 19th, F/L I Richmond took off in T1996 HA-S to carry out the squadron's first sortie, an attack on the aerodrome at Vlissingen (Flushing) on the island of Walcheren at the mouth of the Scheldt. He returned two hours later having completed his assigned task, registering the squadron as a fully-fledged member of 2 Group. Squadron Leader C House also undertook an operational sortie to De Kooy airfield, but was forced by insufficient cloud to abort.

Although for 218 Squadron the time on Blenheim's would be only a brief interlude in a long and varied wartime career, any association with 2 Group operations should be looked upon with pride. Throughout the battles for the Low Countries and France, 2 Group had shared with the AASF the responsibility of trying to stem the irresistible enemy tide, and had suffered the most horrendous losses. The "courage by daylight" displayed by its crews then, and in the time to come before its departure from Bomber Command, was inspirational and unsurpassed, and never were crews asked to undertake more hazardous operations with such little prospect of survival. The first operational loss of a 218 Squadron Blenheim was not long in coming, and resulted from a raid on Brugges on the 23rd. Having taken off at 11.35hrs in T1990 HA-J, S/Ldr House was shot down by a fighter and crashed onto a farm between Hames-Boucres close to the Calais-Boulogne railway. Charles House was buried in the local Cemetery at Guines while his observer, Sgt Percy Lefevre was laid to rest in St. Tricat Churchyard. The survivor, Sgt Howard, spent the remainder of the war as a PoW. What makes this loss intriguing is that at 14.41hrs the crew requested a fix, which was plotted near the south coast of England, near Dungeness. Two of three sorties mounted by B Flight against aerodromes on the following day were completed, and all three Blenheim's returned safely. The squadron flew a modest seventeen sorties during the month, and in comparison with some of the group's other squadrons, it would continue to be under-employed.

September would bring the climax of the Battle of Britain, and with invasion fever still gripping the nation, an even greater number of sorties was sent against invasion transports, making it 2 Group's busiest month until 1944. The squadron was put on Invasion Alert No 1 on the 8th, which required half the squadron to

There are very few photographs of Bristol Blenheims in squadron service. This shows the regular mount of New Zealander Flight Lieutenant Ian Richmond. Bristol Blenheim T1996 HA-S survived its brief service with 218 squadron and finished its days with the Turkish Air force.

be available for operations at immediate readiness. That afternoon the squadron registered its second and final operational loss of a Blenheim, after L8848 crashed in the North Sea during a search for enemy shipping off the Dutch coast. There were no survivors from the crew of Sgt Gerald Clayton, a twenty-three-year-old from County Cork. Only the body of the air gunner, Welshman Sgt Gordon Taylor, was recovered after being washed ashore. Acting S/Ldr Kenneth Ault was posted in as the new A Flight commander on the 4th, two days after his promotion, having previously served with 114 and 139 Squadrons on Blenheims. Flight Lieutenant J Hughes had an inconclusive encounter with three He113 fighters on the 13th while carrying out a photo reconnaissance sortie between Ostend and Flushing. The various reported encounters with the He113 fighter was a result of a deception carefully orchestrated by Joseph Goebbels, the Nazis Reich Minister of Propaganda,there were in fact no He113 fighters operational. On the same day Sgt C Owen attacked a convoy steaming out of the Scheldt Estuary, and dropped a salvo on the biggest vessel. Upon their return the crew claimed hits on an escorting destroyer, which had split in half and sunk. The convoy may have consisted of three German torpedo boats that had set sail from Rotterdam the previous day. Torpedo boat T.2 was attacked and damaged by a Blenheim resulting in serious damage. It limped into port and required major repair.

On the 15th the squadron lost veteran F/L John Hughes DFC who was one of the few surviving pilots from the Hawker Hind days. He was posted first to the Radio Servicing Flight at RAF Biggin Hill then to 25 Squadron based at RAF Wittering. On the afternoon of the 16th P/O W Crosse was briefed to carry out a photo reconnaissance of the coast between Calais and Ostende. A convoy of German E Boats was sighted just leaving Calais, and as Crosse positioned himself for an attack, he was bracketed by intense flak from the port. With the defenses alerted he opted to head for Dunkirk instead, where he took a number of photographs of the town in ideal weather conditions. Continuing on north to Ostende he dropped his bombs on another convoy, and was again engaged by accurate and intense flak from shore batteries and flak ships. The Blenheim received a number of hits to the wings, aileron controls and main spar, forcing Crosse to dive into cloud to escape the barrage. There they were flipped upside down and sent into an inverted roll, causing the bomb sight to leave its mounting and hit the canopy roof, knocking out a panel. Crosse cut the throttles and wrestled the Blenheim back onto an even keel, by which time he was down to a thousand feet. The sensible option at this point was to turn for home, where he landed without further mishap. The squadron lost another pre-war veteran on the 22nd when F/Sgt Charles Owen was screened from operations. Sadly Charles would be killed with 107 Squadron flying from Malta in September 1941. During this, it's first fully operational month with 2 Group, the squadron dispatched fifty sorties, of which thirty were completed.

1940: Fourth Quarter

In October the squadron would share in the continued assault on the Channel ports, while also conducting night raids on airfields, daylight armed reconnaissance sorties and roving commissions. October's operations began on the 3rd with a daylight foray by four aircraft to the Ruhr. The crews were those of Sgt F Hoos, P/O Mansfield, Sgt Morley and F/O Anstey, all of B Flight. Hoos was given the oil town of Sterkrade-Holten to attack but on crossing the Rhine at 3,000 feet he was unable to locate his primary target and selected instead a factory in a wood. The crew returned at 18.15hrs with the distinction of being the first from 218 Squadron to drop bombs on Germany since taking on Blenheims. Sergeant Morley's objective in N6183 was the oil works at Reisholz, but lack of cloud cover forced him to look elsewhere, and he ultimately delivered a successful attack on fifty invasion barges moored at a quayside on the River Maas. Flying Officer Anstey headed for a synthetic oil plant near Homburg, but with cloud becoming almost non-existent, he turned to the north to attack the docks at Rotterdam. Four 250lb bombs were delivered from 5,000 feet, but intense flak made an assessment of the results impossible. Pilot Officer Mansfield and crew encountered insufficient cloud cover and returned with their bombs.

On the following day nine crews were detailed for attacks on the Ruhr and targets in other parts of Germany, including Bremen and Emmerich. Wing Commander Combe was leading from the front in T1865 with Salzbergen as his objective. Weather conditions prevented the primary target from being reached and he attacked a convoy off Ijmuiden instead. Coincidentally, this convoy was also attacked by S/Ldr Ault, who had intended to attack Bremen until his starboard engine sustained flak damage over the seaplane base at Schellingwoude. Squadron Leader J Gillman landed at West Malling after attacking a factory west of Rotterdam, in fact not one of the nine aircraft reached its primary target.

On the 5th ACM Portal relinquished his post as Commander-in-Chief of Bomber Command, and became Chief-of-the-Air-Staff. He was replaced by AM Sir Richard Peirse, an officer of great ability, whose period of tenure would be dogged by misfortune, and the general inadequacies at the time with regard to equipment and the expectations of the exalted. On the 9th F/L Shaw was persuaded by the weather to seek alternative employment when bound for the oil refinery at Homberg near Duisburg in the Ruhr. He found and attacked three ships in the Maas, and on the way home he mixed it with a Heinkel 111, before being forced to call off the fight when the guns jammed one by one. The encounter lasted fifteen minutes, and damage to the Blenheim was limited to one bullet hole in the rudder. On the following day one of the new four engine Short Stirlings landed at Oakington, providing the squadron's air and ground crews and station staff with their first glimpse of the bomber type that they would be operating sometime hence. The type had only recently begun trials with the newly reformed

7 Squadron at Leeming, and would ultimately become the main equipment for 3 Group squadrons. Oakington had been selected as 7 Squadron's new home, and this station was about to be transferred from 2 Group.

On the 16th F/L Shaw had another encounter, this time with a JU88. Engaged on a weather reconnaissance sortie to assess cloud conditions, Shaw pressed on to within thirty miles of the Terschelling lightship before heading back to base. When only fifty miles from the English coast he glimpsed the hazy silhouette of an aircraft in the mist below. He turned towards the still unidentified aircraft, and it was only when two hundred yards distant that he recognised the unmistakable outline of a JU88. Shaw immediately cut across the enemy aircraft to give his gunner, Sgt Gill, an opportunity to open fire from the turret. Two short bursts were fired with indeterminate results and the element of surprise was lost. Shaw now found himself astern of the JU88, and opened fire with his wing gun, only for the JU88 pilot to open the throttles and put himself beyond range. Another to encounter the enemy on this day was S/Ldr Ault, who was outbound for Dunkirk and was about to abandon the operation because of insufficient cloud cover. It was at this point, 16,000 feet over the Channel, that two Bf110 fighters were spotted 2,000 feet above. Ault carefully lost height while keeping the fighters in view, and made it safely back to Oakington, it was a close shave.

The squadron operated Blenheims for the last time on the 31st of October, F/L Shaw and crew taking off at 10.20hrs on a roving commission, during which they attacked Soesterburg aerodrome from 600 feet, before returning safely at 13.05 hrs. The fifty-seven sorties flown during the month demonstrated a more equal share in the group's activities, but it was once more time to move on. On the 29th the first influx of officers and men began to arrive from 7 Squadron at Leeming, and that afternoon two Stirlings landed. The remaining 7 Squadron personnel and aircraft arrived over the next two days. The squadron were shocked to learn that John Hughes one of the squadrons most respected and experienced pilots had been killed while carrying out a black out test over Peterborough on December 7th, the possible result of a collision in bad weather. Having survived the Battle of France the loss of this fine officer under these circumstances was a bitter blow to all those who knew him.

Chapter Four

A New Group:
The Arrival of the Vickers Wellington

O n the 5th of November 218 Squadron joined 3 Group with which it would remain for the rest of the war, and this involved it in flying its third aircraft type in six months. The first Wellington to arrive was a rather battered dual controlled Vickers Armstrong-built Mk I, L4293, which had previously served with both 148 and 75 Squadrons, before spending five months with 15 O.T.U. On arrival at 218 Squadron on November 6th it was allocated to B Flight, and initial impressions were that this machine was a "hack", displaying clear signs of wear and tear. However, the mood changed with the arrival later of the Pegasus XVIII powered Mk Ic, R1009, fresh from 23 Maintenance Unit. This was a new

aircraft, in which the dustbin turret and been removed and two detachable mid-ship guns installed in its place. Two more were taken on charge on the following day, when R1008 and R1025 were flown in by Czech pilots from 311 Squadron, and the squadron immediately set about training. With the conversion underway a number of experienced Wellington crews were posted in, among them that of P/O Dunham from 214 Squadron at Stradishall. Two Weybridge-built Wellingtons, T2801 and T2844, arrived on the 13th, followed on the 14th by a further two, T2885 and R1183 and another dual control Mk Ia, N2937. R1210 was delivered on the following day to bring the total squadron strength up to eight plus the two dual control machines.

On the 23rd the squadron again began the upheaval of changing address, and completed its move to Marham on the 27th. Marham was originally opened in 1916, but like so many other airfields it

Peter Dunham DFC seen here wearing the observer brevet. In 1940 he held the rank of leading aircraftman. During his operational career he served as a gunner, observer and finally pilot. In 1945 he had reached the rank of wing commander.

218. Gold Coast Squadron 1941

1.
At the beacon, at the beacon,
Landing turn is No.9.
And the Aircraft are all saying
One more hour and I've had mine.

Chorus.
O'er the beacon, O'er the beacon,
O'er the beacon come with GEE.
Getting hours in, getting hours in
Just 200 hours for me.

2.
They are calling, they are calling,
They are calling to us all,
So we switch the T.R.9. on,
And the answer is F------- all.

Chorus.

3.
Comes a fighter, comes a fighter,
Comes a Junker 88.
Hurry Campbell, Hurry Campbell
Or you'll be too F----- late!

Chorus.

4.
Hello Darkie, Hello Darkie
There's a fighter giving chase,
Hello Darkie, Hello Darkie
Where the hell's the course for base.

Chorus.

5.
Hello aircraft, Hello aircraft
What's it got to do with me,
Circle beacon, circle beacon
Q.F.E. is 923.

Chorus.

6.
Hello Campbell, Hello Campbell
Aircraft's shooting hard at me,
Hello aircraft. Hello aircraft
Shoot it down says Square McKee.

Chorus.

7.
Hello Campbell, Hello Campbell;
We've received and understood;
Remove fingers, remove fingers,
B----s down in Lady's Wood.

Chorus.

8.
Hello Campbell, Hello Campbell,
Can I now come in and land;
Hello aircraft, hello aircraft,
Would you like the b------ band?

Chorus.

9.
Hello aircraft, hello aircraft,
Get a green when you are near;
Hello Campbell, hello Campbell,
I have left the flare path clear.

Chorus.

10.
To the Op's Room, to the Op's Room,
From dispersal we must go;
What the hells gone wrong with
Transport,
Jesus Christ they're bloody slow.

Chorus.

11.
We are down Sir, We are down sir,
And no thanks to Tony GEE.
Our results sir, Thanks to Met sir
Our results are N.A.P.

Chorus.

SUNG TO THE TUNE OF :-"CLEMENTINE."

was abandoned during the inter-war years until re-opening on April 1st 1937 to accommodate the heavy bombers of 3 (Bomber) Group. 218 Squadron would have to share the facilities here with 115 Squadron, which had been in residence since a few months after its re-opening. Wing Commander Combe was on ten days leave from the 20th, and the burden of overseeing the transfer fell on S/Ldr Gillam. Tragedy struck on the 28th, when one of the longest serving gunners, Sgt Evans DFM, was killed after accidentally walking into a spinning airscrew. Nineteen-year-old Evans had been awarded the DFM for his action on May 14th, when he shot down a Bf109. Squadron Leader Edward Davy was posted in from B Flight of 15 O.T.U at this time. He was an experienced pilot, who had joined the RAF in 1930 and had served with some distinction with 30 Squadron in Iraq during the early 1930s.

November's blustery weather had made conversion training difficult, and the freezing mists of December would pose even greater problems. Twenty-six airmen were posted to the squadron on the 1st to augment the existing manpower, now that the crew complement had increased to six in a Wellington. Over the next two weeks ninety-five training flights were undertaken without major incident. Squadron Leader Davy's time on the squadron was cut short by a posting to 40 Squadron on December 16th, to replace the outgoing commanding officer, W/Cdr Barnett. Flight Lieutenant Richmond was promoted to the unpaid rank of acting squadron leader, a popular appointment as the unassuming New Zealander was one of the squadron's most respected and experienced pilots. In the early hours of December 20th the squadron undertook its first Wellington operation, when S/Ldr Richmond and fellow New Zealander F/O Anstey were ordered to attack the port of Ostend in R1009 HA-L and R1210 HA-B respectively. First away at 04.20hrs was Richmond, followed by Anstey five minutes later, and both crews bombed from between 11,000 and 12,000 feet, observing their six 500lb GP bombs and 120 incendiaries to burst in the docks area and cause large blue flashes and fires. Two nights later the same two crews were joined by F/L Shaw for an attack on Flushing (Vlissingen). Ault was unable

Another of the pre-war New Zealanders who made a name for himself on the squadron, William Anstey. One of a few who survived the bloodbath over France in May 1940. He was awarded a well-deserved DFC in 1941.

to locate his primary target in the prevailing weather conditions, and bombed Calais harbour as an alternative. The two remaining crews did not encounter any problems, and their bombs started a number of fires, which were visible from ten miles away. The squadron's final operation of the year was mounted on the 29th when six crews were briefed to attack the channel port of Boulogne. In the event, severe icing and ten-tenths cloud conditions outbound and over the target area resulted in the attack being abandoned.

1940 was the most difficult year of the war to categorize, having begun with the unreality of the Phoney War, before erupting into unimaginable fury as the Low Countries and then France were swallowed up by the advancing German military machine. Most of the pre-war conceptions had been swept away in the final quarter of 1939, and those that remained in 1940 were subject to rigorous reappraisal. The first attempts at strategic bombing had been attended by great enthusiasm on the part of the crews, and their efforts were much heralded in the press, but in truth, little had been achieved, other than to present a belligerent and defiant face to the, as yet all-conquering enemy. Bomber Command had played its role in the Battle of Britain, and its crews had shown commendable gallantry in flying into the teeth of those defending the invasion embarkation ports, but it was attended by a backs-to-the-wall mentality. It was already clear that this was going to be a long war, and as far as Bomber Command was concerned, the longer the better, to give time to develop the aircraft, weaponry and electronic wizardry that was essential if Britain were ever to go onto the offensive.

1941: January

A second successive harsh winter restricted flying at the start of the year, and those operations which were mounted, were directed largely at German and French ports. The year began for the Command in general with raids on Bremen on the first three nights, two of which were reasonably effective for the period. The first operational activity of the New Year for 218 Squadron involved sorties by S/Ldr Richmond and Sgt Adams, who were briefed to attack Antwerp's port facilities on the 1st. The flight commander found the target in freezing conditions, and dropped his bombs over the docks area, but Adams's flares failed to release and he returned with his bombs. Ian Richmond was attacked while in Marham's circuit on return from an ineffective raid on the 4th. Unseen by the rear gunner, a Bf110 had managed to position itself 500 yards astern of the Wellington before opening fire. A stream of cannon fire passed within feet of the starboard wing, upon which Richmond instinctively turned into the darkness and flicked off the landing lights while opening up the throttles to lose his pursuer, it had been a close shave. Snow and fog curtailed further operations for the squadron until the 9th when a successful raid was flown by six crews with the oil refinery at Rotterdam as the intended target. Weather conditions were ideal and crews reported a number of fires as they left the target. While the squadron was attacking Rotterdam a record 135 aircraft were sent to Gelsenkirchen to attack its synthetic oil plants. Wellingtons made up almost half of the force, and now that 1 and 3 Groups were fully equipped with the type, it would continue to be the mainstay of the Command in numbers until well into 1942.

On the following day the squadron reported that it had ten fully trained Wellington crews available. Remarkably 218 Squadron did not lose a single Wellington during the conversion and working up period, but this fine loss-free record could not last indefinitely. On the 12th F/O Phillip MacLaren, an Australian was posted in from 9 Squadron with over six hundred hours on all types to his credit. Tragedy struck him and the squadron on the morning of the 15th, when P9207 crashed near Wormegay & Pentney, six miles south east of Kings Lynn, just ten minutes after take-off, MacLaren was killed while carrying out his first solo flight in a Wellington. This was also the day on which a new Air Ministry directive was issued, stating an assumption that the German oil position would be passing through a critical period during the next six months. It was suggested that a concerted assault on the centres of Germany's domestic oil production would have a materiel effect on its war effort. A list of seventeen sites was drawn up accordingly, the top nine of which represented 80% of production.

It would be February before Peirse could put his orders into effect, and in the meantime, Wilhelmshaven continued to be the main focus of attention. It was the destination that night for 218 Squadron's first visit to Germany since converting to the Wellington. Six crews from the squadron were briefed to attack the important port, but in the event only two took off, those of Sgts Hoos and Morley in N2844 HA-M and L7798 HA-S respectively. Hoos located and bombed the target in good visibility, but Morley was forced to bomb the secondary target of Rotterdam Docks after developing engine problems. Snow and fog prevented any further operations until the end of the month, during which period there was a flurry of postings-in. 218 Squadron registered no further casualties from either training or operations during this time.

February

February began for the squadron with a change of command on the 6th, when W/Cdr Combe was posted to HQ Bomber Command, and was succeeded by the equally experienced W/Cdr Geoffrey Amison MiD. Twenty-eight year old Amison had joined the RAF in 1932 and gained his Mentioned in Dispatch while serving in Palestine. He joined 38 Squadron as a squadron leader in August 1939, before being posted to 311 (Czechoslovakian) Squadron a year later and then 214 Squadron. He was promoted to acting wing commander on the day he assumed command of 218 Squadron. The Wellington squadrons were kept busy during the first week and a half targeting ports along the occupied coast.

Operations resumed for 218 Squadron when nine crews were briefed on the 7th for an attack that night on the port of Boulogne. Led by S/Ldr Richmond in his now regular R1009 HA–L, all crews managed to locate and bomb the target, causing a number of fires in the harbour area between docks 3, 4 and 5, which were still visible to the crews as they returned over North Foreland. The first major raid of the month to a German target was Peirse's "big night", mounted on the 10/11th, for which 222 aircraft were sent against Hanover. 3 Group detailed over one hundred Wellingtons, ten of them from 218 Squadron, and nine of these attacked the primary target in the face of spirited opposition from both flak and searchlights. A secondary operation on this night involved over forty aircraft, including three Stirlings on the type's offensive debut. The target

Geoffrey Amison's command of the squadron was relatively brief, he was posted to Training Command after 3 months.

was oil storage tanks at Rotterdam, which became the objective for P/O Mansfield. After turning for home he was then set upon by an unidentified night fighter, which followed him over the North Sea for around ten minutes before breaking off. Two other crews had inconclusive encounters with intruders as they arrived in the Marham circuit. Sergeant Morley was attacked by a single-engine fighter, and F/O Crosse by a JU88, which delayed his landing by an hour. The total 3 Group effort for the night amounted to a new record 104 aircraft, the first time that any group had reached, let alone exceeded, a hundred aircraft in one night. A congratulatory message from the A-O-C was duly received at 3 Group stations on the following day.

On the following night, over seventy Wellingtons, Hampdens and Whitleys took off for Bremen, home of the Focke-Wulf Flugzeugbau AG, manufacturer of the Kondor long-range maritime reconnaissance bomber. Eight 218 Squadron Wellingtons took off, and those crews reaching the target found it covered in ten-tenth's cloud and had to bomb on ETA. In all only twenty-seven crews reported carrying out an attack in the target area. Although no losses were incurred as a result of enemy action, despite the presence of night fighters, twenty-two aircraft crashed or were abandoned by their crews on encountering unexpected thick fog on return. Unable to land at Marham the 218 Squadron crews were forced to seek sanctuary further afield, and for some crews this was to prove difficult because of the shortage of fuel. Sergeant Adams managed to crash-land T2885 HA-D on the mud flats near Frampton on the River Severn at 00.40hrs, and he and his crew walked away, and Sgt Smith likewise put T2801 HA-R down safely in a field one mile south of Roos at 01.30hrs. Flying Officer Anstey strayed over London's formidable flak defences, but made it as far as Cumberland before running out of fuel and abandoning R1210 HA-O. The aircraft crashed near Tebay, nine miles north-north-east of Kendal, in Westmoreland's Lake District at 02.15hrs. Ninety minutes later F/O Agar belly-landed R1135 HA-S in a field, again without crew casualties.

Peirse put the oil plan into effect on the 14/15th, when the Ruhr refineries at Gelsenkirchen and Homberg were targeted, but few crews were able to identify the aiming points. 218 Squadron did not participate, but seven of its crews were briefed to attack targets in the Ruhr on the following night. Both flight commanders took part in the operation against the oil plant at Homberg, and fires were already taking hold when they arrived in the hotly defended target area. Thereafter, the Command embarked on nine nights of minor operations, mostly against French ports. 218 Squadron next operated on the 22nd when W/Cdr Amison joined S/Ldr Ault's crew for a raid on Brest. Low cloud forced them to try their luck at Lorient instead, which turned out to be similarly cloaked, and they turned for home with their bomb loads intact. The remaining crews fared little better, although Sgt Morley did eventually bomb through a break in the cloud after stooging around for more than seventy minutes.

Typical of the ineffectiveness of operations at this stage of the war was a raid on Düsseldorf on the evening of the 25th, for which eighty aircraft took off. The city authorities recorded around seven bomb loads falling within the city, and damage was slight in the extreme. On return and while awaiting his turn to land at Marham shortly before 23.30hrs, Sgt Hoos attracted the attention of a JU88 flown by Fw Ernst Ziebarth of I/NJG2. Hoos skilfully managed to crash land his extensively damaged Wellington at a K Site field located near Red Lodge, two miles from Swaffham. All six crew members were initially taken to Swaffham Hospital, five of them with a variety of non life-threatening injuries. Twenty-five year-old Sgt John Stanley was trapped in his front turret and sustained serious burns. He was rushed to Kings Lynn Hospital, where he had a leg amputated, but succumbed to his injuries on March 3rd. Over 120 aircraft were dispatched to Cologne twenty-four hours later, and again, just a few bombs fell onto western suburbs, the remainder finding open country and outlying communities. The month's activities ended with a tilt at the Tirpitz at Wilhelmshaven on the night of the 28th, but the raid was sufficiently inaccurate to warrant no mention in the town's diary.

March

March began for the Command with a return to Cologne on the night of the 1/2nd, an operation which produced some useful damage to the docks area on both banks of the Rhine. The new month began for 218 Squadron, however, with an attack on the 2/3rd on the Hipper Class Cruiser berthed in Brest Harbour, in which six crews participated without loss as part of an overall force of fifty-four. This was the last operation of his tour for A Flight's commander, S/Ldr Ault. He was posted to 15 OTU at Harwell for instructor duties on the 6th, swapping places with S/Ldr William Beaman, who now took over A Flight. Sadly Ault was not destined to survive the war. He would be killed on April 9th 1942, while leading 11(F) Squadron on a suicidal attack against the Japanese fleet moored in the Indian Ocean. Beaman was an experienced pilot, who had served with 70 Squadron in Iraq in 1938 and had been promoted to the rank of squadron leader in June of the same year.

A less convincing attack on Cologne on the 3/4th preceded a period of minor operations, most of which were directed at ports along the occupied coast. On the 9th a new Air Ministry directive brought a change in emphasis, in response to mounting losses of Allied shipping to U-Boats in the Atlantic. From now on, this menace, and its partner in crime, the Focke-Wulf Kondor, were to be hunted down where-ever they could be found, at sea, at their bases, at the point of their manufacture and in the component factories. A new target list was drawn up, which was headed by Kiel, Hamburg, Vegesack and Bremen, each of which contained at least one U-Boat yard, while the last mentioned was also home to a Focke-Wulf factory. The French ports of Lorient, St Nazaire and Bordeaux were also included in the hit list, for housing U-Boat bases and support facilities.

The new campaign began on the night of the 12/13th, when three major operations were mounted, to Hamburg and Bremen in line with the directive, and Berlin. 218 Squadron dispatched nine crews into a freezing moonlit night, three of them, S/Ldr Richmond with S/Ldr Beaman acting as "Second Dickie", F/L Mitchell and F/O Agar heading for Berlin. In the event Richmond was forced to bomb Hamburg docks because of fuel problems, while F/L Mitchell returned after ten minutes with an overheating starboard engine, and only F/O Agar reached Berlin and reported a successful attack in the face of accurate flak and plentiful searchlight activity. Of the six other crews briefed for the Focke-Wulfe Factory at Bremen, one returned early with technical problems, and R1326 failed to return after being shot down by Feldwebel Hans Rasper of IV/NJG1 at 21.46 hrs. The Wellington crashed into the river at Gouwe Sloot near Opperdoes, and twenty-six year old William Crosse and three of his crew were killed. Crosse had joined the squadron in June 1940, and at the time of his death had undertaken thirteen operations, six of which were flown in Blenheims. In 1972 the wreckage of this aircraft was recovered by the Royal Netherlands Air Force. The Hamburg force inflicted some useful damage on the Blohm & Voss shipyard, and started over a hundred fires, a third of them classed as large.

Another effective operation took place against Hamburg on the following night, when the Blohm & Voss yard sustained further damage, and thirty large fires erupted in the city. Nine 218 Squadron crews were briefed for this operation, and they noticed a marked increase in German resistance, beginning as early as the Dutch coast. Flying Officer Agar's R1448 HA-S was attacked by two Bf110s on leaving the target, and the co-pilot, Sgt Vandervord, was wounded in the leg by a bullet. A homebound R1328 HA-V was attacked from below and astern by another Bf110 flown by Fw Hans Rasper of 4./NJG1 while at 15,000 feet, and damage to the hydraulics system left it with undercarriage, bomb doors and flaps hanging down. With gritty determination a wounded Sgt McNeil and his crew managed to coax the Wellington back to Marham, where a successful crash-landing took place. Flight Lieutenant Shaw decided to make a low-level strafing attack on an enemy airfield while homebound, and then found himself being stalked by an intruder over Swanton Morley. On his return Shaw's rear gunner, Sgt Gill, opened fire and the enemy fighter broke off without responding. Meanwhile, two freshman crews were sent to Boulogne to attack the docks, and R1183 became the object of intense flak. Sergeant Donald's wireless operator, Sgt Jack Huffinley, was hit in the leg by shrapnel while standing beside his pilot, and he quickly bled to death, on this, his first operation.

218 Squadron sat out a raid on Gelsenkirchen on the 14/15th, which caused loss of production at the Hydriewerk refinery at Scholven, and also remained at home when the Command returned to matters maritime with attacks on Bremen and Wilhelmshaven on the 17/18th. The squadron contributed eight aircraft to a force of forty-three from the Group to attack the town of Kiel on the night of the 18/19th, when S/Ldr Beaman operated for the first time as captain since joining 218 Squadron. The squadron was briefed for operations to Cologne on the 20th, Lorient on the 22nd and Berlin on the 24th, but each was cancelled just prior to take-off. One freshman operation was carried out on the 27th by P/O Donald to Dunkirk. On the 29th, the German cruisers Scharnhorst and Gneisenau were reported to be off Brest, and by the following morning they had taken up residence. This proved to be the start of an Admiralty-inspired bitter eleven month-long campaign to eliminate this twin threat to the Atlantic convoys.

That night the squadron contributed nine crews to a 3 Group contingent of thirty-eight in an overall force of 109 aircraft prepared for a two-wave attack on the ships, which would be nicknamed "Salmon and Gluckstein" by the British press. The first wave found the target almost free of cloud, while the second encountered difficult visibility, but all crews reported bombing the dry docks and observing numerous explosions, although no hits were scored on the ships. This was the final operation for twenty-two-year-old F/O William Anstey, the New Zealander who had joined the squadron in November 1939. In April Anstey would fly out to Malta and then onto Fuka to join 70 Squadron. Here he would complete his tour and bring his total operations to over seventy operations. The squadron also parted company with the recently promoted F/L Mitchell, who was posted to B Flight of XV Squadron at Oakington, to which station he would fail to return from Berlin on June 2nd.

April

On each of the first three days of April small forces were sent to Brest, but were recalled before bombing took place. The Wellington brigade was not involved, and its turn came on the night of the 3/4th, when fifty-one of the type set out for the port and its guests in company with thirty-nine other aircraft. The warships proved difficult to locate, and again no hits were scored. A further attempt on the 4/5th left an unexploded bomb in the dry dock occupied by the Gneisenau, and on the following morning, its captain decided to move the ship out into the harbour while it was dealt with.

During the first week of April 218 Squadron dispatched thirty-five sorties without loss, and parted company with the experienced Sgt Frederick Hoos on his posting to 20 OTU at Lossiemouth on the 4th. On the 8th ten crews, including both flight commanders, were briefed to participate in an operation to Germany's principle naval port of Kiel, which followed on from the previous night's successful assault on the town's docks area. The squadron was timed to attack during the first wave, between 23.30hrs and 23.59hrs, in company with a further nineteen Wellingtons from the Group. They encountered intense flak over the target, and P/O Lambert's aircraft was hit in the starboard engine, despite which, he still delivered the five containers of incendiaries and three 500lb bombs and one 250lbs. While homebound the damaged engine suddenly seized, and the crew threw out everything possible to reduce the weight and remain aloft. With the coast almost

Officers and men of 218 Squadron outside B Flights hanger, RAF Marham early 1941.

in sight they were attacked by an unidentified night fighter, which they evaded by flying into cloud. Employing radio fixes from Hull, the Wellington was nursed back to England, where a wheels up landing was safely carried out at Horsham St Faith. Kiel recorded another damaging night, with the main weight of the attack falling this time upon the town rather than the port area.

A force of eighty aircraft headed for Berlin on the 9/10th, while the maritime campaign continued at the hands of small numbers of aircraft at Vegesack and Emden. 218 Squadron was not involved, but contributed nine Wellingtons on the night of the 9/10th for the next assault on Brest and its lodgers. Two of the squadron contingent returned early, and R1442 HA-D crashed into the sea just off Brest with the loss of all on board. Pilot, Sgt John Brown, was on his ninth operation, and third as captain. At least, on this occasion, four bombs struck the Gneisenau, and fifty men were killed, while a further ninety sustained injury. The squadron returned to Brest on the 12th and 14th dispatching a total of seventeen sorties without loss. For the remainder of the month, Brest remained the most frequently visited destination, along with Kiel, but it was back to Bremen on the night of the 16/17th, when nine 218 Squadron crews attacked the port area in hazy conditions. Flight Lieutenant Shaw was in a running battle with a JU88 while outbound, and the rear gunner fired over four hundred rounds, inflicting damage on the fighter, which was claimed as a probable.

On the 22nd W/Cdr Amison was notified of a posting to 12 OTU at Benson as chief flying instructor. His replacement was to be twenty-nine year-old W/Cdr Herbert James Kirkpatrick, who was currently serving as a flight commander with 9 Squadron at Honington. A former Oxford University Air Squadron member he had joined the RAF in February 1932 and served with various squadrons, as well as spending time at HQ Fighter Command in 1939. After his time at 12 OTU. Amison would be posted to HQ 6 Group, and finish the war as SASO with 205 Group in the Mediterranean.

Group Captain Herbert Kirkpatrick DFC seen here while serving as SASO at 3 Group HQ. The 29-year-old Scotsman's command of the squadron lasted nine months, in which time he successfully completed 12 operations.

Wing Commander Kirkpatrick presided over his first operation and casualties on the night of his appointment, when another attack took place on the German Cruisers at Brest. The squadron dispatched eight aircraft at around 19.45 hrs on the evening of the 22nd, and they encountered thick cloud and a determined defence in the target area, which thwarted the attack. On return Sgt Adams wanted to divert to Boscombe Down as ordered at briefing, because of the likelihood of low cloud at Marham. Oddly, permission was refused, and with tanks almost empty the Wellington pressed on to find Marham as "socked in" as forecast. Approaching Kings Lynn both engines cut, and the pilot gave the order to bail out. The Wellington crashed near Clenchwarton Station, two miles west of Kings Lynn at 03.15hrs, and all of the crew landed safely in the surrounding area. Flight Sergeant Shaw did land at Boscombe Down with engine trouble, and Sgt Graham forced landed at St Minver in Cornwall with wireless failure and empty tanks. Pilot Officer Mansfield's R1496 HA-O was hit by flak over the target and force-landed at Abington with damage to the tail-plane. This was the fifth operation for the twenty-three-year-old New Zealander Sgt Swain RNZAF, and it proved to be his last. Only the rear gunner survived the crash of Wellington L7798 HA-S north of Trezeguer Farm, Milizac, eleven kilometres north-west of the target.

Two nights later another freshman crew found themselves in difficulty on return from a trip to Ostend. Sergeant Chidgey hit trees and crash-landed T2958 HA-T in a field at Barton Bendish at 00.03hrs after overshooting his second attempt to land at Marham, but he and his crew walked away unscathed. An attack on Kiel was planned for the night of the 25/26th, for which nine 218 Squadron crews were briefed. Wing Commander Kirkpatrick chose this as his first operation, and joined the crew of Sgt McNeil in Wellington P9299 HA-R. This was one of only three crews to find and bomb the target on a night when one crew failed to return. Flying Officer George Agar and his crew were last heard of at 23.56hrs, when an SOS bearing was received showing them to be approximately eighty miles from the Dutch Coast. R1507 HA-V is believed to have crashed in the North Sea, taking with it Agar, who was on his twenty-fifth operation, and the rest of the crew. Squadron Leader Beaman was thrown off course by navigational equipment failures and inaccurately forecast winds, and arrived late over the target. After further navigational difficulties he finally landed at Sutton Bridge at 05.30hrs after more than eight hours aloft.

The month was brought to a conclusion with another attack on Kiel on the night of the 30th, for which the squadron contributed nine aircraft to a 3 Group force of thirty-one Wellingtons. Ten-tenths cloud over the target resulted in the group bombing on flak and searchlights in the general proximity of the target. Squadron Leader Beaman circled for fifty minutes drawing flak throughout, before bombing somewhere north of aiming point A. Squadron Leader Richmond was unable to locate the target, and bombed Wilhelmshaven from 10,000 feet instead. Pilot Officer Lymbery attacked Rendsburg aerodrome from 17,000 feet, starting one large fire and several smaller ones.

May

There was a busy start to May, with a major operation almost every night for the first two and a half weeks. It began at Hamburg on the night of the 2/3rd, when a force of under a hundred aircraft achieved very modest damage and thirteen large fires. A force of similar size produced only superficial damage at Cologne on the following night, while a small, predominantly Wellington effort kept up the pressure on Brest. Sergeant William Adams completed his first operational tour in April, and on May 6th he was posted to 23 OTU at Pershore.

This latter operation signalled the start of the new month's operational activities for 218 Squadron, when nine of its crews took part. Weather conditions were perfect, and all of the aircraft bombed the target in bright moonlight. All returned safely to Marham, where crews reported a number of bomb loads straddling the Scharnhorst. Brest was the main target on the 4/5th, when hits were claimed on the Scharnhorst and Gneisenau but were unconfirmed. 218 Squadron sat this one out but was back in action on the following night when contributing nine Wellingtons to an overall force of 140 bound for Mannheim. Weather conditions were not favourable, with ten-tenths cloud all the way into southern Germany. 120 returning crews claimed to have bombed in the target area, but the local authorities estimated around twenty-five bomb loads only fell within the city. Squadron Leader Ian Richmond dropped the squadron's first cookie (4000lb blast bomb) on this night from a Merlin-powered Mk II Wellington, W5448 HA-Z. However unable to find the aiming point hidden beneath the cloud, he dropped it onto an autobahn one and a half miles south-east of Manheim, and witnessed a terrific explosion.

The disappointing series of major raids continued at Hamburg on the 6/7th, when damage was again slight. Another crack at the Scharnhorst and Gneisenau at Brest took place on the 7/8th, when ten 218 Squadron crews joined a further thirty-four Wellingtons drawn from 99, 149 and 115 Squadrons. The attack proceeded in ideal weather conditions and on his return S/Ldr Richmond reported:

Target BREST cruiser Scharnhorst attacked from 13,500 feet with 5 x 500lb S.A.P + 1 x 250lb G.P S.A.P. Direct hits on ship observed by the crew. Several searchlights shot out on way home. Returned safely to base.

Pilot Officer B Pape and crew in R1596 HA-D also claimed to have hit the cruiser, reporting:

Target Scharnhorst at Brest attacked at 00.31hrs from 15,000 feet one stick of 5 x 500lb S.A.P and 1 x 250lb S.A.P. Three bursts observed on jetty and on stern of ship. Brief engagements with enemy fighter over target area.

The largest effort of the month thus far was directed at Hamburg's shipyards on the night of the 8/9th, when 188 aircraft were detailed, 106 of them from 3 Group. 218 Squadron contributed ten aircraft, whose crews were briefed to attack the Blohm & Voss Werke. Wing Commander Kirkpatrick led the squadron contingent in R1496 HA-O, when they arrived over the target city they found the weather to be excellent. Returning crews reported large fires and numerous explosions, one of which was caused by F/O Smith's cookie, and he recorded "*a pleasing explosion and blue flashes, a wizard bomb*". Not to be outdone, S/Ldr Richmond dropped his cookie on what was reported to be the Blohm & Voss Werke, and he too noted a terrific explosion. This time the bombing results on Hamburg were more encouraging, and the city authorities reported eight large fires and the destruction of a number of apartment blocks. The death toll was put at 185 people, and this was the highest death toll from a Bomber Command attack of the war to date. A simultaneous raid on Bremen by over one hundred aircraft produced widespread bombing throughout the city, but no hits on the U-Boat yards. The total number of sorties for the night was a new Command record, surpassing February's big night at Hanover. A Congratulatory message from Senior Air Staff and the C-in-C of Bomber Command was received at Marham on the 9th, which read:

> "*My congratulations to you and the groups and squadrons under your command on last night's heavy and successful raids over Germany. The skill and daring with which they carried out deserves the highest praise and the scale reveals the growing power of Bomber Command. Archibald Sinclair.*"

On the same day the station records book records the following details:

> *The Commander in Chief desires to bring to the notice of all ranks in the command the coolness and devotion to duty shown by No.938896 Sgt Burke H a Wireless Operator / Air Gunner in No.218 Squadron.*
>
> *On a night on 8/9th April 1941 this N.C.O was a member of a crew of a Wellington aircraft detailed to attack Kiel. In the course of this operation the aircraft was very badly hit and was eventually flown back to England across the North Sea on one engine after all movable equipment and maps had been jettisoned from the aircraft. Great dependence, therefore, had to be placed upon the assistance which could be obtained by wireless in order to bring the aircraft back to England. The fix aerial, however had been damaged by enemy action and before any wireless could be obtained, Sergeant Burke with more than half his body outside the astro hatch repaired the damage. The aircraft returned to England on a course guessed by the navigator, who had no means of sextant and by wireless bearings which were obtained by Sgt Burke once he had repaired his wireless. Throughout the whole trip Sgt Burke's coolness and efficiency resulted in the aircraft being brought safely back to an aerodrome in England. He had to change frequencies and wavebands at*

the pilots request with great rapidity and finally homes the aircraft successfully at Horsham St Faith. It is considered that this N.C.O's coolness and skill resulted in the safe return of this aircraft."

Regardless of the above, Sergeant H Burke did not receive any award for his action.

On the 9th S/Ldr Beaman was posted to 149 Squadron to succeed W/Cdr Powell as commanding officer. His replacement as A Flight commander was an equally experienced and courageous pilot, acting S/Ldr Denis Clyde-Smith, who was posted across the tarmac from 115 Squadron. Mannheim had always featured prominently on the Command's target list, and would continue to do so for the remainder of the war. One of its attractions as the bomber force increased in strength was its geographical proximity to Ludwigshafen, which nestled opposite Mannheim on the western bank of the Rhine. Any attack on Mannheim with an approach from the west would inevitably lead to the bombing spilling over into Ludwigshafen, and in time this would be incorporated into the plan of attack. On the night of the 9/10th 146 aircraft were dispatched for a joint raid on these twin cities, and for the period, a reasonably successful outcome was achieved. A little over fifty buildings were destroyed, but a substantial number sustained damage, and over three and a half thousand people were rendered homeless, although some only temporarily.

The assault on Hamburg in line with March's directive continued on the 10/11th and 11/12th, and the two operations resulted in a combined total of over two hundred fires, seventy of them classed as large. Earlier on the 11th G/C V.E Groom OBE DFC relinquished his role as base commander, having received a posting to the Air Ministry as Director of Plans. He was succeeded by W/Cdr Andrew "Square" McKee DFC AFC, who had commanded 9 Squadron for six months in 1940. Remarkably his tenure would last only a matter of days, as he was replaced on the 18th by the substantial figure of G/C A "Tiny" Evans-Evans, who combined the role with that of commanding officer of 115 Squadron. Mannheim and Ludwigshafen came into the bomb sights again on the 12/13th, but the earlier success was not repeated and many crews bombed alternative targets. The on-going hectic round of operations took a hundred aircraft to Hanover on the 15/16th, before raids on Cologne on the following two nights produced only modest damage. Kiel also escaped lightly on the 17/18th, and this was the final major operation of the month. Tragedy struck on the morning of the 18th, when P/O Brian Lymbery and his crew were conducting a training flight in W5448 HA-W, a Mk II Wellington. The dinghy escaped from its stowage and jammed the starboard elevator, causing the aircraft to crash near Hilgay, five miles from Downham Market. All but the rear gunner died on impact, and he succumbed to his injuries two days later. To survive operations only to die in this manner was tragic, and it was the only blemish in the squadron's otherwise loss-free month. Vickers built W5448 had joined the squadron from 12 Maintenance Unit on April

16th, and was the regular mount of S/Ldr Richmond. It had been this Wellington that dropped the squadron's first 4,000lb blast bomb on May 5th.

On the 24th F/L Herbert Price was posted in from 15 OTU at Harwell, and promoted to the rank of acting squadron leader to assume duties as B Flight commander. On the 26th S/Ldr Ian Richmond was posted to command 27 OTU at Lichfield in Staffordshire at the end of his long association with 218 Squadron. After screening he would be posted to XV Squadron at Mildenhall. On June 29th 1942 he would fail to return from an attack on Bremen and spend the remainder of the war as a PoW. Ian Richmond was the cousin of S/Ldr Leonard Trent, who was to earn a VC during an epic daylight attack on a power station at Amsterdam in May 1943.

June

The performance of the Command over the next two months was to have a significance of which the crews were unaware. Photographs taken during the period's night operations were to be used to assess their effectiveness, and a civil servant, Mr D M Butt, was charged with the responsibility of producing a report for the War Cabinet. The first operation of the new month was a low-key effort directed at Düsseldorf on the night of the 3/4th, for which forty-nine Wellingtons were detailed by the group, thirteen of them from 218 Squadron. Shortly before take-off the squadron's participation was all but cancelled, and only S/Ldr Price flew to the Ruhr in Wellington R1148 HA-L. The target was hidden under ten-tenths cloud, through which heavy flak was bursting, and unable to locate the aiming point Price bombed on an estimated position. Small-scale operations then held sway until the 10/11th, when over a hundred aircraft were employed against Brest, where the Prinz Eugen had now joined its sister ships. The squadron dispatched twelve crews, whose efforts were thwarted by an effective smoke screen and they were unable to assess results.

On the 11/12th Düsseldorf was the intended target for sixty-seven Wellingtons from 3 Group, while eighty others were sent to Duisburg. It seems that neither city was troubled by falling bombs, while Cologne reported a significant number of them, some of which caused substantial damage to the main railway station, while others fell into the docks area. Whether the Rhineland Capital was bombed in error or as an alternative to the briefed targets is uncertain. Pre-empting a new directive a month hence the night of the 12/13th was devoted to attacks on railway targets at Soest, Schwerte, Hamm and Osnabrück, the two latter assigned to forces of Wellingtons. The 3 Group crews were briefed for Hamm just north of the Ruhr one of Germany's most important railway centres, but the attack by eighty-eight aircraft was disappointing. Industrial haze over the target made identification difficult although F/L Stokes and crew glimpsed a railway line and dropped their load from 10,000 feet in one stick. That started three large fires, two of which were still burning vigorously as the crew turned for home. On the credit side only one Wellington was lost from the 150 of the type dispatched on all of the night's activities.

Cologne, Düsseldorf and Bremen dominated the remainder of the month, the first two-mentioned were attacked simultaneously on no fewer than eight nights by forces of varying sizes. Another ineffective assault on Brest and the *Prinz Eugen* took place on the 13th, when haze and the very efficient smoke screen hampered the attempt. This was followed twenty-four hours later by a trip to Cologne, in which twelve 218 Squadron crews took part. Squadron leader Clyde-Smith and crew were the squadron's only contribution to a small-scale attack on Hanover on the same night, when flying in W5447 HA-C. They found the primary target covered in thick cloud, and bombed on a concentration of flak and searchlights. Homebound just south of Amsterdam the Wellington was attacked by a Bf110, which was claimed as destroyed. In fact, the encounter was not as one-sided as the claim suggested, as evidenced by the Wellington's port wing and fuel tank, which were riddled with cannon and machine-gun fire. What the crew didn't know was that their adversary had been Lt Leopold Fellner of 4/NJG1, who had claimed the Wellington as shot down at 03.18hrs. Squadron Leader Clyde-Smith was awarded the DFC for this action, as was his rear gunner, P/O Frederick Chalk.

The squadron sent a respectable fifteen aircraft to Cologne on the night of the 17/18th, when industrial haze made accurate bombing difficult. Both flight commanders were among fifteen crews sent to attack Kiel docks on the 20/21st, and two aircraft failed to return. Both were captained by New Zealanders who had called for help as they struggled with engine trouble during the return flight. They sent out SOS messages which located them in approximately the same position at 54 degrees N – 30 degrees 17' E. Sergeant Gordon Jillett was on his third operation as captain and eighteenth in all, when and his crew were lost in the sea in R1339 HA-J. Sergeant Mason Fraser and crew fell victim to Oblt Paul Bohn of 4/NJG2, who claimed R1713 HA-V at 00.20hrs twenty kilometres off Spurn Head. Twenty-three year old Fraser had joined the squadron on February 10th, and at the time of his death had flown twenty-two operations. He had previously received the following commendation:

"The Air Officer Commanding No.3 Group has highly commended Sgt Fraser, second pilot to Wellington 1328 on the night of 13/14th March, 1941. On his skilful and successful landing of that aircraft with its undercarriage retracted, after it had been severely damaged by enemy action and the first pilot wounded."

As the North Sea was calm an air sea rescue effort was put into action in an attempt to locate the ditched crews. A high speed launch was dispatched from its base in the Humber, while two Wellingtons and three Stirlings also set out to search. Each combed the area for an hour, and a patch of oil and a dinghy were located. The dinghy was empty and there was no sign of any survivors. It was a bitter blow to the squadron to lose two experienced crews.

Briefings took place for a number of targets on the 23rd, among them Cologne, for which eleven 218 Squadron crews were dispatched, led by S/Ldr Clyde-Smith. Wing Commander Kirkpatrick, meanwhile, attacked Kiel harbour where his Mk II Wellington was bracketed by accurate flak during his bombing run. Having dropped his 4,000lb bomb in the general target area without observing results, he put the Wellington into a violent dive and ultimately landed safely back at Marham with a damaged tail. Sergeant Workman and crew were sent to bomb Emden on a freshman trip, and once again thick haze prevented an assessment of results. Thirty-four 3 Group Wellingtons were detailed as part of a force of sixty-four aircraft bound for Bremen on the night of the 25/26th, and twelve of them were provided by 218 Squadron. Electrical storms made conditions impossible and no bombs fell within the target area. The group sent a further seventeen aircraft back to Kiel on the same night, and they encountered the same appalling weather. Icing was experienced almost immediately after take-off, and six aircraft were forced to turn back before or just after crossing the Dutch coast. Three crews bombed targets of opportunity, including Soesterberg and Haamstede aerodromes, while F/L Stokes and Sgts Taylor and Rose battled against the elements to reach the target area and bomb.

On the 29th the group was again handed two targets, assigning fifty-five aircraft to marshalling yards at Bremen, and a further twenty-two Wellingtons to Kiel Harbour. Ideal conditions over Bremen allowed the crews to locate and bomb visually in the face of an intense flak barrage, and German night fighters were also noticeably active. Sergeants Taylor and Skett were among 218 Squadron participants compelled to take violent evasive action over the target to escape the flak, while Sgt Workman was forced down almost to ground level. Unable to deliver his load safely he bombed Bremerhaven as an alternative. One 218 Squadron aircraft failed to return home, T2806 HA-T crashing in Germany without survivors from the crew of twenty-seven–year-old Australian, P/O Francis Bryant who was on his 18th operation. The squadron's sole Wellington crew to be dispatched to Kiel on this night experienced intercom problems while outbound, and this persuaded P/O Lambert to drop his 4,000 pounder on the last resort target of Rendsburg. Analysis showed that not one of the month's raids produced significant results.

July

July would begin as June had ended with the accent on Bremen but the month's first operation was by fifty Wellingtons against Brest on the night of the 1/2nd. During the course of the attack a bomb exploded along side the Prinz Eugen causing considerable damage and killing sixty sailors. 218 Squadron's first operation of the month was again directed against Bremen, to which nine aircraft were dispatched on the night of the 2/3rd. Cloudy conditions over the target made accurate bombing practically impossible for the forty-nine 3 Group crews, and most were forced to bomb through the few isolated breaks in the clouds. Although explosions could be seen below the white stuff, the effects of the bombing could not be observed. Essen, home of the giant Krupp armaments works, had already gained a reputation for being almost impossible to identify and hit, and this was a situation that would not be rectified until 1943. A raid there on the 3/4th by ninety Wellingtons and Whitleys sprayed bombs over a wide area of the Ruhr, and few on the intended target. Bremen was also visited again on this night by Hampdens and Wellingtons, and effective bombing was reported by returning crews.

There followed yet another assault on Brest and its lodgers on the night of the 4th, conducted by a force that included twelve 218 Squadron Wellingtons led by the two flight commanders. An effective smoke screen over the docks created difficulties but Sgts Skett and Forster and F/L Stokes positively identified the dockside and jetty area, and dropped their loads accordingly. Wellington MkII W5447 HA-C developed engine trouble halfway across the channel, but Sgt Taylor opted to press on despite struggling to climb above 5,000 feet. Fierce flak accompanied the bombing run, which frustratingly ended with a total hang-up. Undeterred, a second run was attempted, only for the entire load to fall safe moments before the aiming point was reached. The squadron contributed twelve aircraft to an overall 3 Group force of fifty-four for an accurate raid on the marshalling yards at Münster in ideal weather conditions on the 5/6th. Squadron Leader Clyde-Smith didn't find the aiming point, and bombed the railway at Albersloh as an alternative. T2887 HA-N was attacked by a Bf110 on the return journey, and the rear gunner, Sgt Bain-Killie, claimed it as destroyed. R1436 HA-N also crossed swords with a JU88 while homebound, at which the rear gunner, P/O Cranley, opened fire at thirty yards range with two short bursts. The attacker was seen to dive away with smoke pouring from an engine, and a minute later both the captain and the rear gunner witnessed an explosion in the sea below. The crew claimed the fighter as destroyed. Returning crews reported large fires in the vicinity of the railway yards. Flying Officer Ralph and crew described a tremendous bluish-white explosion which lit up the interior of the aircraft.

For the second night running favourable weather conditions enabled Münster to host what was claimed by returning crews to be a successful attack. Eleven 218 Squadron aircraft were led away by S/Ldr Clyde-Smith in the rather battered R1008 HA-A, and a number of crews reported explosions around the aiming point, including a large one believed to be from a gas holder, which lit up the surrounding area. The target area became a mass of flames and smoke which was still visible from more than sixty miles away as the crews retreated. Reports from Münster, however, mention only twenty-one people killed during the first attack, and thirty incendiaries in the town during the second. On the following night 114 Wellingtons took off for Cologne, and those reaching the target delivered upon the city its most destructive raid of the year. Residential property was badly effected, and almost five and a half thousand people were left homeless, while a number of railway lines were cut, and seven industrial buildings sustained serious damage. Also on this night Wellingtons returned to Münster, where the authorities this time acknowledged many bombs falling.

A new Air Ministry directive was issued on the 9th, which referred to Germany's transportation system and the morale of its civilian population as its most vulnerable points. C-in-C Peirse was now ordered to direct his forces against the major railway centres ringing the Ruhr, to inhibit the movement of raw materials, and the export of finished products. The precision nature of such targets dictated that moonlight conditions prevail, while on moonless nights, the Rhine cities of Cologne, Düsseldorf and Duisburg would be easier to identify. When less favourable weather conditions obtained, attacks were to be carried out against more distant urban targets in northern, eastern and southern Germany.

The first large raid of the war on Aachen employed eighty-two aircraft on the 9/10th, when central districts sustained particularly heavy damage. Almost seventeen hundred dwelling units were destroyed or seriously effected, and scores of commercial premises were hit. Wellingtons played only a minor role, as the majority of those operating on this night went instead to Osnabrück. Fifty-seven Wellingtons took part in the intended attack on the marshalling yards, and ten of these were provided by 218 Squadron. Night fighters were again in evidence, and over Holland a Bf109 attacked R1436 HA-N, which contained the crew of Sgt Banks. The Station Records Book records the following:

> "*For a second time in succession F/O Dunham (flying as Observer to Sgt Banks) captain of A/C 1436 was attacked by a Bf109 which appeared from his starboard beam and opened fire from 300 yards with one cannon firing red tracer and 4 machine guns. Our aircraft turned and front gunner opened fire simultaneously with the E/A in a short burst. Our pilot then turned away and gave the rear gunner a chance to fire a 10 second burst. The enemy aircraft went down in a very steep dive and was seen by the 2nd pilot, 700 feet below still diving steeply. The crew consider that the E/A could not pull out of the dive and are convinced that he piled in*".

Sadly, the operation itself was less successful and the local authorities recorded no bombs falling upon the town.

Almost a hundred Wellingtons were sent to Cologne in poor weather conditions on the 10/11th, and they and a Hampden element managed to find the mark with only three high explosive bombs. After a night's rest Wellingtons began a six night stretch of operations, beginning at Bremen on the 12/13th, again in company with Hampdens. There was a return to northern Germany for 218 Squadron on the night of the 13/14th, when eleven of its crews were detailed to join in an attack on Bremen, while the freshman crew of Sgt Huckle was briefed for Emden. Weather conditions outbound and over the target were unfavourable for accurate bombing, forcing most crews to find alternative targets, including Amsterdam and various airfields. The freshman couldn't find Emden, and bombed Borkum Island as an alternative. An all-Wellington force of sixty-nine aircraft set off for Bremen, Vegesack and Emden on the following night, but thick cloud and icing conditions reduced the numbers reaching their assigned targets to seventeen. A predominantly Wellington force was back over Bremen on the 14/15th, when returning crews reported the whole town to be ablaze. Many fires were also claimed to have resulted from a simultaneous raid on Hanover, to which twenty-one Wellingtons contributed.

Marginal weather conditions and intense flak over Duisburg on the night of the 15/16th created problems for the twelve participating 218 Squadron crews, and the aircraft of Sgt Rose and S/Ldr Price were both hit. The latter, R1448 HA-L, lost an engine and sustained considerable damage to the fuselage. Despite being attacked by a night fighter while homebound at 600 feet over Holland Price and crew brought their mount home to a safe landing at Marham. On board for operational experience was the recently promoted W/Cdr J L Fletcher. Herbert Price was awarded a DFC for his actions on this night, the citation reading:

One night in July 1941, this officer was detailed to attack Duisburg. In spite of searchlight concentrations and heavy anti aircraft fire, he spent 40 minutes over the target, which was eventually successfully bombed. His aircraft was repeatedly hit and his rear turret put out of action. Over Holland and on the return journey his aircraft was intercepted by an enemy aircraft, which was shaken off by skilful avoiding action. The port engine failed and his aircraft began to lose height rapidly. All available articles were jettisoned but S/Ldr Price was compelled to fly at 600 feet. By skilful piloting, however, he landed at his base. He has always shown the utmost coolness, courage and determination.

Less fortunate were F/L John Stokes and his crew, who all perished when R1536 HA-G was shot down over Holland at 00.55hrs by Hptm Werner Streib of I/NJG1. The loss of twenty-three year old John Stokes, who was on his thirty-third operation, was a bitter blow to the squadron. Canadian P/O Cottier RCAF made a heavy landing on return from a training flight on the 15th, stalling Wellington X3217 onto the ground from between 20 and 30 feet, and badly damaging the port undercarriage in the process. The A.M.Form 1180 records that,

"Cottier was posted in from a Stirling squadron, and that he is unlikely to make an efficient pilot. If this was known he would have had been given duel training. Previously been at Wellington OTU 218 Squadron C.O states further tuition has now been given on the Wellington, and it is thought he will make a capable pilot."

Squadron Leader Herbert Price DFC shows Sir Alec Burns around a squadron Vickers Wellington. Note the recently applied Donald Duck emblem and 22 bombing symbols.

Harsh words initially, but W/Cdr Kirkpatrick's intervention would see the young Canadian given the extra hours training he obviously needed. Sadly, Thomas George Cottier failed to return from an attack on Hamburg with 419 Squadron RCAF on January 15th 1942. There would be no further operations for 218 Squadron for six nights, during which period Hamburg was targeted on the 16/17th with Wellingtons constituting half of the hundred-strong force. In conditions of poor visibility only 50% of the force bombed in the target area for little reward. The Cologne authorities reported no serious damage on the 17/18th and 20/21st, and the first major raid on Frankfurt was equally ineffective on the 21/22nd. A force of Wellingtons and Halifaxes was sent to Mannheim on this night also, twelve of the former provided by 218 Squadron. The weather was good, and for once Mannheim's defences seemed to be taken by surprise. A number of crews reported seeing their bomb loads exploding across the railway station just south of the aiming point, but it is unlikely that damage was more than modest. The same two southern cities featured twenty-four and forty-eight hours later, on each occasion with inconclusive results.

A plan had been prepared for a major assault on the German cruisers at Brest, and this was to take place in daylight on the 24th. On the 23rd, however, it was discovered that the Scharnhorst had slipped away and was now at la Pallice some two hundred miles further south. The original plan had called for a co-ordinated attack by Wellingtons from 1 and 3 Groups and Halifaxes from 4 Group, and in the light of the new information concerning Scharnhorst it was decided that the Halifax element would target her, while the original plan went ahead at Brest. Three Fortresses from 2 Group's 90 Squadron were to lead the operation by bombing from very high level, and it was hoped that they, and a diversion by Hampdens under a Spitfire escort at a less rarefied altitude, would draw off sufficient enemy fighters to allow the seventy-nine Wellingtons to bomb unopposed. In the event, the fighter and flak opposition was more fierce than anticipated, and the Wellington crews had to run the gauntlet as they made their final approach. In return for six unconfirmed hits on the Gneisenau, ten Wellingtons were shot down,

The nine participating 218 Squadron Wellingtons were divided into three formations. Squadron Leader Gibbes DFC, who was operating for the first time since joining the squadron, led the first trio with W/Cdr Fletcher as second pilot. They were engaged by two Bf109s, one of which was claimed as destroyed. Pilot Officer Pape landed his flak-damaged R1598 HA-D at Harwell and reported his bombs straddling the quayside. The second formation was also engaged by the defences, following which R1726 HA-O was observed to crash into the sea in the target area. Twenty-three-year-old New Zealander P/O Morrison Jolly and three of his crew were killed, while their two colleagues took to their parachutes to survive as PoWs. It was Jolly's nineteenth operation since joining the squadron direct from 15 OTU in March. Sgt John Knott, the wireless operator, recalls the events leading up to the capture and eventual imprisonment.

On July 24th the target was Brest and the German Battleships. Ack – ack was very intense, and we dropped the bombs with flak exploding all around the aircraft. Having survived the flak thundering under the Wellington we encountered about fifteen Bf109s. The rear gunners all let loose. Our rear gunner gave a running

Wing Commander Augustus "Rod" Gibbes DFC. The Australians tour with 218 Squadron very nearly cost him his life when he ditched on return from Oostende on September 2nd 1941.

commentary over the intercom. Whilst this was going on I was forced to kneel down because the bullets from the fighters were whizzing through the aircraft. I clipped on my chute and adjusted my hardness. I tapped the 2nd pilot on the shoulder and indicated back down the fuselage that a fire had broken out. I opened the escape hatch to bail out, but in my haste the chute opened in the fuselage having caught on something protruding. I gathered the billowing chute in my arms, and during this time the Canadian Observer, Sgt W "Jake" Jacobsen, had left. I followed and remember tumbling through the air thinking, I hope the chute opens correctly. I looked up and was shocked to see that the chute was only partially opened, and I remember the relief when I was jolted upwards as it finally deployed fully. I then started a slow decent watching the action unfold all around me. As I descended a German fighter circled around me, I found out later that this was to indicate where I would be coming down for those on the coast. I inflated the Mae West just before I hit the water. In my shocked state I had forgotten to release my harness and chute and started to slowly sink below the waves, I frantically tried to hit the release gear, and I finally managed it and shot up to the surface, to find my chute was floating nearby. After about half hour a green motor launch arrived, I was dragged aboard and given hot coffee and taken ashore. The beach was full of young French girl's sun bathing with a number of German officers, while above them the battle was still unfolding. A German officer arrived from a nearby Chateau which overlooked the bay I had just landed in. The Luftwaffe officer informed me in perfect English that I was now a Prisoner of War. I was taken to the Chateau and informed my wet clothing would be dried and that I would be fed shortly. While waiting we started to chat about the war, all the time we both watched transfixed as the battle unfolded above us. The Luftwaffe officer loaned me his binoculars so that I could see that the Battleships were still undamaged. He had been using them to try and locate any other survivors from my crew. I was later informed that one chute appeared to open too late, while two chutes were seen but never located. The German officer assured me that the German Authorities will notify the Red Cross of my capture immediately and it would be broadcast. In fact my parents knew I was a PoW before they had received the telegram!! After about two hours in this beautiful Chateau a large black open-tourer arrived with two gentlemen in black shirts and close-cropped hair. They did not look particularly pleasant. I was taken to a nearby Army Barracks, given more food and asked a number of questions. I was then loaded into a large lorry and transported to a nearby airfield to be greeted by the German Bf109 pilots who had shot us down!!!

R1601 HA-T sustained considerable damage from both flak and fighters, and on return Sgt Banks claimed one of the latter as damaged and also a hit on the Gneisenau. Meanwhile the Halifaxes of 35 and 76 Squadrons had experienced an equally bruising time at the hands of enemy fighters and flak at la Pallice, and had lost five of their number, a third of those dispatched, and all of the surviving aircraft had returned with battle damage. In return a number of bombs had struck the Scharnhorst, necessitating her return to Brest, where better repair facilities existed, and this would at least ensure that she posed no threat to Allied shipping for some time. That same night the squadron dispatched six NCO crews to Kiel, five of them reaching the target and the sixth returning early with technical difficulties after depositing the bomb load onto an enemy airfield on the island of Sylt.

During the remainder of the month Wellingtons were involved in fairly minor operations against Kiel on the 24/25th and Hamburg on the 25/26th, before representing over half of the force of 116 aircraft bound for Cologne on the 30/31st. The crews encountered bad weather, and the raid almost entirely missed the city. There were no further operations for 218 Squadron after the 24th, the annual sports day went ahead on the 27th in weather fine enough to allow the squadron dance to be held on the sports field. It was a fitting way to end a hectic month, which had seen the squadron carry out six daylight and ninety-two night sorties totalling 484.25 flying hours, and deliver 317,180lbs of bombs. The award of the DFC to S/Ldr Ian Richmond was announced at the end of the month, the citation read:

> *"This officer has served with his squadron since 1938 and for the past year has commanded a flight with conspicuous keenness and leadership. On the night of May 7th 1941, he dived through heavy and accurate flak to obtain a direct hit on the Gneisenau at Brest. He has at all times, provided an example of efficiency, courage and devotion to duty"*

August

The August account was opened at Hamburg on the 2/3rd, where railway installations were the targets for eighty aircraft, including fifty-eight Wellingtons. A further forty of the type, together with a handful of Stirlings and Halifaxes, carried out a simultaneous raid on Berlin, where haze hampered the bombing. 218 Squadron's S/Ldr Price and P/O Pape were given the German Air Ministry building in the Capital as their target, but they found far from ideal weather conditions over the city, and that rendered the location of the aiming point almost impossible. Even the defences failed to open up to provide a reference, and after what seemed an eternity, both crews bombed targets of opportunity, P/O Pape dropping his cookie on Brandenburg, and S/Ldr Price his over the area of Neusterlitz.

Frankfurt was the intended target on the night of the 3/4th, but the weather prompted a switch to Hanover. Wing Commander Fletcher led a force of nine 218 Squadron participants in an operation that started badly, when, soon after take-off, X9747 HA-E crashed at Salthouse, seven miles north-east of Norwich

A lone German sentry stands guard over the crash site of Wing Commander John Fletcher's Vickers Wellington Z8781 HA-S the victim of Bremen's flak.

after a fire broke out. Pilot Officer John Maxwell, a Canadian, and P/O George Crabb, who was flying as second pilot and at thirty-eight-years of age was one of the squadron's oldest pilots, were killed. The remaining crew all parachuted to safety, but a number of injuries were sustained. Weather conditions in the target area again made pin-pointing difficult, and one aircraft failed to return after falling victim to Bremen's Flak Regiment 22. Z8781 HA-S contained the crew of W/Cdr John Fletcher, who died with all but two of his crew when it crashed in flames near Moordeich, south of Bremen. Only the observer, F/Sgt Alexander, and rear gunner, Sgt Sponge, survived. Glaswegian Alexander, who spoke fluent German, managed initially to evade capture by stealing a civilian jacket and a scarecrow's peaked cap from a local farm close to the crash site. Next day, while casually walking past a public house, he stole a cycle left unattended outside. By August 6th Alexander found himself in Lübeck, where, after a week in hiding, he managed to board a neutral Swedish ship heading out into the Baltic. Nine hours later Alexander's presence on the vessel was radioed back to Lübeck. A German motor-launch was dispatched to collect him. Despite Alexander's protestations that he was on board a neutral vessel he was forced aboard the motor-launch at gun point. Taken to Warnemünde he was put into the cells at the nearby aerodrome until transferred by train to Dulag Luft Frankfurt. Alexander was awarded an OBE in December 1945 for this escape attempt and two others while a PoW.

Wing Commander John Fletcher had joined the RAF in 1930 and spent most of his pre-war career flying fighters. It was only in 1938, when posted to 6 (Auxiliary) Group, that he began his association with Bomber Command. Fletcher is one of numerous wing commanders to pass through the squadron without any explanation in the ORB for their presence. As he does not appear to have been decorated, it seems possible that his wartime service had been undertaken in a non-operational post. The most likely scenario is that he was gaining operational experience prior to being granted a command with a 3 Group squadron, and it is not beyond the realms of possibility, that he was being groomed to replace W/Cdr Kirkpatrick at 218 Squadron.

A busy night of operations on the 5/6th involved seven aircraft attacking three separate targets, Mannheim, Karlsruhe and the docks at Calais. Squadron Leaders Gibbes and Price took the squadron's Mk IIs to Karlsruhe, Gibbes dropping his 4,000lb bomb from 9,000 feet at 01.22hrs in the south-west corner of the town, where it started a number of good fires. Three minutes later Price dropped his from 8,000 feet into the centre of the town, and this resulted in a huge red explosion followed by two large fires, which were visible from eighty miles on the return trip. Pilot Officer Pape and Sgt Banks attacked Calais, causing considerable damage to the docks area and again creating fires visible from England's south-east coast. Railway targets were raided at the same locations on the following night, before an attempt to hit the Krupp works at Essen on the 7/8th caused only light damage within the city. 218 Squadron sent two aircraft to attack Boulogne on this night, and then contributed five more to a low key 3 Group attack on the Blohm & Voss Shipyards at Hamburg on the 8/9th, while a single crew went to Kiel. Railway installations at Mönchengladbach were the objective for twenty-nine Wellingtons on the 11/12th, of which ten were provided by 218 Squadron. They were forced to bomb through scattered cloud, and results were inconclusive. Sergeant Fisher crash-landed R1596 HA-O at Marham on return after sustaining flak damage over the target. Damage to the hydraulic system caused the bomb bay doors to remain open, and along with a buckled starboard aileron and several holes in the fuselage, condemned the crew to a slow and cold return flight.

The squadron contributed six aircraft to an ineffective attack on the Krupp works at Essen on the 12/13th, while S/Ldr Price and Sgt Huckle were handed Berlin as their target in company with thirty-eight other Wellingtons and a contingent of Halifaxes, Stirlings and Manchesters. In the event, the weather conditions dictated otherwise for Price, who bombed the docks at Stettin, while Huckle bombed Kiel and set off six medium fires. Neither operation caused much damage, but one of the Gee trials Wellingtons from 115 Squadron was lost during the former, although the equipment did not fall into enemy hands. Railway stations at Hanover and Magdeburg were the aiming points on the night of the 14/15th, the former claiming two 218 Squadron aircraft. Pilot Officer Winston Wilson's X9753 HA-G crashed near Maquise on the way home, killing all but the rear

The twisted remains of Vickers Wellington X9753 HA-G skippered Pilot Officer Winston Wilson. The Wellington crashed on farm land near Marcquise, south of Calais on August 15th 1941.

gunner, Sgt Roy Barnard. After treatment in St Omer hospital he became a PoW. Wilson had conducted all of his previous ten operations as 2nd pilot to S/Ldr Clyde-Smith and this was his first operation as captain. There were no survivors at all from the crew of P/O Arthur Mitchell, who were on their fourth operation. They were in R1008 HA-A, one of the squadron's longest serving Wellingtons, and sent a message at 00.57hrs stating *"Target bombed"*.

It was on the 18th that the Butt Report was completed, and its disclosures were to send shock waves reverberating around the Cabinet Room and the Air Ministry. Having studied around four thousand photographs taken on night operations during June and July, Mr Butt concluded that only a tiny fraction of bombs were falling within miles of their intended targets. This swept away at a stroke any notion that the Command's attacks were having a materiel effect on Germany's war effort, and it demonstrated the claims of the crews to be over enthusiastic. The report would forever unjustly blight the period of tenure as C-in-C of Sir Richard Peirse, and would provide ammunition for those calling for the dissolution of an independent bomber force, and the redistribution of its aircraft to other theatres of operation.

Typical of the claims of success was a raid on Cologne on the night of the report's release, when crews returned with eye-witness accounts of many fires, while the city authorities announced just one building damaged. 218 Squadron's two Mk II Wellingtons were involved in this operation and one of them failed to return. Sergeant Huckle and crew were in W5457 HA-Z, which fell to Ofw Gerhard Herzog of III/NJG1 over Germany at 02.30hrs. This was Herzog's second victory of the night, having claimed a 149 Squadron Wellington only minutes earlier. All but the wireless operator survived the incident, and it is believed that he was killed during the engagement. A simultaneous attack on Duisburg was supported by seven 218 Squadron Wellingtons, and N2844 HA-M was shot down into the Ijsselmeer by Fw Siegfried Ney of IV/NJG1 on the way home. There were no survivors from the crew of Sgt Kenneth Shearing, who was on his twenty-third operation, but only his seventh as first pilot.

His Excellency Sir Alan Burns, Governor Designate of the African Gold Coast, visited the squadron on August 20th and officially bestowed upon it the title *Gold Coast*. In the Gold Coast a local "Spitfire Fund" had been inaugurated in June 1940, the total contributions to which had reached a staggering £100,000 by June 1942. The choice of name was intended partly as a compliment, and partly as a means of associating outlying parts of the Empire as closely as possible with the general war effort. In an effort to bond the squadron and the peoples of the Gold

The Governor of the Gold Coast Sir Alec Burns is escorted by RAF Marham's station commander, New Zealander Group Captain McKee while inspecting A Flight August 20th 1941. It is believed the visit was to mark the official adoption of the title Gold Coast. Note the smashed windows on B Flight hangers.

Coast even closer, a number of the squadron's Wellingtons had the names of local towns and cities applied to them.

No further operations were undertaken by the squadron until the 26th, but the weather continued to cause problems for those involved in the meantime, and heavy cloud and icing conditions completely nullified an intended attack on Kiel on the 19/20th. Crews returning from Mannheim on the 22/23rd claimed many fires, but the authorities reported only one house seriously damaged. Storms and thick cloud ruined an attempt on Karlsruhe on the 25/26th, but even when there was clear visibility, as at Cologne on the 26/27th, only a few bombs found the mark and damage was negligible. 218 Squadron's Sgt Thomson and crew attacked Boulogne on this night and dropped their six 500lb bombs across docks 4 and 6. Several small fires erupted, which soon merged into a single conflagration that was visible from forty miles away. The final few nights of the month brought plenty of activity but little improvement in performance. Mannheim was the target for the night of the 27/28th, when eight crews were briefed for what turned out to be a rather frustrating night for the squadron. Sergeant Rose taxied R1601 HA-T into barbed wire, ending its participation, and then a JU88 attacked Marham and inflicted minor damage to the Drem Light system and flare path that would cause problems for returning aircraft when landing. Sergeant Banks suffered port engine failure over France and returned early and Sgt Foster experienced difficulties with the bomb distribution arm, which caused his load to overshoot the target by fifteen seconds. Sergeant McBride was diverted to West Raynham and crashed on landing at 04.00 hrs after undershooting his approach, whereupon X9663 HA-D was destroyed by fire. Finally, Sgt Fisher crashed while attempting to land at Marham with an oiled up windscreen, but both the Wellington, R1596 HA-O, and crew were returned to duty. The final operation of the month involved ten 218 Squadron Wellingtons in an ineffective attack on Mannheim, when most bombed on ETA or the glow of the fires below the complete cloud cover. Eighty-two sorties had been flown during the month, delivering a total of 238,530lb of bombs.

September

In the light of what is now known about actual damage inflicted on targets, it is likely, that many of the fires reported by crews were decoys set by the Germans and this was the case at Cologne on the 1/2nd of September, when only one house was damaged despite the claims. Eight 218 Squadron crews were briefed for this operation, of which one failed to take-off through technical difficulties, and another returned early with a port engine malfunction. This was the first operation for S/Ldr Gerald Spence MiD, who had arrived at Marham on the previous day, and was crewed for this one with the experienced B Flight commander, S/Ldr 'Rod' Gibbes DFC.

Gibbes and crew were among four assigned to attack the docks at Ostende on the 2nd. They were aloft in X9810 HA-K, which was hit by flak over the target and sent diving towards the sea. At around 4,000 feet, with both engines racing, Gibbes and second pilot Sgt Helfer managed to level out and bring them under control. Helfer reported considerable damaged to the fuel and oil pipes to both engines, while the open bomb doors and lowered undercarriage suggested a hydraulics failure. All removable objects were jettisoned in an attempt to maintain height, but with both engines misfiring badly and the Wellington losing height in a nose down attitude, Gibbes had no option but to attempt to ditch. At around 90mph the Wellington's tail section hit the sea ten miles off Orfordness, slamming the nose forward and down. The fuselage broke in two, giving four of the crew the opportunity to clamber out. Ten feet under water in the bomb aimer's position, whence he had been catapulted on impact, the dazed Gibbes somehow made his way back to the cockpit to locate the pilot's escape hatch. Finding it jammed he went back towards the astro hatch, but his failing strength left him unable to open it. Finally, with his lungs bursting, he chanced upon a break in the fuselage, and made his escape. He was by then too exhausted to inflate his life jacket, in a similar state his front gunner, Sgt Purcell, was too shocked and exhausted to help. Gibbes ordered his gunner to leave him and make for the dinghy, but Purcell refused and clung on to his soon unconscious skipper until they were both pulled aboard the dinghy.

For three days and four nights they drifted on the current, knowing they had come down within ten miles of the English coast. On the fourth morning they heard a train, then through the morning mist they could pick out the faint outline of buildings. Eventually at 11.45pm the crew managed to coax the dinghy ashore near Margate in Kent. For four of the crew, including the front gunner, this was their first operation. It was Gibbes' thirty-sixth and last with 218 Squadron, and he was posted to Waterbeach on the 27th on completion of his tour. Twenty-six-year-old Gibbes was born in Australia, and joined the RAAF in 1936. Selected to join the RAF Gibbes arrived in England in 1937. He had been awarded the DFC in September 1940 while with 115 Squadron. On August 16th 1943, while serving as a wing commander with 142 Squadron, he would fail to return from an attack on Viterbo, Italy.

A major effort against the warships at Brest originally involved 140 aircraft on the 3/4th, but worsening weather conditions forced a recall of all but the 3 Group crews, who pressed on to deliver an inconclusive attack through a smoke screen. Almost two hundred aircraft set off for Berlin on the night of the 7/8th, seventy-five of them from 3 Group, while others were active over Kiel and Boulogne. The squadron dispatched ten aircraft to the former and two freshman crews to attack the docks at Boulogne. Most of the bombs aimed at the Capital fell into districts north and east of the city centre and returning crews reported brilliant fires in the target area and a number of large explosions. Wing Commander Kirkpatrick's crew witnessed the end of an enemy fighter shot down in flames by an unidentified bomber. Squadron Leader Price had his port engine catch fire over the Dutch coast on the return trip, and the over-worked starboard engine failed suddenly over Norfolk. Price put W5499 HA-Y down safely in a recently harvested wheat field at Hall Farm near Barton Bendish at 04.30 hrs. A number of days later Price described the raid and his subsequent crash landing in a BBC broadcast.

The first large raid of the war on Kassel was mounted on the 8/9th, when a number of important industrial premises were hit along with the main railway station. The 10/11th brought a change of scenery for over seventy crews, with a trip across the Alps to Turin, where the Fiat works, an arsenal and a railway station were the intended targets. 218 Squadron contributed eight Wellingtons to the first-mentioned, each one modified to carry additional long-range fuel tanks. Conditions in the target area were not favourable, mist and industrial haze making positive identification impossible. Squadron Leader Price dropped his bomb load half a mile south of the target, where a number of fires were already visible. Other fires were started and green explosions were seen, and opposition over the target was reported as being negligible. The last crew landed at 05.30hrs after being aloft for more than nine hours. Wellingtons targeted ship yards at Kiel on the 11/12th, before forming more than half of the 130 strong force heading for Frankfurt on the 12/13th. Nine 218 Squadron Wellingtons took part, but Z8865 HA-O's involvement was ended by flak at the enemy coast. Knowing that the aircraft would not be able to climb to the briefed bombing height, Sgt Fisher dropped his load near Ostende. The remaining crews found the target to be blanketed by low cloud, which led to widely scattered bombing, and even the town of Mainz, some twenty miles away, reported receiving many bombs and suffering some fatalities. One of the two Wellingtons failing to return was X9670 HA-N, from which the entire crew of twenty-year-old New Zealander, Sgt Charles Dare, escaped with their lives to become PoWs. Charles was on his twenty-fourth operation having joined the squadron from 20 O.T.U on May 25th.

The larger-scale raids continued at Brest on the 13/14th, when the warships lay concealed beneath a smoke-screen. Hamburg came next on the 15/16th, where a greater degree of damage occurred than had become the norm of late. Returning in the early hours of the 16th, a 57 Squadron Wellington attempted to land at Marham with its brakes shot away. Half way down the runway it swung from the flare path and crossed the airfield to crash into 218 Squadron's R3153, causing both aircraft to burst immediately into flames. Four of the crew managed to escape, but the pilot and wireless operator were trapped and burned to death. Squadron Leader Spence carried out his first operation as skipper on this night, when forty-five freshman crews were sent to le Havre and faced only limited opposition. Gerald Spence had joined the RAF in 1932, when he was granted a short service commission. After a spell with 4 Fighter Training School Egypt he was posted to 70 (BT) Squadron at Himaidi in Iraq.

The night of the 16/17th brought a 3 Group attack on Karlsruhe by forty-one Wellingtons, ten of which were drawn from 218 Squadron. No actual results could be assessed, but numerous small fires were seen west of the target. Squadron Leader Price was frustrated in his attempt to identify the aiming point, and after forty minutes of stooging around he decided to attack a blast furnace at Saarbrücken, where his bomb load caused a large explosion. On the 19/20th 218 Squadron contributed to an attack on the Baltic port of Stettin, which was being extensively used to reinforce the Russian front. The operation started badly for the squadron, when three aircraft failed to take off, two for technical reasons and a third following a taxying accident. The remaining crews found the distant target and bombed the centre of the port, before arriving safely back home after being airborne for over nine hours. Worsening weather forced a recall to be issued to crews outbound for Berlin and Frankfurt on the 20/21st. Marshall of the Royal Air Force, Lord Trenchard, paid a twenty-four hour visit to Marham on the 25th, and all officers were ordered to "dine in". An informal after dinner talk was given by Lord Trenchard to the assemble officers. The following morning he addressed the aircrews and ground personnel of the squadron outside the A Flight hanger.

The last night of operational activity of the month for 218 Squadron involved further cracks at Stettin, Hamburg and le Havre on the 29/30th. Two freshman crews went to le Havre, while W/Cdr Kirkpatrick and S/Ldr Price each took a Mk II Wellington to attack the dockyards at Hamburg. On board with Price was W/Cdr Peter Heath, who was gaining operational experience before being given his own squadron. The remaining crews targeted Stettin's marshalling yards, and all eventually returned safely to Marham. Twenty-four hours later Wellingtons went yet again to Stettin, and a mixed force took another swipe at Hamburg, starting fourteen fires. It had been a busy month for the squadron, launching seventy-four sorties totalling 480.42 hours, and delivering 170,390 lbs of bombs.

October

The first operation of the new month for 218 Squadron took place on the night of the 3/4th against the docks at Rotterdam, when thirteen aircraft joined others to attack in good visibility. Flight Lieutenant Dunham and crew were able to identify their bombs exploding around the warehouses in dock areas 15 and 18. Meanwhile W/Cdr Heath took Wellington R1025 HA-J to Dunkirk, where he bombed at 21.07 hrs from 13,500 feet in the face of a spirited defence. There were no operations at all by Bomber Command between the 5th and the 10th because of bad weather, and it was not until the night of the 10/11th that the squadron next flew in anger. Eleven aircraft took off for an attack on the oil plants at Bordeaux, and two failed to return. X9677 HA-V was homebound when bracketed by heavy flak, which damaged the port engine. With the Wellington losing height and the weather worsening Sg A McLean was forced to sink below the rain-bearing cloud base to less than a thousand feet over the sea. Almost immediately the starboard engine cut, and McLean turned the Wellington into the wind for a ditching. The aircraft broke in two on impact and sank within thirty seconds. The Australian pilot, co-pilot and front gunner managed to clamber into the dinghy, but the wireless operator was swept away by a large wave, the observer went down with the tail section, and the rear gunner was observed to be floating face down. The survivors were picked up by the trawler Grimsby Town, and taken ashore at Portsmouth for transfer to the RN Hospital at Hasler.

The other missing Wellington, R1511 HA-L, shed its starboard propeller without warning while homebound over France, and Sgt V Haley gave the order to bail out. Five of the crew came down safely, but the observer, Sgt Horace Judge, was killed. Last out and with little height to spare, Haley took to his parachute and landed near a farm at le Pizou. The farmer took him into his home, where he was given a drink and time to recover. He was then provided with a pair of dungarees, an old jacket and a hand-drawn map of the area, which showed the route across the line of demarcation. Setting out at 04.30hrs Haley headed for the border, scouting around the village of Very and finally crossing the demarcation line between Mon Pont and St.Remy. Haley's luck held as he chanced upon a farm at St. Remy, where he stayed between October 12th and December 11th. While waiting for the farmer to organise a guide to the Pyrenees he was introduced to an Englishman, who had lived in Lille since the end of the Great War. It was this unnamed Englishman who eventually arranged Haley's journey by taxi and train to the Spanish Border. With the help of a Spanish guide he crossed the Pyrenees on December 12th 1941, initially taken to Miranda and then on to Madrid, before finally reaching Gibraltar on February 28th 1942. Victor Haley was awarded the Military Medal for his exploits, the only one awarded to the squadron. The citation read:

This airman was a member of the crew of an aircraft, which crashed returning from an attack on Bordeaux. Evading capture on bailing out, he showed great resource in journeying across France, and after overcoming many obstacles, he finally made his way without a guide over the Pyrenees into Spain from where, after a period of detention, he was repatriated.

The slight lull in activity enabled Peirse to prepare his forces for a major night of operations on the 12/13th, for which the main course was to be Nuremberg by a mixed force of 152 aircraft, half of them Wellingtons. While this was in progress, a predominantly Wellington effort would be directed at Bremen, while 5 Group attacked a chemicals factory at Hüls. 3 Group put up ninety-three aircraft for this effort and a further twenty-six for Bremen, along with fifteen Wellingtons for Boulogne, bringing its total for the night to a magnificent 134. The total number of sorties, 373, represented a new record for the Command, but sadly, this mammoth effort was not to be rewarded with success. The bombing at Nuremberg was scattered over a wide area up to a hundred miles from the intended target, and the other operations were inconclusive in the face of complete cloud cover. The night's losses amounted to thirteen aircraft, not including 218 Squadron's Z8910 HA-F, skippered by Sgt McGlashan, which was damaged beyond repair when it collided with a 115 Squadron Wellington while taxying on return.

On the following night Düsseldorf escaped serious damage from a scattered attack by a predominantly Wellington force, before eighty aircraft set off to return to Nuremberg on the 14/15th. 218 Squadron supported this operation with ten Wellingtons, one of which, Z8865 HA-O, encountered engine problems soon after take-off. With the port engine feathered Sgt K Fisher turned back, and after misjudging his approach, struck some trees and crashed just short of the runway at 01.00hrs. All of the crew members sustained minor bruising, apart from Sgt Barrowdale, who fractured a leg, Z8865 HA-O was a write-off. Weather conditions outbound and over the target were very bad, and bombs were dropped on ETA or flak explosions. Low on fuel Sgt J Vezina RCAF made a wheels-up landing at Hampton Park near Eastbourne at 06.15hrs, extensively damaging veteran Wellington R1025 HA-J. Bombs were once again spread all across Germany, and only one crew positively identified Nuremburg.

Two nights later eight 218 Squadron aircraft were detailed to attack the main power station at Duisburg, one of them captained by F/L Dunham, flying as observer. Z8957 HA-L took off from Marham at 01.25hrs carrying a cookie, the first occasion on which a 218 Squadron Mk Ic had carried a blockbuster. On his return to Marham the pilot, Sgt Jim Hinwood, recorded the events of that night.

On the 16th of October 1941 I was detailed to air test a new aircraft, which only had flown 2 hours. I remember the controls were very stiff and it all smelt very new. The air test lasted 15 minutes and then the bomb was loaded. Take off was 01.25hrs on the 17th. Take off was up the hill past "Lady Woods", and at the fence I lifted off and then touched down again briefly in the field outside the boundary. It really was touch and go. We climbed rather slowly, and after about 15 minutes as we reached 3,000 feet the port motors started to misfire badly with lots of flames from the exhaust. I throttled back, but the props would not feather on the Pegasus engines. As height could not be maintained on one, we continued to the coast to drop the bomb into the sea. Inside the fuselage, alongside the navigator's position, the aircraft floor had been raised and a bomb beam fitted. The beam, the bomb release hook and a manual release lever were above floor level. Two Vickers hoists were also in place, one in the front beam, the other behind. The hoists were initially used to lift the bomb into the bomb bay by means of two steel cables to the hoist, the hoists and cables being left in place to stabilise the bomb during the take off and climb. Once clear of the coast the co-pilot had slackened off the cables, releasing them from the anchorage point. The co–pilot was also responsible for the manual release in an emergency.

We crossed the coast north of Great Yarmouth and the co-pilot, Sgt McKay, went back to jettison the bomb. The fuselage of the Wimpy is not over large and with the raised floor, bomb beam and hoists there is not a great deal of room for someone wearing an Irvin flying jacket and Mae West. Anyway, when the release was pulled one cable was not clear so that the bomb fell off the hook and the front end dropped into the slipstream whilst the back end push the floor up even higher. There was only one thing to do, using the fire axe the co-pilot Sgt McKay chopped through the ply-wood floor and then through the cable which was resting against the bomb casing. By this time we were down to 1,600 feet, and the good engine running at maximum continuous power was getting very hot. The last strands of the cable parted and we turned for the coast. With the port engine still spitting flames we could not dump the full fuel load. The coast was crossed in bound at Lowestoft, but as we were still losing height, the first crew member was told to jump at 1,300 feet using the rear escape hatch. The co-pilot and rear gunner were followed by the front gunner at 1,100 feet, and the wireless operator at 900 feet. The observer, F/Lt Peter Dunham, was the captain, unusually, but he was on his second tour. So after checking that the rest of the crew were clear, and handing me my chest type parachute, he left from the front hatch. I closed the throttles at 700 feet, trimmed the aircraft and dropped from the seat only to find my harness had caught up in the seat-lowering handle. Struggling free I went out of the hatch head first, well below 500 feet by now, and pulled my rip cord. I landed in a ploughed field impacting on my shoulders with my parachute canopy streaming behind me. The flight had lasted 45 minutes. The aircraft landed in a field in which a potato crop was being harvested. None of the crew was injured, but Sid Turner hurt his knee when climbing over a gate, and Ken Wheeler fell into a dyke. Peter Dunham and I finished the night at the house of a local Policeman in Cantley between Yarmouth and Norwich, while the rest of the crew found a pub. Next day we were collected by personnel from Horsham St Faith and returned to Marham by road.

On the following day 115 and 218 Squadron witnessed the departure of the popular station commander, G/C McKee AFC DFC, whose successor was G/C A.H.H McDonald. Pilot Officer Harper's was the only 218 Squadron aircraft operating on the night of the 20/21st, when he and his crew went to Antwerp. Bremen was the main target on that night and again twenty-four hours later, while Mannheim was the host on the 22/23rd. When Kiel was the objective on the 23rd, S/Ldr Spence was among seven 218 Squadron participants finding the target hidden under cloud. After observing the flash from the explosion of their 4,000 pounder they reported that an estimated twelve flak guns stopped firing. The spate of engine related incidents afflicting the squadron continued on the 29th, when X9833 HA-A crashed near Washpit Farm, Rougham, Norfolk at 12:50hrs, killing

Sgt Reg England. The pilot, Sgt Tomkin and his remaining crew all suffered minor cuts and bruises. Another assault on Bremen brought the month's operations to a close on the night of the 31st, when 3 Group dispatched sixty-two aircraft, eleven of which were provided by 218 Squadron. Once again weather conditions over the target thwarted an accurate attack, and most crews again bombed on ETA or on the flashes of flak. Sergeant Thompson's X9674 HA-H was attacked and badly damaged on the way home by a night fighter flown by Oblt Siegfried Ney of IV/NJG1 at 23.38hrs. The port main tank, tail-plane and cockpit instruments were hit and rendered useless by cannon fire, and the rear gunner, nineteen-year-old Sgt John Northcote, was killed. The Wellington was skilfully coaxed back to Marham, where a successful landing was made. It had been a costly month for the squadron, but with eighty sorties launched, it claimed second place in the group behind 115 Squadron, and top spot for bomb tonnage delivered.

November

November began with a raid on Kiel by 134 aircraft on the night of the 1/2nd, but only half of the force reached the target to bomb through heavy, low cloud on estimated positions. No bombs found the mark, and this situation, recently highlighted by the Butt Report, was about to come to a head. The new month began for 218 Squadron with a low-key attack by two crews against Brest on the 3/4th. Squadron Leader Price and Sgt Webber departed Marham in bad weather, which hadn't improved by the time they reached the target. Price orbited the target for eight minutes, while trying to draw a bead on the Scharnhorst and Gneisenau, and Z8375 HA-Z was hit by flak in the process. Sergeant Webber fared little better and was forced to bomb on ETA in the face of accurate flak. It was back to the Ruhr and Essen on the 4th, when eight aircraft took off and again encountered ten-tenths cloud over Germany. Bombing was carried out on ETA, and once more failed to find the mark.

   No doubt frustrated by the persistently unfavourable weather that had prevented him from having a real crack at Germany, and anxious to erase the stigma arising from the Butt Report, Peirse planned his most ambitious night of operations yet. The original order of battle had allowed for Berlin to be attacked by over two hundred aircraft, while a 1 and 3 Group force went to Mannheim. There were again doubts about the weather conditions, however, which prompted an objection from the 5 Group A-O-C, AVM Slessor, who was authorized to withdraw his contribution and send it instead to Cologne. The total number of sorties for the three main operations and those of a minor nature amounted to a record 392, of which 169 were destined for Berlin, seventy-five for Cologne and fifty-five for Mannheim. Seventy-five aircraft were provided by 3 Group, of which the largest contribution was by 218 Squadron, which sent thirteen Wellingtons to Berlin, and two to the Ruhr. It was to be an ill-fated night for the Command, although in some ways, not for 218 Squadron, whose crews were among the seventy-three claiming to have reached the "Big City". None succeeded in identifying Berlin in the conditions, and bombing was carried out on estimated positions. A few buildings were hit, and fourteen houses were classed as destroyed, but this was a poor return for the effort expended and the loss of twenty-one aircraft. The Wellington of New Zealander, Sgt Phil Lamason was enveloped in accurate heavy flak over the target, and sustained damage to the intercom and heating system, the astro-hatch, both wings and turrets, the port oil tank and Perspex windscreen. Amazingly the crew sustained no injuries and made it back to Marham.

The squadron did, however, post missing the crew of P/O J McGlashan in Z1069 HA-J, which had reached and bombed the target at 20.34hrs. It is believed the aircraft crashed south of Krefeld as result of severe icing. Flying on his first operation with Sgt McGlashan was Australian 2nd pilot Sgt W Fraser. News eventually came through that the entire crew was safe, albeit in enemy hands. It was McGlashan's twentieth operation and the crew's eleventh. The squadron's other twelve aircraft returned without major incident and this praise-worthy performance was doubtless due in part to the quality of leadership enjoyed by the squadron at this time. The 5 Group force fared better at Cologne in terms of casualties, all of its aircraft returning, but Cologne had also escaped damage, while no bombs at all fell into Mannheim, and seven Wellingtons failed to return. A further nine aircraft were missing from the various minor operations, bringing the total to a massive thirty-seven, more than twice the previous highest in a single night. This was the final straw for the War Cabinet and the Air Ministry, and Peirse was summoned to a meeting with Churchill to make his explanations. On the 13th he was ordered to restrict further operations, while the future of the Command was considered at the highest level. This edict would be in force into the coming year, and was quite opportune for 218 Squadron, whose time with the venerable Wellington was drawing to a close. Immediately after this operation S/Ldr Spence was posted to Alconbury to oversee the rebuilding of 40 Squadron, after most of its air, ground and administrative personnel had been posted to Malta. On the 26th of November he would be given command of 149 Squadron, a post which he would hold until the following May.

Other than for training purposes, the entire Command remained on the ground from the 10th to the 15th. That night there was a return to Germany for twelve 218 Squadron Wellingtons, which were part of a force of forty-seven aircraft bound for Kiel, while two others joined an attack on Emden. Both operations proved to be testing in the extreme for 218 Squadron as the weather intervened. Four crews jettisoned their bombs because of icing or technical difficulties, another brought his load home, while the commanding officer and another crew bombed on ETA. The squadron suffered further when R1135 HA-N failed to return with the crew of Sgt Alan Cook RAAF. An SOS message was received at 02.04hrs, fixing their position north of the intended track, no doubt as a result of the night's unexpectedly strong winds, and only one body was recovered after it washed ashore in Norway. The night's ordeal come to an end at 06.00hrs, when

Canadian Sgt Forsyth's Z8853 HA-H made a forced landing at Redcar on the north-east coast, killing the twenty-one year old front gunner, Sgt Charles Collins, and seriously injuring the second pilot.

One 218 Squadron Wellington took part in small-scale operation against Dunkirk on the 23/24th, when weather once again thwarted the attack, and the bombs were jettisoned safe in the sea. Eighty Wellingtons were joined by Hampdens for a raid on Emden on the 26/27th. Just one 218 Squadron Wellington was in attendance, Z1103 HA-A, which reached the target and bombed through ten-tenths cloud. Heavy flak was encountered on the way home, and once over the sea it was discovered that fuel was leaking away at an alarming rate. After a tense flight the pilot descended to 3,500 feet expecting to sight land. Failing to do so a priority fix was acquired, which put them still one hundred miles out. On reaching the Norfolk coast the Wellington was guided by searchlights, but within minutes both engines began to splutter and back-fire through lack of fuel. It was decided to ditch rather than risk encountering anti-invasion obstacles on the shoreline. Sergeant Helfer put the Wellington down half a mile off the shore at 23.06hrs, and the crew clambered into the dinghy. It took two hours for rescue to arrive in the form of an RAF launch piloted by the coxswain of the Wells Lifeboat. One of those rescued was Sgt Jack Purcell, former front gunner to S/Ldr Gibbes, who had also ditched on return from Ostende on September 2nd 1941.

The last operation of the month for 218 Squadron was directed at Düsseldorf on the 27/28th, when nine of its Wellingtons contributed to a 3 Group force of forty-nine. Strong winds hindered the less experienced crews, some of which bombed Cologne, where over a hundred buildings were hit. Damage in Düsseldorf was concentrated around the railway yards. The city authorities, however, reported only two high explosive bombs and light superficial damage. Undertaking his first operation as a squadron leader was Wilfred Williams DFC. Soon after crossing the Dutch coast Williams encountered a problem when the starboard engine blower of Z8431 HA-J failed. This resulted in the heavily laden Wellington's inability to climb above 9,000 feet, and the airfield at Haamstede was attacked as an alternative.

Within a matter of days Williams would take over B Flight on the departure of S/Ldr Price DFC, who was posted to HQ 3 Group as Squadron Leader Operations at the end of the month. Promoted to wing commander he would assume command of 156 Squadron on May 31st 1942, after the loss of W/Cdr Peter Heath, who had cut his teeth with 218 Squadron between October and November 1941. Sadly W/Cdr Herbert Price would also be lost, in his case over the North Sea on return from an attack on Hamburg on July 28/29th 1942. This fine and inspirational officer would have completed sixty-one operations at the time of his death. Williams was a worthy replacement, who had a first tour of thirty-one operations and a DFC with 75 (NZ) Squadron behind him. Born in Napier, Williams had joined the RAF in 1936, and after graduating as a sergeant pilot he was posted to 9 Squadron. In July 1939 he was transferred to the RNZAF to join the squadron tasked with ferrying six newly purchased Wellingtons to Ohakea in their homeland. However, on the outbreak of war the New Zealand government magnanimously allowed the aircraft and crews to remain in the RAF. On completion of his first tour with 75 (NZ) Squadron he was posted to 311 (Czechoslovak) Squadron, where he assisted in the training of Czech pilots.

No further operations were carried out by 218 Squadron during the remainder of a month, in which a total of only forty-eight sorties were flown, and 143,530lb of bombs were delivered. The month ended for the Command with 181 aircraft heading for Hamburg on the night of the 30th, and a further fifty bound for Emden. The former was modestly effective in starting fires, and rendering 2,500 people homeless, but it was achieved at the high cost of thirteen aircraft.

December

December began with a blanket of fog that prevented any operations until the 7th, when twelve crews were briefed as part of a force of 130 aircraft to be sent against the *Gneisenau* and *Scharnhorst* at Brest, while Sgt Gregg carried out a simultaneous freshman trip to Dunkirk. For once the weather over the main target was good, until an effective smoke screen made identification difficult. Pilot Officer Cottier and Sgt McGregor positively identified dock 8 and bombed accordingly. This was the first of a number of raids directed against Brest, and no fewer than thirteen operations of varying sizes would be directed against the port during December. It was on this night that Stirlings of 7 and XV Squadron conducted the first operational trials of the Oboe blind-bombing device.

With the battle of the Atlantic swinging in favour of the Axis, Bomber Command was instructed on December 10th to direct more of its effort against Biscay ports, and this would continue on and off over the next fourteen months, depending on how much pressure the Admiralty applied. The cathedral city of Cologne was the main target on the 11/12th, while 218 Squadron contributed eleven aircraft to a thirty-strong 3 Group attack on Brest. W5727 HA-V developed a port engine fire while outbound at 6,500 feet, and Sgt Brewerton ordered his crew to bale out before carrying out a successful crash-landing at Upavon in Wiltshire. The remaining crews bombed on flares dropped by the Stirlings of 7 and XV Squadrons over a completely cloud covered target. Operating with the squadron for the first time was S/Ldr Beverley Ker in R1436 HA-M.

On the 16th Stirling N6127 arrived at Marham to begin a new era for 218 Squadron, which thus became the fourth 3 Group unit to receive the type after 7, XV and 149 Squadrons. Six crews paid a return visit to Brest that night, led by W/Cdr Kirkpatrick in Z1101 HA-F. Weather conditions were marginally better and returning crews were enthusiastic about the flares that illuminated the primary target. There was only one loss, that of Sgt J.F Vezina RCAF and crew, whose starboard engine caught fire at 11,000 feet while outbound. Unable to extinguish the fire the pilot ordered the crew to bail-out, and all but the observer, P/O Brown, landed in the area around Maiden Newton. Brown landed in the same field as the Wellington, X9785 HA-O, which Sgt Vezina, who was on his nineteenth operation, had crash-landed five hundred yards west of Home Farm, Chilfrome, Dorset. Taken in by Mrs Egerton the dazed and concussed Brown was given hot soup and a set of her son's pyjamas before being sent to bed! Despite the insistence of the authorities that Brown be taken to Dorchester, Mrs Egerton refused. The local Police visited Mrs Egerton to check Brown's identity while he slept, and insisted he could only stay until the morning. On his return to Marham, Brown sent a postcard to Mrs Egerton on which he wrote; *"To the nicest people I have ever dropped in on"*. This was the final Wellington to be written off in 218 Squadron service. Joseph Vezina would be posted to the newly formed Canadian 419 Squadron at Mildenhall in January 1942, and would fail to return from the ill fated "Channel Dash" episode on February 12th.

Stirling N6126 was taken on charge on the 17th and N6128 on the 23rd, but it would be February before the crews were fully converted and the working up period was completed. The year came to an end with another disappointing attack on Düsseldorf on the 27/28th, and a surprisingly effective one on Wilhelmshaven on the following night, which inflicted widespread damage. Two DFCs were announced in December awarded to W/Cdr H Kirkpatrick and F/L Peter Dunham, the latter's citation reading:

> *"This officer has participated in attacks on a wide variety of important targets in Germany and the occupied territory. Throughout he has displayed great courage and leadership, often descending to low attitudes to ensure accuracy of bombing. On two occasions, when acting as captain, fighters have attacked his aircraft, but in both instances the enemy was destroyed and the mission completed. Flight Lieutenant Dunham has displayed great ability and devotion to duty. Although normally employed as an observer, he has also acted as captain of aircraft"*

It had been a year to forget for Bomber Command, ending under a black cloud and with its future hanging in the balance. There had been little significant advance on the performance of 1940, and the three new heavy types introduced into operational service early in the year had all failed to live up to expectations. Each had undergone lengthy periods of grounding as essential modifications were put in hand, and consequently, the re-equipping programme had progressed much more slowly than anticipated. The damning Butt Report had sealed the fate of C-in-C Sir Richard Peirse, who had done his best to fulfil the frequently changing and often unrealistic demands placed upon him by the decision makers. The fate of a strategic bomber force also lay in the hands of the boffins, who were working hard to develop the electronic aids to navigation and bombing, without which, it was impossible to envisage any improvement in performance.

Chapter Five

1942:
A Year of Change

January

The New Year started with the departure of the popular W/Cdr Kirkpatrick DFC on the 1st to take up duties at 3 Group HQ at Exning Hall. Kirkpatrick would rise to the wartime rank of group captain and become a SASO at 3 Group until the end of hostilities. He was succeeded at 218 Squadron by thirty-one-year-old South African-born W/Cdr Paul Holder DFC, who had seen considerable action during the Baghdad coup in April 1941. He had been awarded a DFC in October 1941, and would be awarded a DSO in October 1942. He held an MSc in civil engineering from Bristol University and a PhD from the University of Illinois.

Operationally 1942 began as 1941 had ended with the obsession with Brest and its guests. The assault on the port resumed on the night of the 2/3rd, and by the end of the month a further ten operations would have been mounted against it, including five on consecutive nights between the 5/6th and the 9/10th. Not one resulted in damage to the warships, but this long, drawn-out epic was shortly to be resolved. Fog prevented 218 Squadron from undertaking operations until the 6th, when S/Ldr Williams led five aircraft to Brest with W/Cdr Holder as his second pilot. A British Empire Medal had been awarded to front gunner Sgt Jack Purcell earlier in the day in recognition of his courage in staying with his semi-conscious skipper, S/Ldr Gibbes DFC, following the ditching of their Wellington on return from Ostende in the previous September.

A follow-up raid on Brest on the 8th included five of the squadron's Wellingtons again led by S/Ldr Williams. The well-trodden path to Brest was followed again on the 10/11th and 11/12th, and both assaults on the port and its lodgers involved 218 Squadron. Wing Commander Holder took an all NCO crew on his first operation as captain, when, unable to pinpoint the target, he bombed through nine-tenths cloud on ETA and flak positions. Two crews were briefed for different targets on the night of the 14/15th, one to join ten others in attacking the port of Rotterdam, and the other to bomb the port of Emden. Weather conditions over northern Germany were better than over Holland, and the aiming point at Emden was visually identified and bombed from 16,000 feet. Sir Richard Peirse was removed as A-O-C in C Bomber Command by the Chief of the Air Staff, Air Chief Marshal Charles Portal, in early January, after Portal had become increasingly

The burnt out fuselage of Short Stirling W7535 HA-C photographed May 30th 1942. The aircraft, a victim of Flak, crashed at Colombes, a suburb north west of Paris, killing the entire crew of Flight Lieutenant Arthur Jones. Note what appears to be an unexploded 500lb bomb amongst the wreckage.

concerned and frustrated about the mounting losses and lack of success. Peirse was replaced temporally by 3 Group's own A-O-C, AVM "Jack" Baldwin.

Five 218 Squadron crews participated in a rather disappointing raid on Hamburg on the night of the 15/16th, and two of these returned early. Wing Commander Holder drifted off course outbound through an inaccurate wind forecast at briefing, and he attacked the last resort target. Sergeants Hinwood and Webber found Hamburg covered in cloud, and both bombed on E.T.A from 17,000 feet. Wing Commander Holder mistakenly landed at Docking, a Coastal Command station on the Norfolk coast, where he turned off the perimeter track into soft ground, collapsing the undercarriage of Z1101 HA-F. It was not a auspicious start to his command. A small-scale raid was flown against Emden on the 20/21st, followed by attacks on the French ports of Boulogne and Dunkirk on the 21/22nd and 22/23rd. By the time of the two last-mentioned the squadron had waved a fond farewell to the experienced and respected B Flight commander, New Zealander S/Ldr Wilfred Williams DFC, who departed on the 21st. After continuous service in the UK since 1936 he was repatriated to New Zealand in March 1942. Upon his return and after a number of ground jobs, Williams joined 1 Operational Training Unit, and was killed in a tragic accident on July 15th 1943 while flying a Hudson.

Five crews were briefed to attack Münster on the 28th, of which only three found the primary target. After the bomb load had been delivered, the cockpit instruments in Z1070 HA-B froze, and the Wellington fell from 19,500 to 2,500 feet before Sgt Smithson could bring it back under control. It was then that the starboard engine cut, and soon afterwards the A.S.I. failed. Ordering his crew to stand by to bail out, the pilot was informed that the front bulkhead had jammed and the front gunner could not be extricated. It was a unanimous decision to press on to Marham, where a safe landing was made a full hour after the previous returnee.

February

There was little major activity during the first half of February, and no operations were completed until the 6th. That night sixty Wellingtons and Stirlings carried out an attack on Brest, but only a third of the crews claimed to have bombed in the target area. Heavy snow and frost restricted operations during the first week and a half, but another twenty aircraft tried again at Brest on the 10/11th, before eighteen Wellingtons carried out a further raid late on the 11th. It was within hours of this last attack that Operation "Cerberus" was launched by the German contingent. Scharnhorst, Gneisenau and Prinz Eugen slipped anchor and headed into the English Channel under an escort of destroyers and E-Boats. It was an audacious bid for freedom by Vice Admiral and fleet commander Otto Ciliax, which was undertaken in the most atrocious of weather conditions. It was not until 10.42hrs on the morning of the 12th that the enemy fleet was first sighted. Group Captain Victor Beamish, the commanding officer of Kenley, and W/Cdr Finlay Boyd had taken off in their Spitfires on a Jim Crow sortie, and managed by some miracle to positively identify the German fleet steaming off le Touquet.

The British authorities had prepared a plan for precisely this eventuality under the code name *Operation Fuller*, but it seems that many of those at grass roots level charged with its implementation were not fully appraised of its requirements. The elaborate plans also had one obvious flaw, that no one knew when the break out was going to happen. Bomber Command could not remain on immediate alert indefinitely and on the morning of the break-out the vast majority of Bomber Command's squadrons had been stood down. Twenty-one Wellingtons and three Stirlings of 3 Group had been on four hour's standby since 07.00hrs but thirteen of the former and one Stirling were stood down in anticipation of the coming night's operation. At 11.40hrs an Executive Order from Bomber Command requested all available group aircraft to prepare for an immediate take-off. At 13.18hrs a follow-up order informed group that the night's planned operation was cancelled, and every effort should be made to concentrate on the German battle cruisers. This order excluded any aircraft with TR1335 equipment (Gee), and at a stroke seventy-three 3 Group aircraft were side-lined. The first sorties only got away at

13.30hrs, but the squally conditions and low cloud made it almost impossible for the crews to locate the ships, and even harder to deliver an attack.

218 Squadron's contribution to *Operation Fuller* was six aircraft on what was a landmark occasion. Three Wellingtons were to carry out the final sorties by the type in 218 Squadron service, but two failed to take off and the third was forced to return early. Sergeant Griggs and crew were just five minutes into their sortie in R1448 HA-N, when the front turret hydraulics failed, and they landed back at Marham to have a hasty repair carried out. They were airborne again within minutes, and made for the search area, where, on breaking cloud on ETA, a destroyer was immediately identified. An attack was pressed home from around 300 feet in the face of both heavy and light flak, and the seven 500lb semi-armour piecing bombs undershot by a mere one hundred yards. This day also brought the first 218 Squadron Stirling sorties, flown by S/Ldr Ker in N3700 HA-O, F/O Allen in N6127 HA-T and Sgt Tompkins in N6089 HA-D, who had taken off between 14.30hrs and 15.15hrs. Squadron Leader Ker and Sgt Tompkins were thwarted by the weather conditions, the former catching a fleeting glimpse of the enemy from 3,000 feet. Both crews reported being engaged by enemy aircraft, but escaped with minimal damage. Flying Officer Allan sighted two destroyers and lost them almost immediately in cloud. Patiently he circled for thirty-six minutes, until a further sighting of a large ship was made from 1,500 feet. Undeterred by the heavy flak the crew went in to attack, and the rear gunner reported two red flashes 100 to 150 yards from the starboard quarter of the lead ship. The Stirling was hit in the bomb bay by flak, and was then engaged by three Bf110s, one of which attacked, while the other two held off. A spirited and well-coordinated defence from the Stirling resulted in one of the assailants breaking away in a vertical dive to be lost from sight.

Aircraft were taking off throughout the afternoon and evening in a desperate attempt to halt the ships' progress, but all to no avail, and they passed through the Straits of Dover into open sea. N6089 HA-D was also attacked by a Bf110 but arrived home safely with its bombs, having been unable to locate the ships. Squadron Leader Ker was the last back at 19.00hrs, having caught the briefest glimpse of his quarry before cloud obscured the aiming point. His Stirling was engaged by a Do217 and sustained slight damage, but Ker dived the aircraft into cloud and ended the encounter. Despite the largest daylight effort to date amounting to 242 sorties, the enemy fleet made good its escape, and although the Scharnhorst and Gneisenau struck air-laid mines, which slowed their progress to an extent, all had arrived in home ports by the following morning. It was a sorry day for Bomber Command, which lost fifteen aircraft and crews in the valiant attempt to save the nation's blushes. The whole episode was a major embarrassment to the government, but at least this annoying itch had been scratched for the last time and the Command could now concentrate more of its resources against suitable strategic targets.

Ken Spragg recalls the day's activity and for him, the painful consequences, and his account also illustrates the commitment and conditions under which the ground crews operated:

Two things I did not know on the morning of February 13th, the Toads had left Brest and that I had mumps. I had felt bad the previous night and at breakfast I could not eat or drink anything, I was going to report sick. On the way to the S.S.Q I was grabbed by Peter Kingsbury and he told me that we were off to Lakenheath, as they had a Stirling there and we had to check the bomb gear. I told Peter I was off to the S.S.Q, but his reply was that I could not go sick and we had a job to do. He told me I could go sick on our return! I went, after all he was my Corporal! Weather was foul with thick freezing fog, not the best weather to be out at the best of times. This weather had most of our group's stations u/s, I think only Lakenheath was serviceable. I was by now feeling far worse and my voice had turned into a croak. We found the Stirling parked on rough ground with the bomb bay doors opened and a belly full of 500 pounders. The pilot, I think a flight lieutenant, came up. He had the most beautiful ginger moustache and Peter immediately named him "Electric Whiskers". He was obviously upset and glared at me and said "I can't find the buggers". He had been out twice and brought his bombs back twice. The fog had got worse and it was freezing. I was almost on my knees.

It was now dark, everyone had disappeared and we were alone. There was no transport, so we decided to head off on foot. The fog had by this time got thicker and the temperature had plummeted to below zero, and the only problem was, we did not know where to go. We walked over heaps of soil, fell down holes and clambered over rough ground. We were lost on Lakenheath. I was now feeling seriously ill, but kept going, until finally, after two hours, we stumbled by sheer luck upon a few army huts. Thank god for the army! They, for some reason thought we were spies, bloody army! I must have looked ill as they gave me some cocoa which I could not swallow. Peter got on the telephone to RAF Marham and told them of our predicament, but we were told that we would have to stay overnight at Lakenheath and would be picked up on the following morning. Feeling sorry for us the Army directed us to some huts, which had some beds and blankets. Peter was a sleep in less than five minutes, I could not sleep and spent the entire night walking up and down. The following morning a wagon arrived to collect us, and on reaching Marham I went to see the M.O. The M.O stuck something in my ear and grunted ""what is your name?" I told him and he started shouting "this is the wrong man, and get him into isolation immediately he has mumps". I was taken into a room with a single chair, and a door with a window in it, and from time to time a head would peer in. After what seemed an eternity two orderlies arrived and keeping their distance beckoned me out of the room into a waiting ambulance, and off I went to Ely Hospital. Once booked in I was ushered into a small ward with four beds, three of which were occupied by airman with mumps. One poor fellow was bad, and looked as if he had a pair of bollocks around his neck, and down below was jaw dropping! I stayed for three weeks before I was let out, and the poor fellow with a pair of nuts around his neck was still there when I left. I telephoned Marham to arrange for collection, and I was told that I was not wanted, and I was to go home and would be sent for when I was needed. Two weeks later I ran out of cash, so I wrote a really nice letter to the commanding officer asking for help. He sent me a £5 postal order, jolly nice chap the C/O. After nearly six weeks I received a letter asking for my return, I was back that same afternoon!

On the following day the squadron gained its first experience of the Stirling malaise, when N3713's undercarriage collapsed on landing at Lakenheath at the end of a training flight in the hands of Sgt Lamason RNZAF and his crew. This crew took part in the squadron's second Stirling operation, when two were dispatched on the 14th to bomb le Havre and drop leaflets north east of Paris. Lamason completed the operation in N3700 HA-O, while Sgt Gregg and crew returned short of fuel, having spent too long trying to identify a snow covered target. Extremely poor visibility at Marham forced Gregg to divert to Oakington, where a 500lb bomb fell onto the runway on touch-down, having been jammed between the bomb doors. It failed to detonate, and its tail fin was found next morning embedded in one of the doors.

A new Air Ministry directive had been issued to Bomber Command on the 14th, which authorized the blatant area bombing of Germany's towns and cities, and reaffirmed the assault on the morale of the civilian population, particularly the workers. This had, of course, been in progress for a long time, but could now be prosecuted openly, without the pretence of aiming for industrial and military targets. Waiting in the wings, in fact already at sea aboard the armed merchantman Alcantara, was a new leader, who would not only pursue this policy with a will, but also had the strength of character and stubborn self-belief to fight his corner against all-comers. Air Chief Marshal Sir Arthur Harris was approaching his fiftieth birthday, and had been recalled from his role as head of the RAF delegation in Washington. He took up his appointment on the 22nd, and immediately set about the mammoth task of turning Bomber Command into a war-winning weapon.

Harris had always been an advocate of the pre-war theory, that a war could be won by bombing alone, and he arrived at the helm of Bomber Command with firm ideas already in place about how this might be achieved. It was clear to him, that to destroy an urban target with acceptable losses, it was necessary to overwhelm the defences and emergency services by condensing an attack into the shortest possible time. This meant pushing the maximum number of aircraft across the aiming point in the shortest possible time, and concentrating his strength against a single target, rather than deliver simultaneous pin-prick attacks against multiple objectives. He also recognized, that urban areas are most efficiently destroyed by fire rather than blast, and it would not be long before the bomb loads carried in his aircraft reflected this thinking. This new approach signalled the birth of the bomber stream, and an end to the former practice, whereby squadrons and crews determined for themselves to an extent the details of their sorties.

While Harris considered his options, he continued with the small-scale raids on German ports for the remainder of the month, and it was during one of these, that the war threw up one of its ironies. While attacking the floating dock at Kiel on the 26/27th, one of the participating Wellingtons, Hampdens and Halifaxes scored a direct hit on the bows of the Gneisenau, now supposedly in safe haven after enduring eleven months of almost constant bombardment at Brest. 116 of her crew lost their lives, and the ship's sea-going career was ended for good. Her main armament was removed for use as a shore battery. Later on the 27th an undercarriage collapse at Marham wrote off N3715 after a training sortie, but Sgt Tompkins and his crew emerged unscathed. This was Sgt Tomkins' second incident in less than ten days, having pranged and badly damaged N3718 on return from a cross country flight on the 16th.

With the slow but steady introduction of the four-engine bomber to operational service, a number of squadrons were instructed to organise an additional flight for the purpose of familiarisation and conversion training. 218 Squadron formed its own Conversion Flight on February 28th under the commander of S/Ldr Jo Jo Ker. The flight would be independent of but affiliated to the squadron, but ultimately come under the direct control of the Australian station commander, G/C W Kyle DFC. The flight was initially equipped with four Stirlings, W7454 W, N6128 T, N6129 X and N6078 P, along with seven instructors, S/Ldr Ker and P/O A.W.I Jones looking after the pilots, while gunnery came under P/O P.T Wilkes and Sgt Stephenson, wireless operating under Sgt P.H Barnes, and the post of observer instructor remained to be filled. Flying commenced on March 24th, and the first accident occurred on the 27th as the result of yet another undercarriage collapse.

March

The first unmistakable sign of a new hand on the tiller came at the start of March in a meticulously planned operation against the Renault lorry works at Billancourt in Paris. Launched on the night of the 3/4th it involved 235 aircraft, the largest force yet sent against a single target, and was a three wave attack, led by experienced crews, and with extensive use of flares to provide illumination. In the absence of a flak defence, bombing was conducted from low level, both to aid accuracy, and to avoid civilian casualties in adjacent residential districts. 218 Squadron provided four crews, those of S/Ldr Ker in W7469 HA-M, F/L Humphreys in N3720 HA-B, with S/Ldr A W Oldroyd AFC flying on his début operation with the squadron, F/L Livingston in W7473 HA-F, with W/Cdr Holder as second pilot, and F/O Allen in N3712 HA-Y, and all completed their part in the operation.

Rochester & Bedford built Short Stirling Mk.I R9189 HA-K receiving an engine check. The aircraft was Struck of Charge on February 28th 1943 when it swung on take-off collapsing the undercarriage, it had completed 30 operations.

The attack was an outstanding success, which left 40% of the factory's buildings in ruins, and halted production for a month. Just one Wellington was lost, and the satisfaction was marred only by the deaths of 367 French civilians, a figure which was double the previous highest at even a German city target.

On return to Marham at 22.55hrs two hung-up 1000lb bombs fell from F/O Allen's Stirling and exploded. What was left of the mangled fuselage of N3712 HA-Y immediately burst into flames, but all of the crew survived the initial explosion. Pilot Officer Gales, the bomb aimer, managed to climb out of the blazing wreckage, but on realising that some of his crewmates were still trapped inside, he courageously re-entered the Stirling, despite the handicap of a broken ankle and smashed elbow. He and the second pilot, Sgt Laidlaw, were able to extricate the severely injured flight engineer, Sgt Herring. Tragically, eighteen-year-old Sgt William Gregory and twenty-year-old Sgt Kenneth Harvey both died of their injuries soon after being admitted to hospital, while the remaining crew members suffered from shock and varying degrees of burns and broken limbs. These were the squadron's first Stirling fatalities.

Essen was to feature prominently in Harris's future plans, and, after a spell of severe icing conditions had prevented further operations, a series of three raids on consecutive nights began on the 8/9th against this most important centre of war production, and home of the giant Krupp complex. 218 Squadron contributed four crews to the overall force of 211, the leading aircraft of which were equipped with the TR1135 (Gee) navigation device. The main square of the old town was chosen as the aiming point, and the plan called for the flare force to illuminate the target blindly using Gee. Once illuminated the incendiary force would then follow up to provide the main force with a clearly marked and already burning aiming point. Sergeant Gregg dropped his twenty-two 250lb and four 500lb bomb load from an unprecedented attitude of 18,200 feet. A number of large fires were started in the southern outskirts of the target area, which were visible for many miles on the return journey. On board with F/L Livingston was the respected war artist David Thornton-Smith, who, with Air Ministry permission, had been given the opportunity to gain a first-hand impression of Bomber Command at work. Flak was intense, especially from around the Krupp works, and searchlights were also active and working in tandem with the flak units. Never the less all of the crews returned safely to Marham. In the event the ever-present blanket of industrial haze won out by concealing the city from the bomb-aimers high above, and only light damage was inflicted.

Over the next two nights the squadron returned to Essen with varying degrees of success. On the first occasion, on the night of the 9th, S/Ldr Ker and Sgt Lamason were part of a force of over 180 bombers to attack the cloud-free city. A flak burst over the target destroyed the port-outer engine of Ker's W7506 HA–K, and this resulted in a slower than usual return. Four 218 Squadron crews took part in the second and equally disappointing raid on the following night, when technical malfunctions with Gee combined with cloud cover to prevent a concentrated attack. The cathedral city of Cologne was targeted on the night of the 13/14th, for which 3 Group dispatched thirty-nine aircraft, including five from 218 Squadron. Wing Commander Holder accompanied F/L Livingston in W7475 HA-H, and, on reaching the target area, they found a number of large fires well established in the northern half of the city. To this they added their twenty-one 250 pounders from 17,500 feet. Visibility in the target area was good, and fires from this first successful Gee-led attack were visible from up to fifty miles away on the flight home. It was established later that a number of important war industry factories and fifteen hundred houses had sustained meaningful damage. Following this operation the squadron was effectively stood down, and over the next ten days carried out thirty-seven training flights totalling over fifty-four hours flying.

A period of minor operations saw the Command through to the 25/26th, when a new record force of 254 aircraft, including 123 from 3 Group, was dispatched for another tilt at Essen. 218 Squadron was led by S/Ldr Oldroyd AFC, in an attack that was again delivered in three waves, with the Gee-equipped aircraft of the flare force in the vanguard, followed by the incendiary force and finally the main force. The outbound weather conditions were ideal, but the customary thick haze over the Ruhr Valley prevented visual identification. The defences were active, with flak batteries working in conjunction with searchlights. Flying as second pilot to F/L Humphreys in W7507 HA-F was S/Ldr Harold Ashworth DFC, who, at the age of thirty-nine, was well beyond the average for an operational pilot. He was an experienced civil pilot, who had competed in the 1929 Kings Cup air race.

Having joined the RAF in 1939 as a pilot officer, he had reached the rank of acting squadron leader by March 1942. On this night a decoy fire site at Rheinberg drew off a proportion of the bombing, and the remainder was wasted elsewhere, leaving the intended target almost entirely unscathed.

Within twenty-four hours nine 218 Squadron aircraft were again over Essen, this time in excellent conditions. For once they found the city clear of haze, and the Gee equipment performed as intended, allowing a concentrated attack to develop in the face of an increased defensive effort. Sergeant Tompkins and crew were homebound in W7469 HA-M when they were attacked by a JU88, which the rear gunner, Sgt Howes, peppered from less than seventy-five yards range. The assailant was observed to break-off in flames, but almost immediately a Bf110 was discovered off to starboard, and the mid-upper gunner opened fire, registering hits all over the fighter. This too quickly dived out of range and the crew did not see it again. Despite the enthusiastic reports from returning crews of a successful operation, there was, in fact, no improvement on previous efforts. Harris, however, would not give up, and the campaign would resume in April.

In the meantime, he sought an opportunity to deliver a telling blow against a German city, to demonstrate just what could be achieved, if only his crews could locate their target over a blacked out, hostile country, which was often covered by cloud. He was certain, that if he could provide the crews with identifiable pin-points on the ground, they would do the rest, and the easiest pin-points were coastlines. With this in mind Harris selected the old city of Lübeck on Germany's Baltic coast, where the defences would be weak, and the narrow streets and half-timbered buildings would be ideal for a fire-raising attack. Among the 234 aircraft taking off were nine from 218 Squadron, and the two-thirds incendiary bomb loads reflected Harris's fire-raising intentions. The operation was conducted along similar lines to those employed so effectively at Billancourt at the start of the month, and many crews came down to as low as 2,000 feet to make their attacks. Four hundred tons of bombs rained down onto the historic Hanseatic city, and over fourteen hundred buildings were destroyed, while a further nineteen hundred were seriously damaged. Later photographic evidence suggested that 30% of the built-up area had been reduced to rubble, mostly as a result of fire. Such was the scale of the fires that returning 218 Squadron crews reported, "*it was just one big party*".

Twelve aircraft failed to return, and 218 Squadron's W7507 HA-P was almost the thirteenth. It was severely damaged by flak over the target, before being attacked by a Bf110 over the Kiel Canal on the way home. Damage was sustained to both fuel tanks, the rear and mid-upper turrets, the flaps and the fuselage, and the rear gunner was wounded in the knee. One round hit the pilot's armour-plated head rest and exploded, sending deadly splinters ricocheting around the cockpit. Flight Lieutenant Humphreys brought the damaged bomber down to below 200 feet, and having shaken off the fighter, nursed it back to Marham, where it was declared to be beyond economical repair. The crew's opponent had been Lt Leopold Fellerer of V/NJG2, who claimed a Stirling at 01.02hrs. Arthur Humphreys received the immediate award of the DFC, while the wireless operator was awarded the DFM, the citation reading:

Joint citation with Sgt K WHEELER, as captain of aircraft and wireless operator respectively, Flight Lieutenant Humphreys and Sgt K Wheeler participated in an attack on Lübeck on the night of 28th March, 1942. On the return journey, whilst over the Kiel Canal, the aircraft was subjected to a series of attacks by an enemy fighter. The rear ginner was wounded and the mid–upper and rear turrets were put out of action and other damage was sustained by the aircraft. During the action, Flight Lieutenant Humphrey's aircraft was forced down to some 200ft, but largely due to the excellent collaboration between him and Sgt Wheeler, he finally succeeded in evading his attacker and flew the damaged aircraft back to base where he made a safe landing. Throughout the combat, this officer displayed high skill and courage and was greatly assisted by Sgt Wheeler who steadfastly remained at his post, giving clear directions of the enemy tactics. Both Flight Lieutenant Humphreys and Sgt Wheeler have carried out many sorties over enemy territory.

Another crew attacked on the way home was that of F/Sgt Tomkins in W7503 HA-R. The rear gunner held his nerve and his fire until the JU88 was less than eighty yards astern, and then poured machine gun fire into the fighter, which was claimed as destroyed. The mid–upper gunner engaged a second fighter, inflicting some hits, but no claim was made. This crew had also successfully fought off a fighter attack during the Essen operation on March 26th. It had been a good first full month of Stirling operations for 218 Squadron, in which forty-six sorties had been dispatched for the loss of two aircraft at home.

April

The first operation in April for 218 Squadron was directed at the Ford Motor Matford Factory at Poissy, near Paris on the 2nd. Five crews, including that of the squadron commander, joined a force of forty Wellingtons, sixteen of them provided by 3 Group. Conditions over the target were perfect and crews reported an accurate attack, which left buildings in flames. The first major raid of the month was delivered on Cologne on the 5/6th, for which a new record 263 aircraft were dispatched. 218 Squadron's contribution was ten aircraft, led by S/Ldr Oldroyd. The raid was to be carried out in two waves with the Gee-equipped aircraft opening proceedings with incendiaries. Despite the numbers involved the bombing was scattered across the city with no point of concentration, and a modest ninety houses were either destroyed or seriously damaged. The squadron returned to Essen on the 6/7th once again led by S/Ldr Oldroyd. Only a third of the total force of 150 aircraft reached the target, after dense cloud and icing conditions outbound compelled most crews to return early, and, as a result, damage was described as light.

Yet another new record force of 272 aircraft included six from 218 Squadron, whose crews were briefed for Hamburg on the night of the 8/9th. They encountered icing conditions and electrical storms outbound, but even so almost 190 crews reported bombing as briefed. This was not confirmed by the local authorities, however, which recorded only around fourteen bomb loads falling within the city, and this was another major disappointment. Two further attempts on Essen on the 10/11th and 12/13th repeated the earlier failures and thus far, 1,555 sorties in eight raids had produced scant damage at a cost to the Command of sixty-four aircraft. Five crews were detailed to carry-out the squadron's first Stirling mining operation on the 13/14th, when the target was the Nectarines area. Wing Commander Holder led them away at 21.15hrs, and of the five participants, four completed the operation successfully, while Sgt Davis was unable to pin-point his garden because of malfunctioning Gee apparatus.

Harris turned his attention upon Dortmund on the 14/15th and 15/16th, where the results were equally unsatisfactory. 218 Squadron put up eight and six Stirlings respectively three returning with flak damage from the former, and two returning early with technical problems from the latter. An attack on Hamburg on the 17/18th produced seventy-five fires, thirty-three of them classed by local authorities as large. New Zealander Roy Spear RNZAF joined the squadron from 20 OTU on the 20th. Roy would have a remarkable tour with the squadron, and would epitomise the contribution of the Royal New Zealander Air Force within the ranks of Bomber Command and, especially, 218 Squadron. 218 Squadron contributed a dozen Stirlings, two of them piloted by flight commanders, and all returned safely. Gee had proved its worth as an aid to navigation, and in consideration of its potential as a blind-bombing device, an experimental raid was carried out on Cologne on the 22/23rd. The entire force of sixty-four Wellingtons and five Stirlings carried Gee, but no more than about fifteen bomb loads hit the city. 218 Squadron, meanwhile, put up nine Stirlings for mining duties in northern waters.

The one real success of late had been the raid on Lübeck at the end of March, and so Harris selected another Baltic port, Rostock, as the objective for a series of operations beginning on the 23/24th. The presence nearby of a Heinkel aircraft factory was an added attraction, and a proportion of the force was assigned specifically to this. Six 218 Squadron aircraft were among the force of 161 aircraft, but twenty-seven year-old Sgt Shirley Davidge was soon in trouble, reporting back to base that the port-inner engine had failed. The bomb load of twenty-four 250 pounders was jettisoned in the Wash before Davidge turned back towards base. A ten-year-old eyewitness, John Mann, reported that in his opinion the pilot was attempting to make a forced landing on a narrow strip of pasture at Ingrams Farm, Clenchwarton. The darkness had concealed an oak tree stump on the edge of the field, which the Stirling struck, and this caused the rear fuselage to break-off, and the aircraft to immediately burst into flames. The local Auxiliary Fire Service was quickly on the scene, but equipped only with hand drawn pumps there was very little they could do, and there were no survivors. The bodies of the crew were taken to Ingrams Farm to await collection on the following day.

The eyewitness report would conflict with the RAF Crash Report conclusions, which suggested that the pilot, who was on twelfth operation, had turned into the defective engine, resulting in W7473 HA-F crashing at 23.20hrs. Occupying the second pilot's seat had been Sgt Willem Joseph Gerard Rieter, a twenty-five-year-old Dutchman from Venlo, who had fled his homeland in

Sergeant Willem Rieter the 25-year-old Dutch 2nd pilot aboard Short Stirling W7473 HA-F.

1940 just weeks before the German occupation began. The following day John Mann had to walk past the wreckage of the Stirling. He recalls:

I remember going to school the next morning and seeing the huge single rudder sticking skywards, and ironically, this was the only part of the plane not badly burnt, as it was several yards from the rest. We were told that the rear gunner was alive when the plane stopped skidding but could not operate the rear turret doors as they were buckled and the heat overcome him and he perished along with the rest of his crew. I remember after school going to have a look at the remains, of course there was not much to see, just a big hole in the ground. I remember going to Ingrams Farm shed, where there was a large tarpaulin cover on a bench. I received a terrible shock, as under the cover was the remains of the crew, all horribly burned. It was a sight I will never forget.

The operation had failed to find the mark, and the Heinkel factory escaped damage, but the following night's attack at the hands of over a hundred aircraft, including four Stirlings from 218 Squadron, caused heavy damage in the town centre. When the same target was visited again twenty-four hours later this time with just three 218 Squadron Stirlings in attendance, the town again sustained heavy damage. Also on this night, the 25/26th, flight commanders S/ Ls Ashworth and Oldroyd led a six-strong force of the squadron's Stirlings on the long trek to Pilsen in Czechoslovakia to attack the Skoda armaments factory. They found the target hidden under ten-tenths cloud, which prevented visual identification. Oldroyd came down to fifteen hundred feet and dropped his six one thousand pounders across what was believed to be the aiming point. In the process N3722 HA-E was damaged by light flak, and then during the return trip by a JU88 night fighter, but the Stirling made it back to Marham after a flight of nine hours and eighteen minutes. Oldroyd and his navigator were granted an immediate award of the DFC for "*Displaying skill and courage of a high standard*". Pilot Officer Lamason almost did not return after being attacked by a night fighter and sustaining severe damage to the Stirling's hydraulics system. This rendered the rear turret unserviceable, and a fire broke out below the mid upper turret. Acrid smoke filled the rear fuselage until visibility was practically nil, while still under attack, two crew members attended to the fire and ultimately extinguished it. For displaying "*fine airmanship and great devotion of duty*", Phillip Lamason was also awarded an immediate DFC. W7506 HA-K failed to return with the crew of Canadian P/O Harrold Millichamp RCAF, and is believed to have fallen victim to Obw Karl Haisch of 4/NJG3, and crashed at 00.06hrs near Rudesheim with the loss of all on board. This was Millichamp's seventeenth operation, and his was the first 218 Squadron Stirling to fail to return from an operation. This was a special operation codenamed "Cannonbury", and is believed to have been the only Bomber Command main force operation undertaken throughout the war, which involved the cooperation of a resistance organisation.

The Rostock series concluded on the night of the 26/27th, by which time over seventeen hundred buildings had been destroyed, and 60% of the town's built-up area was deemed to be in ruins. The success was followed up at Cologne on the 27/28th, when five participating 218 Squadron crews were led by S/Ldr Ashworth. The Rhineland city was found clear of cloud and endured a devastating attack, in which some fifteen hundred houses and nine industrial premises were destroyed. A raid on Kiel on the night of the 28/29th inflicted damage upon all three shipyards. The Secretary of State for Air, Sir Archibald Sinclair, accompanied by G/C Sir Louis Greig, paid a formal visit to the squadron on the 29th. After a quick inspection W/Cdr Holder introduced each of the squadron captains to Sinclair, and on his departure the Secretary of State for Air congratulated the squadron on its very fine performance and told them to keep it up!

The last raid of the month took place on the night of the 29th, and was directed at the Gnome & Rhone aero-engine factory at Gennevilliers in Paris. 218 Squadron again put up five crews led this time by A Flight's S/Ldr Oldroyd, who attacked the factory in excellent visibility, and delivered his load from 8,000 feet. All three factory buildings and the adjoining power station were reported to be ablaze. The squadron parted company with F/L William Livingston at the end of the month on completion of his operational tour. Sadly he would be killed while attacking Bremen during the final Thousand Bomber raid on June 25th 1942, while an instructor with 1651

Conversion Unit. These recent operations had produced encouraging results, with improved concentration of bombing and lower than expected losses. 218 Squadron managed a creditable 112 sorties during the month, the highest by any of the four Stirling units, and this was achieved for the loss of just two aircraft and crews.

May

The new month's operations began for the squadron on the night of the 2/3rd, with a return to gardening by five crews, who were briefed to mine the Quince North garden area in the Langelands Belt. It was actually Harris who introduced the use of code names for "gardening", and the mine fields were identified by names of flowers and plants. One aircraft failed to take-off on this night, but the remainder successfully planted their vegetables in the allotted area. On the return flight S/Ldr Ashworth attacked a tanker ship with two 500 pounders and reported a near miss. The squadron was not involved in an attack on Hamburg on the 3/4th, when, despite complete cloud cover and the relatively small number of fifty-four aircraft arriving to bomb, a remarkable amount of damage was achieved and over a hundred fires were created, half of them classed as large.

A three raid series on Stuttgart on consecutive nights began inauspiciously on the 4/5th, and was supported by four 218 Squadron Stirlings, whose crews were briefed to aim for the Bosch factory. W7521 HA-U had been hit by flak over the target, and lost the use of its port-outer engine. On arrival back over England an airlock in the fuel system shut down the good engines, and necessitated a forced-landing, which Irishman Sgt McAuley carried out at 04.55hrs five miles south of Norwich. There was no damage to the crew, but the Stirling was declared to be beyond economical repair. Meanwhile on this night five 218 Squadron Stirlings were sent back to the Skoda armaments factory at Pilsen. Squadron Leader Oldroyd's W7469 HA-M was hit and damaged by heavy flak during the bomb run, but his load was delivered and seen to explode near the power house. During the return flight the aircraft was coned by a number of searchlights in the Rhine area, and further damaged by flak before being intercepted by a JU88 over Brussels. A twenty-minute engagement ended only after contact was broken in cloud. Flight Sergeant Webber attacked the last resort target of Mainz, leaving only P/Os Bullock and Lamason to reach the primary target, where they dropped their loads from 7,000 feet and started one small fire. N6070 HA-A crashed near Frankfurt after being brought down by flak, and F/Sgt William Gregg died with all but one of his crew. The survivor, mid upper gunner Sgt R Macafee RCAF, reported the following upon his return to the UK after liberation.

"Had trouble crossing coast at Ostend, very heavy flak, but no damage. Reached the target a few minutes late, flak very heavy and one large fire on the ground. Had difficulty bombing due to flak and left target with two 1000 pounders. Off

course some time latter and pin pointed Frankfurt dropped remaining bombs from 7-8000ft, then flak barrage came up. Shell burst in cabin and seemed to set fire to all the aircraft in front of the main spar. No Inter-com or lights, aircraft went into a very steep dive, I got out immediately and seemed to hit the ground at the same time. Aircraft exploded very close to where I landed"

Tragically this was the thirtieth and final operation of Gregg's first tour, and if this were not enough, one of those killed was Sgt K Wheeler DFM, who had survived the encounter with the persistent Bf110 over Lübeck on March 28th while flying with F/L Humphreys. One other 218 Squadron sortie on this night involved S/Ldr Ashworth and crew on a nickeling trip to Paris in R9313 HA-Q. Having successfully delivered their load of six hundred bundles of leaflets, they were crossing the English coast homebound when they were attacked over Norwich by a Havoc/Hurricane combination from 1445 Flight. The crew was left with no alternative but to abandon the blazing Stirling, which crashed in a meadow at Gatehouse Farm near Horsham in Essex. What become of the Havoc pilot, S/Ldr Budd, and the Hurricane pilot, P/O Murray, is unknown. The second of the series against Stuttgart was hindered by ground haze, and a decoy fire site lured a proportion of the force away. It was a similar story on the following night, when five 218 Squadron Stirlings participated, and, despite claims of fires by returning crews, no bombs actually fell within the city.

Recent raids on Baltic coastal targets had been a great success, and perhaps this was why Warnemünde and its nearby Heinkel factory were selected for attention on the 8/9th. A force of almost two hundred aircraft was involved, including nine from 218 Squadron. Intense searchlight activity was encountered over the target, which prevented the crews from positively identifying the aiming point. Only F/L Humphreys caught a glimpse of the target, and he reported his bomb load exploding near a row of factory sheds and producing a bright green fire. In the event, the operation was at best only modestly effective, at a cost to the command of nineteen aircraft, four of which were from 3 Group. Bad weather prevented any further operations until the night of May 17th, when the group dispatched fifty-eight aircraft for gardening duties. Eleven crews from 218 Squadron were assigned to mine sea lanes at Hawthorn, Daffodil, Sweet Pea and Rosemary. Two crews returned early with engine problems, and F/Sgt Johnson was unable to open his bomb doors over the release point and jettisoned the mines on the journey home. Two night fighters attacked Sgt Medus while outbound to "Rosemary", but the rear gunner returned fire with two short bursts, and one attacker broke off the engagement, while the other kept its distance and was soon lost in cloud.

Less fortunate was the experienced New Zealander, F/L Arthur Humphreys DFC, who was attacked by Staffel Kapitan Oberleutnant Rudolf Schonert of 4/NJG2 while outbound for the Daffodil mining area. N6071 HA-G had been abandoned by its crew by the time it crashed near Lyne at 00.57hrs. The wireless

Flight Lieutenant Arthur Humphreys DFC (third from left) the New Zealand born skipper of N6071 HA-G shot down by Staffel Kapitan Oberleutnant Rudolf Schonert of 4/NJG2 while outbound for the Daffodil mining area. He survived the war as a PoW.

operator, Sgt Ronald Layfield, was the first to be captured, and he was taken to the crash site by local Danish Police. Layfield pointed out where the second pilot, New Zealander Raymond Hill, lay wounded with a broken ankle and a deep wound to his thigh. Hill was taken to the Varde County Hospital, where his wounds were treated, and he and Layfield were then sent to the local Police Station. At around 05.00hrs, Sgt William Lawrence, the rear gunner, was captured with a broken ankle and a number of superficial wounds, and like his crewmates he was taken to the Varde Hospital to be treated. At 06.00hrs the body of the Australian Observer, twenty-seven-year-old F/O Eliot Barnfather RAAF was discovered underneath his parachute, having died from bullet wounds to the stomach and abdomen area. His body was taken to the Chapel at Varde County Hospital, and was laid to rest on May 23rd in the Fovrfeld Cemetery. George Toynbee-Clarke was captured at 10.30hrs twelve kilometres to the north of the crash site, having sustained a bullet wound to the head that required the attention of Tarms local Doctor, Reinhold Nielson. Finally, at 22.35hrs, the pilot and the flight engineer, Sgt John Taylor, were captured hiding at a farm in Egknud. Like their colleges they were transported to the Varde Police station, where they were eventually handed over to the German authorities. This was F/L Humphreys' twenty-seventh operation of his second tour, his first having been mostly undertaken with 75 (NZ) Squadron in 1940.

Almost two hundred aircraft took off for Mannheim on the evening of the 19th, 103 of them drawn from 3 Group. 218 Squadron's contribution was eight Stirlings lead by the redoubtable S/Ldr Ashworth in N6078 HA-P. The attack was a failure in the face of scattered bombing, most of which ended up in wooded country south west of the target. Flight Sergeant Stanley Coggin and his eight man crew failed to return to Marham after disappearing without trace over the North Sea in DJ977 HA-F. Thirty-two year old Coggin was an experienced pilot, who had cut his teeth serving as second pilot to both W/Cdr Kirkpatrick and F/L Humphreys. At the time of his loss he had completed eighteen operations, seven as captain.

When Harris was appointed C-in-C, he had asked for four thousand bombers with which to win the war. Whilst there was never the slightest chance of getting them, he needed to ensure that those earmarked for him were not spirited away to what he considered to be less deserving causes. This was a time, particularly following the Butt Report, when every branch of the services seemed to be demanding bomber aircraft, among them the Admiralty for use against the U-Boot menace, and the Middle East Air Command to redress recent reversals. Harris knew that he was the only worthy recipient, and needed a major success, and, perhaps, a dose of symbolism to make his point. Out of this was born the Thousand Plan, Operation Millennium, the commitment of a thousand aircraft in one night against an important German city, for which Hamburg had been pencilled in. Harris did not have a thousand front-line aircraft, and would need the support of other Commands, principally Coastal and Flying Training, if he were to reach the magic figure. In letters to Harris on the 22nd and 23rd respectively generous support was offered, but following an intervention by the Admiralty, the Coastal Command element was withdrawn, leaving Harris well short on numbers. Undaunted as always, he, or more likely his able deputy, Air Marshal Sir Robert Saundby, scraped together every airframe capable of controlled flight, or something resembling it, and pulled in the screened crews from their instructional duties. Come the night, not only would the magic thousand figure be reached, it would be comfortably surpassed.

The only question now was the weather, and as the days ticked by inexorably towards the end of May, this was showing no signs of complying. By this time aircraft from the training units had arrived on bomber stations from Yorkshire to East Anglia as the build-up of the giant force progressed, and this gave rise to much speculation and no answers. Harris was acutely aware of the genuine danger, that the giant force may draw attention to itself and compromise security, and the time was fast approaching, when the operation would either have to be launched, or be scrubbed for the time being. On the 29/30th Harris allowed an operation to go ahead against the Gnome & Rhone factory at Gennevilliers in Paris, which had escaped damage a month earlier. 218 Squadron provided a total of ten aircraft for three separate targets on this night, four for the main fare, three for a mining operation in the Nectarines area, and three for an attack on the docks at Cherbourg.

Both flight commanders were involved at Paris, where a combination of low cloud, intense searchlight activity and light flak made identification of the aiming point difficult, and the target escaped with little or no further damage. During the course of the operation W7535 HA-C crashed near Colombes, a suburb of Paris, and acting F/L Arthur Jones and his eight-man crew were all killed, on this, their third operation. Arthur Jones had been instrumental in the forming of 218 conflight.

It was in a tense atmosphere of expectation and frustration that "morning prayers" began at Harris's High Wycombe HQ on the 30th, with all eyes turned upon his chief meteorological adviser, Magnus Spence. After deliberations, Spence was finally able to give a qualified assurance of clear weather over the Rhineland after midnight, with a likelihood of moonlight, while north-western Germany and Hamburg would be concealed under buckets of cloud. Thus did the fickle finger of fate decree that Cologne would host the first one thousand bomber raid in history, and that night the departure of 1047 assorted aircraft began before 23.00hrs, and continued until after midnight. Some of the older training hacks took to the air almost reluctantly, lifted more by the enthusiasm of their crews than by the power of their engines, and some of these, unable to climb to a respectable height, would fall easy prey to the defences, or simply drop from the sky through mechanical breakdown.

218 Squadron put up a magnificent nineteen Stirlings, led by the commanding officer, W/Cdr Holder in W7530 HA-Q, who was carrying as a passenger the most senior officer flying that night. Harris had slapped a ban on A-O-Cs taking part in this momentous operation, but 3 Group's AVM Baldwin chose to ignore it, and worry about the consequences when he got back. The operation was conducted in the now familiar three wave system, and was by any standards an outstanding success. 868 aircraft reached the target to bomb, and they destroyed over 3,300 buildings, and seriously damaged a further two thousand. While living accommodation represented the bulk of the statistics, many public, administrative, industrial and commercial premises were included, along with electricity and telephone installations. The loss of forty-one aircraft represented a new record, but in conditions favourable to attackers and defenders alike, and in the context of the size of the force and the scale of success, it was an acceptable figure. 218 Squadron's W7502 HA-N was badly damaged by flak, and was ultimately abandoned by three of the crew, two of whom attempted to use a single parachute. The navigator, F/Sgt Borrowdale, clung to Sgt Tate RCAF, one of the gunners, but was unable to maintain his hold when the parachute jerked open and he fell to his death. Sergeant Tate and one other survived to be taken prisoner, but P/O Arthur Davis and the rest of his crew perished in the crash near Huppenbroich on the German/Belgium Border. The eight men on board R9311 HA-L had known almost from the outset that they faced a belly landing on return, after damaging the undercarriage on take-off. Having successfully completed their part in the

Operations board for RAF Marham dated May 30th 1942, Operation "Millennium". Note the name of AVM Baldwin.

operation, Sgt Falconer put the Stirling down safely, and all eight men walked away. This was only Sgt Falconer's second operation as captain, having previously carried out ten operations as second pilot to Phil Lamason. The Stirling was struck-off-charge. It had been an expensive month for 218 Squadron, which lost eight aircraft and five crews from seventy-nine sorties.

June

Harris was anxious to use the thousand force again as soon as possible, and after a night's rest, he ordered it to be prepared for a raid on Essen on the night of the 1/2nd. 956 aircraft were available to answer the call, including fifteen from 218 Squadron, led by the flight commanders, S/Ldrs Ker and Ashworth. Sergeant McAuley and his crew were forced to return early when N3753 HA-U developed engine problems, and they walked away from yet another crash-landing. The remainder of the squadron's crews completed their sorties, delivering over 112,000lbs of bombs. Sadly very few of them fell where intended, as bombs were sprayed over a wide area of the Ruhr and damage in Essen was light and superficial. It was a tremendous disappointment after the success at Cologne, and a follow-up raid by a conventional force twenty-four hours later was equally

Luftwaffe personnel gather around the wreckage of Short Stirling W7474 HA-K. Skippered by 19-year-old veteran Pilot Officer John Webber the crew fell victim of a night fighter flown by Oblt Ludwig Becker of 6./NJG2 over Holland crashing at 00.27 hours 2km North of dey Kooy.

ineffective. Some compensation was gained at Bremen on the 3/4th, when the city authorities reported their heaviest and most damaging raid to date. Seven 218 Squadron Stirlings took part, and one of them was among the eleven aircraft failing to return. W7474 HA-K fell victim to a night fighter over Holland, flown by Oblt Ludwig Becker of 6/NJG2. The Stirling crashed at 00.27hrs near Den Helder on the Dutch coast, and only the rear gunner, Sgt K Cox, survived from the eight-man crew of nineteen-year-old P/O John Webber. This was one of the squadron's most experienced crews, and its loss was felt deeply. Webber had commenced operations in September 1941, and by the time of his death had flown thirty operations while the majority of his crew were on their twenty-seventh.

After the recent high tempo of operations there now followed a relatively quiet period for the squadron, during which mining dominated, and such operations were carried out in the Nectarines area on the 7th, 9th, 11th and 18th, all without loss. The only incident was on the 9th, when S/Ldr Oldroyd pranged N3722 on take-off at 11.45hrs. With the throttles wide open and the Stirling moments from becoming airborne, it swung violently from the runway, giving the experienced pilot no chance to correct. As a result the undercarriage collapsed, and the aircraft came crashing to a halt. Thankfully, the crew, which included an additional member, Canadian P/O Turner, who was gaining experience, was able to walk away from the scene, but the Stirling required extensive repair. Harris meantime, was determined to make his point at Essen, and tried three more times during the month, on the 5/6th, 8/9th and 16/17th, thus bringing the number of sorties during June to 1,607. Out of these, eighty-four aircraft had been lost, no industrial damage had been inflicted, and only a modest few houses had been destroyed.

Earlier on the 6/7th, the first of four raids during the month on Emden had produced an excellent return of three hundred houses destroyed, but this success was not to be repeated when the Command returned to the port later in the month. 218 Squadron sat out the first of these on the 19/20th, but dispatched nine Stirlings on the night of the 20/21st. Pilot Officer Medus returned early with technical difficulties, while the remainder pressed on to encounter unfavourable conditions in the target area in the form of five to seven-tenths cloud cover and ground haze. Returning crews reported seeing only scattered fires, but not present at debriefing was the popular B Flight commander, S/Ldr Ashworth, who had fallen victim to Lt Johannes Werth of 7/NJG2 at 02.00hrs. Attacked soon after leaving the target area the Stirling began to burn, and in the face of increasing instability and spreading flames, Ashworth gave the order to bail out. Five of the crew managed to take to their parachutes before the Stirling crashed at Wognun, four kilometres north-north-west of Noorm in Holland, with Ashworth still on board. Squadron Leader Harold John Ashworth was eventually posthumously awarded a well-deserved and long overdue DFC, which was gazetted on July 27th 1943.

One of the survivors was F/L Desmond Plunkett, the second pilot. Captured on the following day near Spierdijk, Plunkett ultimately ended up at Stalag Luft III at Sagan, where he came to the attention of Big X Roger Bushell. Bushell gave Plunkett the role of mapmaker for the forthcoming mass escape. Leading a team of fourteen men Plunkett set about producing not only maps, but forged passes and permits. At his own request he was allocated unlucky number thirteen for the tunnel escape on March 23rd. Managing to reach the local railway station he boarded a train for Breslau, and after several days on the run in Czechoslovakia he eventually managed to reach the border with Austria, where he was recaptured. After a short and rather unpleasant stay courtesy of the Gestapo, Plunkett eventually found himself at Stalag Luft I on the Baltic Sea. It was from this camp that he was repatriated after VE Day.

It was back to Emden for eleven 218 Squadron crews on the night of the 22/23rd, with W/Cdr Holder in the vanguard. The target was found to be cloud-free, and returning crews reported numerous fires in the docks area. Again this target claimed a 218 Squadron victim, twenty-year-old P/O Richard Medus and crew falling to the cannons of Oblt Rudolph Schonert of 4/NJG2 while on their way home at 02.07hrs. It would be learned later that none had survived, and thus another seasoned captain, this one on his twenty-seventh operation, had been lost. He would be posthumously awarded a DFC in July 1943.

The final thousand bomber raid took place on the 25/26th with Bremen as the target. Bomber Command was able to amass 960 aircraft while Coastal Command, ordered by Churchill to participate, sent a further 102 aircraft in what was classified as a separate operation. Never the less the numbers converging on Bremen on this night exceeded those going to Cologne at the end of May. 218 Squadron contributed fourteen Stirlings to what was a moderately successful operation, which fell well short of Cologne, but far surpassed the debacle at Essen. 572 houses were destroyed and many important war industry factories sustained damage, as did one of the shipyards, but the cost in bombers was a new record of forty-eight, including one from 218 Squadron. W7503 HA-A was shot down by Oblt Ludwig Becker of VI/NJG2 at 00.39hrs, crashing onto the banks of the Ijsselmeer in northern Holland, killing the entire crew. Pilot Officer Francis Ball was on his fifteenth operation, and had participated in all of the "thousand" raids. His wireless operator, Sgt Rogers, had completed twenty-four sorties.

Three follow-up operations against Bremen began on the 27/28th, when 218 Squadron contributed ten Stirlings. Flak was responsible for damaging two of the squadron's aircraft, while Sgt Falconer's R9333 HA-F was extensively damaged by two night fighters over Holland. The instrument panel, turret controls and airframe were all hit in the brief but vicious encounter, and Falconer quickly realised he had no option but to jettison the all-incendiary bomb load. This he did at 01.30hrs three miles south-east of Makkum, after which the crew managed to nurse the Stirling out over the Dutch coast to an eventual safe landing at base at 02.47hrs. For his exploits Falconer was awarded an immediate DFM. Sergeant Ralph Waters and his crew were shot down by flak during this operation, and all died in the sea off Hohenstiefersiel. This was Waters' eighteenth operation, and his fourth as captain. The last operation of the month was once again aimed

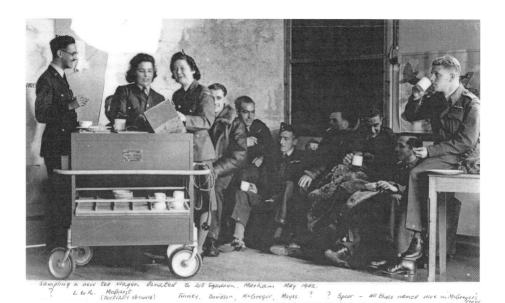

A most welcome donation to the squadron was this mobile tea wagon in May 1942. The crew are those of Flight Sergeant McGregor. Sitting on the table is Roy Spear RNZAF.

at Bremen, for which Bomber Command dispatched 284 aircraft to what proved to be a cloud covered target. 218 Squadron detailed twelve crews led by S/Ldr Oldroyd, who took off at 23.40hrs. Three aircraft returned early but the remainder pressed on and were subjected to the usual barrage of intense flak while on their bombing runs. Despite this they had the satisfaction of observing several large fires and a number of smaller isolated ones around the aiming point. Damage was inflicted on the sheds at the Neustsadt Guter Bahnhof and the Hansa Lloyd Dynamo sheds and Hansa Lloyd Dynamo Automobile factory. In all the squadron dropped a total of 53,640lb of incendiaries without loss.

July

July began with yet another assault on Bremen on the 2nd, 218 Squadron dispatching nine crews, who found visibility in the target area good, and this allowed an effective raid to develop. Sergeant Savage fought off three Bf110s during the return journey, and P/O Farquharson and crew claimed an enemy fighter destroyed. Fate once again played a hand, when yet another experienced crew failed to return. Having taken off at 00.28hrs Sgt Geoffrey Jeary and crew sent an S.O.S shortly afterwards, after which, nothing further was heard. Sergeant Jeary was on his twenty-third operation, and his crew on their eleventh, they had taken part in all three of the Thousand Bomber raids. N3718 HA-C is believed to have come down in the North Sea with the loss of all on board. It is possible that they fell victim to Oblt Heinrich Prinz zu-Sayn-Wittgenstein, who claimed a Stirling fifty kilometres west of Rotterdam. On the following morning Sgt Savage and P/O McCarthy carried out an extensive sea search, but after three and half hours both crews returned to Marham without finding any sign of the aircraft or crew.

Having failed so dismally at Essen Harris would turn his attention upon its Ruhr neighbour, Duisburg, during the second half of July. It had become increasingly apparent to the squadron as well as to Group HQ, that Marham's grass runways were not ideally suited to the Stirling with its clumsy and awkward undercarriage. As a result the squadron was informed that it would be moving to a new airfield still under construction at Downham Market, situated eight miles south-west of Marham. Downham was being built to Class A specification, initially as a satellite to Marham by Messrs W & C French. The new airfield had three concrete runways, two at 1,400 yards and one at 1,900 yards, with thirty-four pan hard standings. Six T2 hangers were to be erected during 1942/43, and 218 Squadron would be the first operational unit to take up residence. The first phase of the squadron's move took place on July the 6th, followed on the 7th by the departure from Marham in pouring rain of thirteen Stirlings. The squadron spent the next few days settling in, and the crews found to their annoyance that some of the facilities were not yet completed. A number of local flights and air tests were carried out, but the first operation from Downham Market would not take place until the 12th.

In the meantime an operation by almost three hundred aircraft took place on Wilhelmshaven on the 8/9th, when many of the bomb loads were wasted on open country. Pilot Officer Farquharson and Sgt Hartley had the honour of launching the first sorties from 218 Squadron's new home, when delivering six mines each by TR fix from 2,000 feet in the Nectarines area. The first of five raids on Duisburg in less than four weeks was mounted on the 13/14th by a little under two hundred aircraft, of which just two belonged to 218 Squadron. Cloud and electrical storms made conditions difficult for bombing, and the city escaped with the slightest damage. Squadron Leader Powell DFM was given a leaflet raid on Lille for his first operation as B Flight commander, having recently arrived to replace S/Ldr Ashworth. Gordon Powell had been awarded the DFM in 1940 while with 115 Squadron, in recognition of his low-level attack on Stavanger aerodrome, which had been pressed home in the face of intense flak and machine-gun fire. Despite being wounded in the arm and torso he bombed the target, before dragging his severely damaged Wellington over three hundred miles across the North Sea to reach home.

Twenty-one Stirlings set off shortly before 19.00hrs on the 16th for an experimental and ambitious dusk attack on the Lübecker Flenderwerke AG U-Boat yard at Herrenwyk, located ten kilometres north-east of Lübeck. All six of the Stirling squadrons provided aircraft for Operation *Pandemonium*, which called for them to fly in formation at low level across the North Sea, until reaching a point where cloud cover could be exploited to carry out individual attacks on the target. 218 Squadron provided six aircraft, while the remainder were drawn from 7, XV, 149 and 214 Squadrons. In the event the raid was not a success, largely because of a lack of cloud cover on the outward flight and ten-tenths cloud in the target area. Only eight crews reported bombing as briefed, and a number of 218 Squadron aircraft were fortunate to survive being attacked by fighters. W/Cdr Holder was attacked outbound by three BF109s, and the following combat report tells the story.

While flying to Lübeck at 2125hrs at 800 feet and positioned at 5520 N 0846 E, two Bf109 aircraft were reported by the rear gunner F/Sgt Steele on the starboard quarter above at 1000 yards away and some distance apart. Shortly afterwards another Bf109 was reported by the mid upper gunner P/O Green on the starboard beam also above and approximately 1000 yards away. One attacked starboard quarter level and fired cannon and machine gun from 600 yards and broke away at 450 yards, when the rear gunner fired a four second burst. Mid upper gunner also fired a good burst. An attack was then made by one of the other fighters from the port beam above and considerably damaged our Stirling by cannon fire, also hitting the hydraulics pipe lines to the rear turret which started to slow down. This aircraft was given a burst by the mid upper and rear gunner with two guns serviceable. Then we were attacked at the rear and starboard beam level. The aircraft on the beam was taken by the mid upper and the one at the rear by the rear gunner who also gave the evasive action to the captain (which was to turn to starboard and climb) These aircraft broke away at 400 yards and were fired at on the break away. The next attack was from the port beam below when the front gunner F/Sgt Bull fired a good burst with the mid upper on the break away. The fifth attack was from the starboard quarter below. The evasive action given by the rear gunner caused the fighters fire to pass behind and below us. The 6th & 7th attacks were made dead astern. When the fighters came into 100 yards the rear gunner fired a couple of good bursts by hand from one gun, as the turret had gone u/s. This fighter is claimed as damaged. The attacks were then discontinued, and we climbed into cloud for a while, and then got back on course and went on to bomb the target.

Wing Commander Holder identified the target, before delivering his six one thousand pounders from five hundred feet. The Stirling was bracketed by both light and heavy flak, which resulted in numerous hits, but thankfully without injuring the crew. Australian P/O Sanderson and P/O Abberton each managed to identify the aiming point, and like their commanding officer, attracted the attention of the port's flak, before managing to weave their way out of the target area. Squadron Leader Oldroyd and P/O Farquharson were unable to identify the target, and jettisoned their bomb loads. Pilot Officer Bullock attacked the aerodrome at Blankensee as a last resort target, and, while homebound, was set upon by no less than five enemy fighters. By sheer determination, crew discipline and good airmanship, which involved flying in tight circles in and out of cloud, the pursuers were eventually evaded, and the Stirling made it back to Downham Market.

An operation was mounted against the Vulkan U-Boat yards at Vegesack on the night of the 19/20th, in which thirty-one Stirlings took part in an overall force of ninety four-engine aircraft. Five Stirlings were provided by 218 Squadron, each of them carrying a second pilot gaining operational experience. Squadron Leader Oldroyd was accompanied by S/Ldr J Shewell, who had previously served in Training Command. The target was cloud-covered, and later photographic evidence revealed that no bombs had fallen near the town. It was back to Duisburg on the 21/22nd, when eight 218 Squadron crews were briefed, and once again the more experienced captains were required to show new pilots the ropes. Squadron Leader Oldroyd was joined on this occasion by S/Ldr Powell DFM, while S/Ldr Shewell accompanied the crew of W/O Johnston. Visibility over the target was excellent, and the aiming point was identified by a number of well placed flares. This allowed accurate bombing, which resulted in a number of fires in the town and docks area. Following his time with 218 Squadron S/Ldr Shewell would be posted to 7 Squadron of the Pathfinders with the acting rank of wing commander, where he would serve as a flight commander. Sadly, in a little over a month's time, he would lose his life during an operation to Frankfurt. Duisburg was attacked twice more on the 23/24th and 25/26th, on both occasions with the participation of 218 Squadron. Cloud cover prevented both raids from inflicting any worthwhile damage, despite the commitment of over five-hundred sorties, of which 3 Group contributed 269.

218 Squadron was not involved in the losses, and prepared itself for two heavy raids on Hamburg on the 26/27th and 28/29th. The former involved the largest non-1,000 force to date of 403 aircraft, including eight from 218 Squadron, which left Downham Market in the hour before midnight. Seven from the squadron reached the target and bombed in near perfect visibility at around 01.00hrs. Returning crews reported a concentration of big fires in the old town, and widespread fires across the city. Such was the apparent success of the raid that some crews compared the area of fire to that of the "thousand bomber" raid on Cologne. Eight hundred fires were started, over five hundred of them large, and more than eight hundred houses were destroyed. Twenty-nine aircraft were missing, but 218 Squadron's casualty occurred at home, when R9354 HA-N lost its undercarriage on landing, happily without casualties among the crew of P/O J Savage.

The second operation ran into difficulties even before take-off, when bad weather over the 1, 4 and 5 Group stations prevented them from taking part. This left just 3 Group and a contingent from 91 Group, although the latter were recalled while still over the North Sea. Now just the Wellingtons and Stirlings of 3 Group, twelve of them from 218 Squadron, continued the operation, and they struggled on in severe icing conditions. Four crews jettisoned their loads before reaching the target, three because of engine failures, Sgt Falconer eventually landed BF515 at Leconfield with two engines feathered. Squadron Leader Oldroyd found a solid mass of cloud covering the target area, and unable to identify the aiming point he and the other crews were obliged to bomb on TR. The city's defenders put up a particularly effective intense and accurate flak barrage, working in conjunction with a ring of searchlights, and twenty-six bombers returned with flak damage. There was also much night fighter activity over the target, and 3 Group recorded twenty-four encounters. It proved to be a bad night for 218 Squadron, which posted missing three crews.

Sergeant John Johnson and his crew had borrowed the Conversion Flight's W7464 HA-Z, which fell victim to Oblt Paul Gildner of Stab 5/NJG2, and crashed into the North Sea twenty kilometres north-west of Terschelling at 01.30hrs. Johnson, who was a thirty-one-year-old Yorkshireman, died with his crew, who were on their fifth operation together. The second loss involved the recently appointed flight commander, S/Ldr Gordon Powell DFM, who was on his third sortie as captain since joining the squadron. There were five survivors from the crew of BF309 HA-M, which was also brought down by a night fighter, and crashed at 01.57hrs in the Waddenzee off Busum. One of the survivors was Canadian wireless operator Sgt H Hawker RCAF, who was on his second operation. He recalls:

"Took off from Downham Market at 22.20hrs. Everything went smoothly until Dutch coast, we were unable to gain altitude due to icing conditions which were very severe at 12,000ft. We still continued on and the nav reported Gee Box

was out of commission. Wireless reception was very bad for the beacon. Around 01.30hrs reached target and we were preparing to drop the bombs and flares when the R/G reported fighters, Ju88 and a Bf109 approaching from the rear, front gunner reported almost simultaneously a 109 fighter from the port. Bombs were dropped and I made certain the flares went out the chute and returned to the wireless set and looked out the Astrodome. Pilot turned plane sharply and went into a long dive levelling out a 3,000 to 3,500ft. Fighters followed us and put our recuperators out of order. The fighters come up from underneath and the mid upper gunner put a burst over the port wing. Soon after the port wing caught on fire, the mid-section was now burning. We reached the coast and the pilot told up to bail out, the fighters were still following and the rear gunner firing along with the mid upper. I helped the pilot on with his chute while the 2nd pilot released the front gunner. I watched the 2nd pilot, Observer, engineer bale out and I followed. I had just pulled the rip cord when the aircraft exploded. I was unconscious until just before landing in the water, I swam until I reach a sand bar and stood on it, trying periodically to make for shore until I was captured in the morning".

The body of S/Ldr Powell was found in the wreckage, and was subsequently buried in the Neun Friedhof Cemetery on July 31st. Finally the experienced P/O Colin Farquharson and crew were shot down in N6129 HA-X, another aircraft on the strength of the Conversion Flight. The Stirling was shot down into the North Sea at 02.01hrs, three kilometres east of the Island of Sylt, by an unidentified night fighter of 4/NJG.3. This was Farquharson's sixteenth operation, eight of which were undertaken as second pilot to S/Ldr Ashworth. It was 218 Squadron's heaviest night loss of the war to date, and to add to the general gloom on the squadron, its former flight commander, the popular Herbert Price DFC, now a wing commander, also failed to return from this operation as the commanding officer of 156 Squadron at Alconbury.

A highly effective raid on Saarbrücken on the 29/30th included five Stirlings from 218 Squadron, and almost four hundred buildings were left in ruins in return for a more acceptable loss of nine aircraft. The month was brought to a close at Düsseldorf on the night of the 31st, when another contribution from the training units swelled the numbers available to take part to 630 aircraft. Of these 484 crews claimed to have bombed as briefed. As would always happen when a large force targeted this city, some of the bombing spilled over into Neuss, and more than nine hundred fires were started, while over 450 buildings were destroyed at the two locations. Losses were again high, at twenty-nine aircraft, but 218 Squadron came through unscathed. This was the last operation for the respected veteran S/Ldr Arthur Oldroyd DFC AFC, who had now completed his tour, he would survive the war. The squadron launched ninety sorties during the month, for the loss of three aircraft and four crews, plus two aircraft from the Conversion Flight.

August

The first major operation in August was undertaken by a force of over two hundred aircraft against Duisburg on the night of the 6/7th. Eleven 218 Squadron crews were briefed, and those arriving early found the target relatively free of cloud. This situation quickly changed however into complete cloud cover, forcing bombing by the later waves to be on ETA. It was yet another disappointing attack that cost Bomber Command five aircraft, among them 218 Squadron's N6072 HA-P, which was dispatched at 02.57hrs by Hptm Ludwig Bietmann of V/NJG1. Four members of the crew lost their lives, while Sgt W.J Laidlaw and two others survived as PoWs. This was Laidlaw's eleventh operation and the majority of his crew's fifth. One of the survivors was F/Sgt David Moffet, a twenty-two-year-old wireless operator from Downpatrick, County Down in Northern Ireland. At the age of eighteen he joined the R.A.F, and on completion of his training was posted to 9 Squadron in 1940, where he completed his first tour of thirty operations. After a spell at 20 OTU he was posted to 218 Squadron in April 1942, and he was at the time of his loss one of the most experienced NCOs on the squadron. It was another disappointing attack on this highly industrialised city, which managed to destroy only eighteen buildings, giving a tally over the five raids of 212 houses destroyed for the loss of forty-three aircraft from 1,229 sorties.

190 aircraft took off for Osnabrück on the 9/10th, and those reaching the town left over two hundred houses in ruins. 218 Squadron put up ten Stirlings, and they

A wonderful photograph of two Short Stirling's carrying out a low level beat up of RAF Downham Market. It is believed this was in preparation of the low level daylight operation to Lingen.

all returned safely. While this operation was in progress, F/L Dodkin and his crew joined seventeen others from 3 Group in a freshman attack on le Havre. Seven crews were detailed to carry out a mining operation in the Silverthorne area on the 10th, when weather conditions proved to be near perfect and all crews reported successfully planting their mines. This was followed by two raids on Mainz on consecutive nights beginning on the 11/12th. Shortly after take-off a fire broke out in the starboard-outer engine of W7568 HA-D, which had reached around 3,000 feet in its climb-out. The crew's efforts to extinguish the fire failed, and the flames began to spread towards the main wing fuel tanks and the electrical wiring in the wing. The bomb load was jettisoned, and P/O John Abberton ordered the crew to bail out. At around 22.55hrs the burning Stirling crashed onto a woodland track at Wiltonhill Wood near Brandon in Suffolk, killing the pilot and his Irish observer, Sgt Jeffrey. Abberton had joined the squadron in March 1942, and undertook his first twelve operations as second pilot to A Flight's commander. He had been alongside Oldroyd on the Pilsen trip, when Oldroyd had earned the DFC. Since taking on his own crew, Abberton had operated nine times. The operation itself was a success that caused extensive damage in the city centre, and this was added to significantly during the latter raid, when industrial districts were also hit. Squadron leader Oldroyd reported; *"Visibility was such that the whole area on both sides of the town was seen blazing long after the target was left"*. Eight 218 Squadron crews joined in the return to the same target on the following night led by the recently

A relaxed looking Squadron Leader Sammy Samson DFC seen here while screened from operations.

promoted S/Ldr Arthur Samson, a native of St John's, Newfoundland, who had just assumed command of B Flight. Fires were still burning when the force arrived in the target area, and damage was again concentrated in the centre of the city and industrial areas.

A new era began on the 15th, with the formation of the Pathfinder Force under the then Group Captain Don Bennett. Harris had always been opposed in principle to an elite target finding and marking force, a view shared by all but one of his group commanders. Harris's staunchest ally was 3 Group's A-O-C, AVM Baldwin, who had opposed the creation of an elite force from the outset, and insisted that selected crews from within each group should be specially trained for the task. Harris, once overruled by higher authority, and in typical fashion, gave it his unstinting support, and his choice of Bennett as its leader, although controversial, proved to be inspired. Given Baldwin's outspoken opposition to the formation of the Pathfinder Force or "Bomber Commandos" as he often referred to it, the relationship between 3 Group and its lodgers was surprisingly cordial, if at times a little fraught. All orders would reach the Pathfinders via Baldwin's 3 Group HQ, but they would remain operationally independent. A lesser man than Bennett might have been fazed, but the Australian possessed a brilliant mind that operated on a plane beyond the reach of most, and although initially still only a group captain, this, and his somewhat humourless character, equipped him to hold his own against all-comers.

Three 3 Group units were hived off, the Wellington-equipped 156 Squadron at Alconbury, 7 squadron with its Stirlings, and finally 109 Squadron and its mixed bag of Wellington Mk.VI and Mosquitos. Each of the Command's four heavy groups would be responsible for maintaining a supply of fresh recruits from among its most promising crews. 3 Group would be responsible for feeding crews to 7 Squadron, while the former 3 Group 156 Squadron became affiliated to 1 Group. 83 Squadron would draw its Lancaster crews from 5 Group, and 35 Squadron was to be supplied with Halifax crews by 4 Group. In addition 109 Squadron moved into Wyton, and this, perhaps, would prove to be the most significant posting of all.

Harris was keen to pitch the Pathfinders into battle at the earliest opportunity, and this arose on the night of the 18/19th, when the west-Baltic port of Flensburg was selected, presumably because of its ease of location on the narrow neck of land where Germany and Denmark meet. 218 Squadron dispatched ten Stirlings, the crews of which encountered unexpectedly difficult weather conditions outbound and in the target area. 218 Squadron's returning crews were unanimous in their disappointment, reporting that flares and incendiaries were scattered all over the target area, and a number of bombs fell on the Danish towns of Sonderdorg and Abenra, twenty-five miles or more north of the intended target. 218 Squadron's W7618 failed to return after been attacked by Uffz Friedel Krause of 8/NJG1 at 00.48hrs over the North Sea west of Esbjerg. Pilot Officer Irven McDaniel, an American from Arkansas, was forced to ditch the severely damaged aircraft, and he and two of his crew alone survived after clambering aboard the dinghy. They were on their first operation together, and endured three days afloat before being chanced upon by the Danish fishing boat E 28 "Dania" out of Esbjerg. On reaching the port the airmen were ultimately handed over to the Luftwaffe at Esbjerg airfield. There is an interesting postscript to this incident. It would appear that the Stirling's gunners had inflicted damage to Uffz Krause's Bf110, because it crashed a couple of kilometres north of Tønder shortly after 01:10hrs while attempting an emergency landing, and Krause and his wireless operator were killed.

A major mining operation was organised for the evening of August 20th involving sixty-five crews from 1, 3 and 5 Groups, who were briefed to deliver 130

A fresh faced Pilot Officer Irven McDaniel of Hot Springs, Arkansas USA striking a menacing pose with his service revolver. The nineteen year was shot down on his first operation as captain. He had previously flown three operations as 2nd pilot including a trip to Lubeck on July 16th with Wing Commander Holder DFC when attacked by Bf109s.

mines in the western Baltic. 218 Squadron contributed nine crews, who could not know that this would be the squadron's worst night for operational losses of the entire war, and, by a cruel twist of fate, result in the loss of four of the squadron's most experienced and long-serving crews with just one survivor between them. Twenty-five year old Australian, F/O Owen Sanderson RAAF and his crew, who were operating together for the tenth time, were victims of the local flak defences situated around the airfield at Schleswig. W7573 HA-U was heading for the "Radish" area at the time, and, with wing tanks ablaze, Sanderson jettisoned the four mines, only to crash almost immediately at 22.30hrs with the loss of all on board. W7615 HA-M was brought down by Lt Rolf Bussman of 9/NJG3, and sent crashing into the sea with no survivors from the crew of Irishman P/O George McAuley DFC, who had run out of luck following the two incidents recorded earlier. Their target had been the "Forget-me-Not" area near Kiel harbour. This was a particularly tragic loss of a pilot on his thirty-second operation, and obviously close to the end of his tour. This operation was the eleventh in the tour of F/Sgt Leonard Hartley and his crew, and they too fell foul of German flak, crashing at 23.56hrs near Hoffnungstal–Mariental while heading for the Kadet Channel. The rear gunner, Sgt Young, was the sole survivor from BF338 HA-Q, which unusually contained four married crew members with an average age of twenty-six. The final loss of the night was that of New Zealander P/O Derek Bullock and crew, who had been briefed to mine in the "Forget-me-nots" area. BF319 HA-C crashed at 00.50hrs near Langwebel, seventeen kilometres south-west of Kiel, again as the result of flak, and all on board were killed. The crew had joined the squadron on April 1st from 1651 Conversion Unit, and were on their twentieth operation, while twenty three year old Derek was on his twenty-ninth. One can only imagine the sombre atmosphere in both messes on the following morning over breakfast, with four crews missing, and twenty-eight airman lost. Not since May 1940 had the squadron lost four crews.

Squadron Leader Raymond DFC arrived to take command of A Flight on the 24th. A New Zealander, Raymond was a seasoned bomber captain, having completed a tour of thirty-nine operations with XV Squadron during 1940/1941.

"Bobby" Raymond arrived having just completed a six month spell as an instructor with 1651 CU, where, as B Flight commander, he had participated in all three of the Thousand Bomber raids, along with another to Düsseldorf. The squadron was called upon to make available nine crews for an attack on Frankfurt on the night of Raymond's appointment, and he was to take the lead. This was the Pathfinders' second operation, which twenty of their number were to open at 23.40hrs with the delivery of 30lb and 250lb incendiary bombs onto the aiming point. In the event, only three aircraft arrived on time, and they, like the rest of the force, found the target under nine-tenths cloud. The results were predictable, and the majority of the bombs fell into open country. Flight Sergeant Robert Yates and crew failed to return from this operation following an encounter with Major Kurt Holler of Stab III/NJG4 at 23.41hrs. W7562 HA-R crashed near Dinant in Belgium, and all eight crewmen, seven of whom were on their eleventh operation, were killed.

New Zealander Bobby Raymond DFC on his wedding day. He brought a wealth of experience when he joined the Squadron, having previously completed 39 operations with XV Squadron. While screened from operations he flew 4 operations with 1651 CU.

Three nights later, the Pathfinders registered their first success, when providing good illumination at Kassel for the main force crews to exploit. 218 Squadron supported the operation with eight Stirlings, and among those taking part were both flight commanders. For once conditions in the target area were favourable, and crews were able to identify the city below, where a number of concentrated fires soon developed. It was still only a moderately successful operation, however, with 144 buildings destroyed, but it was a marked improvement on earlier performances. On the debit side a massive thirty-one aircraft were lost, and the month's misfortunes continued for 218 Squadron with the failure to return of two more crews. Pilot Officer John Gruber and his crew were on their maiden operation together when shot down by Hptm Werner Streib of Stab I/NJG1 at 01.04hrs. BF315 HA-F crashed two kilometres west of Elst and south of Arnhem with just two survivors. One of these, rear gunner Sgt Edward Green, died while in captivity on April 21st 1945. The second loss of the night involved the crew of P/O William McCarthy, and they also fell victim to a night fighter. R9160 HA-G was brought down over the North Sea, west of Bergen aan Zee at 01.40hrs by

The wreckage of F/Lt Du Toits Short Stirling N3717 HA-S at RAF Manston.

Oblt Ludwig Becker of 6/NJG2, Becker's second kill of the night. There were no survivors from the eight-man crew, which again included a second pilot, twenty-year-old Sgt Henry Russell RCAF, who had arrived from 218 Conversion Flight on August 20th. The crew had been on its twenty-fifth operation, and McCarthy on his thirty-first. This brave Australian would not live to wear the DFC so strongly recommended by his commanding officer just three days prior to his death, and it would be almost a year before it was gazetted.

Nuremberg brought the month's activities to an end on the 28th, when six 218 Squadron crews were scheduled to operate against this distant target. A seventh crew, that of Sgt K Ryan, was given the freshman target of Saarbrücken. The Pathfinders employed target indicator bombs for the first time, despite which, the bombing was not concentrated, and much of it missed the city by many miles. At least on this occasion all of the 218 Squadron participants came home. Diverted because of a fuel shortage, South African P/O Du Toit was dazzled by Chance lights as he landed N3717 HA-S at Manston, and with his night vision impaired, he failed to notice a line of parked aircraft until it was too late. The Stirling swept into a line of Spitfires belonging to the Northolt Polish fighter wing, destroying Spitfire Mk.Vb MB566 of 317 Squadron, before colliding with a 841 Squadron Fleet Air Arm Fairey Albacore. The Stirling was written-off, but the crew emerged unscathed to enjoy what would be a temporary reprieve. It had been the squadron's blackest month since those far-off days in France, and had cost eleven aircraft either failing to return or written off in crashes, sadly it also meant the loss of 10 crews some of whom were almost tour expired. At the end of the month the respected W/Cdr Holder was posted to 3 Group HQ. He operated a total of sixty-five times, fourteen of them while commanding 218 Squadron. He would be awarded the DSO on October 27th.

September

The hope was that September couldn't be as bad for the squadron as August had been, although the omens were not encouraging, when N3714 HA-Q went missing from an operation to Saarbrücken on the very first night. The attack, much to the embarrassment of the Pathfinders and the chagrin of the inhabitants, had actually fallen on the non-industrial town of Saarlouis, which suffered extensive damage. By the time the mistake was discovered, the 218 Squadron Stirling, one of eight dispatched by the squadron, was a shattered wreck on Belgian soil. It was the victim of Hptm Walter Ehle of Stab II/NJG1, and F/Sgt Keith Ryan RNZAF and four of his crew lay dead, while two of their colleagues were beginning a period of extended leave as guests of the Reich. This posting of a "black" by the Pathfinders could have portended an unfortunate month generally but in fact, from this point on the Command embarked on an unprecedented run of effective operations, which took it through to mid-month.

In the meantime, thirty-year-old Canadian W/Cdr Montagu F B Read assumed command of the squadron on the 2nd vice S/Ldr Samson. Born in East Wellington, Vancouver, British Columbia, Read was granted a Governor General nomination to join the RAF in 1933. Throughout the thirties he served with both 99 and 83 bomber squadrons, before being posted to the British Forces HQ in Aden in October 1939 to undertake personnel duties. From there he was seconded to the American Legation in Cairo, again in an administrative role. Promoted to the rank of wing commander on the 1st of June 1941, he returned to England a year later. Wing Commander Read had no previous war-time connection with Bomber Command, and had only completed his conversion course at 1651 CU at Waterbeach on September 1st.

The run of successful operations began at Karlsruhe on the night of Read's appointment, when 218 Squadron contributed six aircraft, one of which contained the new commanding officer operating in the role of second pilot to S/Ldr Raymond. A seventh crew, captained by F/Sgt Cozens, was tasked with mining in the Nectarines I area. The main operation wrought heavy damage on the town of Karlsruhe, in which twenty-seven factories were damaged and sixty acres of industrial buildings and yards were devastated. A further 260 acres of residential and commercial properties were also destroyed. While outbound to the target, P/O Du Toit's Stirling was attacked by an enemy fighter, and the rear gunner was killed. An uncontrolled dive then ensued, during which five thousand feet were lost, the bomb load was jettisoned, and the order to abandon ship was given. However, Du Toit regained control and managed to bring the badly damaged aircraft home. Blood stains in the empty mid-upper turret suggested that the occupant had been wounded before baling out. Once on the ground it could be seen that the rear turret had virtually been shot away, and there was much damage to the tail plane. The rear gunner was thirty-year-old Irishman F/Sgt Francis

Rogers, who had been twice Mention in Dispatches. "Frank" Rogers had served in the RAF for over seven years, and had operated in France during 1939-1940. The gunner's body was taken to his home town of Newry, County Down. Pilot Officer Du Toit reported:

"*Up till the encounter nothing much had happened, but when we got just north of Saarbrucken, which we had bombed the night before, I saw one of our bombers shot down by a night fighter, so I knew that we were in a danger area. Then I saw a series of lights on the ground marking our track, and I knew this was a signal to the German night fighters. Next thing I knew was that, without warning, a cannon shell burst over my head and the front cockpit panel was shattered. I did not wait for any more but put the Stirling into a diving turn to port. Down we went, and then I pulled at the stick to change our course and perplex the fighter, but the aircraft was out of control and I could not pull her out of the dive. Down and down went the Stirling, diving steeply all the time, while I was struggling with the controls. I gave up hope of pulling her out of the dive and as the intercom had been shot away I switched on the emergency signal for bailing out. This signal lights up a series of lamps all over the aircraft. But when down to 6000ft, we had already dropped 7000ft out of control, I got control again and brought the Stirling out of the dive. I sent the wireless operator back to tell the rest of the crew to hang on, but the mid upper had already made a dive for it and when my wireless operator came to the rear gunner, he found him lying dead and the turret shattered. The Stirling was not fully under control yet for she was climbing steeply and then diving. All the electrical controls had been shot away and the elevators had probably been damaged. The engineer tied up the controls with the odd bit of rope and that helped a lot.*

We struggled on keeping a fair height and speed. All the compasses were useless except one on the bomb aimer's sight so we had to plot our course from that. The rest of the trip was just a steady struggle to hold the Stirling on course while we all hoped that no more fighters would appear. When we arrived over our base, I found that the wireless was shot away and the undercarriage would not come down. I circled while the undercarriage was wound down by hand, wondering all the time how we would land with most of the controls shot away. When the time came, I just pushed the stick forward and down we came to make a fair landing all things considered. I got out of the aircraft and looked at it. The rear turret was shot to pieces, the elevator and tail plane was riddled, the wireless aerial had gone and there were holes all over the fuselage."

The Command returned to northern Germany on the 4/5th with Bremen as the intended target. 3 Group dispatched sixty-three aircraft, including seven from 218 Squadron, with W/Cdr Read once again accompanying S/Ldr Raymond. The Pathfinders adopted the three-phase system of illuminators, visual markers and backers-up for the first time, and returning crews were once again enthusiastic about the flares. They remarked on their concentration and high visibility, but also reported that flak over the target was intense. By the end of the attack at 02.20hrs 480 buildings had been destroyed, including some of an industrial nature, and almost fourteen hundred others had sustained serious damage. A return was made to the Ruhr on the 6/7th, with Duisburg selected as the target. The five 218 Squadron crews found the city cloaked in ground haze and the Pathfinder flares scattered, but a number of large fires could be seen developing in the docks area. 114 buildings were destroyed, and whilst this was a modest haul, it still represented something of a victory at this most elusive of targets. While their colleagues were over Duisburg, two other 218 Squadron crews were successfully planting their four mines in the Rosemary mining area.

The run of successes was halted temporarily at another notoriously difficult target, Frankfurt, on the 8/9th, for which 218 Squadron put up six Stirlings with S/Ldr Raymond in the lead. A combination of a very dark night and ground haze in the target area resulted in the flares being scattered east of the intended aiming point. Düsseldorf brought a return to winning ways two nights later, when the training units contributed to the 479-strong force, and 3 Group put up sixty-six aircraft. The Pathfinders employed "Pink Pansies" for the first time, and over nine hundred houses were destroyed in the city and neighbouring Neuss. This was the most destructive operation since the thousand-bomber raid on Cologne, but at thirty-three aircraft, the losses were also the highest from a non–1,000 effort. Two 218 Squadron crews failed to return, one of them, that of F/Sgt Geoffrey Milligan RCAF, were on their first operation, having been on the squadron for less than forty-eight hours. They were unfortunate to meet Luftwaffe ace, Hptm Heinrich Prinz zu–Sayn–Wittgenstein of 9/NJG2 at 23.54hrs. BF351 HA-C crashed near St Philipsland (Zeeland), there were no survivors. For F/Sgt Cozens and crew this was their twentieth operation, and they were outbound when forced to ditch R9357 HA-E thirty miles off the Dutch coast. An explosion in the starboard-inner engine almost tore the Hercules from its mounting, and blasted away a large section of fuselage. To add to his worries, both outer engines began to lose power, giving Cozens no alternative but to ditch. Sadly, the navigator and front gunner drowned. At 22.46hrs an SOS was received and a 2nd class fix obtained, which enabled the surviving crew members to be located in their dinghy and rescued by an air-sea rescue launch.

Bremen was attacked for the second time during the month on the 13/14th, when 848 houses were destroyed, and many important war industry factories suffered varying degrees of damage. This result by around four hundred aircraft surpassed that achieved by the thousand force in June, and this was a sign of the burgeoning effectiveness of the Command. The only casualty for 218 Squadron was W7622 HA-P, which ran into a ditch on landing at 05.00hrs. Six of the squadron's crews set out in company with over 190 others to attack the docks at Wilhelmshaven

Wing Commander Montague Read occupancy as squadron commander lasted just a month before his death over Denmark.

on the 14th, when well-placed Pathfinder flares illuminated the naval docks area, giving the crews an ideal opportunity to inflict serious damage. The all incendiary loads were delivered from between 13,000 and 16,000 feet in the face of reported intense flak and tracer. A large explosion was reported by a number of returning crews, and the glow of fires was visible for up to eighty miles from the target. Local authorities reported the town's heaviest raid of the war, and specified the central districts as those hardest-hit. While over the target the starboard-inner engine of N3725 HA-D failed, forcing P/O Frankcombe RAAF to make the return trip on only three engines. While in the circuit over Downham Market the starboard-outer cut, and the Stirling crashed at 00.55hrs, one mile east of Stoke Ferry. There were just two survivors, the wireless operator, who lost both legs, and the mid-upper gunner, who sustained only slight injuries. This was John Frankcombe's sixteenth operation. On the following day ACM John Baldwin CB CBE DSO was succeeded by AVM the Hon Ralph Cochrane, CBE AFC, and the effects of the change at the top would be immediately apparent.

Even Essen received what was probably its most destructive raid thus far, when attacked on the 16/17th by over three hundred aircraft, including five from 218 Squadron. The Krupp complex was hit by fifteen high explosive bombs, and thirty-three large fires were reported in the city, but the defenders fought back to bring down thirty-nine aircraft, the Wellington brigade proving itself to be particularly vulnerable. However, it can be no coincidence that this series of effective operations came at a time when the Pathfinder Force was emerging from its unconvincing start, and its crews were coming to grips with the complexities of their demanding role. There was to be no overnight transformation, and failures would continue to outnumber successes for some time to come, but the encouraging signs were there, and it boded ill for Germany in the years ahead. On the 18th the squadron bade farewell to Sgt Sidney Godfrey Falconer DFM, who was posted on completion of his first tour to 21 OTU, and was one of the few to have completed a tour over the summer. Falconer returned to operations in 1943 with 214 Squadron were he was awarded a DFC on completion of his second tour. He was killed in an accident while flying as a passenger in a Horsa glider with 81 O.T.U in May 1944.

Four of 218 Squadrons most distinguished pilots throughout 1942. Left to right F/Lt Roy Spear DFC RNZAF, F/Lt Geoff Corser DFC RAAF, F/Sgt Henderson, S/Ldr Phil Lamason DFC RNZAF and F/O Don Thomson DFC RNZAF.

Bomber Command carried out two separate raids on the 19th, on Saarbrücken and Munich. Nineteen 3 Group aircraft were assigned to the latter, including four from 218 Squadron. The Pathfinder flares were concentrated and illuminated the target well, allowing the aiming point, the railway station, to be easily identified. The squadron's all-incendiary loads went down from between 10,000 and 13,000 feet, and most of the high explosive tonnage fell onto the southern and eastern suburbs, where damaged was heavy. On the way home S/Ldr Samson was bracketed by accurate flak of such intensity and ferocity, that he ordered the crew to stand by to abandon the aircraft. The navigator did, in fact bail out, and ended up as a PoW at Stalag Luft III. A number of those on board sustained wounds, but after what seemed an eternity, the Stirling left the flak behind and eventually landed at West Malling after eight hours and thirty-two minutes aloft. The attack on Saarbrücken included two crews from 218 Squadron after a third returned early. Once again they found the target easy to identify, due, on this occasion, to the bright moonlight. On arriving over the target, the 218 Squadron boys found the bombing to be scattered, and noticed only a few isolated fires, whereupon they delivered their loads of 4lb incendiaries from 6,840 feet, before returning safely to Downham Market.

The squadron contributed ten Stirlings to operations on the night of the 23/24th, five heading for the Bremer-Vulcan ship yards at Vegesack, while five all NCO crews went gardening in the Nectarines II and III areas. The mining force met with an electrical storm outbound, and ultimately planted their vegetables with the aid of Gee. The Vegesack force encountered the same weather conditions, and F/L Spear RNZAF, who was on his ninth operation in sixteen days, jettisoned his bombs because of icing. Pilot Officer Stubbs returned with his bomb load still on board, Sgt Griffiths bombed the last resort target of Oldenburg from 1,000 feet, having been unable to identify the primary target through the low cloud, and P/O Du Toit dropped his load from 2,000 feet over the eastern part of the briefed target. It is not known whether or not S/Ldr Cuthbert Raymond bombed the primary target. What can be ascertained is that he was shot down by Uffz Karl-Georg Pfeiffer of 6/NJG2 at 03.55hrs, and crashed into the sea forty miles off Nordeney. It was Pfeiffer's first victory, and there were no survivors from R9187 HA-U. At the time of his death twenty-six-year-old S/Ldr "Bobby" Raymond DFC had flown fifty-eight operations, eight of them with 218 Squadron. A number of mining operations saw the month out, and the tally for 218 Squadron was one hundred sorties dispatched at a cost of a more tolerable five aircraft, but this still involved the loss of four complete crews. Sergeant pilot Reginald Elsom DFM completed his tour of thirty operations in September, but would be killed while instructing with 22 OTU on October 13th 1942, before he could collect his award.

October

October began with a small-scale all-Stirling raid against the U-Boat yards at Herrenwyk near Lübeck. Twenty-five Stirling's were drawn from XV, 149 and 218 Squadrons, 218 waving off nine crews between 19.45hrs and 20.05hrs. There was the almost inevitable early return, but the remaining eight crews crossed the North Sea, keeping as low as the conditions would allow. Visibility was initially poor in the target area, and an estimated twenty-five search lights were active, although without the usual accompaniment of flak. Once the first bombs began to explode, however, the flak defences opened up with an accurate barrage aimed at the Stirlings bombing from around 6,000 feet. Sergeant Thompson made three runs across the target before his bomb aimer was satisfied, and dropped the five one thousand pounders onto

Twenty six year old South African Flight Lieutenant Johannes Du Toit.

the slip-way. His experiences mirrored those of the rest of the attacking force, who all found identification problematic. Two crews failed to return, and among the missing crewmen was the squadron commander, W/Cdr Montagu Read. He was flying as second pilot to the popular and respected F/L Johannes Du Toit, who was on his seventeenth operation. W7613 HA-N was homebound when it was intercepted and shot down at 01.40hrs by Major Gunther Radusch, Kommandeur of II/NJG3, and there were no survivors. The Stirling is believed to have crashed to the north west of the island of Rømø. The bodies of the recently promoted F/L Du Toit and W/Cdr Read were found washed ashore near Hvidding on October 17th. Flight Lieutenant Du Toit sent a letter home to his parents dated September 28th, in which he told them with some pride,

Welshman Wing Commander Owen Morris DSO seen here while a group captain. He was station commander of both RAF Station Mildenhall and Tuddenham on posting from 218 Squadron.

"I have my promotion, still very lucky to get my double stripe up. It also means I am duty flight leader, a bit of extra work, but it is what I like."

The second loss of the night was that of Sgt Maldwyn Griffiths and crew, who fell victim to Naval Flak units I/161 and I/259. N3763 HA-Q crashed near Hubertus in Germany between 00.18hrs and 00.24hrs, and once again there were no survivors. The crew was on its sixth operation, although the pilot was on his ninth.

Wing Commander Owen Morris assumed command of the squadron on October 5th, on completion of his conversion course at 1651 CU at Waterbeach. Welshman Aubrey "Busen" Morris had joined the RAF in June 1931, and by 1941 had reached the rank of temporary wing commander. He had carried out operations on Whitleys with 102 Squadron during 1940/41, and experienced a number of close shaves. Between April 1941 and July 1942 he had commanded the station at Cranage in Cheshire.

On the 2nd the conversion flight moved from Marham to Stradishall, where it would amalgamate with other conversion units to form 1657 Heavy Conversion Unit. That night a return to the Ruhr brought Krefeld into the bomb sights of a force numbering over 150 aircraft. Six 218 Squadron crews were detailed, but Sgt Hill lost control of W7636 on take-off after over-correcting a swing, and the aircraft came to grief and was written-off, thankfully without injury to anyone on board. Within days, Sgt Hill would become F/Sgt Hill, and a few days later he and his crew would go missing. Another aircraft turned back with engine failure, while the four remaining Stirlings pressed on to encounter considerable ground haze in the target area, which made identification impossible. Crews bombed on scattered Pathfinder flares, and a number of small fires were reported along with some larger ones, but Krefeld escaped serious damage.

Aachen was the objective on the night of the 5/6th, when weather conditions over the stations were made marginal by an electrical storm. Among the forty-four 3 Group aircraft on duty were eight from 218 Squadron, four of which carried second pilots gaining experience. Tragedy struck almost immediately, when BF322 HA-F crashed at 19.45hrs at Icklingham Marshes, Barton Mills, killing the entire crew of Sgt Phillip Hall. Eyewitness reports suggested that BF322 had exploded in mid-air after being struck by lightning. Sergeant Hall and crew had arrived on the squadron from 101 Conversion Flight during the week of Friday the 11th of September, and this was their fourth operation together. The operation was not a success, and Pathfinder flares were scattered as far as the Dutch town of Lutterade, seventeen miles from Aachen. A moderately successful attack fell on Osnabrück on the 6/7th, and then came a lull in main force operations, during which extensive "gardening" activities involved the Stirling brigade.

A series of mining operations began on the 8th, when five aircraft were dispatched to Nectarine I. This was the last operation carried out by F/L Roy Spear RNZAF

The funeral on October 1st of Sergeant Joseph Curle bomb aimer aboard R9190 HA-E. His crew mates Sergeant Richards and Sergeant White attended the funeral.

on completion of his first operational tour, and after a well deserved period of leave, he would join 1657 HCU as an instructor, and be awarded a well-earned DFC for his tour with 218 Squadron. Wing Commander Morris undertook his first operation as commanding officer on the 10/11th, when accompanying S/Ldr Samson in R9184 HA-U on a mining sortie in the Deodars area. A large-scale mining operation took place on the 11/12th, when twenty-five 3 Group Stirlings contributed to a force of over eighty aircraft. 218 Squadron put up seven aircraft, two allocated to the Pollock area in the Baltic Sea, and five to the Geranium area. R9190 HA-E was hit by flak, and the previously mentioned F/Sgt Hill found it necessary to carry out a ditching in shallow water off Siø, during which the bomb-aimer died. Hill and four others clambered aboard the dinghy and started paddling away from the island, which they apparently could not see in the dark. However, the ditching had been observed from Rudkøbing and Langeland Island, and a search was immediately organised by the local German garrison. Within a few hours the dinghy was located and the crew taken to Rudkøbing. Four of the airmen were wounded and were escorted to the local hospital, while Sgt White was placed in the jail. The mid-upper gunner, F/Sgt Richards, had lost contact with his comrades during the ditching, but a couple of eel fishermen had witnessed the ditching and decided to sail over to the wreck. They found Richards next morning, wading confused off shore, and suffering from concussion and exposure.

Moderate success was achieved at Kiel on the 13/14th, when W/Cdr Morris was once again flying in S/Ldr Samson's right hand seat, but a decoy fire site probably spared the town from a more severe pounding. A similar ruse at Cologne drew away most of the bombs on the 15/16th, so that damage in the city was light. The disappointment was compounded by the continuing rate of early returns, a problem not confined to 218 Squadron. The whole of 3 Group was experiencing an increase, and the matter had already been raised by AVM Cochrane in a memorandum to the C-in-C dated September 19th….

Dear C-In-C,

I hope you will not mind me sending you these few impressions after being in the group such a short time. This has always been a first rate group, but all in it now realise that the leadership has passed to 5 Group. Equally, everyone is determined to wrest it back. The staff and station commanders are all good and the majority have recent operational experience, I am, however, losing McKee, who is stalwart, to your headquarters.

The squadron and flight commanders are also good, but in crews we are getting very close to the vicious circle. The squadrons have had fairly heavy casualties over a long period and the percentage of inexperienced crews is high. This is leading to many unavoidable troubles as well as, in some squadrons, a lack of determination to press home attacks. The Essen raid came as a shock. Out of 72 detailed, 4 failed to take off and 19 turned back. I took the opportunity of a stand down the next day to interview the captains of these crews and their flight commanders, I found only two cases in which the captain took the correct action in returning. The remainder returned because of minor or imagined defects!

Ralph Cochrane then records his disappointment regarding serviceability:

Air serviceability is bad, in fact shocking. Much of it is due to engine trouble, which I believe to be mainly caused by over driving the engines when climbing, or overheating them on the ground. This again is caused by inexperienced crews. The airframe and the electrical systems have also been giving trouble, partly due to bad workmanship, but also to inexperienced maintenance crews faced with the task of maintaining what is probably the most complicated aeroplane in the service. I am changing the Group Engineering Office and a competent electrical engineer has also been posted to the headquarters.

The group commander had pulled no punches in the face of the unacceptably high number of early returns, but Cochrane was the right man to confront the situation. The new initiatives were not immediately felt at squadron level, where return rates were still high, but the number of early returns would decrease over the ensuring months.

A new campaign began on the night of the 22/23rd, after Harris was instructed to give priority to targets in northern Italy in support of the forth-coming invasion of North Africa, code named "*Operation Torch*". Harris, typically, was not in favour of diverting attention away from Germany, and raised his objections with Portal, who, in equally typical fashion, instructed Harris to make his Command available. These distant raids would occupy much of the Command's attention until mid December, and the campaign opened on October 23rd against the port of Genoa. 3 Group dispatched thirty-nine Stirlings and eleven Wellingtons, which, together with fifty-three 4 Group Halifaxes, made up the main force. Nine Stirlings left Downham Market between 18.20hrs and 18.35hrs, but within an hour one was back in the Downham Market circuit with a feathered starboard-inner engine. BF375 HA-Q was hit by flak while crossing the French coast at 8,000 feet, and despite a wing fire and leaking tanks and oxygen system the Stirling made it home. BF342 HA-M was also hit by flak just inland of the French Coast, and it too came home after jettisoning its bomb load. With the Alps in sight and only a hundred miles from the target, F/Sgt Thomson's starboard-outer gave up after misfiring for most of the outward flight. A three engine Stirling was incapable of crossing the mountain range, and its load was jettisoned north-east of Notre-Dame-De-Briancon. Of the nine aircraft dispatched only four are believed to have reached and attacked the target, among them the one captained by the commanding officer.

Genoa was easily identified, and the town and its port area were bombed between 22.12hrs and 22.43hrs. Wing Commander Morris went in from just below 5,000 feet, dropping his two one thousand pounders and ninety-six 30lb incendiaries into the Sampierdarena marshalling yards. Flight Lieutenant Hickling identified the harbour and docks, and his bomb load started a fire in the south-west corner of the harbour. It was this fire that a number of crews reported, along with two large explosions seen near the electrical power station. Wing Commander Morris's W7616 HA-J was intercepted by a Bf109 while flying at 8,000 feet in the Campiegne area on the way home, but after an aggressive response from the rear turret, the enemy aircraft disengaged. R9184 HA-U failed to return with the crew of F/O Reginald Studd AFC, having crashed into the sea off Dieppe without survivors. It had probably fallen victim to Hptm Karl-Hans Godbersen of E. Stab/NJG2, who claimed a Stirling at 02.50hrs. It was only after the event, that it was discovered that the attack had actually been aimed at the town of Savona, some thirty miles away from Genoa.

On the 24th seventy-one aircraft of 1 and 3 Groups took off for Milan. Crossing the Alps was never a picnic for the lower-ceilinged Stirling, and on this night the crews encountered storms during the outward flight, which prevented almost half of them from reaching the target. Seven 218 Squadron crews were briefed, but only six made it to take-off. After thirty-five minutes in the air, F/Sgt Higgott RNZAF noted that the port outer exactor was not working. He shed height and ordered the bomb aimer to jettison the bomb load, which fell un-armed into the sea off Harwich. Shortly afterwards, while at 3,000 feet, the starboard-outer engine burst into flames, and it was soon apparent that the fire was uncontrollable. The order was given to bail out, but sadly it came too late. R9241 HA–L broke up and crashed at 19.29hrs east of Colchester, taking Frederick Higgott and six of his crew to their deaths. One of the gunners just managed to escape by parachute at the last second, and was injured in the heavy landing. Frederick had joined the squadron from 218CF on August 10th, and had flown on six operations as second pilot, before completing a further six as crew captain. Other early returns again depleted the squadron's effort, and it was left to Sgt Richards and F/Sgt Thomson to attack a cloud covered Milan. Fires from the earlier daylight raid by 5 Group were still burning, and provided the crews with an ideal reference point to bomb. There was heavy flak in the target area, where Pathfinder flares were unmistakable but scattered.

The squadron sent seven aircraft mining on the 26th, led by the recently promoted acting S/Ldr Peter Hickling DFM, who had assumed command of A Flight and taken over the crew of the tour-expired Spears. Twenty-eight mines were successfully planted without loss, the squadron stayed at home until the 31st, when two more crews undertook gardening sorties in the Gironde Estuary. The squadron despatched ninety-four sorties during the month, the highest by any Stirling squadron, for the loss of seven aircraft and six crews.

November

Squadron Leader Waldo "Wally" Hiles DSO DFC was one of the squadrons more aggressive pilots with a fondness for low level attacks on German military transport.

November began quietly for the Stirling squadrons in general, but an element from 218 Squadron was selected for a rather secretive affair, a hastily organised special daylight raid against the railway workshops at Lingen on the 3rd. The crews of P/O Hiles DFC, F/Sgt Thomson and Sgt Gough were selected, each accompanied by a second pilot, which, given the fact that this was a highly risky daylight undertaking, was somewhat surprising. The Stirlings were airborne from Downham Market by 15.50hrs, each carrying six one thousand pounders and twelve 30lb incendiaries. Over Holland they came down to as low as 200 feet, and Dutch workers waved at them as they raced towards Lingen. Over the Dortmund-Ems Canal Sgt Gough's gunners opened fire on a number of barges, but the cloud that had cloaked their presence so far now proved to be a hindrance. None of the crews could find the workshops in the low cloud and failing light, so using the Dortmund-Ems Canal and the River Ems as pin points, the crews found the railway leading directly to Lingen. Sergeant Gough's crew made two bombing runs over the general target area, finally dropping his bomb load four hundred yards from the railway station. Pilot Officer "Wally" Hiles DFC came down to below a hundred feet in an attempt to identify the workshops, and finally, after a number of runs, dropped his load, which was seen to explode near some buildings south of the target. Thirty minutes after Hiles and Gough had turned for home, F/Sgt Thomson and crew were still being frustrated by the visibility. Three runs across the target area failed to provide a pinpoint in the conditions of ground haze, low cloud and failing light and the decision was taken to abandon the attempt and head for home.

Five aircraft took off for the "Deodars" mining area on the 6/7th, and only four came back. R9185 crashed into a hill near Lambarquet at 21.00hrs, killing the bomb-aimer and navigator outright. The pilot, Sgt Galbraith Hyde RNZAF, who was operating as crew captain for the first time, was found lying dazed beside the wreckage. Two Frenchmen carried him to their home, where he was treated for his wounds. Next morning Hyde started on what would be an eight-day trek north-east towards Paris. On November 15th he stole a bicycle near Rennes and continued towards Paris, living on the land and eating mainly apples. At Fecamp Hyde became ill with flu, and was cared for by the Varme family. It was while being sheltered that Hyde was betrayed by the local barber, Louis Villebratee, and captured by the German Feldgendarmerie on December 31st. Sergeant Hyde was sent to the notorious Amiens jail, where for the next thirty-two days he was questioned by both the Gestapo and the SS. Found wearing civilian clothing Hyde was told by his captors that he would be shot for spying, but, undeterred by the threat, Hyde only gave his name, rank and number. His defiant and dogged determination to keep quiet, and protect the identity of those who had bravely helped him, finally resulted in his transfer to a PoW Camp. In 1943, while a PoW at Stalag 344 Lamsdorf, Hyde managed to change identity and joined an army working party at Gleiwitz aerodrome. On October 13th, together with P/O Bragg RCAF and Sgt McLeod RCAF and T O'Shaunessy RN, Hyde attempted to steal a single engine Junkers JU 34, which had been parked away from the main runway almost out of site of the control tower and German sentries. Scrambling aboard the Junkers the crew were familiarising themselves with the controls, when they were found and recaptured. They had been within a few minutes of starting the engine and flying to natural Sweden. The four were given a full dress Court Martial, and were sentenced to a two-year civil imprisonment. It was while awaiting the confirmation of the sentence that Sgt McLeod, a former Spitfire pilot, managed to escape to Switzerland. In Switzerland McLeod made a case to the Red Cross, which in turn put pressure on the German authorities, who reduced the sentence to six-months military imprisonment. In 1946, in recognition of his escape attempts, Sgt Galbraith Hyde RNZAF was awarded the MBE, the citation reads,

Warrant Officer Hyde's aircraft crashed near St Marlo in November 1942. He walked for eight days in a south easterly direction, obtaining food and clothing from pheasants. Eventually he stole a bicycle near Rennes and made towards Paris. At Fecamp became ill and was sheltered by a French family but was betrayed and arrested with his hosts in December 1942. In the summer of 1943, Warrant Officer Hyde and three others, having changed their identities, went to Gleiwitz on a working party. They made a daring attempt to seal an aircraft and where in the aircraft for ten minutes before they were detected. The Germans treated this escape as sabotage and meted out a very severe punishment. Warrant Officer Hyde was still serving his sentence when liberated in January 1945.

The Command returned to northern Italy on the 7th, when Genoa was again the target. Six 218 Squadron crews took off, and met a solid mass of ten-tenths cloud at the French coast. One aircraft dropped out thirty miles south-east of Paris with exactor trouble, but the remainder crossed the Alps to find conditions quickly improving. The docks area was easily identified, and a number of fires sprang up. All five 218 Squadron crews bombed the target between 21.16hrs and 22.09hrs, and S/Ldr Hickling reported a number of buildings ablaze, while Sgt Richards more expansively declared *"The whole town ablaze"*. Returning crews reported that the fires at Genoa could be seen from the French Alps. BK606 HA-N was hit by flak in the starboard wing fuel tank while homebound, but quick action by the flight engineer saved most of the remaining fuel. Sergeant Richards nursed the Stirling back across the Channel, only to undershoot his approach to Oakington as a result of two fuel-starved, dead starboard engines. After colliding with trees the aircraft crashed, but remarkably, only the rear gunner sustained severe injuries.

On the following night a special Nickel raid was undertaken, for which W/Cdr Morris took what was presumably a freshman crew, to deliver "toilet paper" to the residents of the Toulon area of France. Twenty-four Stirlings from XV,149,214 and 218 Squadrons were tasked to drop over twelve million leaflets informing them of the Allied invasion of the Vichy French-controlled North Africa on the previous day. The only casualty of the night was the aircraft flown by the 218 Squadron commanding officer. W7612 HA-T was short of fuel as W/Cdr Morris attempted to land at Tangmere, and it turned into an emergency when his engines cut and the Stirling clipped treetops before crashing. Thankfully all of the occupants were able to walk away. Northern Germany was the destination on the 9/10th, when Hamburg was the target. Four 218 Squadron aircraft took off and encountered a combination of ten-tenths cloud, icing and strong winds, which made the whole process of accurate bombing impossible. Squadron Leader Hickling DFM failed to return after W4775 HA-H was brought down by flak thirty kilometres east-north-east of Osnabrück. Twenty-eight year old Hickling was on his fourth operation with the squadron, and had been awarded the DFM in 1941 while serving with 4 Group's 10 Squadron. This all NCO crew had previously been captained by the tour-expired F/L Spear DFC, and was on its twenty-eighth operation. It was a bitter blow to the squadron to lose such an experienced crew so close to the completion of their first tour, and with them yet another flight commander.

The Italian campaign continued with main force Stirling involvement at Genoa on the 15/16th and Turin on the 18/19th. Turin was the target again on the 20th, when eight 218 Squadron Stirlings joined an overall force of 232 aircraft. It was the largest operation directed at Italy during this campaign, but the weather did nothing to assist the crews as they crossed the French coast at le Crotoy. The journey to the Alps was undertaken in ten-tenths cloud, but east of the Alps the route to Turin was almost clear, allowing the crews to identify the River Po and pinpoint the Fiat steelworks located in the east of the city. Dense smoke was rising up to a height of nearly 7,000 feet from a series of large fires in the target area, and a large explosion was witnessed, which was thought to be the end of a gas holder near the Royal Arsenal. While this operation was in progress four other 218 Squadron crews were minelaying in the mouth of the Gironde River. All successfully delivered their mines and returned safely, and on the following night six crews returned to the estuary, and successfully planted a further twenty-three mines without incident.

A force of over two hundred aircraft delivered a disappointing attack on Stuttgart on the 22/23rd, before the month's final major effort. The Fiat works at Turin was the target for 228 aircraft on the night of the 28/29th, for which 3 Group's contribution was a disappointing thirty-four aircraft, eleven of which were from 218 Squadron. The group had been selected to attack the Fiat Mirafiori Factory, located three and a half miles south-west of Turin's old city, but four crews were forced to abort their sorties over France, among them S/Ldr Hiles, whose BK607 HA-X suffered an engine fire. Wing Commander Morris led the remainder to the target, which, despite haze over the aiming point, was identified visually. Pilot Officer Jerromes straddled the plant with his 500 and 1,000 pounders from 2,000 feet, while F/L Sly AFM dropped his 5,000lbs of high explosives onto the north-western corner of the Fiat Works from 4,000 feet, and P/O Bickenson watched as his bombs exploded in the northern part of the factory complex on his third pass. All the time he was subjected to light flak emanating from the factory roofs, but thankfully the gunners' aim was off. The last three 218 Squadron crews to arrive on target attacked the town as instructed, and the operation was a complete success. On return to Downham Market with only three good engines at 00.25hrs, S/Ldr Hiles overshot the landing and lost his undercarriage. No one on board was hurt, but it proved to be the end of

The over worked ground crew seen here undertaking an inspection on the starboard inner engine of Stirling R9189 HA-K RAF Downham Market 1942.

the line for his Stirling. Waldo Hiles was promoted to acting squadron leader on the 22nd, and he assumed command of A Flight.

Bomber Command had intended to carry out a full scale return to the Fiat Mirafiori works at Turin on the 29/30th, but deteriorating weather over much of England left just 3 Group and a Pathfinder element heading towards the departure point of Dungeness on the south coast. 3 Group managed to put up just twenty aircraft, of which eight returned early. Seven 218 Squadron aircraft left Downham Market between mid-night and 00.20 hrs, and three turned back before reaching the target. Thick cloud during the outward flight had thinned by the time the target approached, but a blanket of thick haze combined with smoke from the previous night's attack to cover the target area. Squadron Leader Hiles dropped his 5,000lb bomb load into the centre of the city from 8,000 feet, and B Flight commander, S/Ldr Samson, brought his aircraft down to 3,000 feet in an attempt to identify the factory. He made a number of passes before his bombs were seen to explode close to a large building. This was not an effective operation, and was carried out in the face of a much-bolstered flak defence, but 3 Group losses amounted to just two aircraft and one crew.

218 Squadron launched the second highest number of sorties during the month, eighty-two, but was just pipped to first place by 115 Squadron with eighty-three. 218 Squadron did deliver the highest tonnage of bombs, however, but came second again to 115 with the number of mining sorties. The Monthly Summary of Events publication, which was distributed throughout the group, was openly critical of the group maintenance and early return levels. Cochrane once again pulled no punches in his views, and he ordered the re-issuing to all squadrons of the 3 Group Tactical Notes, and instructed crews to *"read, then re-read, and to discuss and argue until they are understood by everyone"*. Cochrane was under the opinion that a lack of tactical knowledge was the cause of a number of preventable operational losses. He was also concerned about the number of early returns due to icing, *"some captains are inclined to exaggerate the dangers of icing and abandon their mission as soon as ice forms"*. To improve bombing results a new group table was introduced in November, by means of which the accuracy or otherwise of each squadron would be recorded for all to see. The criticism did not stop there, gunnery and the apparent lack of a basic understanding of when and where to shoot was also discussed in some detail. In the opinion of Cochrane the failure laid squarely with the squadron gunnery leaders! Cochrane was proving to be a hard task master.

December

December began with an attack on Frankfurt on the 2/3rd, when weather conditions once again prevented all of the groups from participating. None the less, 112 aircraft were dispatched, of which seven represented 218 Squadron. Frankfurt was covered by a thick layer of cloud, which made accurate marking impossible, and consequently the bombing was reported to be generally scattered. Sergeant Smith's BF401 HA-N was coned and held while on the bomb run at 12,000 feet, and was repeatedly hit in the fuselage and wings, miraculously without damage to the fuel tanks and engines. It was while on the homeward leg that the stream was attacked by what was described as "particularly persistent fighters". Three 218 Squadron aircraft were attacked, among them the above-mentioned BF401, which was north-east of Koblenz when a Ju88 carried out five separate attacks. Close co-operation between the gunners and the pilot, Sgt Smith, allowed only a few rounds to hit the wings and fuselage before the fighter finally broke off the chase. The Stirling's undercarriage collapsed on landing, but none of the crew was injured. Perhaps the crew's deliverance was due in part to the efforts of Sgt Holland in the rear turret.

3 Group carried out an extensive mining operation on the 4/5th, which involved twenty-three aircraft in the Nectarines area off the Frisian Islands. 218 Squadron dispatched four crews, all of whom identified their respective gardens and delivered six mines from between 500 and 900 feet. Mannheim escaped with all but the most superficial damage on the 6/7th, when the eight participating 218 Squadron crews were forced by ten-tenths cloud to bomb on scattered flares and the glow of a few isolated fires beneath. Two crews returned to the Frisian Islands on the 7/8th, P/O Cozens and Sgt Smith delivering their six mines from below 900 feet without encountering any problems. Oddly, Downham Market's Station Records Book records this operation as cancelled. Eighty aircraft were dispatched for a large-scale night of mining in northern waters on the 8/9th, twenty-seven of which were provided by 3 Group. 218 Squadron made the Group's largest contribution by putting up eight Stirlings, which were allocated to the Kattegat Channel (Silverthorne), each carrying four 1,500lb magnetic mines. Fighters were active as were flak ships, and of the eighty aircraft dispatched five were lost, three of them from 3 Group. On the positive side, 218 mines were delivered into the busy enemy shipping lanes.

With the end of the current Italian campaign in sight, the Command targeted Turin on the night of the 9/10th, for which the 3 Group element was assigned to the main railway station area. Three 218 Squadron crews took off, and found the skies over France to be free of cloud. Only three Pathfinder aircraft arrived over the target area at the appointed time, and this caused the initial stages of the attack to be rather scattered. However, later Pathfinder arrivals kept up the continuity of flares, and a successful attack developed. All three 218 Squadron representatives identified the River Po, and bombed between 21.34hrs and 22.16hrs on a number of flares south-east of the town centre. On leaving the target three particularly large fires could be seen to have taken hold in the centre of the city, and they were visible from two hundred miles on the return journey.

Four crews carried out an air-sea rescue search on the 13th over the North Sea, when weather conditions forced the crews down to below 500 feet. Nothing was found. Squadron Leader Samson experienced a few anxious moments when two single engine fighters and a twin engine aircraft were sighted, but they turned out to be friendly. This would be the final operation undertaken by the courageous Canadian after a hectic operational tour.

Pilot Officer Ted Gough's rear gunner, Bill Jackson, recalled the end of tour party.

"It was always an occasion when a crew finished a tour, because it didn't happen too often. This occasion called for a real party, as we were determined to see this popular Newfoundlander off with a bang! The party started off early in both the Sgts and officers messes, and it was not long before the CO and Sammy arrived in our mess, complete with the whole commissioned caboodle. Everyone wanted to make a speech about the amiable Canuck, but only a few stalwarts could keep their balance on the chair. As usual Ted started singing, and eventually fell off the chair, and stayed in the horizontal position giggling his head off until the crew came to his assistance and positioned him on the couch, where he continued singing and conducting as if the audience were suspended from the ceiling. I had always thought that aircrew NCOs threw the craziest parties, but the officers took the cake. At least we didn't go around pouring pints into our friends' trousers to cool them off! When I eventually left the mess to try and find the way to my hut, Sammy was lying fast asleep in the place of honour, the lounge table, and the carpet was strewn with bodies of officers and NCOs, the cream of the Commonwealth, either passed-out, asleep or stiff and unmoveable."

Sammy would be awarded a well-earned DFC in January 1943, and return to operations later in the year when taking command of 3 Group's 514 Squadron. Sadly, he would lose his life in September 1945, while commanding 117 Squadron in the Far East.

Eight 3 Group aircraft were sent to attack the aerodrome at Diepholz on the 16/17th, three of them from 218 Squadron. Over Germany, Canadian P/O Pettit experienced engine trouble that forced him to bomb the last resort target, a military camp near Furstenau. The all-incendiary load was dropped from less than 2,000 feet, and was seen to explode amongst a group of buildings. Flight Lieutenant Sly was also unable to locate the aerodrome, and he too attacked the last resort target. Pilot Officer Jerromes managed to locate Diepholz aerodrome in failing weather, and the all-incendiary load went down from 4,000 feet to straddle the hangers and start a small fire. On the way home they were attacked by a JU88, but gave as good as they got, and the damaged enemy aircraft was seen to dive away and break off the engagement.

The K.D.F Opel works at Fallersleben was attacked on the following night, and this was another all 3 Group effort. Of the twenty-two aircraft involved, almost half were drawn from 218 Squadron. They traversed the North Sea at low level, and on crossing the Dutch Coast over the Zuider Zee at 300 feet, Sgt Gough's Stirling sustained a hit from a flak ship, which caused the port wing to immediately burst into flames and the port-inner engine to misfire and vibrate. For the next five minutes the crew worked frantically to extinguish the fire, and were ultimately successful in bringing BF406 home, where it underwent extensive repairs at 54 Maintenance Unit. Only four crews attacked the primary target, among them that of S/Ldr Hiles, who had sped across Holland and Germany at 300 feet shooting at anything on road or rail, and on reaching the target had climbed to 3,000 feet to deliver two 1,000 pounders and five 500 pounders on what was believed to be the factory complex. They then descended again to 300 feet to make their way home, shooting up any manor of transport. Pilot Officer Cozens' aircraft was badly hit by flak while in the target area, causing severe damage to the fuselage and port aileron. Turning away from the target Cozens found the Stirling vibrating violently, and he struggled with the controls to bring it down to less than 100 feet to attempt to avoid any prowling night fighters. With the enemy coast in sight the Stirling was bracketed by light flak, and the starboard-inner engine immediately burst into flames. The flight engineer battled for the next fifteen minutes to extinguish the raging fire, and at last managed to subdue it. The flight across the North Sea was made with a smouldering engine, but they eventually landed at Marham after a flight of six hours. Sadly two crews failed to return from what proved to be a rather ineffective raid. W7614 HA-J was shot down by flak north of Hanover, and F/O Marshall RNZAF survived with three others of his crew. It was the eleventh operation for the crew as a whole, and F/O Marshall's eighteenth. BF403 HA-R contained the crew of fellow New Zealander, F/Sgt Leonard Shepherd RNZAF, and was brought down by a flak ship to crash into the Waddenzee between Den Helder and Texel without survivors. It was Shepherd's seventh operation and his third as captain.

The squadron was involved in only one more major night operation before the year closed, and this came on the night of the 20th, when Duisburg was the objective for over two hundred aircraft. The squadron dispatched six aircraft, which arrived in the target area in near perfect weather conditions. They were met by intense flak, but the Pathfinder flares were plentiful and accurate, and, taking full advantage of the clear conditions, the crews identified and bombed the Ruhrort Docks. Night fighters were active over the target, and F/Sgt Beecroft described seeing *"a fighter chasing a bomber out of the target area"*, while F/Sgt Thomson reported nine bombers shot down. In fact twelve aircraft were lost in return for particularly severe damage in the south of the city. Unnoticed as this operation proceeded, a contingent of 109 Squadron Mosquitos carried out an Oboe calibration exercise on a power station in the Dutch town of Lutterade, to ascertain the device's margin of error. Sadly, unanticipated bomb craters from a previous attack on Aachen, (as mentioned earlier), invalidated the results, but the trials programme would continue into the coming year, and its success would ultimately change the course of the bombing war. The year ended for 218 Squadron with a mining sortie by F/L Treves and crew in BF405 HA-S on December 28th.

Accompanied by five Wellingtons of 115 squadron, the crew successfully mined the Nectarines area without incident.

It had been a difficult month operationally for the squadron, with weather conditions restricting activity to just eleven raids, totalling fifty-four sorties. Thankfully, in contrast to previous months' severe losses, only three aircraft and two crews had been lost. It had been a testing year for the squadron, and one in which it had lost fifty-two Stirlings on operations, more than any other operator of the type. More alarmingly, the squadron had the third highest casualty rate in the group and suffered the fifth highest casualty rate in Bomber Command, while 3 Group as a whole had a significantly higher casualty rate than any other group within Bomber Command. Although the losses had been grievous over the preceding twelve months, morale remained relatively high, and this was largely due to the influence of the experienced commanding officers and flight commanders. The squadron had been fortunate in having among its ranks a number of pre-war regulars, whose professionalism and courage instilled confidence throughout the squadron. Officers in the mould of S/Ldr "Sammy" Samson and S/Ldr Oldroyd were the back bone of the squadron, and the newly promoted S/Ldr Waldo Hiles was of a similar calibre.

The coming year would bring with it huge advances in the development of new bombing aids and marking techniques, which would ultimately result in Bomber Command fulfilling its long awaited potential. The squadron was honoured with the announcement of a number of awards in December, S/Ldr Waldo Hiles, Australian F/L Edward Corser and New Zealander A/F/Lt Roy Spear, were awarded the DFC. Not to be out done, three DFMs were awarded to NCOs. Air gunner, F/Sgt Bernard Bull received his in recognition of an operational tour which started in February 1941 and finished in August 1942. Between these dates he completed a remarkable fifty-six operations. Wireless Operator F/Sgt William Street's DFM was in acknowledgment of also completing fifty-six sorties.

Chapter Six

1943:
A Year of Attrition

January

The New Year brought a brief respite from operations for the squadron, after a weather front postponed its first raid of 1943 for a week. In the meantime the Canadian 6 Group officially came into being on New Year's Day, and the Pathfinder Force finally attained group status as 8 Group on the 8th. That night nine 218 Squadron crews were detailed to mine the Kadet Channel and the north-eastern Frisian Islands, but three were forced to abandon their sorties due to engine problems. The port-outer propeller of veteran Stirling N3721 HA-P flew off over the North Sea, resulting in an engine fire, which S/Ldr Ernest Sly AFM managed to bring under control, before making a safe return to Downham

Short Stirling MkI N3721 HA-P seen here with "Digger James and Johnnie Wortley. N3721 completed a further thirteen operations before being sent to 1651 CU. John Wortley would train as a flight engineer and return to 218 Squadron in 1945 to commence a tour of operations on the Avro Lancaster.

Market on three. The remaining crews all planted their mines as briefed, albeit with considerable difficulty in atrocious weather conditions.

A new Air Ministry directive issued on the 14th called for the area bombing of those French ports acting as home to U-Boat bases and support facilities, and a list of four such targets was drawn up accordingly. It was headed by Lorient, and the campaign against it was put immediately into action that very night, when a mixed force of over a hundred aircraft, including six from 218 Squadron, delivered a scattered and only modestly effective attack. It was a different story on the following night, however, when a force of 157 bombers was sent back to the port, among them eight Stirlings from 218 Squadron, two of which returned early. The Stirlings were the last wave over the target, and they found the port area ablaze. Flares and incendiaries were considered to be well placed, and the Stirling element had no difficulty in identify the aiming point. Opposition had increased markedly since the previous night's attack, and light flak in particular was evident, as were additional searchlights. Over eight hundred buildings in the town were destroyed, but fortunately most of the residents had fled during the day.

Stirlings were excluded from two disappointing raids on Berlin on the 16/17th and 17/18th, but they continued with their very profitable mining operations. Four crews carried out a successful mining operation on the 18/19th, when fourteen mines were planted in the Nectarines II area. It was back to Lorient on the 23/24th, when 116 aircraft attacked in good visibility, and inflicted yet more damage upon the town. Eleven 218 Squadron aircraft eventually made it into the air, but one was soon back in the circuit with an engine problem. Those reaching the target found it well marked by a series of accurately placed red target indicators, and S/Ldr Sly watched his bomb load explode directly on the docks. The squadron was left off the order of battle for Düsseldorf on the 27/28th, when Oboe ground marking was employed for the first time, but participated in mining operations instead. Two Garden areas were chosen, Sweet Peas in the Baltic, to which five 218 Squadron crews were assigned, while three others were sent to the Nectarines area off the western Frisian Islands. 3 Group's chief medical officer, W/Cdr Huins, accompanied S/Ldr Hiles to conduct a trial of the stimulant, Benzedrine to observe its effects at first hand. Each crew member was given a tablet two hours after departure, but the results were inconclusive. Half felt no discernible change, while others claimed to feel less sleepy. Huins added in his report that the results may have been effected by the fact that the crew members were delighted and excited at operating a new aircraft, BF443 HA-H, which had only been on the squadron a matter of days. A Flight's S/Ldr Hiles DFC reported that *"the aircraft was 25 mph faster than any other on the squadron!"*

Among the trio heading for the Nectarines garden were F/O G Berridge and Sgt G Ratcliffe, both of whom were on their maiden operation. Sadly this final raid of the month resulted in the squadron's first operational loss of the year. N6077 HA-V flew into high ground in Germany during the return flight, and only the rear gunner, Sgt Jackson, survived from the eight man crew of twenty-year old P/O Arthur Gough. "Jacko" Jackson had arrived with the rest of the crew from 1651 Conversion Unit on August 23rd 1942, and they had completed nineteen operations together. The squadron welcomed S/Ldr Anthony Beck in late January, and his arrival heralded the addition of a third, or C Flight, to the squadron, which he was to command. 218 Squadron was required to launch forty-nine sorties during the month, and suffered the loss of the aircraft and crew just mentioned.

February

February started with a series of high level training flights on the 1st, followed on the 2nd by a number of Bullseye exercises. Hamburg opened the month's operational activities on the night of the 3/4th, and involved eight 218 Squadron crews led by W/Cdr Morris. Severe icing was encountered outbound, and this resulted in an alarming twenty-five early returns from the group, two of which were from 218 Squadron. Wing Commander Morris was attacked by a JU88 while outbound, and on return the crew claimed it as a probable. Accompanying the commanding officer was S/Ldr Beck as second pilot, and occupying the rear turret was the squadron gunnery leader, F/L Birbeck. The target was hidden by ten-tenths cloud, and, as no ground features could be identified, bombs were delivered on the glow of flares from the 7 and 35 Squadron Pathfinder element. In the event W/Cdr Morris was unable to drop his full load of incendiaries after experiencing technical difficulties with a bomb door. Two aircraft failed to return from this disappointing attack, and there were no survivors from the crews. BF406 HA-E crashed at 20:41hrs near Deelen airfield in Holland, possibly as the result of an encounter with Oblt Horst Pause of 1/NJG1. Sergeant Leslie Dodd and his crew, which included two Americans, were on their fourth operation. The second crew to be lost was that of F/L Stanley Treves, whose BF408 HA-T came down in the English Channel off the Straits of Dover. Flying as 2nd pilot was F/O Peter Astrosky who was on his first operation with the squadron.

The Command returned to Italy on the night of the 4/5th for an attack on Turin. The operation involved 188 aircraft, of which six Stirlings were provided by 218 Squadron, led by B Flight commander S/Ldr Sly. Solid cloud was encountered for most of the route out, with tops over the Alps at 17,000 feet. Once across this natural barrier the conditions cleared, and visibility became perfect in the target area. A concentrated bunch of red target Indicators and a modest defence afforded the crews an ideal opportunity to inflict serious damage on the Fiat works. Returning crews reported a number of large fires north of the aiming point, and there were no losses from the squadron or group. An all 3 Group mining operation was carried out on the following night involving nineteen Stirlings drawn from 75, 90, 149, 214 and 218 squadrons. The crews were briefed to target Young

Lorient on the receiving end. Pilot Officer Ratcliffe's all incendiary load is dropped over the docks on January 16th from 13,000ft, note the bend in the river and bridge.

Yams, the shipping lanes north of the West Frisians. 218 Squadron was represented by S/Ldr Beck and Dutchman P/O Ter Averst, both of whom were on their first operation with the squadron as crew captains. Low cloud over the entire route and target area resulted in both crews having to deliver their six mines on ETA, before returning without incident.

A devastating two-phase attack was carried out on Lorient on the 7/8th, for which the 3 Group contingent attacked in the second phase, with the Keroman submarine base as its aiming point. Nine 218 Squadron aircraft took part, led by S/Ldr Beck on his second freshman trip. Two returned early, while in contrast, P/O Pettit RCAF, despite the loss of his starboard-inner engine while outbound, opted to continue on to the target, where the all-incendiary load was delivered onto the aiming point from 7,500 feet. A number of well-established fires were evident across the target area and old town, and a particularly large blaze was seen at the Port Militaire complex. Returning crews reported that the fires in Lorient could be seen from half-way across the Channel. Just two 3 Group crews operated on the 12th, both of them from 218 Squadron. Pilot Officer Davies and Sgt Webb each successfully dropped their six mines in the shipping channels off the West Frisian Islands.

Bomber Command carried out its heaviest attack of the war on Lorient on the 13/14th, when around 450 aircraft delivered a record one thousand tons of bombs. 218 Squadron supported the three phase operation with fifteen Stirlings, and proceedings opened with the marking of the aiming point by twenty-four Pathfinders, after which over 200 aircraft from 1, 3 and 6 Groups attacked the old town and the Keroman peninsular. Finally, a further 230 aircraft from 4 and 5 Groups hit the same aiming points in the face of what was described as heavy naval flak operating in conjunction with searchlights. Pilot Officer Cozens reported flak damage, and S/Ldr Beck's BF446 HA-H sustained a shattered windscreen, which resulted in a very draughty trip home. Visibility was perfect over both aiming points, and most crews reported dropping their loads from between 6,000 and 13,500 feet, and described the target as a mass of flames.

The long awaited debut of the Mk III Stirling was finally realised on this night. The Austin Motors-built BK650 had arrived from 44MU on February 6th, followed by BK687 on the day after. BK650 was allocated the individual letter L and BK687 R. The honour of being the first to become airborne on operations was won by BK650, with A Flight's S/Ldr Hiles DFC at the controls. On leaving the target area Hiles impulsively descended to ground level to shoot-up and stop a train ten miles east of Lorient. On his return Hiles commented that he was "*very pleased with the Mk III*", a sentiment echoed by S/Ldr Sly in his report.

Wing Commander Morris took command of Downham Market from G/C "Square" McKee on the 14th, on the latter's posting to 3 Group Headquarters for duties as S.A.S.O. An inconclusive attack was carried out on Cologne that night, involving twelve 218 Squadron aircraft and all three flight commanders. Once over enemy territory German fighters were active throughout, and two crews had encounters. Another large-scale attack was unleashed upon Lorient on the 16/17th, when the eight 218 Squadron crews carried out a timed run from north to south using the lattice B or C lines in good visibility. Large fires, explosions and a dense volume of smoke were seen in the target area, on a night when the flak was described as weak and ineffective. Contrary to orders S/Ldr Hiles brought BK650 down to below 4,500 feet in an attempt to pinpoint the target, and, with the majority of aircraft operating above 8,000 feet, he was extremely fortunate not to be hit by falling bombs. While this operation was in progress three other 218 Squadron crews were engaged in the mining of the Deodars area at the mouth of the Gironde Estuary.

The important port of Wilhelmshaven was attacked on the 19/20th, when crews encountered thick haze in the target area. The raid opened with Pathfinder sky markers, but this was changed to ground markers, a decision which may have been responsible for most of the effort finding open country. Considerable opposition was encountered from both night fighters and flak in the target area, and later the flak defences of Heligoland and a convoy sailing near the North Frisians. Squadron Leader Hiles' aircraft was hit by light flak from the convoy which holed the port wing tank and cost the right thumb of F/Sgt De Silva, the 22 year old rear gunner born in British Guiana. The Hon Mr Hodge of the Colonial Office inspected the squadron on the 19th, he spoke at length with the crews during his inspection and informed all present that the work and contribution of the squadron was of great interest and pride to all those on the Gold Coast. The following day after a brief period as SASO at 3 Group Headquarters G/C McKee returned to Downham Market to relieve W/Cdr Morris as station commander.

Nuremberg, the scene of Nazi pre-war rallies, was attacked on the night of February 25/26th. Over three hundred aircraft set out for this distant target, but bad weather on the outward journey and a misunderstanding at the rendezvous point caused the Pathfinders to arrive late. The initial ground markers were dropped two miles north-north-west of the aiming point, and subsequent marking fell well short. One group of TIs was concentrated on a village five miles from the target, and they attracted the majority of the bombs. Fourteen 218 Squadron

Stirlings supported the operation, but soon after crossing the coast three of these were forced to jettison their bombs and turn for home. The remainder arrived over Nuremburg just after 23.00hrs, and it was immediately obvious that the marking was scattered. The recent run of loss-free operations ended on this night, after Sgt Raymond White and his crew were shot down by flak at 01.14hrs local time. BF450 HA-X crashed near the Mannheim power station on the right bank of the River Rhine, and there were no survivors. Next morning the only wreckage visible was the tail section which was found still occupied by the nineteen-year old rear gunner, Sgt John Hearn.

Eight 218 Squadron Stirlings joined an operation to Cologne on the 26/27th, when slight haze in the target area made pinpointing almost impossible, and none of the returning crews was enthusiastic about the prospects of a successful outcome. On the same night Sgt Hailey carried out a successful mining sortie in the Young Yams area, delivering six mines from 1,000 feet. Flying Officer Stewart was also gardening when attacked by a FW190 twenty miles east of Rotterdam at 20.40hrs. The gunners opened fire at 150 yards range, and numerous strikes were seen all over the engine and wings of the fighter, which immediately dived into the haze below, and was not seen again. A large scale mining operation involving ninety-one aircraft was carried out on the following night, when two areas were allocated to the 218 Squadron element. Four crews each were briefed to sow their mines in the Gironde Estuary and the West Frisians, but one was forced to abort before the English coast was reached. The remaining aircraft planted a total of 55,500lb of mines, and all returned from what appeared to be an incident-free operation.

Having dealt with Lorient, Bomber Command now turned its attention upon St Nazaire on the last night of the month, and an estimated 60% of the town was destroyed on this one night alone. Ten 218 Squadron crews were briefed, but R9189 HA-K swung violently to starboard without warning when almost airborne, and the attempt to straighten it up caused the undercarriage to collapse. Fortunately there was no fire and the crew of Canadian P/O Cozens was able to walk away, but R9189 was beyond repair. Another aircraft returned early with a defective engine, but the remaining crews found the target and carried out a successful operation. Numerous fires were reported in the docks area, particularly on the east side of the complex, and a large one on the southern side with black, acrid smoke billowing upwards.

It had been a record month for 218 Squadron with 124 sorties, the highest among the Stirling squadrons. In the process it had dropped a new record of 628,000lb of bombs, the second highest in the group to 214 Squadron. The squadron also topped the table of gardening sorties with twenty-six, 94% of which were successful. This increase came as a direct result of the formation of the third flight, which had been made possible by the gradually increasing production rate of the Stirling. At the same time Bomber Command was undergoing expansion, and both 218 and XV Squadrons were increased to a strength of twenty-four aircraft plus reserves. There was a change of command at 3 Group HQ on the 27th with the departure of AVM Cochrane to 5 Group as A-O-C. Cochrane's forthright and no-nonsense approach had given the group the impetus it so desperately needed, at a time when it had reached a low ebb. The group's new commanding officer was fifty-year-old Yorkshireman, AVM Richard Harrison CBE DFC AFC. Prior to Harrison's appointment he had served as SASO at HQ 1 Group from December 1940 until his appointment as Deputy SASO at HQ Bomber Command in January 1942. Harrison had been considered as successor to Baldwin back in 1942, but Harris wanted Cochrane and got his wish. In a letter to Portal dated July 5th 1942 Harris wrote of Harrison:

> *"Alternatively, Harrison my Deputy SASO would entirely suit me as AOC 3 Group. He is a fine commander, though rather junior. He would be the first AOC in this war with personnel operational experience of the war, and that of itself has many attractions."*

March

March would bring with it the first major bombing campaign of the war for which Bomber Command was adequately equipped and prepared. By the beginning of 1943 Harris had a predominantly four-engine bomber force at his disposal, with an unprecedented bomb carrying capacity. The blind bombing device, Oboe, had

Short Stirling R9189 HA-K flown by Pilot Officer Cozens RCAF the morning after it swung off Downham Markets runway while taking off for St Nazaire. The Stirling was Struck off Charge after completing 31 operations with 218 Squadron.

demonstrated its potential to negate the ever-present industrial haze blanketing the Ruhr, and protecting the likes of Essen and Duisburg. Bombers, particularly Lancasters, were now rolling out of the factories in large numbers, while the Empire Training Scheme guaranteed an endless supply of fresh, eager crews, and all of this meant that the time was right to demonstrate just what Bomber Command could achieve.

Before Harris embarked on the Ruhr offensive he committed his crews to a major operation against Berlin on March 1st. A force of three hundred aircraft set off for the Reich Capital either side of 19.00hrs, among them nine Stirlings belonging to 218 Squadron. As briefed the squadron contingent crossed the North Sea below 5,000 feet until a hundred miles from the enemy coast. It was during this leg that two of them turned back with technical problems. The force was arranged according to aircraft type, the Halifaxes of 4 and 6 Groups opening proceedings, followed by the Stirling force with the Lancasters of 1 and 5 Groups bringing up the rear. Visibility was good over the target, and several fires were reported in districts east of the centre, while a large explosion was witnessed in the Spandau area. The attackers were subjected to heavy and accurate flak over the target, and Sgt Cobb and crew reported seeing the demise of a bomber. So clear was the visibility that they could count the parachutes of its crew. On return BK666 HA-Q struck trees near Fakenham in Norfolk and crashed, but F/O Berridge and his crew were able to walk away. This was the first Mk III to be written off by the squadron.

An attack on Hamburg followed on the 3/4th, when over four hundred aircraft took part in excellent weather conditions. 218 squadron provided eleven Stirlings, 3 Group's largest contribution, although two returned early. The Stirlings were part of the third wave, and the crews identified the Alster Lake and bombed on a number of scattered green TIs in moderate to intense flak. The squadron dropped thirty tons of bombs, but the raid was largely disappointing, after the Pathfinders misidentified the target. The majority of the crews bombed the town of Wedel, situated some thirteen miles north-east of the intended target, and only Sgt Tomkins among the 218 Squadron contingent managed to bomb within two miles of the correct aiming point.

The Ruhr campaign began on the night of the 5/6th, when 442 aircraft took off for Essen. For the first time in a main force operation Mosquitoes equipped with Oboe would be used to locate and ground mark the target. The heavy crews had been informed at briefing that a new marking method was to be used, and that they should only bomb on red markers using maximum precision. The main force was to bomb in three waves according to aircraft type, with the Halifaxes of 4 and 6 Groups taking the lead between 21.02hrs and 21.20hrs. The Wellingtons and Stirlings of 1, 3 and 6 Groups were briefed to attack between 21.15hrs and 21.25hrs, before the Lancasters of 1 and 5 Groups concluded the attack between 21.25hrs and 21.40hrs. Three of 218 Squadron's eleven Stirlings were forced to return early with technical malfunctions, P/O Pettit, S/Ldr Sly and P/O Fennell all making it safely home. On reaching the target the 218 Squadron crews were confronted by a carpet of flames and intense flak, the latter accounting for R9333 HA-Y, which crashed in Essen-Kray, an eastern suburb, and there were no survivors from the crew of P/O George Ratcliffe. Pilot Officer Ratcliffe had completed twelve operations and his crew nine. An unusually high number of early returns reduced the size of the force arriving over the target, and just 367 crews bombed as briefed. Damage was exceptionally severe and widespread, with at least fifty-three separate workshops of the Krupp works sustaining heavy damage, while thirteen main buildings were virtually destroyed. Several smaller factories were partially gutted, together with gasworks, power stations and the municipal tram depot.

The squadron was not required to operate for the next two nights, and crews took a well-earned breather from operations while the hard working ground crews caught up on long-overdue servicing and repair work. The respite did not last long of course, and the squadron was called upon to operate again on the 8th. The target for this night was the distant southern city of Nuremberg, for which the squadron provided twelve Stirlings. One returned early to Downham Market with an undercarriage malfunction, but the remainder pressed on by an almost straight route across France to the target. Sergeant Webb was attacked by a twin engine fighter, which the rear gunner beat off, and was able to report the fighter diving away with what appeared to be flames emanating from the fuselage. Pilot Officer Smith and crew were attacked by a JU88 at 01.28hrs, ten miles east of Laon, but crew discipline and accurate shooting by the rear gunner, F/Sgt Holland, resulted in the fighter being shaken off.

The red and green Pathfinder flares were found to be scattered across Nuremberg, and two fires were seen to be burning, one in a northern district and another to the south. Flak was moderate but accurate, and Sgt Webb and crew watched a bomber explode over the target, while BF446 HA-H was severely hit by flak on the run into the target area. Damage in Nuremberg was not on the scale of Essen, but over six hundred buildings were destroyed, and the M.A.N and Siemens factories sustained damage. Ten crews joined a disappointing raid on Munich on the 9/10th, when inaccurate marking by the Pathfinders resulted in bombing being rather scattered. On the positive side the squadron dropped 44,640lb of bombs without loss. On the 10th Sgt Bryans and crew undertook their first freshman operation since being posted to the squadron from 1651 CU on February 28th. They were one of four crews to carry out a successful mining operation in the Deodars area.

For a fourth consecutive night, the squadron was required to operate on the 11th, when contributing ten aircraft on the third trip in a row to southern Germany. This time the target was Stuttgart, which the crews found covered in haze. Although impossible to identify the aiming point, fairly concentrated Pathfinder flares were seen and bombed in the face of intense light flak. Pilot Officer Cobb was on his bombing run when another Stirling was shot down in flames less than four hundred yards ahead. The pilot took violent evasive action, which resulted in overshooting the markers, and the bomb load was dropped on surrounding fires. Flight Lieutenant Pettit's BF468 was badly hit by flak over the target, while S/Ldr Sly reported seeing seven bombers shot down in the area. If accurate flak in the target were not enough the crews had to contend with night fighters all the way home. Fijian F/O Davis was attacked by a JU88, and F/L Pettit by a Bf110 a few miles from the French coast. The mid-upper gunner, Sgt Sommerville, was wounded in the hand and leg in the encounter. On return he was transferred to the RAF Hospital at Ely. The squadron lost the experienced crew of F/Sgt Gerald Parkinson RNZAF on this night, while on their twenty-first operation. BF343 HA-M crashed south of Dieppe, possibly the victim of a prowling night fighter, and there were no survivors.

Eager to take advantage of his earlier success at Essen, Harris returned on the night of the 12/13th with over four hundred aircraft. Again 218 Squadron was required to operate, and provided eight aircraft for this Oboe ground marking attack. On reaching the target the crews found a concentrated mass of red and

Canadian Mo Pettit at the controls of his regular aircraft Stirling R9189 HA-K aloft over the East Anglian countryside. On completion of his tour of 26 operations Maurice Pettit was awarded a well-deserved DFC. After a spell as instructor he return for a 2nd tour with No.432 RCAF Squadron flying Halifaxes, he completed a further 22 operations and survived the war and was award a Bar to his DFC.

green markers. Flak and searchlight activity was intense, but some crews bombed from below the briefed height in an effort to achieve better accuracy. Flying Officer Arthur Davis was coned on his bomb run and bracketed by both light and heavy flak, which inflicted damage to his port wing. His all-incendiary bomb load was dropped into a mass of flames and markers from 6,480 feet. A number of aircraft were hit by ground fire on the way home, and Arthur Davis came back at less than two hundred feet, shooting at everything that moved. This was in fact, the final operation with 218 Squadron for the Davis crew, as they were about to be posted to 7 Squadron of the Pathfinders. They would fail to return from an operation to Wuppertal on June 24th. The squadron had dropped a total of 62,280lb of bombs during the Essen raid without loss. Wing Commander Morris again assumed command of Downham Market on the 12th, as G/C McKee departed on some well-earned leave, and S/Ldr Anthony Beck took temporary command of the squadron. There was a lull in major operations during the mid-month period, and the squadron was not required to operate again until March 22nd. On the 20th McKee was attached to Mildenhall, and four days later was promoted to the acting rank of air commodore to assume command of Base HQ at Mildenhall.

A return visit to the U-Boat yards at St Nazaire was planned for the 22/23rd, and ten 218 Squadron aircraft took off in marginal weather conditions. Such were the conditions, in fact, that group sent out a recall message to all crews, who were by then within twenty miles of the French Coast. Pilot Officer Becroft and crew did not receive the recall signal, and continued on to the target to deliver their all-incendiary load. This was the last raid undertaken by one of the squadron's more press-on and audacious captains, S/Ldr Waldo Hiles DFC, who was posted to 3 Group HQ at Exning Hall. Waldo "Wally" Hiles would be awarded a DSO in recognition of completing his second tour. Occupying the second pilot's seat on Hiles' final operation was W/Cdr Jack Sims, who had been attached to the squadron from 1657 Conversion Unit for operational experience since March 11th. On March 30th he would take command of the Lancaster II-equipped 115 Squadron. A Flight would be taken over by the experienced acting S/Ldr Geoff Rothwell DFC.

A small-scale mining operation was laid on for the 23/24th, for which four 218 Squadron crews were allotted the Nectarine I area. It was an opportunity for four recently arrived captains to gain operational experience, P/O Meiklejohn, F/Sgt Richards and P/O Crooks, who came from training establishments, and P/O Brown, who had operated before. Pilot Officer Leslie Smith was posted to 1657 Conversion Unit as an instructor on the 26th on completion of his tour of twenty-three operations, and he would be awarded a DFC in May. Sadly he was to lose his life on September 7th 1943, when he entered a blazing Stirling to extricate a trapped crew member. In doing so Leslie Smith sustained such terrible burns that he succumbed to his wounds on the following day.

3 Group dispatched sixty-six Stirlings and six Lancaster Mk IIs to Berlin on the 27/28th, for what turned out to be a disappointing raid. Twelve 218 Squadron crews participated, and they found the defences around the Capital as formidable as always. BF452 HA-Y was hit by flak on leaving the target area, and the bomb aimer sustained a leg wound. Flight Lieutenant Neilson lost his starboard-outer engine, and had to make the long flight home without it. The Squadron ORB simply recorded *"A Good Show"*. While this operation was in progress, three other 218 Squadron aircraft successfully planted nine mines in the Young Yams area.

On March 28th W/Cdr Morris moved on attachment to Mildenhall, and was succeeded as "station master" at Downham Market by G/C "Speedy" Powell DSO OBE. Group Captain Powell was the well-known wing commander from the 1942 propaganda film, "Target for Tonight", which starred G/C Percy Pickard as the captain of Wellington F for Freddie. Powell was an inspirational leader, who liked to lead by example. On the departure of W/Cdr Morris the squadron welcomed thirty-nine-year-old Australian W/Cdr Donald Saville DFC. Saville was born in 1903 in Portland, New South Wales, and joined the RAAF in May 1927 at Point Cook. He was granted a short service commission in the RAF in February 1928, and served with a number of fighter and bomber squadrons in the UK until his transfer back to the RAAF in February 1932. On leaving the RAAF he became a flying instructor with the Tasmanian Aero Club, and in 1937 joined the Australian National Airways, where he remained until the outbreak of war. On re-joining the RAF Saville was posted to 2 Ferry School, where he could utilize his vast experience of 8046.35 flying hours.

In August 1941 Saville got his wish to be put in the front line, and after completing his course at 21 OTU at Moreton-in-Marsh, he was posted to 12 Squadron at Binbrook to fly Wellingtons. On December 2nd 1941 he was posted as a flight commander to the newly formed 458 RAAF Squadron at Holme-on-Spalding Moor, and in early 1942 was given command of a detachment of the squadron sent to operate in the Middle-East. When 458 was handed a new role in August 1942, he was posted to command 104 Squadron at Kabrit. He was awarded a DFC, and by the completion of his tour in February 1943, he had forty-seven operations to his credit. Inexplicably Saville was not screened from operations for the usual six month rest period, and within weeks of his arrival back in the UK, the tough, no-nonsense Australian was commanding 218 Squadron. Some found his style of leadership refreshing, while to others he was a typical Aussie, loud, rude and self-opinionated. However, all agreed he was a first rate pilot and a true leader of men.

Another crack at St Nazaire was undertaken on the 28/29th, when 322 aircraft were dispatched, including six from 218 Squadron, with W/Cdr Saville accompanying C Flight's S/Ldr Beck. The crews found red and green target indicators concentrated over the docks area and the U-Boat yards, and bombed accordingly in good visibility. Pilot Officer Howlett reported two aircraft going down in flames over the target, and others said that the glow of the fires from St

Nazaire were visible from mid-Channel on the way home. Ten of the squadron's aircraft took off for Berlin on the 29/30th, the second trip to the Capital in three nights. 3 Group's contribution amounted to fifty-three Stirlings and eight Lancaster IIs of 115 Squadron. Weather over the North Sea and the Continent was bad, with severe icing conditions, and this may have contributed to the high number of early returns afflicting the group. It was only during the last twenty miles to the target that the weather began to improve. Crews pinpointed Berlin's largest lake in the haze, and red TIs were initially well-placed in preparation for the arrival of the main force. Unfortunately, they did not turn up in sufficient numbers to capitalize on the opportunity, and the majority of bombs fell into open country, after flares dropped by H2S were six miles south-east of the intended aiming point attracted attention. This last operation of the month accounted for the loss of two 218 Squadron aircraft without survivors. Nothing was heard from F/O John Harris and crew in BK716 HA-J after take-off, and it is believed they were shot down over the North Sea on the way home. Harris and his crew had completed eight operations together. Tragically, of the seven men on board, five, including twenty-nine-year-old Harris, were married. Flak claimed Sgt William Hoar RCAF in BK702 HA-O, which crashed south of Bremen at 03.42hrs. The crew was on its fourth operation together, and Hoar was on his sixth. Two DFCs

The crew of Sergeant William Hoar RCAF. William was initially attached to the squadron during December 1942 for operational experience on posting from No.1651 Con Unit. He returned with his crew on February 8th 1943.

were awarded to the squadron in March, one to the gunnery leader, F/L John Birbeck, and the other to mid-upper gunner, P/O Lionel Newbury.

April

April would prove to be the least rewarding month of the Ruhr period, but this was largely because of the number of operations to targets in regions of Germany beyond the range of Oboe. It began in encouraging fashion, however, with another successful tilt at Essen on the 3/4th, which destroyed over six hundred buildings. The Stirling brigade sat this one out, but ninety of them, including twelve from 218 Squadron, were included in a raid on Kiel on the following night, which employed a new record non-1,000 force of 577 aircraft. Weather conditions were unhelpful, and, unable to identify any ground details, the crews had to rely on yellow Pathfinder route markers. At the target bombing took place on Red Wanganui TIs (skymarkers), which drifted away from the aiming point in the strong wind and caused the bombing to be scattered. 218 Squadron delivered 80,880lbs of incendiaries, but returning crews reported the raid to be a failure.

Wing Commander Saville DFC captained one of three aircraft from the squadron to carry out a successful mining operation in the Deodars area on the 6/7th, before Bomber Command switched its attention back to the Ruhr on the 8/9th. Nine 218 Squadron crews took part in the attack on Duisburg, after two had returned early, and in total fifteen out of fifty-four 3 Group aircraft abandoned their sorties. Once again unfavourable weather conditions contributed to the early returns, and also resulted in scattered bombing. Wing Commander Saville was leading the 218 Squadron element, and, finding the target covered in thick cloud, had to bomb on scattered TIs in the face of an intense flak defence. Among the nineteen missing aircraft from this raid, and lost without trace was BF502 HA-P, flown by twenty-two year old Sgt Douglas Tomkins. This all-NCO crew had arrived on the squadron on Christmas Eve, and had flown a total of sixteen operations, including two to Berlin. While the majority of the squadron's crews were over Duisburg, two others made a return visit to the Deodars area, where eight mines were successfully planted.

Downham Market was visited on the afternoon of the 10th by the Secretary for Air, RT Hon Sir Archibald Sinclair and the A-O-C of 3 Group, AVM Harrison,. Both arrived by air to watch that night's briefing for an operation to Frankfurt. Fourteen crews departed Downham and almost immediately disappeared into thick cloud that persisted for the entire outward flight. An unusually high number of early returns depleted the force of five hundred aircraft, and within fifteen minutes the first of four 218 Squadron "boomerangs" was back over the aerodrome. The remaining crews found the target blanketed in cloud up to 8,000 feet, which made identification impossible. To add to the problems the Pathfinder sky markers were quickly lost in the clouds, and illuminated whole swathes to further confuse the

Squadron Leader Geoff Rothwell DFC "A" Flight Commander. Together with S/Ldr Ryall DFC steered the squadron through its toughest period.

bomb-aimers and hinder accurate bombing. Squadron Leader Rothwell reported that the flares over this notoriously difficult target were scattered and confusing, and the raid ultimately became a failure after all but a handful of bombs fell into open country and outlying communities. The disappointment was compounded by the loss of nineteen bombers, 3.8% of the force dispatched. Second tour veteran Geoff Rothwell DFC had arrived from 75 (NZ) Squadron on April 1st. He was an experience pilot, having completed his first tour with 99 Squadron flying Wellingtons in 1940. He began his second tour with 75 (NZ) Squadron in February 1943, but as New Zealand policy required that all senior commanders on the squadron be New Zealanders, Geoff was posted to Downham Market with forty-six operations already under his belt.

Sergeant Allan and crew carried out a mining sortie off the Frisians on this night, and a similar small-scale operation took place on the following night involving three 218 Squadron crews in the Deodars area. Sergeant Hoey was on his way home at 01.40hrs when he was attacked by a JU88, which was hit by return fire from the rear turret, and broke off the engagement. Later the Stirling was attacked again by two FW190s, which were also driven off. The only damage to BF413 HA-T was a bullet hole in the perspex of the mid-upper turret and a hole in the loop aerial. All three crews returned safely to Downham Market. On the early evening of the 11th W/Cdr Saville led two other aircraft on a fruitless air-sea search, it is believed for the crew of a 75 (NZ) Squadron Stirling that had ditched short of fuel on return from Frankfurt.

Sixteen 218 Squadron crews were briefed for an attack on Stuttgart on the 14th, and this was the largest contribution from the group. A new tactic was to be employed to confuse the German defences, in which the Lancaster force would fly at 20,000 feet, with the Halifaxes at 10,000 feet and the sixty-nine Stirlings at tree-top level until climbing to bombing height for the attack. The Pathfinders were to open proceedings at 00.45hrs followed by the Lancasters of 1 and 3 Groups. The third wave, comprising the Stirlings and Wellingtons of 3 Group and Wellingtons of 6 Group, were scheduled to attack next, followed by the Halifaxes of 4 and 6 Groups, and finally the Lancasters of 5 Group to bring the curtain down between 01.17hrs and 01.27hrs. The Stirlings were to attack from between 12,000 and 13,000 feet, almost 5,000 feet below the Halifaxes and Lancasters, and timing was therefore critical. Once again a high number of early returns blighted the squadron's effort, and three came back with various technical problems.

A fourth crew had other reasons for not making it to the target. Geoff Rothwell was hedge-hopping his way across France and Luxembourg in almost daylight conditions, shooting up a train, a signal box, river barges and a military camp along the way. On approaching the town of Junglinster in central Luxemburg, they chanced upon a slow moving train travelling into the town. Without hesitation the bomb-aimer, Sgt "Wal" Fielding, manned the front turret and opened up, registering strikes all over the engine, which almost immediately gushed steam. While Rothwell's attention was momentarily distracted, he failed to notice until too late that he was on a collision course with an electricity pylon. With sheer brute strength and a fair degree of luck Rothwell managed to avoid a head on collision, but he could not avert contact altogether, and a six foot long section of fabrication starting just below the bomb-aimer's compartment was ripped off to the accompaniment of blue and white sparks. One of the incendiaries damaged in the collision burst into flames, forcing the jettisoning of the entire incendiary load. Having regained control Rothwell turned for home, climbing to an altitude of 5,000 feet in preparation to re-cross the coast. However, ten miles north-east of Sedan they were attacked by a JU88, but crew discipline, superb airmanship and accurate return fire saved the day. It was a close shave, evidenced by a cannon shell smashing the cockpit canopy and sending a piece of shrapnel into Rothwell's neck. The gunners poured fire into the fighter, which was seen to shudder and omit red and orange flames as it was lost to sight. BK650 eventually landed safely after being aloft for a hectic four and a half hours.

At the target the Pathfinders dropped a number of concentrated red TIs over the aiming point by H2S, in the face of what was reported to be a surprisingly subdued defence, with only moderate flak and practically no searchlight activity. More by luck than judgement the bombing crept back over the industrial suburb of Bad Canstatt, and some useful damage was inflicted. A number of 218 Squadron aircraft were hit by flak in the target area, while others took advantage of the low-level return trip to indulge themselves in ground strafing. It was an exhilarating and unusual raid for the Stirlings of 3 Group. Given the opportunity to operate at low level, the crews had needed very little encouragement to take the war directly to the Germans on the ground.

Bomber Command had two main targets for the night of the 16/17th, the Skoda works at Pilsen, to which over three hundred Lancasters and Halifaxes were assigned, while 271 Stirlings and Wellingtons were given Mannheim as a diversion. 3 Group contributed ninety-five aircraft to Mannheim, and ten Lancaster IIs of 115 Squadron to Pilsen. The largest individual contribution was again by 218 Squadron, which dispatched seventeen aircraft led by W/Cdr Saville, and, unusually, just one returned early. The tactics used against Stuttgart were employed again on this night, with the group instructed to reach 13,000 to 15,000 feet over Dungeness, and then lose height and gain speed to cross the enemy coast. Once over enemy territory they were to maintain an altitude of no more than 2,000 feet until reaching a predetermined point, then to climb quickly to a bombing altitude of 9,000 feet. At the coast the weather conditions were found to be ideal for the German defenders with little cloud and a near full moon.

Flight Sergeant Richards was attacked by two unidentified single engine fighters at 23.20hrs just north-west of Compiegne. A series of attacks developed in which one fighter attacked, while the other held back and fired from long range with cannons. Return fire from the Stirling's rear turret was seen to enter one of the fighters, which dived to port and a minute later the wireless operator reported an explosion on the ground, which developed into a fire. At 00.14hrs BF514 HA-X was attacked and shot down by Major Kurt Holler of Stab III/NJG4. It crashed near Raucourt, ten miles south of Sedan, there were just two survivors from the crew of P/O David Howlett, who were on their fourth operation. Both men ultimately made their way to Switzerland, and remained there until being repatriated on August 20th 1944. The raid was relatively successful after accurate Pathfinder marking allowed some well-placed bombing, and over 130 buildings were totally destroyed, with a further three thousand reported damaged to some extent. Destruction was particularly heavy around the inland port area, and over 5½ acres of the Joseph Vogele A.G tank and tractor factory was reduced to rubble.

The squadron lost the services of the experienced Australian P/O Meiklejohn and crew on the 20th, on their posting to 7 Squadron of the Pathfinders. Sadly the crew failed to return from an attack on Krefeld on June 21st 1943, the victim of Hptm Siegfried Wandam of Stab I/NJG5. This was the second crew from 218 Squadron to join 7 Squadron, and the second to be lost on operations.

With the departure of G/C Powell in early April to the Middle East, the responsibility of running the station fell to W/Cdr Don Saville DFC, while S/Ldr Beck ran the squadron. This change of role was short lived, however, and ended with the arrival of G/C Eric Delano Barnes AFC, MiD on April 23rd. The night of the 26/27th brought an operation against Duisburg by over five hundred aircraft, fourteen of which represented 218 Squadron. A disappointingly

Photograph of Arthur Aaron seen here while in training at Love Field, Dallas, Texas 1942.

high number of four crews returned early to Downham Market with various technical malfunctions. Flying on this night with F/L Berridge was a young Sgt Arthur Aaron, who had arrived from 1657 CU on the 17th. Returning crews were enthusiastic about the outcome of the operation, which took place in conditions of intense flak and searchlight activity. There were also night fighters, and a number of the squadron's aircraft returned with battle damage. Reconnaissance showed the main weight of the attack to have fallen to the north-east of the city, but three hundred buildings had been destroyed at this elusive target. Three crews were dispatched to the Nectarines mining area on the 27/28th, for what was the largest mining operation to date involving 160 aircraft. It was on this occasion that Sgt Aaron operated as crew captain for the first time.

On the following night the Command undertook an even larger mine-laying operation, which involved 207 aircraft from all groups. They managed to deposit 593 mines in enemy sea lanes, but lost twenty-three of their number in the process, a very high price and one which illustrated the dangerous nature of mine-laying. It was the final operation of a hectic month for 218 Squadron, which dispatched eight crews to the Sweet Pea II area in the Fehmarn Belt, lead by S/Ldr Sly. Tragically the squadron was to lose three crews under circumstances that would be officially investigated post raid. The operation began favourably, and there was little opposition in the target areas, but the homebound leg would see a desperate battle between the Stirlings and the JU88s and Bf110s of NJG3. BK447 HA-F was shot down near Vronding in Denmark, after being attacked from below by Lt Gunther Holtfreter of II/NJG3, while crossing the east coast of Jutland at 00.12hrs, and there were just two survivors from the crew of P/O Denis Brown, who were on their tenth operation.

Three-quarters of an hour later BF515 HA-N exploded in mid-air during an encounter with Uffw Berg of 7/NJG3, and crashed near Taagerup Moor, north of Skelledjerg, taking with it to their deaths F/L Gordon Berridge and his crew. This had been Berridge's twenty-second operation and the crew's eighteenth together. A little over an hour after this incident, EF356 HA-O was attacked and shot down by Lt Gunther Rogge of 12/NJG3, crashing near Aadum, south-east of Tarn in Denmark. The wireless operator had requested a fix at 01.48hrs, which was received at Hull, and, interestingly, the Bomber Command loss card also records an SOS being received at Tangmere at 02.30hrs. There was only one survivor from the crew of Sgt Kenneth Hailey, who were on their twelfth operation together, and that was Sgt Harry Bliss, the mid-upper gunner. He was taken into captivity, and died on March 30th 1945 from acute appendicitis, while travelling in a filthy rail cattle wagon bound for Fallingbostel. Squadron Leader Sly was very nearly the fourth casualty, after his aircraft was attacked by an unseen night fighter at 01.45hrs. Thankfully, the first burst of cannon fire missed the port wing by a few feet, and Sly immediately dived into the clouds just a 1,000 feet below to pull off a narrow escape.

Immediately following this operation an investigation was carried out by Bomber Command to try to establish the cause of the high loss rate. 3 Group had the highest losses with eight failures to return, the New Zealanders of 75 (NZ) Squadron being particularly unlucky with four missing crews, while 90 Squadron made up the numbers with a single loss. An official enquiry concluded that the squadrons assigned to the Cadet Channel and Fehmarn Belt were given return routes that brought them over a number of very heavily defended areas. All aspects of the operation were investigated in detail, including the number of operations flown and the experience of the participating pilots and crews. After an extensive examination of all available information the eight page report concluded that the major cause of the losses was light flak and sheer bad luck! It was also observed that 3 Group's track down the Great Belt appeared to bring its aircraft closer to the enemy coast than was desirable.

The squadron topped the group for sorties during April with 127, and this produced a new record of 708 flying hours. It also topped the table for monthly mine-laying sorties with twenty-six. Four DFMs were awarded to the squadron in April, all to experienced wireless operators and air gunners, three of which had completed their tours. Flight Lieutenant Maurice Pettit RCAF and P/O Colin Jerromes were both awarded the DFC during the month in recognition of their courage and conduct. Both had encountered their fair share of danger and near misses over the previous few months.

May

May would bring a return to winning ways, with a number of spectacular successes, and it began with a new record non-1,000 force of 596 aircraft taking off for Dortmund in the late evening of the 4th. Eleven Stirlings represented 218 Squadron, and on arrival at the target the crews found a number of well placed green TIs delivered by seven Oboe Mosquitoes. However, these quickly became extinguished, and the following crews were obliged to bomb on a number of red TIs, which, as it turned out, were two miles north of the intended aiming point. Never the less, the target was left with fires raging and covered in smoke. Over twelve hundred buildings were destroyed, and a further two thousand sustained serious damage. On the debit side the loss of thirty-one bombers was the highest to date in the campaign, and one of the missing aircraft belonged to 218 Squadron. BF505 HA-Z was attacked by Lt Robert Denzel of 12/NJG12, and exploded in mid air over Holland. Twenty-eight year old Canadian, F/L Wilbur Turner was one of the squadron's most experienced captains, having joined the squadron from 218 Conversion Flight in August 1942, since which time he had completed twenty-two operations as crew captain, and a further seven as second pilot. Just three men survived from the eight on board, and these were taken into captivity.

Flight Lieutenant Turner had been heavily involved with a recent investigation into the problems encountered by the squadron with the Mk XIV bombsight. In early April the squadron had reported problems in the form of a frequent de-synchronisation of the standard repeater on the then relatively new Mk XIV device, when used in conjunction with the compass system. Other squadrons within the command had expressed similar concerns, and a full-scale investigation began on April 23rd. The task of finding a solution was given to the boffins at R.A.E. At the time over three hundred Mk XIV bomb sights were in service, and of these only six showed consistent de-synchronisation, and all of these were on 218 Squadron. The Boffins of R.A.E worked feverishly to resolve the problem, which, by early May, was becoming wide-spread throughout the Command. By June 3rd the fault had been eliminated throughout Bomber Command by the simple expedient of fitting a suppressor to the master unit transmitter. A R.A.E report dated December 1943 compiled by F Twiney B.Sc., made particular mention of 218 Squadron:

The de-synchronisation failure reported in this note was cured only through the assistance of 218 Squadron, Downham Market, before universal fitting of the Mk.XIV bombsight could make it generally available in Bomber Command. The trouble was discovered because of the excellent maintenance there showed that a definite causes must exist, and the co-operation in making flight tests enabled the simplest remedy to be introduced quickly. Acknowledgment is due, in particular to F/Lt Turner (pilot of I-Ink) F/Lt Jones and P/O Ambrose (Electrical Officers) and F/Sgt Jacobs (Instrument N.C.O)

Four all-NCO crews were dispatched to the Nectarine I and II mining areas on the 5/6th, and twenty-four mines were successfully planted in their allotted positions. The squadron was not required to operate again until the 12th, and this lull in operations gave the squadron the opportunity to catch up on urgently required maintenance. Perhaps more importantly it gave the influx of recent arrivals the chance to carry out a number of fighter affiliation exercises. It was back to Duisburg on the 12/13th for 562 aircraft, for the fourth operation against the city since the Ruhr campaign began. 3 Group contributed seventy-five Stirlings, eleven of them from 218 Squadron. There was just one early return to Downham

Market, a marked improvement on recent experiences. The squadrons of 3 Group were scheduled to be the last over the target, by which time it was blanketed in smoke and difficult to identify. Fortunately this was not important, as the Oboe-equipped Mosquitoes of the Pathfinders had dropped a series of extremely well placed red TIs. Flak was heavy and accurate, and it was estimated that more than two hundred searchlights were active. Five 218 Squadron aircraft were coned and hit during the bombing phase, but none of these incidences resulted in injury to crew members. A spectacular explosion was reported by two crews at 02.18hrs, and this may have been from a munitions factory located in the old town.

Over forty-eight acres of built-up area were left devastated, and damage to the local industry was particularly severe. Four factories owned by the Vereinigte Stahlwerke A.G (August Thyssen) were badly damaged, as were a number of chemical workshops and coke and benzol purification plants. Further damage was caused in the docks area, where a number of timber yards and storage facilities were destroyed. Twenty-one barges and thirteen smaller ships were also destroyed, with a further sixty reported as damaged. Also hit were marshalling yards, in which rolling stock was destroyed and railway tracks torn up. For the first time Duisburg had endured an effective and destructive attack, which brought to an end what had seemed to be a charmed life. The defenders fought back to claim thirty-four aircraft, another new record for the campaign, and 218 Squadron was again represented. BK705 HA-K was shot down into the North Sea by Lt Robert Denzel of 12/NJG1 at 03.28hrs, and there were no survivors from the crew of P/O Robert Bryans RCAF, who were on their thirteenth operation.

It was the turn of Bochum to host a visit from the Command on the following night, when fourteen 218 Squadron crews participated, including all three flight commanders. Three aircraft returned early on this night, all with engine malfunctions, while the remainder joined the other Stirling contingents bringing up the rear of the attack. Sergeant Carney lost his Gee set outbound, and the Stirling stumbled into the Düsseldorf defences, where it was coned by over twenty searchlights. The pilot struggled to find a way out as the aircraft was hit by flak, and believing in his agitated state that there was no escape, he gave the order to bail-out. Tensions between the pilot and bomb-aimer, Spud Taylor, had surfaced during the previous operation when the pilot had opted to return early because of oxygen problems. Taylor had written,

> *"Set out for Duisburg tonight but had to turn back because Jock (Rear Gunner) and Len (Mid Upper) could not get any oxygen. They had forgotten to withdraw their bobbins. Shorty (Nav) and I egged Bill on to complete the trip at 10–11,000 feet, but he is too damn windy".*

Taylor pointed out that they would not reach the ground alive in such heavy flak, but Carney was beyond reason and began to extricate himself from his seat harness and make for the front escape hatch. Seizing the control column Taylor brought the Stirling onto an even keel, and steered a straight course through the inferno of flak until they were clear. With no Gee set and the navigation charts and equipment in disarray, the crew struggled to locate the target. They found themselves over the outskirts of Essen, and again the target for trigger-happy flak crews on the ground. Lucky to survive, they spotted a number of red TIs in the distance identifying Bochum, and the Stirling was steered directly towards the markers with complete disregard for the briefed approach. The bombs were delivered, and on clearing the defences Taylor called each crew member to check on their status. He received no answer from the rear gunner, so handed back the controls to the pilot, who had regained his composure and made his way down the fuselage. On reaching the rear turret Taylor found Sgt Stewart jammed half in and half out of the escape hatch and being buffeted by the slipstream. Stewart had attempted to comply with the bail-out order, but had pulled his ripcord too early and become jammed in the doorway. Taylor managed to drag the dazed and frozen gunner back inside, and took him to the rest station to recover, while the pilot set a course for home. We will return later to this crew.

The rest of the 218 Squadron contingent found the city covered in smoke and flames, with a large billowing tower of black, acrid smoke hanging over it. Bombing from a little over 10,000 feet and well below the majority, P/O Cochrane's BF452 HA-M was hit in the wing by three 4lb incendiaries, which thankfully passed through without damaging the fuel tanks. An inspection at home on the following morning found the tails of the incendiaries still embedded. EF367 HA-G skippered by Sgt Nicholls was attacked and damaged by a night fighter while crossing the Belgian-German border outbound. Sergeant John Howard, the rear gunner, was killed instantly. The badly damaged Stirling managed to evade further attention from the fighter, and, after the bomb load was jettisoned, it turned for home. Nicholls nursed the aircraft over the English coast with diminishing fuel reserves from ruptured tanks, and decided to divert to Chedburgh. With flaps and undercarriage damaged, he lined up for a belly landing, but in the final moments of his approach all four engines cut out, and the Stirling crashed on the edge of the airfield after hitting a tree. Five of the crew were flung clear of the wreckage, which began to burn, but the pilot had to be pulled out in a severely injured state. He was admitted to the West Suffolk Hospital in Bury St Edmunds, and categorized as dangerously ill. Three of the crew died on impact, and a fourth succumbed to his injuries shortly after being admitted to hospital. Miraculously, the navigator, who had not been catapulted out on impact, sustained only a sprained left ankle and emotional shock. It was not all one-sided, however, as S/Ldr Sly claimed the destruction of a Bf109 north of Terschelling at 02.51hrs.

Having endured the defences of Düsseldorf, Essen and Bochum, the Carney crew arrived over Downham Market at 04.55hrs with fuel gauges showing almost zero. With no means to communicate with the ground, the landing was undertaken

Short Stirling BF480 HA-I "Ink" seen here on the morning of May 14th 1943.

without permission, and initially, everything appeared to be under control. Inexplicably at the last moment, the pilot took his hands off the controls and placed them over his eyes. The Stirling swerved suddenly to port cutting a parked lorry in two and then ploughed into two parked cars. With the undercarriage collapsed the bomber hit and partially demolished the briefing room, killing two airmen, who had just returned from a mining operation. The Stirling finally came to a halt with the port wing embedded in the watch office. The crew of BF480 managed to scramble clear, dazed but otherwise uninjured, and "Spud" Taylor's dairy records the sombre and emotional scene on the following morning:

> *"The kite I'm afraid has had it. We walked around counting flak holes and there were about 100, several extraordinarily close to where we were sitting. Len's turret has 5 or 6 holes in it, one piece of shrapnel grazed his nose on its way through. The astro dome was whipped away while Paddy was looking through it and Jock has a deep cut on his head. I was lucky to escape injury myself as a six inch piece of metal from my compartment hit me on the head, fortunately my leather helmet saved my bacon."*

On the morning of May 16th Spud Taylor and the remnants of his crew were ordered to report to W/Cdr Saville's office. Spud recalls:

> *"After breakfast we were told to report to the wing co. In his officer we gave our account of events to do with the raid on Bochum. I told him I had no confidence in*

Bill and did not wish to fly with him again. The Wing Co looked at some papers on his desk and told us that we were Bill's sixth crew and that he had crashed the lot. This was news to us, but the main thing we were granted our wish. This interview was followed by a morale flight which went off ok. Jock is in the sick bay at present and Bill is hanging on in the hope that we will have him back."

The pressure of operational flying had obviously taken its toll on this young pilot. He had volunteered for aircrew and successfully managed to achieve his wings, but the demands were obviously just too much for him, and he was posted from the squadron.

Six crews were briefed for a mining effort in the Nectarine II area on the 16th, but P/O Ter Averst crashed on take-off when the starboard-inner engine cut as he was about to become unstuck. The Stirling swung wildly off the runway, before crashing into a building, fortunately without seriously damaging the crew. EF353 HA-O was damaged even beyond the capabilities of the squadron's ground crew's, and it was taken away for repair by SEBRO, and was ultimately returned to service with 1657 CU on November 3rd 1943. The remaining five crews each planted their six mines in their allotted garden areas and returned safely. The squadron was stood down thereafter, until mining operations involved seven and four crews respectively on the 20/21st and 21/22nd. The target for the former was the Deodars area in the Bay of Biscay. Two crews had encounters with German

Squadron Leader Ian Ryall DFC and crew. Ian commanded B Flight from the early summer of 1943 and bucked the trend of the squadron losing flight commanders.

night fighters, one indecisively, while BF519 HA-E, piloted by Sgt Davis, was attacked multiple times by a persistent ME210, which eventually knocked out its starboard-inner engine. After a tense and exhausting series of engagements, the night fighter was eventually shaken off, and the Stirling made it safely back to Downham Market.

It was back to "Happy Valley" and the city of Dortmund on the night of the 23/24th, and the 826 aircraft represented the largest non-1,000 raid so far in the war. 3 Group contributed a respectable 118 aircraft, and for the first time put up over one hundred Stirlings for a single operation, although early returns reduced the number by ten. Four of these were from among 218 Squadron's contingent of seventeen, all of which suffered engine malfunctions. The main force was divided into three waves, the first of which consisted of 250 aircraft, whose crews were deemed to be the best from each group. The second wave consisted of the remaining Stirlings, Halifaxes and Wellingtons, and the Lancasters brought up the rear. The clear conditions over the target area were perfect for accurate marking, and by the end of the raid the city was blanketed by smoke, with one column reaching up to 12,000 feet. Flying on his first operation with the experienced Sgt J Hoey and crew was F/O Overton, and this was the start of a long and remarkable association with the squadron. BK706 HA-Y crashed in the target area, probably the victim of flak, and there were no survivors from the crew of F/O John Phillips. Post raid reconnaissance showed large parts of Dortmund to be devastated, with nearly two thousand buildings destroyed, and Germany's biggest steel works, the Hoesch AG, and the city's second largest, the Vereinigte Stahlwerke AG, enormously damaged. Operations over the Ruhr were never one-sided, and the defenders claimed thirty-eight bombers, six of them from 3 Group.

Düsseldorf was the target on the night of the 25/26th, when another large force of 759 aircraft was dispatched. 3 Group put up 117 Stirlings and Lancasters, of which fifteen of the former were drawn from 218 Squadron. An alarming five crews returned early, the highest abort rate in the Group. Dense cloud made ground marking impossible, and this resulted in a scattered and disjointed attack. Some red TIs were reported to have fallen twenty miles north of the intended aiming point, and Düsseldorf was spared serious damage. EH887 HA-Z fell victim to Major Walter Ehle of Stab II/NJG1, and crashed near Düren with just one survivor from the crew of Sgt Norman Collins. The two previous raids had shown an alarming increase in early returns on the squadron, amounting to a worrying 28% of those dispatched. The vast majority of them were due to engine failure. By late May the squadron was almost totally equipped with the Mk III Stirling although a number of Mk Is were still soldiering on, most notably N3721, which had joined the squadron back in February 1942.

Following a visit by the King and Queen on the 26th, three crews were given the Frisian Islands to mine on the 27th. Flight Sergeant William Mills and crew did not return from this, their first operation, having been shot down by Uffz Karl-

Georg Pfeiffer of 10/NJG1 at 00.55hrs. BF405 HA-U crashed in the North Sea forty miles north of Terschelling, and there were no survivors. The Barmen half of Wuppertal was the target for the last big raid of May, when 719 aircraft were dispatched, including 109 from 3 Group. Fifteen 218 Squadron aircraft departed over Southwold, among them BK712 HA-D skippered by W/Cdr Saville DFC, who had alongside him G/C E Barnes, Downham Market's Station Commander, and for once there were no early returns! What followed was the most successful attack of the campaign to date. The initial marking was extremely accurate and it was backed up by the heavies of 83, 156 and 405 Squadrons, which kept the aiming point well marked for the following main force. It was one of those rare occasions when an operation proceeded exactly according to plan, and it was the most devastating raid of the war thus far, laying waste to 80% of the town's built-up area, and the catalogue of destruction included four thousand houses, five of the town's six largest factories, and over two hundred other industrial premises. Unusually, more buildings suffered complete destruction than serious damage, but whatever the statistics, it was a tragedy in human terms, and around 3,400 people lost their lives. Thirty-three aircraft were missing on this night, nine of them from 3 Group.

The success of the raid was marred for 218 Squadron by the loss of two crews, both victims over Belgium of Lt Heinz-Wolfgang Schnaufer of Stab II/NJG1. There were no survivors from the crews of twenty-one-year-old P/O Stanley Allan RAAF in BF565 HA-H, who were on their tenth operation, and F/Sgt William Davis RAAF in BK688 HA-P. Davis was a thirty-one-year-old married man from

The burial of the crew of Flight Sergeant William Davis RAAF. Shot down by Lt Heinz Wolfgang Schnaufer, there were no survivors from BK688 HA-P. The crew had mixed fortunes since their arrival on the squadron on April 23rd, two of their number were removed due to flying stress.

Victoria. His crew on this night was a rather mixed bag, the rear gunner, a replacement for the sick regular gunner, was forty-one-year-old F/L Abbiss, who, at the time, was the oldest man on the squadron. A gardening operation brought down the curtain on the month's activities on the 30/31st when S/Ldr Beck and Sgt Aaron delivered six mines to the Deodars area.

The statistics told their own story of ten aircraft and eight crews lost from 113 sorties. The tempo of operations and above average losses were chipping away at morale, especially amongst the inexperienced crews. It was a testament to the leadership of the squadron that morale remained relatively high, even under such testing times. Apart from a few isolated cases, moral was holding, and the station Senior Medical Officer recorded in his monthly summery, *"No new cases of "Flying Stress" have been notified to Group HQ, but the prospects for the coming months are less satisfactory, as some deterioration has been noticed in the quality of some of the recent crews posted to the squadron"*. The squadron had slipped down to third place on the group table for sorties, but was in a healthy second place for mining sorties, with twenty-six carried out and a completion rate of 87%. The squadron had come second behind its old rivals XV Squadron in the monthly group bombing competition. One new record set by the group for May was the delivery of 783 mines.

Bomb aimer aboard BK688 HA-P's was Sergeant William "Bill" Howes, the father of three young children. His letters home were more concerned about the strain on his wife than the dangers over Germany.

June

June began with the departure of S/Ldr Ernest Sly DFC AFM to 1665 HCU on completion of his tour. On November 25th 1943 S/Ldr Sly would return to operations as C Flight commander with 514 Squadron. At the time the squadron was commanded by W/Cdr Arthur Samson DFC, a former flight commander with 218 Squadron. Ernest would be shot down and killed on his fourth operation, during an operation to Braunschweig (Brunswick) on January 14th 1944, the victim of Hptm Walter Barte of Stab III/NJG3.

June's operations got under way on the night of the 1/2nd with a small-scale mining effort carried out by F/L Fennell and F/Sgt Richards in the Nectarines I area. Two nights later F/L H Saunders led a relatively inexperienced bunch of sergeant pilots to the Cinnamon garden area off la Rochelle, where the only incident in an otherwise quiet operation was the explosion of Sgt Smith's first mine on impact. On June 6th the remnant of the Carney crew, including Sgt "Spud" Taylor, was posted to Stradishall, where they would pick up a new skipper and rear gunner. Their future lay with 90 Squadron at Tuddenham, with which they would complete a full tour. Spud would return for a second tour in late 1944 with 149 Squadron, and would survive the war.

The moon period restricted major operations until the 11th, when 783 aircraft set off for Düsseldorf, among them fourteen Stirlings from 218 Squadron. Cloud conditions in the target area were ideal, but stronger than forecast winds contributed to some wayward bombing. A number of well concentrated red TIs in the north and south of the town were bombed from between 12,000 and 15,000 feet to the accompaniment of a comparatively ineffective flak defence. Shortly after leaving the target Sgt Taylor was attacked from the starboard quarter by a Bf110, which opened fire with cannons and machine guns. Return fire from the Stirling resulted in the fighter breaking off its attack with its starboard engine ablaze, and it was claimed as destroyed. Damage in Düsseldorf was heavy, with over 130 acres of the city centre devastated, and a further one-thousand acres seriously damaged. On the debit side Bomber Command losses amounted to thirty-eight aircraft.

Another trip to the Cinnamon mining area involved four crews on the 13th, when twelve mines were delivered. As part of the continuing quest to find the optimum marking method, Cologne was marked by H2S on the 16/17th for a force of Lancasters to follow up with moderate success. The Stirling squadrons returned to action on the 19/20th, when they joined Halifaxes to attack the Schneider Armaments Factory and Breuil Works, located at le Creusot. Operation Lunar required bombing to take place close to a residential area, and it was made very clear that, "operational crews must find their aiming point and hit it. No other target will do!" Wing Commander Saville led twelve aircraft away from Downham Market for the five hour outward leg, and by the time they reached the target the Pathfinders were illuminating the area with hundreds of flares. This provided the opportunity for the first wave to bomb visually, and W/Cdr Saville bombed from 3,500 feet, well below the minimum altitude instructed by group, and, as a result, he was able to see his payload straddle the factory. Flight Lieutenants Saunders and Ryall reported their bombs falling into the factory complex, and accompanying the former as second pilot was W/Cdr Donald Lee, who had arrived on the 15th for operational experience before taking command of the recently formed 620 Squadron at Chedburgh.

Conditions in the target area steadily deteriorated as the attack progressed largely, because of the smoke from the vast number of flares. To add to the problems most of the crews had little or no experience of visually identifying and bombing a target. Returning crews were sceptical about the success of the raid, believing that the greater part of the bombing had fallen on the town itself. Post raid reconnaissance showed that the majority of bombs had indeed fallen into a residential area three to four miles from the target. There was, however, some damage to the factory. Daylight reconnaissance showed the steel and processing works to be destroyed, while the steel foundry was severely hit. A further thirty-one buildings were damaged some of them severely. The Breuil Steel Works was also hit, and four large machine shops were left damaged and burning, but eleven large buildings and around 130 business/apartment buildings were destroyed in the residential district. Squadron Leader Denys Maw AFC arrived on the squadron on the 19th from 1657 Conversion Unit to assume command of B Flight. Maw had been granted a commission in the RAF in 1934 and had served with various units in the UK before being posted to Canada as an instructor. Sergeant Martin's Stirling was attacked by a Bf110 near Rennes on the way home from a mining sortie in the Deodars area on the 20/21st. The crew fought off four determined attacks, and claimed the Bf110 as damaged, but BK737 HA-W sustained damage to flaps and undercarriage, and the port-inner engine had to be feathered.

A hectic round of four operations in the space of five nights began at Krefeld on the 21/22nd, when a force of seven hundred aircraft included fourteen 218 Squadron Stirlings. The Stirling contingent arrived over the target area unable to identify any ground details, so they focussed on a large mass of fires concentrated around three red TIs, and dropped their all-incendiary loads from between 10,000 and 14,000 feet onto a rather subdued Krefeld. By the end of the raid the target was a mass of flames with smoke rising up to 15,000 feet. Over 50% of the town centre was destroyed, more than one thousand people lost their lives, and five and a half thousand houses were destroyed, rendering twenty-five thousand apartments uninhabitable. Damage was reported as heavy in the industrial part of the city also, where eleven factories and a large gas works were severely damaged or destroyed. It was not a one-sided contest, however, and some of the 72,000 homeless residents of the city would have been cheered at the news that forty-four bombers would not be returning home either. 218 Squadron lost two aircraft, BK712 HA-D having the misfortune to encounter the Bf110 of Heinz–Wolfgang Schnaufer of Stab I/NJG1. His cannon shells started a conflagration in the fuselage, and soon thereafter both wings began to burn, sending the Stirling diving into the ground near Langdorp at 01.33hrs. There was no survivors from the eight man crew of Australian P/O William Shillinglaw. The following morning Lt Kuhnel, the German fighter control officer instrumental in the demise of BK712 HA-D, visited the crash scene. The entire crew was found in the smouldering wreckage, the rear turret of which was located some 1,500 yards away. The body of the rear gunner, twenty-year-old Sgt Arthur Hart, was still strapped in his seat.

Flying as second pilot aboard BK712 was Dane, F/O Helvard, who had arrived from 1657 CU on June 13th. Arne Rhoar Helvard was born on March 10th 1915 in Hobro, Denmark. He had joined the Danish Navy and trained as a pilot in the Naval Air Service, but he was demobilized following the German occupation. He found employment at the Kastrup Airport, where he monitored arrivals and departures of German aircraft. On 28 March 1942, Arne and Thomas Sneum escape to Sweden by crossing the Sound, which, at the time, was covered by ice. They were immediately arrested by the Swedish police and imprisoned for almost two months. By luck they manage to avoid being turned over to the German authorities in Denmark. They managed to get to England, where they were initially incarcerated in London's Brixton Prison. Arne was released in mid-June 1942, and accepted in the Royal Air Force.

BK722 HA-G was attacked and shot down south-east of Eindhoven by Oblt Eckart-Wilheim Von Bonin of 6/NJG1 at 01.50hrs. Australian P/O Donald Rich and two of his crew were killed, and the body of the rear gunner was found near Sterksel on the 25th next to his unopened parachute. On March

Flying Officer Arne Helvard seen in the uniform of the Danish Naval Air Service. This brave young Danes time on the squadron was tragically brief failing to return from his first operation.

19th 1945, a fourth member of the crew, Sgt John McDonald RCAF died of diphtheria while imprisoned in Fallingbostel. The crew was on its ninth operation together. Geoff Rothwell was Rich's flight commander, and recalled one amusing incident relating to him.

With the Christian names Donald Robert, and initials, therefore, D.R, the only possible nickname for the chap was Doc, and, with the exception of the station commander, he was known to everyone as Doc Rich. One evening after returning from a sortie from the nearby taverns in Downham, we felt the pangs of hunger. After all, we were young and healthy and war time rations were pretty basic and far from filling for more than a couple of hours. Fortunately my New Zealand navigator had just received a food parcel from home, containing, amongst other goodies, a tin of lamb stew. The very thought of the succulent contents of the tin made my mouth water. The officers mess was a requisitioned rectory and had a large garden in which a small church was situated, unused in the war, of course! Next door to the old rectory was a hunting house, which was used by the officer commanding the station. Whilst we were congregated in the kitchen of the rectory waiting for the lamb stew to heat up, someone, I think Doc, suggested the accompaniment of some fresh asparagus would go down very well. Accordingly a foraging party set off to procure the delicious vegetable from the large kitchen garden attached to

Australian Sergeant Donald Robert Rich
RAAF seen here a few months before his death.
He was along with his crew shot down by
Oblt Eckart-Wilheim Von Bonin of 6./NJG1
at 01.50 hours. Their Short Stirling BK722
HA-G crashed near Eindhoven. Note the
Horsa gliders in the back ground.

the commanding officer's quarters. It is often the way with those who have consumed a quantity of ale that they are quite unaware that their normal voices have increased in volume by a surprising number of decibels, even though those involved would deny they were conversing in anything more than mere whispers. It was in this rather euphoric condition and producing a substantial amount of noise that we set our plan in motion. Four of us, including Doc, set off to harvest the asparagus from the kitchen garden. All was going well, or so I thought, and the asparagus was in prime condition for eating. I could not wait to get back and polish off the lamb stew and our fresh veg. All of a sudden the shutters on the first floor windows were flung open, and the imposing figure of the Group Captain in his pyjamas gazed down on the scene below. We froze for a second before legging it for the brick wall, which separated the old rectory and the garden. In a thunderous voice the Group Captain assured us that he knew who we were, and he would deal with us the next day. The remainder of his ramblings was lost to our ears as were climbed over the wall and regrouped, and it was then we discovered one of our number was missing. We quickly discovered that the missing person was Doc Rich, our Aussie mate, who embraced the "press–on regardless" school of behaviour, and delayed his departure to pick up the asparagus we had dropped in our desperate flight. We shouted to him from behind the wall to get his skates on, while trying to hide our identity, and he finally emerge with an armful of asparagus, blowing like a bellows. Happy with our lot we set off back to the stew.

The following morning I received the expected summons from the station adjutant to present myself at the Group Captain's office immediately, and to bring with me those involved in the incident the previous evening. I told him as impolitely as possible, that there was no way I was bringing anyone with me, and the C.O could employ his own Gestapo agents, as I certainly had no intention of doing his dirty work for him. Outside the C.O's office I found the station medical officer, S/Ldr Bachelor, waiting. In a jocular manner I asked him if he had come to repair the damage my disagreement on the telephone had inflicted on the adjutant's heart and ears. The S.M.O was an extremely pleasant person who, at all times, behaved in a correct and professional way, but was devoid of a sense of humour. He did not take kindly to my facetiousness, but said he had been told that the group captain wished to see him. After a few moments the C.O's door opened, and the adjutant ushered both of us into the presence of the mighty one. I was addressed in the most scathing terms, and told that my crew and I were a disgrace to the Air Force, and if anything untoward occurred on the station, such as the ringing of the church bells, setting fire to Daily Routine orders on the mess board, or causing a nuisance in Downham Market, he, the station commander, did not have to wait to find out who was responsible, he knew it would be me and my crew.!! I cheekily objected strongly to the accusation that we had caused any nuisance in the local town. Unfortunately, I was unable to absolve my crew and myself from the other crimes he had mentioned. I told him it was just harmless high spirits being allowed to escape after the rigors of the battle over the Ruhr, in which the squadron was involved nightly. My explanation was not accepted, and the C.O then turned his attention to the Medical Officer, who had been standing beside me, quite nonplussed.

I too had been wondering what the reason was for Bachelor's presence. The reason soon become clear, when the C.O, referring to the night's escapade, said that he was surprised that a M.O had been party to such a disgraceful behaviour, and that he thought more highly of him as an officer. Bachelor was completely speechless. It then dawned on me what had happened. The station commander was more involved with administration than the operational side, which was left to the squadron commanders. He was quite unaware that there was an Australian F/O D R Rich, who was nicknamed Doc, and he assumed it was his SMO S/Ldr Bachelor, who was involved in the asparagus raid. The C.O referred to all his services medical officers as Doc. It was with a heavy heart that I had to dob in my friend Rich, and a relieved S/Ldr Bachelor walked a free man. I and "Doc" Rich were duly punished with extra Station Duty Officer and Orderly Officer duties, and Rich being the type of bloke he was, did not say a word.

While six crews went mining in the Nectarines area on the following night, the 22/23rd, eight others from the squadron joined in the night's major operation at Mülheim. 3 Group contributed 104 aircraft to the total force of 557, and they encountered an increased measure of heavy and light flak on the way to target, with searchlights and night fighters particularly active. Oboe Mosquitos had delivered a number of accurate red TIs for the crews to aim at, but the bombing run was accompanied by well-aimed flak. Returning crews reported the fires to be as concentrated and intense as those at Düsseldorf on the 11th. Yet another of 218 Squadron's Australian pilots failed to return, and this time it was twenty-year-old Sgt James Smith. He and his crew were the victims of an encounter with Hptm Heinrich Wittgenstein of Stab IV/NJG5, who at the time was on detachment to II/NJG1. BF572 HA-K crashed into the sea north-west of the Hoek Van Holland at 02.09hrs and only the rear gunner survived. It was the crew's eighth operation and the pilot's eleventh. This had been a rather unlucky crew, who had received more than their fair share of bad luck. Their original pilot was a Sgt F Robinson, who had failed to return from his second dickie operation with F/L Turner on May 4th. Then two other crew members had been killed on May 14th in the earlier-mentioned crash-landing incident involving BF480 HA-I and Sgt Carney.

The Elberfeld half of Wuppertal was selected as the target for the 24/25th, when 218 Squadron contributed fourteen Stirlings to another highly successful attack, in which thirteen factories and 137 other industrial concerns were destroyed or damaged. Residential districts were also hit severely, and it was estimated that 94% of Elberfeld had been reduced to ruins. Again it was not a one-sided affair, and thirty-four bombers failed to return, of which two were from 218 Squadron. EH892 HA-U contained the crew of S/Ldr Anthony Beck, and was attacked at 01.50hrs by Uffz Herbert Hubatsch on detachment to I/NJG1, before crashing into a forest near the village of Vettelschob near Kalenborn Germany. After the war F/O R.N Nuttall, the rear gunner and one of just three survivors reported that the Stirling had already been damaged by flak prior to the fighter attack, and that the bomb aimer had suffered a head injury, which required him to be taken to the rest position for medical attention. It was his opinion that the front escape hatch

The crew of Sergeant James Hoey RCAF at the rear exit door of Short Stirling BK613 of 1657 Conversion Unit. The crew would not survive their tour falling victim to Oblt Hans Autenrieth of 6./NJG4 on June 26th 1943.

was either damaged or jammed, because S/Ldr Beck's order to bail out was clearly heard by all the crew, and yet none of those in the front of the aircraft managed to escape. This was the twentieth operation undertaken by the flight commander, who was thirty-one years of age. BF501 HA-N was shot down at 01.59hrs by Oblt Hans Autenrieth of 6/NJG4, and crashed west of Diest with no survivors from the eight-man crew of Sgt James Hoey RCAF. This was the twenty-two-year-old Canadian's seventeenth operation and his crew's fifteenth. Squadron Leader Geoff Rothwell had S/Ldr Maw alongside him in BK803 HA-D, and they ran into searchlights over Düsseldorf while closing in on the target. For five minutes the Stirling was bracketed by flak, and Rothwell used every bit of his experience as a pilot to escape it. Finally, after surrendering three thousand feet of altitude, he managed to slip away, but it had been a close call, which would be self-evident in the cold light of the following morning, when twenty holes would be found in the wings and fuselage, some of them the size of dinner plates. A few days later Rothwell was told to report to W/Cdr Saville, which he duly did, uncertain as to the reason for the summons. Expecting the worst, Rothwell was delighted to hear from his commanding officer and friend that he was now to be screened after completing his second tour. Elberfeld had been his fifty-fifth and final operation.

There was to be no let-up for the hard-pressed men of Bomber Command as attacks on the Ruhr continued with a visit to the thus far elusive oil town of Gelsenkirchen on the 25/26th. Weather conditions deteriorated as the Dutch coast was reached, and ten-tenths cloud covered the track to the target. The seven 218 Squadron crews attempted to bomb on the skymarkers, some of which appeared above and behind them. Equipment malfunctions among the Oboe Mosquitos contributed to ineffective marking of the target, and Gelsenkirchen escaped again. Losses, however, remained high and the thirty aircraft missing from this operation represented 6.3% of those dispatched. 218 Squadron again posted missing two of its own, the first of these to go down was EH898 HA-G, which stumbled across Oblt Werner Husemann of Stab NJG1 while outbound at 13,000 feet. The encounter resulted in a raging fire in the cabin, which forced the New Zealander navigator, P/O Boulton RNZAF, to bail out from the front hatch seconds before the Stirling exploded over Zieuwent, in Holland, taking with it Sgt Eric Hughes and the rest of his crew. The second loss occurred soon afterwards and involved EF430 HA-W, which had S/Ldr Denys Maw AFC at the controls. An attack by Oblt August Geiger of 7/ NJG1 started a fire within the all-incendiary load, and it became immediately apparent to Maw that the Stirling was not going to recover. He quickly gave the order to bail out, and the entire crew responded and arrived safely on the ground. The Stirling crashed at Empe, five kilometres north-north-west of Zutphen, and the crew was taken into captivity. It was Maw's second operation as captain since his arrival from 1657 CU on 19th June. While a PoW Maw was involved in the Great Escape from Stalag Luft III at Sagan on March 24/25th 1944. His escape number was 81, and he was almost at the foot of the ladder and about to leave the tunnel when escapee 77 in front of him was discovered. He was fortunate in being able to get back to his hut without being discovered, and he spent the remainder of the war as a prisoner. Flight Lieutenant Ian Ryall was promoted and given command of B Flight.

A series of three operations against Cologne spanning the turn of the month began on the night of the 28/29th, and involved six hundred aircraft, including seventy-five Stirlings. Ten 218 Squadron aircraft took off, and one returned early. Those crews reaching the target were greeted by complete cloud cover, and only six of the Oboe Mosquitos were able to mark as planned. Despite this, the much bombed city suffered the most horrendous assault of the war thus far, with a level of devastation quite unprecedented at a German urban target. 6,400 buildings were reduced to rubble and forty-three of them were of an industrial nature. A total of fifteen thousand buildings were damaged to some extent, 4,377 people lost their lives while a further 230,000 were rendered homeless at least for a period. There were no losses this time for the squadron, for which this was the last operation of a month costing seven crews, including two captained by flight commanders. The squadron came third in the monthly group table with an impressive 107 sorties dispatched, but it topped the table with a remarkable 98.1% completion rate. The squadron's mining efforts throughout the month also received some welcome praise from Group HQ; *No.218 Squadron's contribution being outstanding in quality and quantity*". The squadron had finally pipped its old rival XV Squadron into first place with twenty-eight sorties completed with a 100% success rate. The announcement of the DSO to S/Ldr W Hiles DFC was gazetted in June, part of the citation read; "*He always presses home his attacks in the most determined manner flying at low level regardless of enemy opposition*".

July

July began with the posting in of the veteran S/Ldr Frederick "Bunny" Austin, who had been in temporary command of 620 Squadron at Chedburgh, and was now to take over A Flight. He had flown an impressive sixty-six operations since 1940, and had served in both the Middle and Far East. Flying Officer Frederick Fennell was posted to 11 OTU on the 2nd on completion of his tour, and he would be awarded a well-earned DFC in August. The second operation against Cologne went ahead on the night of the 3/4th, when the squadron dispatched thirteen Stirlings led by the recently promoted Canadian S/Ldr Howard Saunders, who was now C Flight commander. They contributed to another disastrous night for the city which suffered the destruction of 2,200 houses and twenty industrial premises. A mining operation was carried out on the night of the 4/5th, before the final raid of the series against Cologne took place at the hands of an all-Lancaster force on the 8/9th. Once the dust had settled and the fires had burned out, the city authorities were able to assess that eleven thousand buildings had been destroyed over the three raids, five and a half thousand people had been killed, and 350,000 others had lost their homes. While the main force was at Cologne on this last occasion, further mining operations were conducted, and again twenty-four hours later, and all 218 Squadron aircraft completed their sorties without loss.

On the 10th S/Ldr Geoff Rothwell DFC was given fourteen days well-earned leave, and Saville signed off his Form 414 Assessment of Ability as "Excellent", high praise indeed from someone of Saville's stature. Such are the fortunes of war that, sadly, these two friends would never meet again. Rothwell had been among the most charismatic officers in the squadron, and had passed on the fruits of his operational experience to those under his care. When not on duty he and his crew, the "Rothwell's Ruffians" were the life and soul of the mess and local pubs. The Ruhr offensive had now effectively run its course, and Harris could look back over the past five months with a genuine sense of achievement at the performance of his squadrons. Perhaps he would derive particular satisfaction from the part played by Oboe in the devastation of Germany's industrial heartland. Losses had been grievous, and "Happy Valley's" reputation well earned, but the factories had more than kept pace with the rate of attrition, and new crews continued to flood in to fill the gaps.

With confidence high in the ability of the Command to deliver a knockout blow at almost any target, Harris sought an opportunity to send shock waves through the Reich by destroying one of its major cities in a short, sharp series of raids until the job was done. Having been spared by the weather from hosting the first one thousand bomber raid in May 1942, Hamburg was the ideal choice to host *Operation Gomorrah*. As Germany's Second City, Hamburg's political status was undeniable, as was its position of prominence as a centre of industry, particularly with regard to U-Boat construction. Its location near a coastline was an obvious aid to navigation and it could be approached from the sea without the need to traverse large tracts of hostile territory. It was also close enough to the bomber stations to allow a force to approach and withdraw during the few hours of total darkness afforded by mid summer. Finally, beyond the range of Oboe, which had proved so crucial at the Ruhr, it boasted the wide River Elbe to provide a strong H2S signature for the navigators high above. In each year of the war to date, Bomber Command had visited Hamburg during the last week of July, and so it would be in this year.

In the meantime, Lancasters were sent to Turin on the 12/13th, while a mixed force, including over fifty Stirlings, raided Aachen on the following night, largely because of its importance as a communications centre. Nine of the ten participating 218 Squadron crews were captained by NCOs, and they contributed to a devastating attack. The target lay beneath seven-tenths low cloud, but excellent Oboe marking put red TIs over the aiming point. The crews dropped their all-incendiary loads from between 11,000 and 15,500 feet over a city in flames. Almost three thousand buildings were reduced to a state of ruin, and many large industrial premises and public buildings sustained heavy damage. Apart from a large Halifax operation against a motor factory in southern France on the 15/16th, minor operations then held sway until Harris was ready to launch his "Big Week".

Operation *Gomorrah* began on the night of the 24/25th, and was attended by the first operational use of Window, the aliminium-backed strips of paper, which, when released into the air stream, descended slowly in great clouds, swamping the enemy's night fighter control, searchlight and gun-laying radar with false returns. The device had actually been available for a year, but its employment had been vetoed, lest the enemy copy it. The enemy had, in fact, already developed its own version code-named Düppel, which had also been withheld for the same reason. A force of 791 aircraft stood ready for take-off in the late evening of the 24th, twenty of them Stirlings from 218 Squadron, led by W/Cdr Don Saville on his ninth operation with the squadron and his fifty-seventh in all. Take-offs began at 22.15hrs, and just one crew returned early, while the remainder encountered little contact with enemy night fighters during the outward flight. A number of aircraft were shot down during this stage of the operation, but each was many miles off course, and outside of the protection of the bomber stream.

The efficacy of Window was immediately apparent to the crews on their arrival in the Hamburg defence zone, where the usually efficient co-ordination between the searchlights and flak batteries was absent. The defence was accordingly random and sporadic, thus giving the Pathfinder crews a rare, almost unhindered run at the aiming point. The markers were a little scattered, but most fell close enough to the city centre to provide a strong reference point for the main force crews, and over the next fifty minutes, almost 2,300 tons of bombs were delivered. The bombing began near the aiming point, but a pronounced creep-back developed, which cut a swathe of destruction from the city centre along the line of approach, across the north-western districts, and out into open country, where a proportion was wasted.

The 218 Squadron crews dropped their high explosive and incendiary payloads from heights ranging from 14,500 to 16,500 feet. The attack was highly destructive and conducted for a loss of a very modest twelve aircraft, for which much of the credit belonged to Window. At a stroke the device had rendered the entire enemy defensive system impotent, but an advantage was rarely held for long before a counter-measure was found, and this would eventually see the balance swing back in Germany's favour. It was a sad night for 218 Squadron, whose crews waited in vain for the return of their popular commanding officer. BF567 HA-P had been shot down by Fw Hans Meissner of 6/NJG3 at 01.10hrs, and crashed one kilometre south-west of Einfeld in Germany. There was just one survivor from the eight man crew, the bomb-aimer, F/O Cedric Eyre, who was flying with his commanding officer for the first time. Having landed on a Luftwaffe station building and smashed his knee cap, he was destined to spend the rest of the war in captivity. As often happened when a commanding officer went missing, section leaders were lost also, and 218's gunnery and signals leaders, F/L Birbeck DFC and F/L Stanley DFC respectively had been on board. It was reported that Birbeck and F/Sgt Adam Howat, S/Ldr Rothwell's former rear gunner, had died in hospital.

S/Ldr Rothwell, himself an experienced and battle-hardened veteran, had this to say about Saville.

> "*The lack of bull and his friendliness were features that endeared Don to all who served under him. I remember how I admired the way he was able to run the squadron so effectively without relying on tight discipline as many others in his position did. It was the free and easy atmosphere which brought out the best in the crews.*"

Squadron leader Ian Ryall said of his former squadron commander:

> *I knew Don Saville well. I was his senior flight commander on 218 squadron. He was a good chap and I remember him as a good friend. He was a good CO, the sort of chap that made Bomber Command tick by giving the lead both on and off duty. He liked his pint and was always there with the boys when there was a night off. I had lots of commanding officers, but quite honestly, he was the most outstanding, without a shadow of doubt.*

The loss of Donald Saville was a blow not only to the squadron but to Bomber Command too, as men of his calibre were few and far between. He would almost certainly have risen through the ranks, and might easily have become a house-hold name, just like Gibson and Cheshire. Shortly after his death Saville was awarded the DSO, the citation for which is quoted in A.M.B.10952, dated July 1943.

> *This officer has completed a large number of sorties, and has displayed outstanding determination to achieve success. He is a fearless commander, who invariably chooses to participate in the more difficult sorties which have to be undertaken. Whatever the opposition, W/Cdr Saville endeavours to press home his attacks with accuracy and resolution. By his personal example and high qualities of leadership, this officer has contributed materially to the operational efficiency of the squadron.*

Within twenty-four hours a new squadron commander had arrived from 620 Squadron. Wing Commander William Gordon Oldbury had only completed his conversion to the Stirling on July 9th, before being posted to Chedburgh with the rank of acting squadron leader. His promotion to wing commander had followed quickly thereafter, and by the time of his departure from 620 Squadron he had undertaken just a single mining sortie. Wing Commander Oldbury had learned to fly in 1936 at the Airwork Reserve Training School in Perth. He had been granted a short service Commission in the RAF in March 1936, and in 1937 joined his first unit, 38 (B) Squadron. The prospect of taking over 218 Squadron would have been daunting for the relatively inexperienced Oldbury, who must have been aware of his predecessor's reputation.

Geoff Rothwell returned to a very subdued Downham Market on the 25th to learn that his friend, Don Saville, was missing. There was an air of disbelief that the loss of a pilot and commander of Saville's stature was even possible. Rothwell took the news very hard, and instinctively wanted to remain with the squadron, but orders dictated otherwise. Fortunately, he did not have time to dwell on the matter, as S/Ldr Ian Ryall flew him and his remaining crew to 11 OTU at Westcott later that afternoon.

It had been Harris's intention to follow up the success at Hamburg immediately, but lingering smoke over the city and less favourable weather conditions persuaded him otherwise. Instead he switched his force to Essen, to take advantage of the body blow dealt to the enemy's defences by Window. It was another massively concentrated assault on this city, and the Krupp complex sustained its heaviest damage of the war, while over 2,800 houses and apartment blocks were destroyed. It was on this night that 218 Squadron's longest serving Mk I Stirling N3721 ended its service after being hit by an incendiary bomb. The tail sustained damage and the port flap was set on fire, but the flight engineer brought the fire under control, and Sgt Goodman opted to continue to the target, where a successful attack was carried out. N3721 HA-J had been taken on charge on February 23rd 1942, and would be struck off charge on May 1st 1944 while serving with 1651 Conversion Unit. The Stirling had participated in sixty-two operations, all with 218 Squadron, amassing a grand total of 610 hours 55 minutes flying time.

After a night's rest, 787 aircraft took off to return to Hamburg, eighteen of them from 218 Squadron, of which one returned early. What followed the force's arrival over the city was both unprecedented and unforeseeable, and was the result of a lethal combination of circumstances. A period of unusually hot and dry weather had left tinderbox conditions in parts of the city, and the initial spark to ignite the situation came with the Pathfinder markers. These fell two miles to the east of the planned city centre aiming point, but with unaccustomed concentration into the densely populated working class residential districts of Hamm, Hammerbrook and Borgfeld. The main force crews followed up with uncharacteristic accuracy and scarcely any creep-back, and delivered most of their 2,300 tons of bombs into this relatively compact area. The individual fires joined together to form one giant conflagration, which sucked in oxygen from surrounding areas at hurricane velocity to feed its voracious appetite. It is believed that at least forty thousand people died on this one night alone, on top of the fifteen hundred killed three nights earlier, and the horrific events triggered the start of an exodus of an eventual 1.2 million inhabitants from the city. A number of 218 Squadron crews were involved in inconclusive brushes with enemy night fighters, but all returned safely.

The third Hamburg raid took place on the 29/30th, for which eighteen 218 Squadron aircraft contributed to a total force of 777 aircraft. One returned early with a number of malfunctions, but the remainder were among 707 aircraft to arrive over the city from the north with 2,300 tons of bombs to deliver. The markers again fell two miles east of the intended aiming point, and a little to the south of the firestorm area. A creep-back developed across the devastation of two nights earlier, before falling onto other residential districts beyond, where a new area of fire was created, although of lesser proportions. The city's fire service was already exhausted, while access to the freshly afflicted districts was denied by rubble-strewn and cratered streets, and there was little to be done, other than to allow the fires to burn themselves out. The defences were beginning to recover from the shock of Window, and as they did so, the bomber losses began to rise. Once again a number of 218 Squadron crews returned with reports of being harassed by enemy fighters, but two others were among the twenty-eight that failed to return at all. BF578 HA-A was damaged by flak before falling into the clutches of Uffz Walter Rohlfing of 9/NJG3, who shot the Stirling down at 01.26hrs south-west of Buxtehude. Sergeant Raymond Pickard and his rear gunner lost their lives, while the remainder of his crew became PoWs, after what was just their second operation. EE825 HA-S was brought down by flak and crashed near Billstedt in Hamburg's eastern suburbs. There were no survivors from the crew of Sgt James Clark, who was on his fifth operation, while his crew were on their fourth.

July ended with an attack by a fairly modest force of 264 heavies and nine Mosquitoes on Remscheid on the night of July 30th. 218 Squadron put up eighteen Stirlings as part of the second wave, and they benefitted from concentrated Pathfinder flares, which had been scattered in the early stages. Flight Sergeant Aaron's aircraft was hit by two incendiaries during the bombing run, which caused a fire to break out in the fuselage. The starboard-inner engine sprang a major fuel leak, but Aaron pressed on with his run while the flight engineer and wireless operator tackled the fire. Having dropped the all-incendiary load from 15,000 feet they were coned by searchlights and bombarded with flak, but managed to drag themselves clear and ultimately extinguish the fire. Such was the damage to BK761 HA-Q that it required major repair, and would not return to front line service until mid-August. Arthur Aaron would receive a DFM for his effort. BF519 HA-E fell victim to Fw Helmut Ternieden of E/NJG2 at 01.50hrs while homebound, and crashed near Dinteloord Holland. Sadly there were no survivors from the crew of F/Sgt Robert Taylor, who were on their sixteenth operation. The night ended with Sgt Knight making a heavy landing upon his return to Downham Market, and BF440 HA-T was declared a write-off. This highly successful raid, which brought down the final curtain on the Ruhr offensive, destroyed or damaged over three thousand houses, an estimated 80% of the town's built-up area, and killed eleven hundred people.

The Stirling brigade sustained the highest numerical and percentage losses for this operation, and it was a trend that would continue. It was becoming apparent to Harris that the Stirling was not suitable for further development, and the type's future was the subject of a meeting on July 30th. The squadron set a new record of 130 sorties during the month, second overall in the group to 75 (NZ) Squadron, which managed 135. It was the same in the mining category, with 75 Squadron in first place with eighteen sorties, followed closely by 218 Squadron on fifteen. Seven DFCs were announced in July to former squadron officers, sadly, four of whom had already been killed on operations. S/Ldr Harold Ashworth, P/O Richard Medus, P/O William McCarthy and, finally, P/O George McAuley, would never wear their awards. There were, however, three DFC recipients who were able to collect their awards, Canadian F/L Ross Campbell, bomb-aimer F/L Dennis Booth, who had just completed his first tour, most of which was undertaken as the squadron's bombing leader, and P/O Henry Morrison, wireless operator who had completed his tour of thirty-one operations.

August

Operation Gomorrah was concluded somewhat inauspiciously on the night of the 2/3rd, when violent electrical storms and icing conditions persuaded many crews to abandon their sorties and turn for home. Some bombed alternative targets, while others jettisoned their bombs over the sea, and little fresh damage was inflicted on Hamburg. 218 Squadron dispatched fifteen crews, of which one returned early, eight jettisoned their loads and four pressed on to bomb the target. 218 Squadron's contribution to the campaign was seventy-one sorties, fifty-seven of which were completed as briefed, with three aircraft failing to return.

The squadron was not called into action to support operations against Italian targets on the 7/8th or Mannheim on the 9/10. The squadron welcomed the arrival of F/L Arthur "Peter" Piper from 1651 CU on the 9th, an experienced gunner, who would fill the vacant post of gunnery leader. Before the squadron went into battle again, and in an effort to expand the number of squadrons within the group, it was decided that XV and 218 Squadrons would lose a flight each to help form two new Stirling units to be numbered 622 and 623 Squadrons. Both units would be to establishment WAR/BC/337, with sixteen aircraft and four in reserve. 623 Squadron was formed on August 10th from 218 Squadron, and would share the facilities at Downham Market. Seven crews, including one flight commander, and eight Stirlings formed the nucleus of the squadron, and the pilots were as follows; S/Ldr F Austin, F/O J Overton, F/O N Humphreys RNZAF, P/O G Jenkins, F/Sgt K Shaw RNZAF, F/Sgt J Wallace RAAF, and Sgt M Nesbitt. Ground crews painted out the red HA code and applied the new code of IC. Until the arrival of 623 Squadron's own commanding officer, it fell under the control of W/Cdr Oldbury, and the two units would be linked over the

Seen here at Bone airfield, Arthur Aarons Short Stirling EF452 HA-O. Note the ground crews pointing at the bullet holes in the cockpit canopy.

next few months. As the seven transferred crews were operationally experienced, 623 Squadron was able to operate alongside 218 on the very day of its formation, when the target was the distant southern German city of Nuremburg.

Wing Commander Oldbury led fourteen crews from 218 Squadron and four from 623 Squadron, but three of the 218 Squadron contingent returned early suffering from engine malfunctions. The Stirlings were scheduled to attack in the third wave, at which point they found the target to be largely obscured by cloud, and inadequately illuminated and marked. While running in to the aiming point EE885 HA-W was hit by incendiaries from above, and the wing tanks immediately caught fire. The Stirling crashed near Offenhausen east of the target, and all but the pilot survived to become PoWs. The body of the twenty-four-year-old captain, F/L Stuart Fillmore RCAF, was found with his partially opened chute on the following day. One of the survivors was the second pilot, Sgt Moyneux, who was on his first operation, having arrived from 1651 Conversion Unit on August 5th.

An all-3 Group operation to Turin was mounted on the 12th, for which 218 Squadron provided thirteen Stirlings and 623 Squadron four in an overall force of 112 aircraft. The Downham Market contingent was still intact as it made its way across France, where a number of combats took place with enemy night fighters, one of which was claimed as destroyed. On approaching the target with the bomb doors open, EF452 was hit by fire from another Stirling 250 yards ahead.

The navigator, Sgt Cornelius Brennan RCAF, was killed instantly by a bullet through the heart and the pilot, F/Sgt Arthur Aaron, was hit in the face, chest and arm. His jaw was shattered and exposed and he was unable to use his right arm which had been almost severed below the elbow. Other crew members transferred him to the rest position away from the freezing air blasting through the shattered windscreen. The flight engineer, F/Sgt Larden, took over the controls of the Stirling, which now had only three good engines. The bomb load was jettisoned, and with the crew unsure of their exact location, it was decided to attempt to reach the North African coast. The Stirling steadily lost height, but it held together, and was within forty miles of the Italian coast by the time a QIM was picked up.

A course was set for Bone aerodrome in Algeria, and, after what seemed an eternity, the crew could make out the pyramids in the early morning light, and finally Bone was in their sights. For the next forty-five minutes they circled the aerodrome, until Aaron, who was unable to speak, insisted on trying to take control. Although in a desperate condition, he wanted to carry out the landing, and made a number of unsuccessful approaches. Conscious of the lack of fuel, Larden seized the controls and pointed the aircraft towards Bone's seven hundred foot-long runway. He pulled off a belly-landing at 06.15hrs on rough ground north of the runway, and they came to rest fifty yards from a lightly raised flood bank. Aaron was taken away by ambulance, and sadly succumbed to his wounds nine hours later. Had he rested and not insisted on taking control himself, he may well have survived. The landing was a remarkable example of airmanship by Larden, and it was discovered only afterwards that two bombs had hung up and were still in the bomb bay. For his devotion to duty Aaron became the second and last Stirling crewman to be awarded the Victoria Cross. He had arrived at the squadron from 1651 CU on April 17th 1943, and by the time of his death had flown three operations as second pilot and eighteen as captain, including all four raids on Hamburg. MZ263 HA-Y was also forced to head for the safety of Bone, after suffering a starboard-outer engine failure over the Alps while at 15,000 feet. The propeller eventually flew off, and F/O McAllister ordered the all-incendiary load and ammunition and guns to be jettisoned to reduce weight. The journey to Bone was carried out at 500 feet, and a safe landing was made at 05.15hrs in another fine display of airmanship.

After a four day break a 3 Group force returned to Turin with a Pathfinder element to conclude the campaign against these distant Italian targets. In a force of 140 aircraft nine were from 218 squadron and five from 623 Squadron, and by the time they reached Southern France they were bathed in bright moonlight. It was while approaching Amberieu at around 00.43hrs that EH884 HA-X was attacked and shot down by Oblt Hans Kulow of 9/NJG4. A raging fire developed in the bomb bay area, which the flight engineer, Sgt Deans, fought with the extinguishers until realizing it was a lost cause. He instructed the pilot to jettison the all-incendiary load, by which time the fire had completely engulfed the engineer's cabin and was working its way back towards the mid upper turret. Twenty-three-year-old W/O Stanley Chudzik RCAF ordered the crew to bail-out, but only the rear gunner and the navigator managed to do so safely before the Stirling crashed. The pilot and the mid-upper gunner were still on board, and the remainder had jumped too late for their chutes to save them. The navigator managed to evade capture and returned to the UK in January 1944.

The rear gunner, Sgt McKinnon RCAF, recalls the events:

> *"We were flying at 6,000ft crossing enemy coast, the weather was clear with a full moon. There were numerous aircraft in the air around us which were identified as four engine bombers. Nothing out of the ordinary happened until attacked by an enemy aircraft, I did not see anything until the guns opened up. I was hit in the left eye, left leg and lost all senses. I then tried to contact the pilot over the inter-com but failed to do so. The aircraft was on fire at this time and it was impossible to reach any of the crew. I then put on my chute and went out through the turret. On the way down I saw what appeared to be our aircraft crash. I landed in a ploughed field and was later picked up by the Germans"*

This had been Stanley Chudzik's eleventh operation and his crews tenth. The remaining crews pressed on and arrived over Turin to find it accurately marked with green marker flares. The Downham Market crews bombed from between 4,000 and 5,000 feet in hazy conditions, S/Ldr Saunders making six runs across the target before dropping his all-incendiary load on a well-grouped cluster of green TIs. The city's defences had slightly increased since the previous attack, but were generally inaccurate.

Since the start of hostilities, intelligence had been filtering through concerning German research into rocket weapons. Through the interception and decoding of signals traffic, the centre for such activity was found to be at Peenemünde, an isolated location on the island of Usedom on the Baltic coast. Regular reconnaissance flights helped to build up a picture of the activity there, and through listening in on signals, the brilliant scientist, Dr R V Jones, was able to monitor the V-1 trials being conducted over the Baltic, and gather much useful information on the weapon's range and accuracy. Churchill's chief scientific adviser, Professor Lindemann, or Lord Cherwell as he became, steadfastly refused to give credence to rockets as weapons, and even when confronted by a photograph of a V-2 on a trailer at Peenemünde, taken by a PRU Mosquito as recently as June, he stubbornly remained unmoved. It required the urgings of Dr Jones and Duncan Sandys to persuade Churchill of the need to act, and it was finally agreed that an operation should be mounted at the first available opportunity. This arose on the night of the 17/18th of August, for which a detailed plan was meticulously prepared.

The Peenemünde research and development establishment consisted of three main areas, the housing complex, where the scientists and workers lived, the assembly buildings, and the experimental site. The operation was, therefore, to take place in three waves, each wave assigned to a specific aiming point, beginning with the housing estate, and the Pathfinders were charged with the responsibility of shifting the point of aim accordingly. 3 and 4 Groups were to go for the housing estate, 1 Group was assigned to the assembly sheds, and 5 and 6 Groups were to bring up the rear at the experimental site. The entire operation would be controlled by VHF by a Master of Ceremonies, or Master Bomber, in the manner of Gibson at the Dams, and the officer selected was G/C John Searby of 83 Squadron. He would be required to remain in the target area throughout the raid, within range of the defences, directing the marking and bombing, and exhorting the crews to press home their attacks.

Many of the Stirling contingent involved in the previous night's operation to Turin had arrived home late, and some were dispersed on airfields to which they had been diverted due to the wide spread fog over East Anglia. This meant that they could not be made ready in time to participate in this most important of operations, and in the event, only sixty-nine of the group's Stirlings and Lancasters were available, of which just five were from Downham Market. Sadly, the initial marking of the housing estate was inaccurate, and the first markers fell onto the forced workers camp at Trassenheide, more than a mile beyond the planned aiming point. This inevitably attracted a proportion of the 3 and 4 Group bombs, and heavy casualties were inflicted upon the friendly foreign nationals trapped inside their wooden barracks. Wing Commander Oldbury had been forced to return early with a malfunctioning intercom, but the four remaining crews bombed on schedule, S/Ldr Ryall commenting on a red glow beneath the clouds as he departed the target area. Once rectified, this phase of the operation proceeded according to plan, and a number of important members of the establishment's technical staff were killed.

1 Group attacked the V-2 construction sheds, and despite a crosswind, managed to inflict substantial damage. It was while 5 and 6 Groups were in the target area that the night fighters belatedly arrived on the scene, and they proceeded to take a heavy toll both in the skies above Peenemünde and on the route home towards Denmark. Twenty-nine of the forty missing aircraft were from this final wave, but the losses were deemed acceptable in the light of the importance of the operation, and the fact that it took place in bright moonlight. Flight Lieutenant Kingsbury and F/Sgt Adams reported the glow of large fires still visible from between fifty and seventy miles on the return trip. The operation was sufficiently successful to set back the development program of the V-2 by a number of weeks, and the testing was moved east into Poland, out of reach of Harris's bomber force, while production was transferred to hastily constructed underground facilities.

On the following day W/Cdr Edwin "Jack" Little DFC arrived from 1657 CU to assume command of 623 Squadron. Jack Little had joined the RAF in 1936, and was an experienced pilot, who had served with 101 Squadron pre-war and completed a tour with 40 Squadron in 1941, when he had been awarded the DFC. On completion of his first tour he was screened and posted to 22 OTU as an instructor, eventually becoming chief flying instructor with 11 OTU in 1942. By January 1943 he had been three times Mentioned in Dispatches. Unlike most of his contemporaries Little was a devout Christian, who regularly visited the local church and on many occasions took the service.

Harris had long believed that Berlin, as the seat and symbol of Nazi power, held the ultimate key to victory. He maintained the belief that bombing alone could win the war, and if this could be achieved, it would remove the need for the kind of protracted and bloody land campaigns that he had personally witnessed during the Great War. At the time it was a perfectly reasonable theory, and Harris was the first commander in a position to put it to the test. On the night of the 23/24th Harris embarked on the first stages of what would be the longest and most bitterly fought campaign of the war. Nothing before or after came closer to breaking the Command, and it would bring about the end as a front line bomber for the Stirling.

127 Stirlings and thirteen Lancasters represented 3 Group's contribution to the first attack of the campaign against the "Big City". Thirteen 218 Squadron aircraft took part with a further five from 623 Squadron. Among the 218 Squadron contingent was S/Ldr Waldo Hiles DSO DFC, who it will be recalled, had completed his tour back in March. He was currently occupying a post at 3 Group HQ at Exning Hall, and why he was back at Downham Market with his name on the battle order is a mystery. He collected a number of spare 218 squadron airman and formed a scratch crew, who, apart from his old rear gunner, F/Sgt De Silva DFM, who had not flown since 19th February when injured by flak had only one or two operations under their belt. The eighteen aircraft departed Downham Market in light showers and headed towards the east coast. Two of the 218 contingent were forced to return, but the remainder pressed on to encounter increasing fighter activity during the outward flight. The Stirlings were part of the third wave.

Problems with interpreting the H2S returns meant that the Pathfinders were unable to locate and mark Berlin's centre, and marked the southern outskirts instead. The main force crews, many of which approached from the south-west instead of a more southerly direction, deposited many bomb loads onto outlying communities and open country. This would become a feature of the entire campaign, but at least on this night considerable damage was inflicted on the southern districts, where 2,600 buildings were destroyed or seriously damaged, and this represented the best result yet at the "Big City". EE937 HA-S was attacked by a twin engine fighter thirty miles south-east of Berlin, and sustained numerous hits. A fuel tank was holed and the mid-upper turret was knocked out, but an unidentified Stirling caught up with it and passed alongside firing a continuous burst of machine gun fire at the enemy fighter. A grateful F/Sgt Knight and crew ultimately arrived home none the worse for their experience.

Three crews failed to return to Downham Market from this operation, among them that of S/Ldr "Wally" Hiles DSO DFC, whose EH925 IC-C was brought down by a fighter three kilometres south of the target, and there were no survivors. A number of books ascribe this crew to the strength of 623 Squadron. The confusion arises out of the fact that the aircraft was indeed on the strength of 623, but the crew members themselves, other than Waldo Hiles himself, were from 218 Squadron. The second loss involved EH986 HA-X, which also had a fatal encounter with a night fighter, and crashed near Berlin's Tempelhof airfield, with just two survivors from the crew of F/Sgt Walter Williams. Both sustained injuries, one in the form of severe burns and the other a broken ankle. BF522 HA-N was on its way home over the North Sea, when it crossed swords with a night fighter. Flight Sergeant William Martin RCAF and crew sent an S.O.S at around 03.34hrs, stating that they were preparing to ditch and they came down some 160 miles north-west of Heligoland.

While the RAF bombers were on their way home from Berlin, elements of the Luftwaffe were already over East Anglia, and a Me410 of V/KG2 dropped one heavy bomb on Downham Market at 03.10hrs, causing a crater on a runway, and also scattered anti-personnel bombs over the aerodrome. No injuries were reported, but upon their return the aircraft were diverted to Waterbeach and Stradishall. On the morning of the 24th three Downham Market dispersals lay empty, as did fifty-three others on bomber fields from County Durham to Cambridgeshire. This was a new record loss for the Command, and a tragedy for the Stirling brigade, which had lost sixteen aircraft, an unsustainable 12.9% of those dispatched.

Later in the day an aircraft each from 149 and 199 Squadrons chanced upon F/Sgt Martin's dinghy during an air-sea search. It appeared that five survivors were on board, and two Hudsons of 279 Squadron were sent from Bircham Newton to patrol the search area. Some two hours later the dinghy and the circling Stirlings were sighted, and a special lifeboat was dropped at 16.00hrs, into which the survivors clambered. Both Stirlings then turned for home, but two Bf110s arrived on the scene at 16.30hrs, and opened fire on the lifeboat. The two Hudsons closed in to provide protection, but it was not long before one was shot down into the sea. Seven more Bf110s approached the area, but did not join in the attack, and the second Hudson ultimately managed to evade the enemy and land back at base at 17.54hrs. Ofw Brannicke and Ofw Statzinger of ErpKdo 25 reported a combat with a Lockheed and a Beaufighter. Sadly, the crew of HA-N, having survived the ditching, were all lost under these tragic circumstances. Twenty-four-year old William Martin was on his fifteenth operation, and his crew had completed fourteen.

A series of small scale mining operations were mounted over the next few days, until the next major operation was launched on the 27/28th, when Nuremburg was the target. 112 Stirlings and ten Lancasters were due to represent 3 Group, but this number was reduced by the failure to take off of eight aircraft and the early return of nine more. It was to prove a bad night for Downham Market, which waved off eight aircraft of 218 Squadron and five from 623. EE944 HA-O was involved in a take-off incident, which was witnessed by Eric Basford, a corporal engine fitter:

I was on the ground crew of O-Oboe in B Flight. EE944 was our new O-Oboe, which replaced the one so tragically lost on August 12th with F/Sgt Arthur Aaron. It was detailed for a bombing attack on Nuremburg. Only twelve days had elapsed since we took charge of EE944, but they had been busy days. During that time it had completed two mining operations and one raid on Berlin. We had also changed two engines, port-outer and starboard-inner because we had found metal in the oil filters. On this evening I happened to be on "seeing off" duty and was watching the line of fully loaded Stirling's taxiing along the perimeter track towards the long east/west runway. As I watched, Sgt Bennett positioned O-Oboe on the end of the runway and began his take off run. The Stirling gathered speed, the tail began to lift, and then there was an orange flash followed by a loud bang. The port wing dipped, the aircraft slewed to port and hurtled across the grass towards the maintenance hangar. I dashed under the other aircraft now stationary on the perimeter track, past the end of the runway across the grass to where O-Oboe had come to rest. The port wing was only three feet above the grass and there was a huge pile of earth in front of the port leg, which had gouged a track through the soft soil. Just as I got there a small pickup was leaving, but the crew were all uninjured, and were just standing around looking a bit shaken, until rapidly recovering their composure. Already the rest of the squadron had begun to take-off. I soon heard that whilst swinging to turn into the end of the runway, Sgt Bennett had run over one of the FIDO pipes which were being laid at Downham throughout the summer. The flight engineer had jumped out and examined the wheel, saw no damage and it was decided to press on with the take-off. However, as soon as the tail wheel lifted and put the full load on the main wheels, the port wheel burst with disastrous results. This was the end of EF944's life as O-Oboe because major repair work was necessary on the undercarriage. Later, after repair at the MU, it returned to the squadron, eventually being written off completely after a crash at Tempsford in March 1944.

The weather was clear as the remaining bombers crossed into Germany, and this brought the night fighters out in numbers. Combats took place all the way in to the target, where the attack was scattered, and most of the bombing fell beyond the city limits or across its south-eastern districts. The disappointment was compounded by the loss of thirty-three aircraft, eleven of each type, and this represented a 10.5% loss rate among the Stirling brigade. 623 Squadron posted missing its first crew on this night, the experienced Welshman P/O G Jenkins. EF448 HA-P also failed to return, having crashed in a railway culvert at Munstermaifeld in Germany, with only the wireless operator and rear gunner surviving. Flight Sergeant Noel Davis RAAF and crew had been on only their second operation together.

Bomber Command was due another success, and this came on the night of August 30/31st with a two-phase attack on the twin towns of Mönchengladbach and Rheydt. The operation started badly, when F/O J Wiseman of 623 Squadron swung on take-off and severely damaged his Stirling, but the crew walked away unhurt. At the target the main force crews exploited accurate marking to destroy over 2,300 buildings in the two locations, but another twenty-five aircraft failed to return home. 218 Squadron posted missing the crews of F/Sgt William Clague in BK650 HA-T and Sgt Stanley Bennett in EF903 HA-Q. The former was shot down by Lt Wilheim Hensler of 4/NJG1 at 03.30hrs, and fell near Wickrath, four miles south-south-west of the target area. There were no survivors from this inexperienced crew, which was on only its third operation. BK650 was engaged by Hptm Kurt Fladrich of 6/NJG4 while on the way home over Holland, and with the starboard wing on fire, the twenty-six-year-old pilot ordered the crew to bail-out. The rear gunner, navigator and wireless operator all successfully complied, but it transpired that the pilot, F/Sgt Clague, had taken off without his parachute, and there was no spare aboard the aircraft. The bomb-aimer, Sgt Lorne, pleaded with the pilot to jump attached to him, but he refused, and with the Stirling now starting to nose over, he had no other option than to leave the brave young pilot to his fate. Almost immediately the aircraft blew up, crashing into the farm "De Voorhoeve" near Dorplein. Sergeant Lorne was showered with burning wreckage as he parachuted down, and such was the force of the explosion that a piece of the Stirling struck and fractured his foot and shredded his flying boot. The wireless operator was found dead on the ground with severe head injuries, believed to have been caused by the explosion. It had been the crew's eighth operation together. Sergeant Fredrickson RCAF, the rear gunner, describes the events leading to the Stirling's demise.

> *"Everything was fine all the way to the target. We just about 20 minutes of the target on the way back when a Stirling crossed our path about 800 yards astern and below. Just at the same time the M/U called myself on the intercom asking if I had seen a plane below us. I told him what I had seen and was re-checking when there was a flash of fire from 11.30 O'clock. I fired a return burst instructing the pilot to dive to port. At the same time the servo feed began to flood the turret. Flames had started to come down the starboard side. A second burst of fire from 11 O'clock was observed, the M/U called for the pilot to dive to starboard, almost immediately the pilot gave the order to bale out, the engineer reported the fire could not be put out. I called up the pilot to see if any help was needed up front, I was told to get out quickly, I then heard the bomb aimer asking the pilot if he wanted help. The pilot replied to get out, I went out through the side hatch".*

Group Captain E Barnes AFC was succeeded as station commander by G/C H Downs AFC on the 29th, pending an overseas posting. The respected and equally well liked Barnes would become the A-O-C, No.1 (Training) Group RAAF. The last operation of the month was a GOODWOOD effort against Berlin, 3 Group supplying 101 Stirlings and five Lancasters, of which an alarming twenty-five returned early for a variety of reasons. Three of these were from Downham Market, and the two belonging to 218 Squadron returned with feathered engines. The raid was rendered ineffective, after problems with H2S led to the markers falling well to the south of the city centre, and the creep-back extended thirty miles along the line of approach. A new tactic was employed by the Luftwaffe in the form of bright flares, which were dropped above the bombers over the target area to illuminate them. The Command paid the heavy price of forty-seven aircraft for the failure, and seventeen of the missing were Stirlings, a massive 16% of those despatched. Remarkably, 218 Squadron came through unscathed, and only F/L Kingsbury reported an engagement with single and twin engine enemy night fighters, which ended inconclusively. There was one loss across the tarmac. 623 Squadron's commanding officer, W/Cdr Edward John Little DFC and crew, were brought down near Werdig in Germany, and there were no survivors.

Seven 218 Squadron crews had been lost on operations during the month from a modest 107 sorties. The number of sorties was well down on previous months after the posting of seven crews, equivalent to a complete flight, to form 623 Squadron. The squadron had delivered just over 149 tons of bombs during the month. On the plus side an unprecedented five DFMs were awarded during the month, two of them immediate, and two DFCs were also awarded.

September

The current phase of the Berlin offensive was concluded by an all Lancaster force on the 3/4th, in an attack which again largely undershot the target. However, some of the bombing hit the Siemensstadt district, where a number of important war industry factories suffered a serious loss of production. 623 Squadron welcomed Canadian W/Cdr Wynne-Powell on the 9th on posting from his flight commander duties with 199 Squadron. The creep-back that attended most heavy raids was incorporated into the plan of attack at Mannheim and Ludwigshafen on the 5/6th, when the aiming point was in the eastern half of Mannheim, with an approach from the west. Nine 218 Squadron Stirlings took off, but three of them were forced to return early. The city appeared to be a ringed by searchlights, which were working closely with night fighters. Flight Lieutenant Cochrane's EE888 HA-K was struck by a 4lb incendiary in the starboard inner-engine while on the bomb run, and this was an ever-present danger for the lower flying Stirlings. BF472 HA-D had its port-outer propeller almost shot off by flak also while closing in on the aiming point, and then the all-incendiary load hung-up, forcing Sgt Spencer RCAF to order it to be jettisoned over the target. Precisely according to plan the bombing spread back over the western half of Mannheim, before spilling across the Rhine into Ludwigshafen, and thousands of buildings were either destroyed or seriously damaged in both cities. The Stirling losses on this raid reached 7%, and the alarm bells continued to ring at Bomber Command.

The Stirling brigade took part in what became a controversial operation on the 8/9th. *Operation Starkey* had been devised to mislead the enemy into believing that an invasion was imminent, and it involved all of the services, including the RAF. Harris was not amused at being ordered to participate in what he described as play-acting, and when the time came, he gave it less than his full commitment. Starkey began in mid August with highly visible troop movements, and the assembly of glider fleets and landing craft, which any self-respecting enemy reconnaissance crew could not fail to notice. Attacks on heavy gun emplacements on the French coast were to have begun in the final week of August, but poor weather conditions continued into September and it was not until the night of the 8/9th that operations could take place. By this time the Air Ministry had revised its demands on Harris, and in the interests of keeping civilian casualties at an acceptable level, reduced the commitment of heavy bombers. The targets for this night were two batteries, code-named Religion and Andante, situated respectively north and south of the small resort town of la Portel near Boulogne. Phase I, against the northern site, involved Oboe Mosquitos and Pathfinder Halifaxes marking for fifty-seven 3 Group Stirlings and sixty-one Wellingtons from 91 and 93 Training Groups.

218 Squadron contributed six crews, including W/Cdr Oldbury, who was accompanied by Downham Market's station commander, G/C Downs. All six crews carried out their assigned tasks and returned safely, having dropping thirty-six one thousand pounders and a similar number of 500 pounders. The phase II force was of similar size and make-up, except for a number of 6 Group Wellingtons, and 92 Group representing the Training Groups. Three 218 Squadron and five 623 Squadron Stirlings took part in the attack on the Andante site, and all returned. The operation was a failure, neither battery was damaged, and la Portel suffered grievously with around five hundred of its inhabitants losing their lives.

There were no further operations for the main force crews until the night of the 15/16th, when 369 crews drawn from 3, 4, 6 and 8 Groups were briefed for an attack on the Dunlop Rubber factory at Montlucon in central France. The operation was controlled by W/Cdr "Dixie" Dean of 35 Squadron acting as Master Bomber, and he presided over an accurate attack, which left every building in the factory complex damaged. All fourteen 218 Squadron Stirlings returned safely, having carried out their bomb runs from as low as 3,800 feet. Flight Lieutenant Kingsbury reported the target to be a *"Mass of flames"*, while F/L Cochrane commented on *"Scattered fires over whole of target area, also town and marshalling yards"*. On the following night a similar force tried to repeat the success at the important railway yards at Modane, on the main route into Italy. The squadron dispatched fourteen Stirlings led by W/Cdr Oldbury, and for the second night running there were no early returns, and, more importantly, there were no 218 Squadron losses. Downham Market's contribution was over 70,000lb of bombs, but the location of the target in a steep valley thwarted the crews' best endeavours, and the operation failed. There followed a four day respite from operations for both Downham Market squadrons, during which period, on the 20th, Canadian S/Ldr Garfield Prior DFC arrived from 1657 CU to take over the vacant A Flight commander's role.

A series of four major operations against Hanover over a four week period began on the 22nd at the hands of over seven hundred aircraft. 218 Squadron dispatched fifteen Stirlings led by S/Ldr Ryall, and they were part of an element of 137 Stirlings scheduled to attack during the second wave. Flak in the almost cloud-free target area was moderate at most, but fighter activity was reported as large-scale. Stronger than forecast winds pushed the marking and bombing onto the south-eastern outskirts, and the city escaped major damage. Two 218 Squadron Stirlings were among the twenty six missing aircraft. EF139 HA-B was believed to have been attacked and shot down by Lt Ernest-Erich Hirschfeld of 5./JG300 at around 23.30hrs crashing 3 miles south of Pohle killing twenty-one-year-old Canadian Sgt Norman Spencer and four of his crew. The two survivors were blown out of the aircraft, flight engineer, Sgt Morement, being found in a wounded condition the next day, having come down in a cherry tree near Meinsen. Sergeant Morement states that the aircraft was bombed from above and exploded mid-air, the resulting explosion blew him out of the doomed Stirling. He was at the time wearing his parachute, which ultimately saved his life. Sergeant Baker, the rear gunner, was found by school children, he was sitting on the remains of

The size of the Stirling is shown to good effect in this view of Squadron Leader Howard Saunders DFC aircraft taken at Downham Market October 1943.

his parachute in a ditch along the Hulsede – Meinsen road suffering from shock. The crew, who had arrived from 1651 CU on August 19th, had completed eight operations before their loss.

The second loss involved BK700 HA-L, which was hit by flak soon after leaving the target area, and there were no survivors from the crew of Canadian, Pilot Officer Carman Colquhoun, who were on their fourteenth operation, having arrived from 1651 CU on June 13th. EJ105 was hit flak as it left the target area, and two of the crew bailed out. The body of a third member of the crew, the rear gunner, F/Sgt R Gehrig RAAF, was found by the Germans on the following day without his parachute. A number of pieces of wreckage were recovered by Luftwaffe troops, who concluded that they were from EJ105. The largest item found was the rear turret, and it was suggested that the damaged Stirling may have hit the ground near Bernstorff, while flying low on the return journey. What is clear is that F/Sgt Ronald Duffy and his remaining crew somehow managed to coax the Stirling across Germany and France and back to East Anglia, where tragically, it crashed near Hall Farm, Barrow, five miles from Bury St Edmunds, killing all on board.

Mannheim was raided for the second time during the month on the 23/24th, for which 218 Squadron put up twelve Stirlings. 106 other 3 Group aircraft contributed to the force of over six hundred, but once again 218 Squadron was beset by early returns, which on this occasion amounted to four. The Stirlings were part of the second wave, and returning crews reported a number of well placed green TIs, concentrated fires and masses of smoke, and there was general enthusiasm about the outcome of the attack. Not at debriefing was the crew of EJ104 HA-G, which exploded at 23.00hrs over Kirchheimbolanden, Germany after a possible encountering Lt Heinz Wolfgang Schnaufer of 12/NJG1 . Only the wireless operator, Sgt R Smith, survived from the crew of F/O Adrian Brace, who were on their tenth operation. The raid was a success with over nine hundred houses destroyed, along with twenty industrial premises, including the important I G Farben chemicals factory located in the northern part of Ludwigshafen.

A force heading for round two at Hanover on the 27th included 116 Stirlings, of which ten returned early. The remainder found the city clear of cloud, and the defences much improved since the previous raid, with the searchlights working in conjunction with fighters. A number of fighter flares had been dropped north and north-east of the target area, and this was where most of the encounters took place. Wrongly forecast winds misled the Pathfinders, who dropped their TIs up to five miles north of the intended aiming point. The following main force crews bombed these, and consequently the majority of the effort landed in open country. The squadron lost two aircraft within minutes of each other, and both contained experienced crews. EE937 HA-A is believed to have been shot down by Uffw Ernest Reitmeyer of 3/NJG5. It crashed south of the target area at 23.25hrs, and there were no survivors from the crew of P/O William Knight, who were on their nineteenth operation. Short & Harland built BF472 HA–D was attacked by Oblt Robert Plewa of 2/JG300, and witnesses then observed the Stirling to be hit by local flak while at medium altitude, before falling into a steep dive and crashing near Bothfeld at 23.30hrs with the loss of F/L Balding, RAAF and his crew. Twenty-seven year old Keith Balding had arrived at the squadron on April 16th, and was on his twentieth operation. In October 1943 the London Gazette announced that both pilots had been awarded the DFC. The loss of two such experienced crews was particularly hard on those who were still in the early stages of their tours. It had been another testing month for the Stirling squadrons. 218 Squadron had launched ninety-four sorties for the loss of seven aircraft and six crews. The award of a bar to S/Ldr Geoff Rothwell's DFC was announced at the end of the month, the citation reads:

> *"Throughout many attacks on enemy targets, Squadron Leader Rothwell has consistently displayed courage and determination of a very high order which has had an influence on the results obtained by the whole of the squadron. He is now on his third tour of operational duty, which has consisted mainly of attacks on major targets in Germany".*

The award of the Conspicuous Gallantry Medal to Canadian Alan Larden, bomb aimer to F/Sgt Arthur Aaron, was also announced.

October

October began in hectic fashion for the Lancaster squadrons, which were called on to provide crews for six operations in the first eight nights. Hagen and Munich opened the month's account, before the Halifaxes and Stirlings were called into action at Kassel on the 3/4th. This was the first truly major assault on the city, for which 218 Squadron sent nine crews led by S/Ldr Prior DFC. The Downham Market contingent joined ninety-eight other Stirlings for this "Derby" operation. A spoof raid on Hanover by ten Mosquitoes drew off the majority of the night fighters, and this enabled the Stirlings to bomb a number of well-grouped green TIs relatively unmolested and in good visibility. 218 Squadron's EH984 was homebound when coned by searchlights, which F/Sgt John Riley initially managed to evade by corkscrewing. However, a series of flak bursts finally damaged the rudder, and shortly afterwards a large hole appeared outboard of the port-outer, and the engine erupted in flames. Riley held the bomber steady while his crew baled out, and he was the last to leave. The crew landed south of Cologne, but F/Sgt Riley sustained a broken leg and pelvis on landing. He was ultimately repatriated due to the severity of his injuries, and was awarded a DFM in May 1944 for his bravery in keeping the Stirling aloft, while his crew parachuted to safety. Two crews from 623 Squadron also failed to return from this operation, both victims of prowling night fighters.

Frankfurt suffered under a heavy assault on the following night, when 341 aircraft delivered a most concentrated attack, which devastated the eastern districts and inland docks area. S/Ldr Prior led five Stirlings from 218 squadron, and returning crews reported a number of large fires and two violent explosions that illuminated the city. A major 3 Group mining operation was undertaken on the 7/8th involving forty-eight Stirlings, of which ten were from 218 Squadron. It was to northern Germany that the crews of 3 Group headed on the 8/9th, briefed to attack the city of Bremen as a diversion for the third assault on Hanover by Lancasters and Halifaxes. The crews of one hundred Stirlings, twelve Lancasters and two B17s of the 422nd Bomber Squadron were briefed for the operation, which followed on the heels of an 8th Air Force effort against the city during the afternoon. 218 Squadron put up eight aircraft, and for once, there were no early returns. The main force found the target area almost completely cloud-covered, and the H2S-equipped blind-marker element of the Pathfinders was hampered by a combination of cloud and smoke from the earlier American raid. BK687 HA-R was shot down by Lt Hans-Heinz Augenstein of 7/NJG1 at 01.42hrs near the village of Ebersdorf, seven kilometres north-west of Bremervode. It was his seventeenth victory. The largely Canadian crew of twenty-one-year-old F/Sgt Eric Rogers RCAF were on their fourteenth operation. One of the squadron's most experience flight commanders, S/Ldr Howard Saunders RCAF, was posted on completion of his first tour on the 11th, after undertaking twenty-eight operations. The young Canadian was posted to 1665 CU, and was one of the few to survive a tour during the five months he was operational. He would be awarded a well-deserved DFC.

A few nights of mining operations began on the 20/21st, after which fog settled over East Anglia, curtailing any further activity for a month in which 218 Squadron had launched forty-nine sorties. The squadron found itself in third place in the group sortie table, which was a considerable achievement considering that joint leaders 75 (NZ) and 90 Squadrons were both three flight units. In terms of sorties successfully completed, however, 218 led the group with an impressive 95.9%. The reduction in operations meant a fall in operational losses, and this is exactly what the squadron needed. Since June twenty-six crews had failed to return from operations, which meant, on paper at least, that it had lost one and a half times its strength.

November

November began as October had ended, with the Stirling squadrons sitting out the few bombing operations mounted. It was the Lancasters and Halifaxes which carried out a destructive raid on Düsseldorf on the 3/4th, while two dozen Stirlings mined the sea lanes around the Frisians. On the 4/5th the coastal waters between Denmark and Norway were targeted, and W/Cdr Oldbury took G/C R.E de T Vintras as his second pilot for a sortie to the Kattegat Channel. The crews were airborne from Downham Market at 16.00hrs, and headed north in deteriorating weather conditions.

Wing Commander Oldbury became involved in a prolonged engagement with a JU88, at which over six hundred rounds were fired, and it was claimed as damaged. The German crew was unfortunate to have encountered 218 Squadron's gunnery officer, "Peter" Piper DFC, who had seen action in the Battle of Britain in Blenheims. The commanding officer's usual gunner, Murray Bell, was off operations at the time due to illness.

Harris was now ready for the resumption of the Berlin offensive, and in a minute to Churchill on the 3rd, he had stated that he could "*wreck Berlin from end to end*". That was, of course, if the Americans were to join in. Harris acknowledged that it would cost between them four to five hundred aircraft, but he asserted that it would cost Germany the war. There was no real prospect of enlisting American support, and Harris would, therefore, go to Berlin alone.

The night of the 17/18th brought the resumption of the Berlin campaign for the

218 Squadrons gunnery leader Flight Lieutenant Arthur "Peter" Piper DFC. A veteran of the Battle of Britain F/Lt Piper's operational career spanned five years.

Lancaster squadrons, while the Stirling and Halifax brigade provided the main force for a raid on the Command's favourite diversionary targets of Mannheim and Ludwigshafen. 3 Group's contribution to the night's activities was fourteen Lancasters for Berlin, and an impressive 122 Stirlings and thirteen Lancasters for Mannheim. The recent lull in operations had given the hard-pressed ground crews an ideal opportunity to bring the squadrons up to full operational strength, and 218 Squadron was able to put eleven Stirlings into the air, led by A Flight's S/Ldr Prior. Night fighters were active during the almost straight route across France, and thirty-six interceptions were recorded, with the majority taking place between Cambrai and Trier. The force, already depleted by the early return of fourteen Stirlings, including three from Downham Market, was now set upon by Wilde Sau (Wild Boar) single seat fighters in the target area, which was found to be almost free of cloud. The marking was inaccurate, and fell between two and four miles north-north-west of the planned aiming point. 218 Squadron's EE884 HA-B crashed between the towns of Hofheim and Bodstadt, and there was only one survivor from the crew of P/O Alan Hine, who were on their tenth operation. Bomb-aimer F/O A Powell managed to travel over seventy miles from the crash site before being captured.

The chemical works at Leverkusen was the intended target on the 19/20th, for which 112 Stirlings were detailed. Twenty-six of these failed to take off, and a further nine returned early, an alarming proportion, the impact of which was not wasted on the A-O-C. Ten-tenths cloud over the target and the failure of the blind marking equipment resulted in a rather scattered attack. 218 Squadron dispatched nine aircraft, which delivered over thirty tons of bombs, and all returned safely, albeit to diversion airfields.

A maximum effort was demanded for the next raid on Berlin, which took place on the 22/23rd. 764 aircraft took off, among them an unimpressive fifty-three Stirlings, of which an alarming fifteen returned early. Nine 218 Squadron aircraft departed Downham Market led by the flight commanders. The first of five early returns headed for home soon after crossing the English Coast, and one even reached the German frontier before having to turn back. Icing and a variety of technical malfunctions were to blame. The remaining crews took an almost direct route to Berlin and encountered little fighter opposition on the way. The Stirlings arrived over the target at between 13,000 and 17,000 feet to find it completely cloud-covered. Flak was intense as the crews made their bomb runs and aimed at red sky markers. A number of crews observed a very large explosion at 20.20hrs, and those returning were generally optimistic about the success of the raid, reporting the glow of many fires visible through the cloud. In fact, this was the most devastating assault of the war on the Capital, destroying at least three thousand houses and apartment blocks, along with twenty-three industrial premises, while two thousand people lost their lives, and a further 175,000 were rendered homeless. Five Stirlings were among the twenty-six missing aircraft, and this represented a 10% loss rate for the type. 218 Squadron lost its A Flight commander, S/Ldr Garfield Prior DFC, who died with his crew when EF180 HA-D crashed in the target area. Canadian Prior was an experienced bomber pilot, who had completed a tour with 10 Squadron during the first year of war. Garfield Prior had a reputation on 10 Squadron for his tenacity in trying to identify and bomb the target, not an easy feat in a Whitley in 1940, for this he gained the nick-name "Pin-point Prior". Prior and his crew had arrived on the squadron from 1657 CU on September 20th, and were on their sixth operation.

The crew of Pilot Officer Alan Hine stand in front of Stirling EF884 HA-B "Bertie". They failed to return from Mannheim November 18th 1943.

Squadron Leader John Overton, with pipe. This photograph shows the crew on return from Berlin on November 23rd 1943. The stain is clearly etched on the faces. The crew were at the time operational with 623 Squadron. Seated center with a mug of tea is Canadian Sergeant Leonard McCann RCAF. He would fail to return from Berlin in March 1944 while serving with 115 Squadron.

He had completed a total of thirty-nine operations at the time of his loss, and his experience would be missed.

The Group's apparent inability to contribute a worthwhile number of aircraft regularly for operations, along with its high rate of early returns and heavy losses among the Stirling brigade, proved to be the final straw for Harris. He made the decision to withdraw the type from further operations over Germany, effectively relegating them to secondary, if useful duties. To be taken from the front line was a bitter blow to 3 Group, which, from the very start of hostilities, had been in the vanguard of the Command's campaigns. For both Downham Market squadrons the decision to remove them from attacks on Germany was beyond their control, but over the coming winter they would come to realize that the decision was the right one. The crews, like most of war time Britain, would read with increasing dismay of the burgeoning losses being sustained by Bomber Command.

As the decreasing tempo of operations during the latter stages of the month combined with the decision to remove the Stirlings from attacks on Germany, it meant that the group's monthly sorties figures were down on the September and October totals. 218 Squadron was placed fourth with forty-four sorties, and had slipped down to joint sixth place for mining sorties with fourteen dispatched and forty-seven mines delivered with a 92% success rate. From now on, Stirlings were to play an even greater role in mining operations, and, in fact, had already been responsible for around 50% of such sorties during 1943. A new role also beckoned at this time, as support increased for the resistance organisations in the occupied countries. This was already a 3 Group preserve in the hands of 138 and 161 Squadrons, the so-called "Moon" squadrons, operating out of their secret station at Tempsford in Bedfordshire. The restrictions placed on Stirling operations applied only to Germany, and this left the way clear for bombing operations over France, where a new menace was being prepared for use against Britain. V-1 launching sites were being constructed, and these would become targets for 3 Group's Stirling contingent during December and January. The month of November would see the posthumous award of the Victoria Cross to F/Sgt Arthur Aaron DFM. It was not only a tremendous honour to the squadron, but also to the group, and Aaron was also the first member of the Air Training Corps to be awarded this highest of decorations. The citation read:

The KING had been graciously pleased to confer the
VICTORIA CROSS on the under mentioned officer in
recognition of conspicuous Bravery

145818 Acting Flight Sgt Arthur Louis Aaron DFM, RAFVR.
No.218 Squadron (Deceased)

On the night of 12th August, 1943, Flight Sgt Aaron was captain and pilot of a Stirling aircraft detailed to attack Turin. When approaching to attack, the bomber received devastating bursts of fire from an enemy fighter. Three engines were hit, the windscreen shattered, the front and rear turrets put out of action and the elevator control damaged, causing the aircraft to become unstable and difficult to control. The navigator was killed and other members of the crew were wounded. A bullet struck Flight Sgt Aaron in the face, breaking his jaw and tearing away part of his face. He was also wounded in the lung and his right arm was rendered useless. As he fell forward over the control column, the aircraft dived several thousand feet. Control was regained by the flight engineer at 3,000 feet. Unable to speak, Flight Sgt Aaron urged the bomb aimer by signs to take over the controls. Course was then set southwards in an endeavour to fly the crippled bomber, with one engine out of action, to Sicily or North Africa.

Flight Sgt Aaron was assisted to the rear of the aircraft and treated with morphia. After resting for some time he rallied and, mindful of his responsibility as captain of the aircraft, insisted on returning to the pilot's cockpit, where he was lifted into his seat and had his feet placed on the rudder bar. Twice he made determined attempts to take control and hold the aircraft to its course but his weakness was evident and with difficulty he was persuaded to desist. Though in great pain and suffering from exhaustion, he continued to help by writing directions with his left hand.

Five hours after leaving the target the petrol began to run low, but soon afterwards the flare path at Bone airfield was sighted. Flight Sgt Aaron summoned his failing strength to direct the bomb aimer in the hazardous task of landing the damaged aircraft in the darkness with undercarriage retracted. Four attempts were made under his direction; at the fifth attempt Flight Sgt Aaron was so near to collapsing that he had to be restrained by the crew and the landing was completed by the bomb aimer.

Nine hours after landing, Flight Sgt Aaron died from exhaustion. Had he been content, when grievously wounded, to lie still and conserve his failing strength, he would probably have recovered, but he saw it as his duty to exert himself to the utmost, if necessary with his last breath, to ensure that his aircraft and crew did not fall into enemy hands. In appalling conditions he showed the greatest qualities of courage, determination and leadership, and, though wounded and dying, he set an example of devotion to duty which has seldom been equalled and never surpassed.

December

The main force went to Berlin on the 2/3rd, and received a bloody nose at the hands of the defences, and then inflicted a heavy blow on Leipzig on the following night. Some Stirlings mined in northern waters on the night of the 1/2nd, and around the Frisians on the 4/5th, before a period of inactivity took the Command through to mid-month. The changes within the group finally caught up with Downham Market, when, on December 6th, 623 Squadron and its Servicing Echelon 9623 was officially disbanded. It was a bitter blow to the whole squadron, especially the new commanding officer, W/Cdr Milligan AFC. The squadron establishment stood at twenty-one crews, and almost immediately six crews, including that of S/Ldr Overton, the only surviving operational pilot and crew from the squadron's formation back in August, was posted back to 218 Squadron to take over the recently vacated A Flight commander role. On the night of the 16/17th Lancasters raided Berlin, while twenty-six Stirlings, including four from 218 Squadron, joined in the first of a series of attacks on flying bomb sites, this one at Tilley-le-Haut near Abbeville. Other Stirlings carried out mining sorties around the Frisians and in French coastal waters, and the squadron's EE888 HA-K failed to return from the latter, disappearing without trace somewhere in the Bay of Biscay with the crew of F/Sgt Dennis Williams. The crew were on their first operation with the squadron since transferring in from 623 Squadron. Aboard was P/O John Taylor RCAF who was standing in for the crews bomb aimer, twenty-two–year old Taylor was W/Cdr Oldbury's regular bomb aimer. MZ263 HA-B arrived back over Cornwall short of fuel, and in the kind of bad weather conditions that were to blight the night's efforts for the whole Command. It was crash-landed at St Eval by F/O I Locke RNZAF and his crew, who all sustained minor injuries. The Stirling was struck off charge. The raid on the flying bomb site failed, despite being marked by Oboe Mosquitos, and this highlighted the limitations of Oboe as an aid to precision bombing. Although ideal for urban areas, where a margin of error of a few hundred yards was considered to be pin-point, a small target required absolute precision.

On Christmas Eve eight crews were detailed to carry out an attack on a special target in the Cherbourg area, while a further three crews were to mine the waters off the Ile de Re, but thankfully for all concerned, the operations were cancelled. The Station Records Book records that Christmas Day was *"Bang-on in the Camp"*. The fifth wartime Christmas came and went in relative peace, and the year petered out gently for the Stirling squadrons. Not so for the Lancaster Brigade, however, which faced three trips to Berlin in the space of five nights spanning the turn of the year. 218 was the least employed of the Stirling units during the month, and despatched only twenty-five sorties for the loss of two aircraft and one crew. It had been a year of steady and persistent losses for 218 Squadron, with a few bad nights, but unlike many other units there had been no catastrophes, and the coming year would bring a drastic reduction in missing aircraft and crews. Away from the station the future role of the squadron was being decided, and a memorandum dated December 10th from HQ Bomber Command stated the intention to equip 218 and 214 Squadrons who had taken up residence on the disbandment of 623 Squadron with the then new and still secret G-H apparatus.

The wreckage of Short Stirling MZ263 HA-B flown by New Zealander Flying Officer Ian Locke. Miraculously the crew walked away from this crash the aircraft was unsurprisingly written off.

Leave was usually six days every six weeks, and the majority of crews headed south for London if money permitted. This was particularly true for the Dominion and Commonwealth crews, who, not unnaturally, wanted to visit the shows and bars of the war-time capital. The capital was where almost anything went and often did, and was fast and exiting, unlike rural Norfolk. Squadron Leader Ryall DFC, one of the squadron's more colourful characters, recalls an incident just before Christmas 1943:

I was on leave with one of the girls from the Stow Bardolph Hospital, and we came out of one of the seedy afternoon clubs, in which there seemed to be so many full of the joy of alcohol. This one was one of those off the Shaftesbury Avenue. Outside the club was a chap winding a barrel-organ, playing a popular tune of the day called "Oh Johnny" I asked him if I could play it and he was happy to let me. I then suggested that I push it down to the corner of Piccadilly. He thought this a bit daring, and he was reluctant to do so because he only had a license for playing in the side roads. However, I dropped him a quid, and the sporting chap agreed, and the effect was quite amazing. There was hundreds of uniforms around, with many Yanks, British and others gathering around to see this squadron leader playing a barrel-organ, while his girlfriend collected money in his hat. A huge crowd soon formed, and people were singing, and soon there was the beginning of a traffic jam. My hat was bulging with money, pound notes and the occasional fiver I noticed. The whole thing only lasted about five minutes. Traffic was at a standstill, and something had to give. On the outer edge of the crowd a couple of red caps appeared, trying to force their way through the crowd, and we though it time to leave. We tipped the contents of the hat, probably more than he earned in a whole year, into the man's collection box, and then, conveniently, a brewer's dray slowly rumbled passed, low slung with small wheels, and we jumped up onto the back, slowly pulling away to the cheers of the now massive crowd.

Chapter Seven

1944:
A New Role and the Avro Lancaster

January

Flying Officer Doolan RAAF opened the 1944 mining offensive for 218 Squadron in the early evening of January 1st, with Texel as the intended destination, and six mines were dropped successfully during an otherwise quiet trip. From 1942 the German Air Force had been developing an unmanned aircraft, which became known as the V1 flying bomb. This was the first of three "Vergeltungs" or vengeance weapons being developed, the others being a stratospheric rocket, the V2, and a subterranean supergun at Mimoyecques in France, the V-3. In order to launch the V1, the Germans began work in the spring of 1943 to construct four large bunkers and ninety-six bases along the French and Belgian coasts. These sites, and their supporting infrastructure, would become a target for Harris's bombers over the ensuring months in a campaign codenamed "Crossbow". The V1 ski sites themselves were referred to as "No Ball" targets and each was given its own unique code name. The first bombing operation of the year for the squadron took place on the 4/5th, when twelve crews were briefed for a raid in the Pas-de-Calais area. The target was a V1 site codenamed 'Blackcap', which was situated just south-west of the town of Hazebrouck. A Flight Commander, S/Ldr Overton, led the crews out over Beachy Head, and found the target in good visibility and well-marked by Oboe-equipped Mosquitos. Enemy opposition was described as negligible, but danger was never far away, and LJ472 HA-K was raked by an overzealous rear gunner in another Stirling. One engine was put out of action and minor damage was caused to the nose section, but thankfully without injury to F/O Brentnall and his crew.

Apart from another mining effort on the 6/7th, which took place off the entrance to the River Adour just north of Biarritz, bad weather curtailed any further operations for 218 Squadron until the 14th. On this night nine crews were ordered to attack the constructional works at Bristillerie, codenamed 'Blackbird D', which was situated south of Cherbourg. In the event eight crews took off, and carried out what appeared to be a successful attack on the primary target.

A blanket of fog prevented further operations until January 20th, when the main force returned to Berlin, and three 218 Squadron crews were given the Nectarines I garden to mine north of Den Helder and around Texel. Oddly, three

214 Squadron aircraft were used by the squadron for this operation, EF215 BU–M, BF727 BU–S and LK445 BU–D. In the early evening of the 21/22nd S/Ldr Ryall led twelve aircraft in two sections against the constructional sites at "Blackbird" D and " Blackcap". Each was attacked by six crews in good visibility, and bombing appeared to the accurate, although returning crews were of the opinion that the targets would be easier to bomb accurately if fewer aircraft were over the target at the same time. The main operation on this night was carried out by over six hundred Lancasters and Halifaxes against Magdeburg, when, in return for an inconclusive raid and almost certainly little damage, a new record loss of fifty-seven aircraft was incurred. 218 became the sole occupant of Downham Market when 214 Squadron departed on January 24th for Sculthorpe. As a part of the ongoing restructuring within the group, 214 had been chosen to join 100 (SD) Group in a radio countermeasures (RCM) role.

Weather conditions had improved sufficiently for ten crews to be briefed on the 25th for a small scale attack on "Blackbird D". Seven aircraft actually took off in marginal weather conditions to join up with ten more from 90 Squadron. The Pathfinders delivered their green TIs a few minutes ahead of zero hour, and this forced the bombing element to orbit until the target was re-marked. Fortunately the flak defences were light, but crews remarked on an increase in searchlights positioned south of the target area. Australian P/O J Webster finally managed to bomb on a number of concentrated green TIs from 14,000 feet, and reported, *"A Good Show, if TIs correctly placed."* A major mining operation was undertaken on the 27/28th for which 218 Squadron contributed fourteen of seventy-six Stirlings. It was an extensive diversionary operation in support of a large-scale all-Lancaster attack on Berlin. Ten 218 Squadrons crews were given the Heligoland Blight to mine, and the remaining four were assigned to the Esbjerg Approaches, while twenty-one Pathfinder Halifaxes carried out a diversionary raid on Heligoland docks. The flares from the last-mentioned allowed the minelayers to pinpoint their position, and seventy-two mines were delivered without loss in a total for the group of an impressive 269 mines. Another major minelaying operation was laid on for the 28/29th, for which 218 Squadron supplied twelve aircraft. Two returned early, but the remainder pressed on to pinpoint the Aero Island, which had been marked by the Pathfinders. This was the first occasion on which the Pathfinders had actively participated in a minelaying operation undertaken by 3 Group.

So ended January 1944, during which the squadron had flown seventy-eight bombing sorties, elevating it to first place among the Stirling squadrons with a 91% success rate. It stood joint third behind its old rivals, 75 and 90 Squadrons, in mining sorties, but all were accomplished without loss, and it was an encouraging start to the year. The influx of new crews and the switch to targets in the occupied territories was welcomed, and the mood within the squadron was buoyant. The squadron's strength at the end of the month stood at twenty-three fully operational Stirlings. They would be needed for the forth-coming period of operations, in which the squadron would be given a number of new challenges that would test crews and senior officers to the limit. The installation of Sodium Funnel lighting was completed at the east end of the main runway during the month, in a system that would become known as FIDO. Installation had started back in September 1943. William Press the contractors had been tasked with laying thousands of yards of piping along the East – West runway, initial results were encouraging and throughout the winter of 1943, improvements were carried out.

February

The first operation of February took place on the 3rd, when two crews headed for the waters off le Havre. Seven crews were aloft by 11.30hrs on the 6th for a daylight cross-country exercise in conjunction with RAF fighters. Up until then the squadron had been relegated almost to the bottom off the group ladder for training and fighter affiliation flights. Life was not all about operations and training, and there were some light hearted moments. Harry Pinnell, navigator to F/L Goodman, recalls some such incidents.

> "I was at Downham Market when the powers-that-be built a new officers mess. It really was quite deluxe for those days. It was built in a hollow presumably so that any bomb blast would go over the top. This was OK, but my crew started up a steam roller standing there minding its own business. We were having some fun when we lost control of it and it smashed through the new mess wall, fortunately it went through two pillars, but did leave a rather big hole! On another occasion we managed to get the Peter Piper DFC the squadron gunnery leader's fiat sports car into the mess by turning it on its side and pushing it in. We then cleared the furniture and succeeded in driving around the ante room … eight point turns as well."

Partially successful mining operations were carried out on the nights of the 10th and 11th in the Cinnamon, Brest Peninsular and Cherbourg areas, while eight aircraft from the squadron planted forty-seven mines in the Hyacinth and Greengage gardens on the 12/13th. Wing Commander Royd Fenwick-Wilson AFC arrived on attachment on February 8th from 31 Base to assume temporary command of the station on the departure of G/C Down, who was awaiting a posting on the 10th to 33 Base, Waterbeach. The move would bring with it a promotion to Air Commodore. Canadian Fenwick-Wilson had enlisted in the Air Force in 1934, and by the outbreak of war he was instructing at 12 Service Flying Training School, where he was eventually awarded the AFC and promoted to wing commander. Eager to get "stuck-In" Fenwick-Wilson found himself in England in early 1941 and flying Wellingtons with 405 Squadron RCAF, the squadron he would eventually command. On completion of his first tour in February 1942 he was sent back to Canada, where he toured the various training stations north and south of the border. Succeeding him at 405 Squadron was fellow Canadian W/Cdr Fauquier, who would eventually command 617 Squadron during the final months of the bombing war. The new base commander's first official duty was to welcome HRH the Duke of Gloucester and the A-O-C on February 13th. A full tour of the station was undertaken, and a selected number of senior officers were introduced to the Duke.

Thirteen crews successfully carried out a mining operation in Kiel Bay on the 15/16th, and a total of thirty-nine mines were delivered to the primary target, the Forget-me-Nots area. Flying Officer Webster RAAF and crew were attacked by a JU88 while at 15,000 feet, and the crew returned to claim it as destroyed. The Combat Report recalls,

> *"Our aircraft was doing a gentle weave when the rear gunner F/Sgt Howes saw two unidentified aircraft flying together on the starboard side up at 800 yards. He told the pilot to corkscrew to starboard and on doing so the mid upper gunner F/Sgt Clarkson saw the two a/c. The rear gunner opened fire at the aircraft, which was at this time at 400 yards. He gave a 5 second burst and saw his tracer strike the enemy aircraft which continued to come in firing with tracer. The rear gunner gave another burst and saw the aircraft suddenly turn over and dive towards the ground. While the rear gunner was firing at this aircraft the mid upper gunner saw the other aircraft dive away to starboard and was not seen again. Both aircraft had twin engines and are believed to be JU88's. At time of this combat other combats were seen to take place by tracer in the sky by other members of the crew. The enemy aircraft is claimed as destroyed."*

Eight 218 Squadron crews returned to Kiel Bay on the 19/20th, and delivered thirty-two mines, while the main force of over eight hundred aircraft headed for Leipzig, and the greatest disaster to afflict the Command thus far in the war. Part of the enemy night fighter force met the bombers as they crossed the Dutch coast, and remained in contact all the way to the target. It was impossible to assess the results of the attack, but there was no question over the scale of the defeat for Bomber Command. A massive seventy-eight aircraft failed to return, a new record loss by a clear twenty-one aircraft.

Six 218 Squadron crews enjoyed a successful night of mining off the island of Borkum on the 20/21st, while the main force went to Stuttgart, and produced an effective and damaging raid. Twenty-four hours later five aircraft went back to the Borkum area, and one was claimed by flak from the island. Returning crews reported seeing an aircraft burst into flames about two miles north of the island, and fall in flames into the sea. Twenty-four year old Scotsman F/L James "Red" Wiseman had begun his operational career with 623 Squadron back in August 1943, having joined from 1657 CU. He and his crew had completed eleven operations before the unit's disbandment, and they had flown four further sorties before being lost. It was initially thought that EJ125 HA-J had been brought down by flak, but information from historian Dr Theo Boiten indicates that it may have been the victim of Uffz Lorenz Gerstmayr of 4/NJG3. A large-scale mining operation in Kiel Bay on the 24/25th was intended to act as a diversion for the main force operation taking place against Schweinfurt. Ten 218 Squadron aircraft joined forty other Stirlings and more than ninety Halifaxes from 4 and 6 Groups. Flak and fighter opposition appeared to have increased, and F/L T Knapman RNZAF reported an exchange with a prowling FW190.

On the 25th 121 ground crew departed Downham Market by road and headed south to Gibraltar Farm, otherwise known as Tempsford in Bedfordshire. Once there they would make ready for the arrival of the squadron's detachment for a period of "Special Duties". February had been a rather quite month for the squadron with only fifty-nine sorties undertaken, all of which were mining. Squadron Leader Overton and eleven other crews, eight from A Flight and three from B Flight, were dispatched to Tempsford on the 28th for operations over the forthcoming moon period. Tempsford was home to two Special Duties squadrons, 138 and 161, both of which were engaged in clandestine operations over occupied Europe under the direct control of 3 Group. These two squadrons were known within the group, but not so outside. With the invasion of Europe only months away, supplies of weaponry and equipment were urgently needed by the various resistance organisations. The removal of the Stirlings from front line operations left them available to supplement the efforts of the designated SOE squadrons and those of 38 Group.

March

March began with the majority of the squadron still on detachment, and the remaining crews at Downham Market non-operational, awaiting a move to Woolfox Lodge in the county of Rutland. The main force went back to Stuttgart on the night of the 1/2nd, and lost only four out of 557 aircraft in return for a highly destructive attack. Thereafter, the majority of the Command stayed at home until mid-month, and it was during this interlude that 218 Squadron began its SOE flights over France, and the first salvoes were fired in the pre-invasion campaign as part of the Transportation Plan. SOE sorties were particularly arduous, and often required crews to fly low to pinpoint the drop zone, often in difficult visibility, and this made them easy targets for light flak. Seventy-six aircraft were involved in SOE sorties on the 4/5th, on return from which, 218 Squadron's EE944 HA-H lost its port-outer engine during final approach to Tempsford. Pilot Officer Elwyn Edwards tried to overshoot, but was unable to prevent the port wing from dropping, and the Stirling side-slipped into the ground. Edwards and four of his crew died in the wreckage, while the two gunners sustained injuries.

On the night of the 6/7th Halifaxes of 4 and 6 Groups carried out the first of the interdiction raids in preparation for the forthcoming invasion. The systematic dismantling by bombing of the French and Belgian railway networks would occupy much of the Command's attention from now until the end of the summer, but with the Lancasters still fully engaged in the winter campaign, it was left to the Halifaxes to open proceedings on this night. The target was the railway yards at Trappes, where heavy damage was inflicted on installations, track and rolling stock. Later on the morning of the 7th, the 218 Squadron remnant completed its move from Downham Market, which was transferred to 8 Group, and took up residence at Woolfox Lodge, recently vacated by 1665 HCU. On its departure 1665 HCU had declared Woolfox Lodge to be unserviceable, but 218 Squadron signalled group that the aerodrome was serviceable, but for day operations only because of the incomplete state of the Mk II Drem light system. With Woolfox Lodge now housing a front line operational squadron a change in station

Wing Commander Royd Fenwick-Wilson AFC. The Canadian enlisted in the RAF in 1934, his experience was put to good use during his tenure as commanding officer. His organisational skills and his style of command did much to change the fortunes of 218 Squadron.

commander took place, S/Ldr Lidstone stepping aside on the 7th in favour of G/C Heard.

On the March 9th W/Cdr William Oldbury concluded his tour as commanding officer, and was posted to HQ Bomber Command prior to attending 13 Intermediate Course at the Army Staff College at Camberley. He was succeeded by the previously mentioned W/Cdr Fenwick-Wilson, whose tenure as station commander at Downham Market had ended with the arrival there of the Pathfinders. Following further operations on the nights of the 5/6th, 6/7th and 7/8th, the Tempsford detachment carried out another one on the 10/11th, when ten crews were tasked with S.O.E drops in France. On the 11th the squadrons former commanding officer, Air Commodore H Kirkpatrick DFC, now SASO 3 Group, paid a visit to the station and the squadron, and he was followed the next day by 3 Group A-O-C AVM Harrison CBE DFC AFC. The squadron, which had been partially equipped with G-H since December 1943, carried out a series of G-H training flights on the 18th, and a number of local cross country flights. At the time only one flight of eight plus two Stirlings was fully equipped. It would be left to 218 Squadron to re-introduced G-H operationally into the Group after both 115 and 514 had their sets withdrawn. These sets would find their way to the squadron over the coming weeks. The final Tempsford operation was undertaken on the 15/16th by three crews, none of which was successful.

During the squadron's short period at Tempsford it launched forty-four sorties, and a top secret report drawn up at the time recorded the extent of the SOE operational activities of 3 Group's Stirling squadrons, including 138 and 161, during the moon period between February 28th and March 16th. A total of 509 sorties was carried out, of which 265 were successful, resulting in the dropping of 3,553 containers and 709 packages for the loss of five Stirlings, one Halifax and one Lysander. The Tempsford detachment arrived at Woolfox Lodge on the 16th to bring the squadron back to full operational strength.

A period of relative calm settled over Woolfox Lodge for the remainder of the month, and this was in contrast to the activity elsewhere in the Command. The final operation of the war against Berlin was carried out on the 24/25th, and resulted in the loss of seventy-two aircraft. Squadron leader Ian Ryall DFC was posted to 1651 CU on the 26th on completion of his second tour. His leadership qualities and determination instilled confidence not only to "B" Flight but to the whole squadron. He had proved himself to be a first rate flight commander during an intense period of heavy losses against well-defended targets. Happily he would survive the war and be awarded a bar to his DFC. The very next day S/Ldr Poulter MiD arrived with his crew from 31 Base to assume command of B Flight. The winter campaign came to an end on the night of the 30/31st, with a standard maximum effort raid on Nuremberg. The operation went ahead despite grave doubts about the forecast cloud, and in the face of a hotly disputed 5 Group-inspired straight-in route. The operation became the greatest disaster to afflict the Command during the entire war, with the loss of ninety-five aircraft, more than eighty of them falling to night fighters before the target was even reached. Over a hundred crews bombed Schweinfurt in error, and Nuremberg escaped with only insignificant damage.

Squadron Leader Cecil Poulter MiD, B Flight Commander. His selfless act of keeping his stricken Stirling aloft saved the lives of his crew over Soissons, France.

In a Top Secret memo dated March 31st, the future role of 218 Squadron was finally decided. The squadron had one of its flights equipped with G-H back in December, and was now to be totally equipped with the device to assist in the marking of any target within range. This could be carried out in conjunction with Oboe marking, by the PFF or on its own for 3 Group, and, if required, the Command as a whole. G-H would become a 3 Group preserve from the autumn, and in its hands, it would prove to be a highly effective blind bombing device. The system was based on a G-H equipped lead aircraft releasing its bombs as a signal to the following gaggle to do likewise, and it would be developed by the group into a fine art, with a particular application against oil and railway targets. This did not mean, however, that the squadron would no longer be required to participate in bombing and mining operations. G-H training was to be carried out as a matter of urgency, and the pilots, navigators and air bombers were to attend lectures at the Navigation Training Unit (NTU) at Warboys, a Pathfinder station.

The squadron was to remain under the operational and administrative control of 3 Group, but it was evident that close co-operation with 8 Group would be necessary. 3 Group was ordered to make arrangements for the installation of a G-H type 77 trainer at Woolfox Lodge for the training of both pilots and navigators on curved-track bombing approaches. At the time there was only one type 77 in existence, and it was for the Air Ministry to decide who had priority, the A.E.A.F, or 218 Squadron. After some lengthy discussions and numerous meetings it eventually arrived at Woolfox Lodge! March had been a busy month for all concerned, and had included a change of commanding officer, a change of station and a temporary change of role with the detachment to Tempsford.

April

That now facing the main force crews was in marked contrast to what had been endured over the long winter months. The Transportation Plan was now the priority for the whole Command, and the long slog to Germany on dark, often dirty nights was to be replaced by largely shorter range hops to France and Belgium in improving weather conditions. These operations would prove to be equally demanding in their way, however, and would require of the crews a greater commitment to accuracy, to avoid unnecessary civilian casualties. The main fly in the ointment was a decision from on high, which decreed that most such operations were worthy of counting as just one third of a sortie towards the completion of a tour, and until this flawed policy was rescinded, mutterings of discontent pervaded the bomber stations. Despite the prohibitive losses over the winter, the Command was in remarkably fine fettle to face its new challenge, and Harris was in the enviable position of being able to achieve what his predecessor had sought but failed to do. This was, to attack multiple targets simultaneously, with forces large enough to make an impact. Such was the number of aircraft and crews available to him, that he could now assign targets to individual groups, to groups in tandem or to the Command as a whole, as dictated by operational requirements. Although invasion considerations were the priority, Harris still favoured city-busting as the key to victory, and while he remained at the helm, he would pursue this line of attack whenever an opportunity arose.

The new month opened with an intensive G-H training programme, while the station ground staff continued preparing the station for operations. The first signs of tension between 8 Group and 3 Group came on the 2nd, when 8 Group chief, AVM Don Bennett, fired off a top secret memorandum to HQ Bomber Command demanding that 8 Group have full control and sole responsibility in both the training and operational marking role of 218 Squadron. It was the start of a simmering dispute. The new campaign got into full swing on the night of the 9/10th, when Halifaxes, Lancasters and Stirlings of 3, 4, 6 and 8 Groups attacked the Lille-Delivrance goods station, while elements from all the groups went for the railway yards at Villeneuve-St-Georges on the outskirts of Paris. The former in particular was highly successful, and involved ten Stirlings from 218 Squadron, whose crews found a number of well-placed TIs, which despite a thin layer of cloud, they managed to pin-point and bomb from between 11,000 and 13,000 feet. Pilot Officer H Seller EF249 HA-H, P/O L Gillies RAAF LJ481 HA-B, F/L C Doolan RAAF EF259 HA-G and F/L A King RNZAF EF184 HA-A all used their G-H equipment for the first time on a main land target. Crews reported a concentration of explosions over the target, F/L Brentnall reported *"Wizard bombing"* on his return. Post raid reconnaissance revealed that over two thousand items of rolling stock were destroyed, along with buildings and installations. Sadly, the satisfaction was marred by very heavy casualties among French civilians in adjacent residential districts, and this was a problem that would never satisfactorily be addressed.

Two mining operations were planned for the night of the 10th, but one was cancelled to leave four 218 Squadron aircraft assigned to the waters off Ile de Re. The Transportation Plan continued on this night at five railway centres in France and Belgium, before an area raid on Aachen devastated the town on the 11/12th, and killed over fifteen hundred people. A high-level G-H mining operation was carried out on the 12th, when four 218 Squadron crews went to the waters around Den Helder and north of Egmond. Wing Commander Fenwick Wilson AFC flew with F/L Brentnall aboard LJ472 HA-K on this operation. Both F/Ls Brentnall and Funnell dropped their six mines from between 14,800 and 15,000 feet. The operation was only partially successful after two crews were unable to receive G-H reception.

From the 14th the Command became officially subject to the demands of SHAEF, and would remain thus shackled until the Allied armies were sweeping towards the German frontier at the end of the summer. No further operations took place until the 18th, when thirteen aircraft from the squadron joined a contingent of 4 Group Halifaxes for a high level mining trip to Kiel Bay. The German

The crew of Australian F/Lt Gregory Doolan RAAF. Twenty three year old Doolan seen here back row right failed to return from an attack against Chambly on April 20th 1944, it was his 18 operation.

defences were alert, and fighter activity was reported all across Denmark to the target area. The crews reported seeing one aircraft shot down near the town of Ribe, only minutes after F/L King RNZAF had been attacked by an unidentified fighter. The enemy managed to manoeuvre behind and below the Stirling without being detected, and its first burst of cannon fire rendered the rear and mid-upper turrets unserviceable, and wounded the rear gunner, Sgt Hancock, in the right knee. Flight Lieutenant King managed to shake off the fighter by carrying out a diving turn to the port, and continued on to deliver the payload at an alternative location west of Fano Island. Sergeant Hancock was given a morphine injection, and it was found that his knee had been almost shot away.

218 Squadron sent fourteen Stirlings on the 19th, to conduct a G-H raid on the important railway depot at Chambly situated north of Paris. Weather conditions outbound and in the target area were good with no moon, but, disappointingly, only three crews reported a successful reception on G-H, and they each brought home an aiming point photograph. Post raid reconnaissance established that two bombs had severed railway lines at two points, and there was severe damage to a stores building. LJ448 HA-D was hit during the bombing run, and an explosion near the flight engineer's panel was the first indication of any danger. The flight engineer informed the pilot, F/L Doolan RAAF, that a fire had taken hold forward of the mid-upper turret. The twenty-three-year-old Australian skipper gave the order to bail-out, and five of the crew left through the front hatch at 6,000 feet.

The Stirling crashed near Asnieres-sur-Oise, where the bodies of Gregory Doolan and his flight engineer, Sgt Cecil Bishop, were found two hundred yards from the wreckage. Four of the crew, who were on their fifteenth operation, ultimately evaded capture, while one became a PoW.

Two small-scale mining operations off the Dutch coast were carried out successfully on the 21/22nd, during which forty-eight mines were delivered. It was back to the interdiction campaign for 218 Squadron on this night, when thirteen crews took off to attack the marshalling yards at Laon. Three aircraft returned early with technical malfunctions, but the remainder joined thirty-seven other Stirlings from 149 and 90 Squadrons to attack two aiming points. Wing Commander Cousens of 635 Squadron was Master Bomber for the occasion, and the initial marking was carried out by Mosquitos. 218 Squadron was assigned to the second wave with the northern aiming point as its objective. The markers went down late, and W/Cdr Cousens instructed the main force to orbit while he confirmed their accuracy. That done he instructed the crews to bomb from 7,000 feet, and to aim at a number of well-placed green markers. Fighters were evident in the target area, but for once there was practically no opposition from flak. Crews bombed in good visibility and reported the target to be well ablaze. EH942 HA-M was attacked by Lt Otto Fries of Stab II/NJG1 soon after leaving the target area. Cannon fire left the port wing tanks ablaze, and five members of the crew managed to bail out before the Stirling crashed south-west of Soissons at 00.26hrs, killing the pilot and mid-upper gunner. The pilot was the recently appointed B Flight commander, S/Ldr Cecil Poulter MiD, who was operating with the squadron for the first time. It was an experienced crew with eighteen operations behind it, but its first with S/Ldr Poulter, who, it is understood, had not operated since completing eight sorties in 1940/41. All five survivors managed to escape and return to the UK, a remarkable feat. The following is Harry Fisher's, the crews wireless operators own account of that fateful night and the days and weeks that followed.

After successfully bombing our target, we were attacked by enemy aircraft. Both the port inner and outer engines were ablaze and we had lost altitude to about 10,000 feet. There was no way we were going to make it back to base and the order was given to bale out. I made my way to the forward escape hatch only to find it open, and the navigator and bomb aimer had already gone. I looked up at our pilot, S/Ldr Poulter, and received a tap on the shoulder indicating to me that it was time to go! I naturally thought the pilot would be following me but he was either too badly injured or lost control of the aircraft. He went down with the plane. The injured mid-upper gunner also died in the crashed plane, and the five other members of the crew, including myself, parachuted into France to meet differing fates. For me, it was the start of an incident-packed attempt to reach neutral territory – and one that almost succeeded while trying to recall details of pre-operational training on how to deal with such events. I had landed at midnight, in a field near the village of Vic-sur-Aisne, situated between Compiegne and Soissons. After hiding my parachute and Mae West in tall grass, I followed the railway line for almost two kilometres to a farmhouse but the family was too frightened to let me in. However, the young couple at the next farmhouse answered my door-knocking and kept me overnight. The following morning, they made contact with Allied sympathisers at another farm, where I discovered our bomb aimer was already being given shelter. For ten days, we hid in a mushroom cave and food was brought to us at this hide-out.

We were then taken by farm cart, hidden under straw, to the house of a resistance leader in Vic-sur-Aisne where we were vigorously interrogated. From there, we were moved to another farm in a village named Morsain, where we were hidden for a further few days. Plans were made to get us into occupied Paris so we could be guided to safety by the French underground. Dressed in civilian clothes, we were accompanied to Paris by the farmer's wife. She took us to her mother's home, and then we were moved to a nurse's house. Staying there for about a fortnight, we passed some of the time by listening to BBC broadcasts at a nearby clinic. On 25th May 1944, armed with bogus identity cards supplied by the underground - mine stated I was 75% disabled and unable to speak (I only had schoolboy French), we were taken by a girl from the underground movement, along with a few others, on a 27 hour train journey to Toulouse. Included in this group was my flight engineer who turned up in Paris, having arrived via a different route within a similar elaborate network.

We were always very careful to keep our distance from the guide. If we were suspected and caught, she would hopefully keep walking and evade capture. There was nothing more she could have done for us in any case by hanging around and there was always some chance for us to attempt escape in the future. It was understood that if caught, she would be tortured to extract information before being eventually shot - the grim fact being, that no amount of torture would yield useful information to the enemy because each guide had only very limited information sufficient for the immediate task in hand. Each contact was very much an individual cell who did not know the identity of the next underground member in the chain leading to freedom. Arriving without incident at Toulouse, we changed trains heading for Pau near Lourdes, close to the Spanish frontier. Although arriving after the official curfew time, our luck held. I was issued with a pass by the German guard at the exit, to enable me to get from the station to my place of residence. From the railway station, we were taken to an underground movement house in Pau. Several others had successfully made it to this point and we travelled by car up into the mountains where Basque guides were expected to take over. Basque guides were not always the most reliable and there were now a fairly large numbers of people including a Jewish group, all attempting to cross the Pyrenees in their bid to escape. It was early June, yet we were so high (about 8,000 feet), we reached the snow-line.

Eventually we travelled into a valley where the guides pointed in the direction of the Spanish frontier. There was still a considerable distance to go but the guides indicated they were about to return to the pick-up point and therefore we were now on our own. We spent that night alone in the open without the guides. Next morning, we discovered that, without guides, the large group had split into smaller groups. The following morning, as a member of one of the small groups, we headed towards what we thought was the Spanish border. Too late! In our weary and tired condition we had failed to notice the German soldiers, although only 200 or 300 yards away, until they started to fire at us. We were hungry and exhausted having been in the mountains for 10 days and we didn't stand a chance. Four of us were captured and I think it was on Spanish territory. The four included me, our flight engineer, a bomber pilot from Portsmouth, and an American from Pasadena, California. Our bomb aimer was some way behind our small group and managed to evade the Germans. He later made it into Spain and returned to the UK by way of Gibraltar. The four of us were taken back by three German soldiers to a small mountain village where we were interrogated.

We were lying in the cell where we had been placed when the door opened and an immaculately dressed German Officer, jackboots and all, walked in. In perfect English, he asked, "Who is the 'English' officer here?" As no one else moved, I rose to my feet and said "I am" only to be told, "Stand to attention when you speak to a German Officer!" We were then taken to a room for interrogation. I was asked questions such as "Where was your base?" Which type of aircraft were you flying and where was your target? Where were you shot down and who helped you?" Predictably, my replies were, "I cannot give you that information" and quoting the Geneva Convention on the requirement to give only number, rank and name. The others gave the same answers. I then heard the lines that were to be caricatured many times in the future but were extremely threatening and sinister given the situation of airmen being captured in civilian clothes. I quote verbatim, "Huh! So you won't talk, well it is not my job but we have ways and means of making you talk!" We were threatened with torture and the firing squad but we never revealed any details of the people who had helped us. From the mountain village, we were then taken back to Pau, and as I subsequently found out later, spent some time in Gestapo headquarters. Curiously enough, during our short spell there, we were given the best meal in all the time we spent in German hands. Mind you, that wasn't saying very much. From Pau, we were taken under escort by train to a civilian prison in Toulouse. During the train journey, another incident of note occurred. We were in a compartment by ourselves with armed German guards when the door opened and a Luftwaffe Officer came in. He looked at us and said in English, "Who are you?" At this point, the German soldiers were obviously unhappy but as he was an officer, they were limited in what they could do or say. On being told we were RAF airmen who had been shot down he replied, "I thought perhaps you were". He took out a pack of cigarettes, gave us a cigarette each, and said "Good Luck!" before leaving. Had we witnessed an example of the special bond between flying types

Having walked through the Pyrenees escape route for 10 days, we were hungry and exhausted, and no match for the German soldiers who captured us on the Spanish border. We then spent 75 days in what appeared as a nightmare prison. 250 grams of stale black bread and two bowls of weak cabbage soup per day, with 'always the threat to shoot.' With the Allies pushing south after D Day, the Germans suddenly decided to evacuate the prison in a frantic hurry, leaving us in our cells. We were freed by the Maquis who broke down our cell doors on August 19th 1944. By that time, I had lost about three stone in weight, and helped myself to food, still hot on the stove, left by the fleeing Germans. It was indeed fortunate I had stopped to have some food, as the first of my fellow-prisoners who had dashed outside, were machine-gunned down by passing Germans who were themselves evacuating the city. Many fellow-prisoners were killed or wounded, and having seen what was happening, some of us managed to hide behind stone pillars, with bullets flying around us. French Forces of the Interior (Maquis) took charge of the town, as there were no Allied forces close by. However, Germans were being cut off from that part of France, hence the reason for their evacuation in sudden panic. I was with the Maquis until September 3rd 1944, and was expected to accompany them on some of their missions to blow up bridges, railway-lines etc. An aircrew member like me (?) who could never hit anything with a rifle at the best of times!

At one point, we were driven through the streets of Toulouse in an open truck by the Maquis who were shouting 'Anglia's et Americans' while the people lined the streets cheering and shouting. Allied troops had still not arrived in the Toulouse area, the Maquis were in full control, and I had been given a 'Pass' by the Free French stating I was a British Officer liaising with the Maquis. At this time, we witnessed what happened to traitors, or females who had collaborated with Germans; they were stripped to the waist, had heads shaved, paraded through the streets and humiliated. On September 3rd, we were taken into the countryside to a site used by RAF Special Duties aircraft who had delivered arms & supplies to the Maquis, and even landed on improvised runways if need be. On this night, a Hudson landed with the help of only a few flares, and with engines still running ready for a quick get-away, boxes and crates was hurriedly chucked out. To the utter amazement of the crew, I scurried quickly across the grass towards the plane. "Where the hell have you come from?" was all they could utter. One minute later before being spotted, we were taking off across the field. On the flight back, I can still remember being astounded by the sheer mass of shipping we could just see in the dawn light across the English Channel. Massive quantities of supplies were still being ferried across to France 3 months after D Day. On landing back in U.K., I was taken to London for interrogation, given back-pay and leave, and then sent to a Rehabilitation Unit near Nairn. As I had never been classified as a POW the only news my mother had received was that I was 'missing.' I still have the telegrams to that effect. On my return to UK in September 1944, I became an active aircrew member again, but according to RAF policy, I was not sent on flying operations over the area where I had been previously shot down. It struck me later, the extent to which indoctrination had been applied over the previous 11 years under Nazism. When captured in the Pyrenees, one of the first questions asked was "Are you Jewish?" This question from ordinary German soldiers who considered this to be of paramount importance. I shudder to think of the consequences if the answer had been "Yes!" but it did illustrate the powerful influence exerted by the Nazi regime.

The experienced F/L Philip Brentnall was promoted to acting squadron leader on the 23rd, and he assumed command of B Flight. Unlike the majority of their predecessors, Brentnall, and the A Flight commander, S/Ldr John Overton, would survive their time in the roles, and over the ensuring months contribute to the success of the squadron. A switch to a Belgian target on the 23/24th focussed attention on the Luftwaffe signals Depot at Vilovorde, located three miles north-east of Brussels. This was an all 218 Squadron G-H attack carried out by twelve aircraft led by S/Ldr Overton. Flight Lieutenant Lock RNZAF was involved in an incident at take-off, when, having just become airborne, the port-inner engine of LJ481 HA-B cut suddenly and without warning. The prompt action of jettisoning the bomb load gave the crew a few extra feet, and the Stirling brushed through tree tops on the perimeter. Lock managed to land the Stirling without further incident in a marvellous display of airmanship by the twenty-one-year-old from Kawa Kawa. The bombs landed in a field alongside No.2 Site, and were dealt with by the armoury on the following morning. The remaining crews found the target clear of cloud, and good G-H reception allowed the bombing to fall all across the target area. There was practically no opposition, and all the crews had landed safely back at base by 01.50hrs. The target was, in fact, completely untouched, and the only encouraging feature of an otherwise disappointing raid was that over 50% of the bombs were within 550 yards of the aiming point.

The squadron was asked to operate again on the following night, when the target was the Chambly railway yards. This was the fifth night of action in succession, and the four crews who were briefed would be the only ones attacking the target. Squadron Leader Overton, P/O Coram RAAF, P/O Seller and F/L Goodman DFM departed England over Orfordness in good visibility, and G-H reception was good in the target area. Three crews bombed from 14,000 feet, and there was a tremendous explosion when Overton's load hit the aiming point, which momentarily enveloped the whole area in a red glow that illuminated the surrounding buildings. Post raid reconnaissance showed heavy damage to installations and plant, and that a bomb had exploded on the railway lines near the storage yard. A return to Chambly railway depot took place on the 26/27th, and 218 Squadron was once again the only unit involved. Sadly, the raid was a failure after none of the crews was able to obtain G-H reception. The last operation of the month was carried out by four crews on the 29/30th, to deliver mines by G-H off Den Helder and north of Egmond. The squadron dispatched 103 sorties during the month, of which thirty-three were mining.

May

3 Group opened its May account on the night of the 1/2nd with a return to Chambly by predominantly Lancasters, while 218 Squadron provided all sixteen Stirlings. After initial difficulties with the marking, the raid was outstandingly accurate, and one of Europe's most modern and important depots was severely hit, sustaining heavy damage to installations, plant and buildings. It was a bad night for 218 Squadron, losing three aircraft, one of which crashed in England. B Flight's EF504 HA-P was subjected to repeated attacks over a fifteen minute period, during which the rear gunner, F/O E Twinning, managed to draw a bead on the attacker, and he informed the pilot *"I've got him, he is going down in flames.* Sadly it was too late, as a fire had begun in the starboard-outer engine, which spread along the wing. Twenty-nine year-old Flying Officer Ieuan Jones ordered his crew to bail out, and two managed to comply as the Stirling passed through 3,000 feet. It exploded on hitting the ground near Poix at 00.47hrs, about thirty yards from where the navigator landed. He and the flight engineer were aided by

"A" Flights Flying Officer Ieuan Jones and crew. The crew had various operational experience when they arrived from No.31 Base on April 16th. Within two weeks of their arrival they were shot down while attacking Chambly Railway Depot, only two of the crew survived.

"A" Flights Pilot Officer Noel Elliot RAAF and crew pose with the ground crew besides Short Stirling LK387 IC-P of 623 Squadron November 1943. The crew completed four operations with 623 before transfer to 218 Squadron where they completed a further 9 operations.

the resistance, and managed to return to England, arriving at Northolt in mid August. Flight Lieutenant Jones was on his third operation, having been posted in from 31 Base on April 16th.

Having successfully bombed the target, EF259 HA-G was attacked by two fighters, reported to be FW190s. It is believed that Hptm Fritz Sothe of 4/NJG4 shot down the Stirling near la Houssaye, taking with it four members of the young, skippered by experienced F/O Noel Elliot RAAF. There were four evaders, including the pilot, who stated in his escape and evasion report that the tail section had been almost shot off, and the port–outer engine set on fire before the order was given to bail-out. On board was Sgt Wilson, who was officially still attached to Training Command, but went on the trip for the experience. EF184 HA-G was attacked by two JU88s soon after leaving the target, and extensive damage was sustained in the encounter. The flight engineer was killed and both gunners injured, but P/O Scammell nursed the Stirling back to the emergency airfield at Woodbridge, where he landed at 02.10hrs. EF184 HA-G was struck off charge and scrapped. This proved to be the only bombing operation to be carried out by the squadron during the month.

Three crews carried out a mining operation on the 2/3rd, and successfully planted eighteen mines off the West Frisians. No further operations took place until the 7/8th, when four Stirlings delivered twenty mines with the aid of Gee off the coast of Terschelling, while five others headed south across France to mine the waters off Courbre Point in the Gironde Estuary. Both operations were completed in excellent visibility without encountering any opposition. Four aircraft returned to the Gironde Estuary on the following night, and each delivered four mines in bright moonlight. On return F/Sgt Samuels attempted to land on three engines, after the port-inner engine failed over France, but overshot and wrote-off EF249. The squadron was asked to provide six aircraft for three gardens on the 9/10th, when Australians F/Sgt J Corlis RAAF and Sgt R Ecclestone were given the Sultanas area to mine. Both crews had collected ten special mines from Tuddenham, which were designed to be dropped from a higher attitude. Both aircraft carried five mines, and successfully dropped them from 14,000 feet. In all twenty-seven mines were planted by the squadron. It was similar fare for two crews on the following night, and for five more on the 11/12th.

The main force, in its constituent parts, began to concentrate in greater detail on pre-invasion targets, thus coastal batteries, airfields, ammunition dumps and military camps and depots all competed with railways for the bombers' attention. The coastal batteries were generally in the Pas-de-Calais, and well away from the planned invasion beaches, in order to maintain the deception. Deception was to play a major part in the actual landings, and 218 Squadron was one of a number of units to be selected for an important and special role. 617 Squadron was approached in early May to evaluate the feasibility of carrying out a major deception operation, which, by its very nature, would call for a high degree of flying ability and navigational accuracy, and above all crew discipline.

A meeting had been held on Sunday May 7th at 54 Base, Woodhall Spa, to discuss the forthcoming operation. A number of high-ranking personnel from the Air Ministry and senior Bomber Command officers were present. The meeting was chaired by Air Commodore Dalton Morris, (Chief Signals Officer, HQ Bomber Command). Also attending the meeting was Air Commodore H.A.Constantine, (Operations, HQ Bomber Command), Air Commodore Sharp, Base Commander 54 Base, and, finally, the commanding officer of 617 Squadron, W/Cdr Cheshire DSO, DFC. A number of points were raised by Cheshire, who expressed his concerns about the complexity of the operation and the strain it would place upon his crews. The assembled senior staff listened to Cheshire's concerns, and decreed that a second navigator would operate with each of the selected crews. An extra GEE set would be fitted to each Lancaster, along with an additional flare chute to deliver the required amount of Window. Within a matter of days the new modifications had been carried out, and an intense period of training began.

This decision to select 218 Squadron was made in the light of the squadron's familiarity with both the GEE and G-H systems. 218 Squadron was the only front line heavy bomber squadron fully operational and trained to use the G-H device. The squadron's early success with G-H was in no small part due to the involvement of one of the "boffins" of ORS, Sebastian Pease, known to his friends as Bas. Bas joined Bomber Command in 1942, and had worked tirelessly on blind-bombing equipment, and was, at the time, one of Bomber Command's leading experts in the field. While at High Wycombe he was also involved with the development and use of Window. Bas was one of those lucky individuals who managed a more "hands-on" approach to his research, resulting in him spending a lot of time with the squadron assessing the accuracy and complexities of the temperamental G-H apparatus under operational conditions. His knowledge of the G-H system was eagerly passed onto the crews, who benefitted from his vast experience, and this was to pay dividends.

On Wednesday the 17th a special meeting was held at HQ Bomber Command, High Wycombe. Once again the meeting was chaired by Air Commodore Dalton Morris. Twenty-two senior Bomber Command and Royal Navy officers were in attendance, including the Vice Admiral of Dover, Commodore Jessel RN. This meeting was again attended by W/Cdr Cheshire, and, for the first time, W/Cdr Fenwick-Wilson, and finalised the planning of the forthcoming operation. On the 19th, HQ Bomber Command issued instructions to 218 Squadron to commence timed training flights. Six experienced senior crews with two reserves were selected. Normal operations still had to be carried out, however, and on the evening of the 19th four crews were given the now familiar Greengages garden off

"Happy" Funnell and crew stand beside their regular aircraft EF124 HA-R. The crew completed a full tour of operations with 218 Squadron. Frederick Fennell DFC was one of the squadron's characters when not operating.

Cherbourg. Ten mines were dropped with the aid of G-H, while F/L R "Wag" Walker and F/L Rycroft dropped ten mines in the Scallops garden area.

Training commenced on the following day under the watchful eye of W/Cdr Fenwick-Wilson AFC, and within the short space of eleven days 119 training flights had been undertaken. It was soon apparent that the exacting requirements of the operation demanded a larger crew complement, and it was increased accordingly to two pilots, three navigators, one wireless operator, one flight engineer, two gunners, two Window droppers plus two reserves, a total crew compliment of thirteen. For the remainder of the month the selected crews spent their time in preparing for the big day, the training flights being recorded in their log books as "special local flying" or something similar. The speed with which the squadron reached the stringent operational requirements confirms the very high standard of all those who served on the squadron. It also pays tribute to the special leadership qualities of the squadron's Commanding Officer, W/Cdr Fenwick-Wilson. Life on the squadron was not all training, and there were some stress free nights. Flying Officer Roy Hine, bomb aimer to F/L King RNZAF, recalls one of the many squadron characters who did much to ease the tension and anxieties of operational flying during this period,

> "One of the more notorious characters was Happy Funnel, I clearly remember his doleful voice announcing "Funnel in the Funnel" as he made his final approach. In the mess "Happy" was completely wonderful. I clearly remember in the Mess at Woolfox Lodge Happy with his tunic inside out, his trouser leg rolled up "Masonic Fashion" hanging in a bat like manor from one of the rather low girders drinking pint after pint. Both he and his pint seemed to defy the laws of gravity for at least an hour."

The squadron carried out forty-nine sorties during the month, well down on previous months, but this resulted from the squadron's operational stand-down from the 19th. Even so, the squadron was top of the 3 Group board with a 97.9% completion rate.

June

The weather at the start of June was less hospitable than had been hoped for, and delayed the launching of the invasion. Training for 218 Squadron's part in Overlord continued with practice flights on the 2nd, 3rd and 4th, during which, twenty-eight sorties were carried out by the eight selected crews. Their role was one of supreme importance, which would have a direct bearing on the enemy's response to the approaching invasion fleet. If 218 Squadron's *Operation Glimmer* and 617 Squadron's *Operation Taxable* were successful, it meant that the armada of Allied ships would probably reach its position off the Normandy beaches unopposed, and be able to disembark the invasion forces in relative peace. The plan was for six 218 Squadron aircraft in two lines of three abreast, to fly a meticulously accurate succession of overlapping elongated orbits for up to 2¾ hours, each one advancing gradually towards the coastal area between Boulogne and le Havre, north of the genuine landing grounds. At precise intervals, Window would be dispensed into the slipstream at a rate of a bundle every twelve minutes, and to the enemy radar, this would appear as a large convoy of ships heading across the Channel at a speed of seven knots. These six aircraft plus two reserves would represent only a tiny fraction of the Command's contribution to the invasion, and in all, a record 1,211 sorties would be dispatched against coastal batteries, and in diversionary and other support operations.

It was 23.39hrs when LJ522 HA-N took off from Woolfox Lodge in the hands of F/L Chaplin and F/L Webster, to launch Operation Glimmer. Two minutes later S/Ldr Brentnall and P/O Ecclestone departed in LJ472 HA-K, to be followed at 23.44hrs by S/Ldr Overton and F/L Funnell in EF133 HA-A. The reserve aircraft were next away at 23.50hrs, F/Ls Locke and Coram in LJ449 HA-E, and

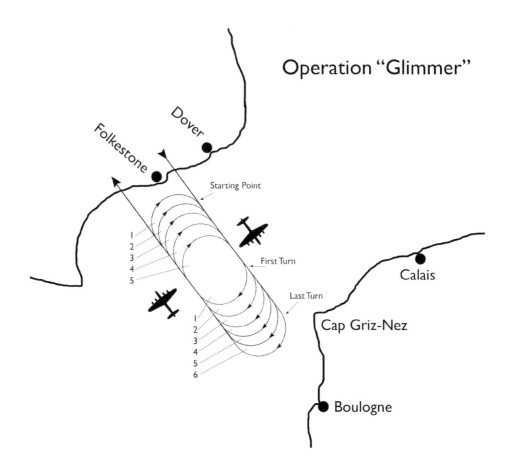

F/L Knapman with the appropriately named F/L Stirling in LJ517 HA-U, both of these pilot combinations RNZAF/RAAF. An hour after the departure of the first aircraft, F/Ls McAllister and Young initiated the second wave in LK401 HA-I , to be followed three minutes later by F/Ls Seller and Scammell in LJ632 HA-J, and F/Ls King and Gillies in EF207 HA-F at 00.43hrs. By the time the second wave reached its beat, the first wave had completed eight of its eventual twenty-three orbits and the final fifteen would be conducted in tandem. If a single crew faltered in its course or the timing of turns and Windowing, the enemy would see the operation as a spoof, and be alerted to a landing elsewhere. In the event, the crews of both 218 and 617 Squadrons performed to the high standards expected and demanded of them, and the operations were a complete success. The German reaction to Glimmer was immediate. Official Air Ministry and Naval documents state that the Germans mistook this raid for a genuine threat unlike 617 Squadron activities, German long-range guns along the French coast opened fire on Glimmer's imaginary convoy. German searchlights were also pressed into service, as too were a number of E-Boats dispatched into the convoy area.

At around 19.30hrs on the evening of June 6th a message was received from HQ No.3 Group:

"I HAVE RECEIVED THE FOLLOWING MESSAGE FROM C IN C FOR AIRCREWS...

"YOU DID FAMOUSLY LAST NIGHT IN THE FACE OF NO MEAN DIFFICULTIES. FIRE FROM COASTAL BATTERIES WHICH WERE YOUR TARGETS HAVE BEEN VIRTUALLY NEGLIGABLE.""

A further message arrived on June 7th at 10.55hrs from the C in C Bomber Command to Officer Commanding No.218 Squadron:

"IT IS ALREADY ESTABLISHED THAT THE OPERATIONS ON WHICH YOU ENGAGED ON THE NIGHT OF 5/6TH JUNE WERE VERY SUCCESSFULLY AND IT MAY WELL BE WHEN THE FULL FACTS ARE KNOWN IT WILL BE FOUND THAT YOU ACHIEVED RESULTS OF EVEN GREATER IMPORTANCE THAN CAN BE KNOWN AT PRESENT. THIS CAN ONLY HAVE BEEN BROUGHT ABOUT BY INTENSIVE TRAINING AND ATTENTION TO DETAIL AS A RESULT OF WHICH CREWS CONCERNED ACQUITTED THEMSELVES ADMIRABLY. THE NAVAL COMMANDERS HAVE EXPRESSED THEIR GREAT APPRECIATION OF THE SUPPORT OF NO.218 AND 617 SQUADRONS, AND IT IS NOW DISCLOSED THAT THE PATROL CARRIED OUT BY 101 & 214 SQUADRONS SUCCEEDED TOGETHER IN DELAYING THE ENEMY'S

APPRECIATION AS TO THE ACTUAL POINT OF ASSAULT, THEREBY ASSISTING THE MEASURE OF TACTICAL SURPRISE GAINED FOR OUR MAIN ASSAULT FORCES."

A thousand aircraft were aloft on D-Day Night to attack communications targets in and around the towns leading to the beachhead. It was similar fare on the next two nights, as 218 Squadron returned to the business of mining, a role to which it would devote itself exclusively for the remainder of the month. The campaign against railways would continue, but would run alongside two new offensives, one of which was to make particular demands on the Command's resources over the summer. This was the renewed campaign against flying bomb launching and storage sites, which would begin on the 16/17th, but first, 1, 3 and 8 Groups opened a new oil campaign with stunning success at Gelsenkirchen on the 12/13th. All production of vital aviation fuel at the Nordstern plant was halted for several weeks, at a cost to the German war effort of a thousand tons per day. The first daylight operations since the departure of 2 Group a year earlier, were mounted against E-Boats and other fast light craft at Le Havre on the evening of the 14th. It was a predominantly 1 and 3 Group show, the former attacking first, with 3 Group following up at dusk, both under the umbrella of a Spitfire escort. The operation, and a similar one against Boulogne on the evening of the 15th, were entirely successful, and few craft remained sufficiently intact to pose a threat to Allied shipping supplying the beachhead.

The first bombing operation of the month for 218 Squadron was an all-Stirling attack on the 15/16th against the marshalling yards at Lens, for which the squadron put up sixteen aircraft. The crews found the target to be well marked with red TIs, and S/Ldr Overton reported that a number of explosions were observed. On the 17th 90 Squadron conducted its final Stirling sorties, leaving only 218 and 149 Squadrons to carry the banner in 3 Group as Stirling bomber units. For the remainder of the month the Command was active by day and night against railways, oil refineries, V-Weapon sites and fuel and ammunition dumps, each raid accompanied by Pathfinder Mosquitos and or Lancasters to carry out the marking. Apart from its eight sorties on behalf of Operation Glimmer, 218 Squadron flew forty-nine mining sorties, which resulted in two Stirlings being written off at home on the night of the 12/13th. EF181 HA-J crashed when the Starboard tyre burst during take-off for French coastal waters, but F/L Young and his crew walked away, while EF299 HA-Z came to grief when attempting to overshoot on return, striking a ridge resulting in the u/c to collapse and F/L Funnell and his crew also emerged unscathed. As events were to prove, these were the final Stirling casualties to be suffered by the squadron as its two and a half year association with the type neared its end. A WAAF Anniversary dinner and dance was organised in the WAAF dining hall on the 28th, in honour of the fifth anniversary of their forming. A cake was made, and the station commander, G/C R.A.T Stowell, did the honours of cutting it. Messages from Her Majesty the Queen, the Duchess of Gloucester, the Chief of Air Staff and the A-O-C in C Bomber Command were read out to all ranks.

July

With the capture of the Cherbourg peninsula by the advancing allied armies, the onetime safety of the Channel ports had been compromised. German naval units were being harried, and any movement was becoming hazardous. The German U-Boot headquarters was moved to Brest, and Bomber Command consequently began a short campaign to extensively mine the waters off the port. Light rain and drizzle curtailed operations until the 3rd, when four 218 Squadron Stirlings took off for Brest. One aborted, but the remaining three delivered their mines from 14,000 feet using G-H. Six Stirlings returned on the following night to plant thirty mines, when the weather conditions over the garden area were such that F/L Gilles was able to follow fellow Aussie F/L Young visually, and successfully plant his five mines, despite having lost the use of his G-H apparatus while outbound. Returning crews reported what appeared to be rockets bursting at 14,000 feet while on their bomb run. Four crews were given individual targets on the 6/7th, Knocke, Ijmuiden, Noordwal and Gravelines, and all were serviced successfully. Flying bomb sites and railway targets would keep the rest of the Command busy during the first two and a half weeks of the month, although the first tactical operations in support of the ground forces took place on the evening of the 7th. Over 450 aircraft attacked enemy strong points in fortified villages north of Caen ahead of a British and Canadian advance.

Four 218 Squadron crews returned to Brest on the 8/9th, and delivered twenty mines. There was a determined effort from the defences to hamper the operation with accurate heavy and predicted flak as well as rockets, and LJ440 HA-E, captained by F/L Scammell, sustained damage to its front turret. Four crews were briefed for Goulet-de-Brest on the 9th, and three of them planted twelve mines using G-H.

No further operations were carried out until the 13/14th, when six crews were sent back to Goult-de-Brest, and five of them laid twenty-five mines in their allotted positions on G-H. Weather condition were ideal, with a solid cloud base at 10,000 feet. The last of the current series of operations against Brest was carried out on the 16/17th, when four crews returned again to Goult-de-Brest. There was only one incident to an otherwise quiet night, and this resulted from a training flight. Flight Sergeant Hibbard RAAF lost radio communications while returning to base, and when the navigator informed him that they were at Woolfox Lodge, he lined up for an approach. A near perfect touchdown was followed soon after by the end of the runway, much to the surprise of the pilot, who soon discovered the Stirling had landed at the 9th USAAF Troop Carrier base at North Witham, ten miles north-east of Woolfox Lodge. EF291 HA-C overshot the runway, which was four hundred yards shorter than the one at Woolfox Lodge, and ended up imbedded in a ditch. The aircraft was declared CAT AC/FB, and sent to SEBRO for repair, returning to the squadron in late August.

Squadron Leader Overton led an early evening take-off of fifteen Stirlings on the 17th, for a dusk attack on the flying bomb site at Mont Candon located south of Dieppe. On reaching the target area the crews easily identified the Pathfinder markers in the slight haze. The Master Bomber, S/Ldr Attwater DFC of 156 Squadron, ordered a one second delay in bombing the selected TIs south of the aiming point, and the delay took the bombs even further away, leaving the target unscathed. Eight 218 Squadron crews were given the task of mining between Ile de Groix and Lorient on the night of the 20th. Weather conditions outbound were terrible, with heavy rain and dense cloud over the Channel. Fortunately, conditions improved in the target area, and twenty-eight mines were laid with the aid of Gee from around 500 feet. This was followed by a small-scale mining operation on the 23/24th, when two crews returned to the waters off Goult-de-Brest to deliver ten mines with the aid of G-H.

A select number of B Flight pilots began their Lancaster conversion on the 24th, and the squadron's B Flight ground crews began the move to the squadron's new home on the 25th, Methwold having been chosen to accommodate the squadron during its long awaited conversion to the Lancaster. One flight of 3 Lancaster Finishing School at Feltwell moved to Woolfox Lodge for the purpose of training and converting the crews of A Flight. The Lancasters intended for 218 Squadron were initially allotted to XV and 514 Squadrons for acceptance and installation of G-H. Once accepted and modified the Lancasters were to be collected by the converted 218 Squadron crews, or to be ferried directly to Methwold. It is believed that the squadron's first Lancaster was Armstrong Whitworth built Mk I LM257, which arrived from XV Squadron on the 25th. An early problem was that the recently installed G-H equipment interfered with the operation of TR1196 sets. TRE and 3 Group's own radar specialists were soon on the job, and developed a suppresser that was found to cure the problem. With Methwold now being occupied by a front line squadron, it was upgraded to the full status of an independent station under direct operational and administrative control of Group HQ, rather than remain a substation to Feltwell.

The squadron was called upon to carry out another early evening operation on the 27th, when eight Stirlings were detailed to attack the flying bomb site at les Landes Vieilles et Neuves. The attack was divided into two waves, each consisting of two G-H aircraft followed by eight from 149 Squadron and a further two from 218 Squadron. Everything went to plan until the last turning point, when the G-H aboard the lead aircraft of the first wave failed. Squadron Leader Overton ordered his rear gunner to fire a green verey flare, which was the signal for the deputy leader F/L Gillies RAAF to take over. This delay resulted in the first wave being south of its intended track, and the bombing appeared too scattered to be effective. Complete cloud cover over the target meant there was no opposition from either flak or fighters. This was the first occasion that the G-H leader method of attack had been employed by the group, and although the operation appeared to be disappointing, group believed that this method of attack had potential, and the squadron and G-H would be given the opportunity to develop the technique further. Wing Commander Rogers was posted onto the squadron from 3 Lancaster Finishing School on the 27th. It is not known if the posting was to gain operational experience or for flight commander duties, but his stay was relatively short-lived, and he was posted to command 214 Squadron in 100 (RCM) Group on September 28th.

The flying bomb sites at Wemaers Cappel and Fromental were attacked in the late evening of the 28th. Seven aircraft were dispatched, each carrying twenty 500lb bombs, four of them acting as G-H leader and deputy pairings for each target. The other three crews together with thirteen from 149 Squadron made up the rest of the formation. The aircraft formed up in pairs, line astern over Cambridge, and proceeded on their respective routes. G-H reception was good, although the Wemaers Cappel element drifted off course, which brought it close to Ostend, where the flak defences gave a good account of themselves, and inflicted damage to four of the squadron's aircraft. The flak dispersed the formation, but this did not prevent accurate bombing. The attack on Fromental was carried out in excellent visibility, and the G-H leader saw his bombs burst across the target area, which was confirmed by the deputy.

"B" Flight Commander, Squadron Leader Phil Brentnall DFC and crew. Phil brought a wealth of flying experience when he arrived on the squadron in October 1943. A number of former flying instructors found their way onto the squadron, their skill and experience was a major factor in the squadron's success.

Four crews were selected to lead an attack on the flying bomb storage dump at Foret de Nieppe on the 29th. The operation, which would prove to be the last of the month, was again carried out in two waves, each with a G-H leader and deputy from 218 Squadron and twelve Stirlings from 149 Squadron. Bombing was carried out over ten-tenths cloud with tops up to 13,000 feet. Heavy flak was encountered at le Touquet, but the gunners' aim was off, as the flak was seen to burst 1,000 to 1,500 feet below the formation. Five Lancasters arrived at Methwold at the end of the month, LM281 and PD223 on the 30th from XV Squadron, and PB291 from 514 Squadron. PD234 arrived direct from AV Roe on the 31st, while NF906 came from Armstrong Whitworth. It had been a busy month for the squadron, during which eighty-two operational sorties had been carried out, and over 162 tons of bombs and 145 mines had been delivered without loss. The squadron had also undertaken 130 non-operational sorties, totalling some 138 hours. Three crew members of S/Ldr John Overton DFC crew were the recipients of awards in July, two DFC's and a DFM thus making the squadrons most decorated crew of the war.

August

V-Weapon-related targets dominated proceedings at the start of August, and on the 2nd, twenty Stirlings joined 370 other aircraft in attacks on one launching and three supply sites. Six from 218 Squadron paid a return visit in daylight to Mont Candon in company with fourteen from 149 Squadron. Weather conditions outbound and over the target were perfect, and G-H reception was good. The first bomb hit the wooded aiming point, while the remainder overshot, but the following bomb loads were seen to be accurate, and sent up plumes of earth, debris and uprooted trees. The second formation approached the target, which was now covered in smoke, and bombed from 13,000 feet. The bombs were mostly well placed, but dense smoke had by then obscured the target area. This was the final operation for the Stirling in 218 Squadron service, and also the last to be undertaken from Woolfox Lodge, as the move to Methwold would shortly be completed. On the departure of the squadron, RAF Woolfox Lodge was reduced to a care and maintenance basis under the command of the American IX Troop Carrier Command. The squadron's brief stay at Woolfox was a happy one, characterized by low losses, good leadership and decent facilities on and off the station. The period in Rutland had provided the whole squadron with the tonic it needed before its return to operations over Germany.

Over the next few days the squadron's conversion to the Lancaster was carried out in overcast and drizzly conditions, and the move to Methwold was completed with the arrival of the rear party on the 9th. Since the start of the year 3 Group had been gradually emerging from its "winter of discontent", as one by one, its squadrons took on Lancasters, and soon it would regain its rightful place at the forefront of operations.

The group's squadrons were divided into three bases, 31 at Stradishall, 32 at Mildenhall and 33 at Waterbeach. Control of 218 Squadron was directed from 31 Base Station at Stradishall under the able command of Air Commodore J Silvester CBE. Joining 218 in the months to come would be 186 Squadron at Stradishall and 195 Squadron at Wratting Common. After its short period of screening, 218 Squadron returned to the fray as a fully-fledged Lancaster unit on the night of the 9/10th, when seven aircraft took off to attack a flying bomb storage site at Fort d'Englos, located west of Lille. The squadron participants joined a further ninety-three Lancasters drawn from 32 and 33 Bases, which made up 3 Group's effort on this target. Oboe Mosquitos opened proceeding by marking the aiming point with red TIs, before the 218 Squadron Lancasters delivered eighty-four one-thousand pounders on a number of well-placed markers from between 13,000 and 14,000 feet. There was no flak or fighter opposition on this raid, and all of the Lancasters returned safely to base. The operation was a success, which left the target area a mass of craters, and the concrete and earth structure protecting the fuel badly damaged. A daylight raid on Lens marshalling yards was undertaken on the 11th, when six 218 Squadron Lancasters joined a further 114 from 3 Group. They picked up an escort of 11 Group Spitfires at the south coast, and carried on to deliver an accurate attack on a number of accurate red and yellow target indicators. A large cloud of smoke began to obscure the target as the crews turned for home, and once again there was no opposition from flak or fighters.

On the night of the 12/13th eight 218 Squadron Lancasters were made ready for an operation against the Opel works at Rüsselsheim in southern Germany. This was to be the squadron's first venture into Germany since November 1943, and for the majority of the crews now serving with the squadron, it would be their first ever foray over Germany. Each Lancaster was carrying a 4000lb cookie, a new experience for former Stirling crews, plus six 500lb bombs and 540 x 4lb incendiaries. The force departed England over Orfordness to join thirty-eight other 3 Group Lancasters heading towards the French coast in conditions of ten-tenths cloud. There was one early return, but the remainder pressed on to the target, where, in view of the small size of the factory site, the marking was to be by controlled by visual ground marking.

The attack opened punctually, but thick ground haze prevented the Master Bomber and his deputy from visually identifying the target, and the subsequent marking was not concentrated. The squadron was part of the second wave, and crews reported that the markers were scattered, and that a number of fires were evident but isolated. Flak over the target was intense, and night fighters had already been active since the force had passed by Brussels. PD252 HA-D failed to return home and thus became the first Lancaster to be lost by the squadron, and the first crew to go missing since May. The Lancaster crashed forty miles west of Frankfurt-am-Main, possibly the victim of a prowling night fighter. The bodies of the twenty-three-year-old pilot, P/O Vernon Humphrey RAAF, and his navigator,

F/Sgt Alan Chew, were found in the wreckage the following day, and it is believed that all of the remaining crew members managed to bail out as ordered. Two of these succumbed to their injuries, and three survived to become PoWs. The crew's regular rear gunner, Sgt Knopp, was in Ely Hospital with an eye problem, and was replaced by Sgt Westbrook DFM, rear gunner to P/O Scammell. Leslie Westbrook had received his award in June for his actions over Chambly. The fortunate Knopp went on to complete thirty-five operations with the squadron. Pilot Officer Humphrey had joined the squadron from 31 Base on May 9th, and he had completed six operations when lost on what was his first Lancaster operation.

One of the squadron's longest serving and most respected crews completed its tour mid-month. Squadron Leader John Overton DFC, A Flight Commander, was posted to 1657 CU on the 13th. John Overton had joined 218 Squadron from 1657 CU on 21st May 1943, and undertook his first operation as second pilot against Dortmund two nights later. Together with his crew he completed thirty one operations over a fifteen month tour.

Over eight hundred aircraft were involved in support of Canadian ground forces on the afternoon of the 14th, as they advanced on German positions around Falaise. Three 218 Squadron Lancasters were involved at Hamel, a strong point north-east of Falaise, along with a further ninety-seven 3 Group Lancasters. In clear weather the bomber stream collected their 11 Group Spitfire escort and headed almost directly to the target. Crews bombed a number of well-placed green TIs from 9,000 feet, and clouds of dust soon enveloped the whole area to obscure the results. It was during these attacks that some stray bombs fell among Canadian troops, killing thirteen of them, and wounding over fifty others.

In preparation for his new night offensive against Germany, Harris launched a thousand aircraft by daylight on the 15th, to attack nine night fighter airfields in Holland and Belgium. 218 Squadron supported the attack on St Trond, initially with three Lancasters, but W/Cdr Fenwick-Wilson was forced to return early when the port-inner of NN704 HA-S over-heated. The operations took place in conjunction with almost a thousand American bombers, and under the umbrella of both RAF and USAAF fighters. On the night of the 16/17th over four hundred aircraft destroyed fifteen hundred houses and many industrial buildings at Stettin, and sank five ships in the harbour. 218 Squadron provided five crews, and three newly arrived pilots flew their maiden operations as second pilots. A simultaneous attack on Kiel by three hundred aircraft was partially successful, many of the bombs falling within the docks area and ship-building yards. Bremen was left devastated by an assault on the 18/19th, which left more than 8,600 houses and apartment blocks gutted by fire, and well in excess of a thousand people killed. Eight 218 Squadron Lancaster's took part, and one of them sustained flak damage during its run-in to bomb.

The campaign against flying bomb sites would be concluded by the end of the month, as the Pas-de-Calais returned to Allied hands, but in the short term the weather conditions over 3 Group bases curtailed any further operations until the 25th, when six crews were detailed to carry out a daylight G-H attack on the flying bomb site at Vincly in the Nord Pas-de-Calais region of France. The crews were dispatched to RAF Waterbeach, where they would be briefed and joined by crews of 514 Squadron. The intention was to attack the target in three waves of five aircraft, each with a G-H leader from 218 Squadron, but problems with the take-off and identification of the G-H leaders forced a reduction to two waves. Flight Lieutenant Arbury arrived over the aiming point four minutes after zero-hour, and was the first to bomb. With G-H working perfectly the crew watched from 13,000 feet as their load of eleven one thousand pounders and four five hundred pounders exploded in two distinct clusters across the aiming point. Flight Lieutenant "Happy" Funnell identified the wood and road, and he too saw his bombs explode across the target area. It was impossible for the following crews to gauge the accuracy of the bombing as low cloud and smoke drifted across the target.

The small gaggle of eleven Lancasters encountered heavy accurate flak from St Omer on the way home, and F/L Knapman lost an engine to it. LM258 HA-Q was also hit, and it seems that F/L Douglas Haggis had to feather one or both engines on the port side. The Lancaster was coaxed across the North Sea to within sight of the Suffolk Coast, where a number of witnesses in Felixstowe observed it approaching low from the north-west with its undercarriage lowered and both port engines stationary. Witnesses also reported that the pilot was apparently looking

The crew of Flight Lieutenant Douglas Haggis taken just prior to their arrival on the squadron.

for somewhere to ditch as the Lancaster was circling near the New Pier, when it suddenly banked to port, side slipped and dived into the sea at 21.15hrs. Two dull explosions followed and a fire broke out on the water. A Walrus aircraft was soon on the spot, as were two launches, but sadly, only one survivor was located. The critically injured gunner was brought to Felixstowe docks and then transported to a local RAF Hospital, where he succumbed to his injuries at 00.30hrs. The pilot had been on his eleventh operation, and his and his crew's bodies were recovered over the following weeks as they were washed ashore.

That night, four hundred aircraft from 1, 3, 6 and 8 Groups returned to Rüsselsheim, to try again at the Opel factory. Seven 218 Squadron Lancasters took part, and they encountered considerable opposition in the target area from both flak and fighters, but returned safely. Considerable damage was inflicted upon the forge and gear-box assembly workshops, and both were out of action for over seven weeks, despite which, there was no effect on lorry production. The night's activities were no yet over, as seventeen 115 Squadron Lancasters were diverted from Witchford to Methwold on return from the raid due to unfavourable weather over their own base. The following morning the squadron was visited by the A-O-C, AVM R Harrison CB CBE DFC, AFC, to discuss with the crews the daylight operation to Vincly.

1, 3 and 8 Groups delivered a destructive attack on Kiel in hazy conditions on the 26/27th, for which 218 Squadron provided ten Lancasters. Flak and searchlight activity over the target was described as heavy, and fighters were active all along the route to and from the target. Severe damage was inflicted on the naval dockyard and arsenal, and the Germania Werft A.G and Deutsche Werke Kiel A.G factories were also hit. The final acts of the flying bomb campaign were played out in daylight at twelve sites on the 28th.

A follow up raid on Stettin was undertaken on the 29/30th, for which the squadron put up nine Lancasters, three of which returned early. A fire broke out in the fuselage of PD259 HA-A during the outward flight, caused by the ignition of three incendiaries. Prompt action by the flight engineer, P/O Shorter, prevented the fire from spreading, and F/L R "Taffy" Ecclestone and his crew were able to continue on and bomb the target. Considerable flak was experienced, particularly over Denmark and the target, and fighter activity was reported from Denmark to the target area. There was also a spirited response as the force made an incursion over neutral Sweden. W/O B Aves reported "*A very considerable flak barrage on route over Sweden, they were just not playing cricket!!*" All 218 Squadron crews returned home after being aloft for over nine hours.

August was brought to a close with daylight attacks by almost six hundred aircraft on nine V-2 stores on the 31st. Eleven G-H crews carried out a daylight raid on the flying bomb supply dump at Pont Remy. Two aiming points had been selected, one north of Pont Remy, and one slightly south. 218 Squadron was given the southern target, and attacked first at 16.00hrs. Cloud covered the target as the crews bombed from 15,000 feet, and they were unable to report on the accuracy

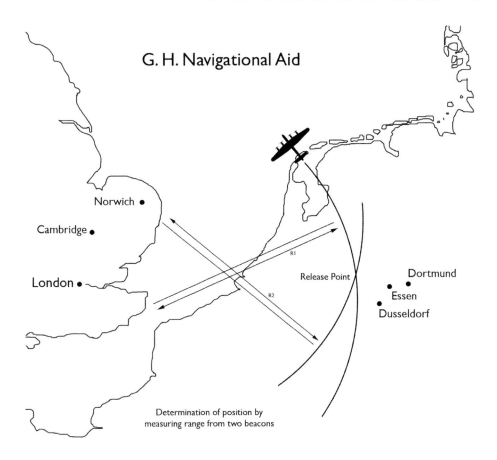

G. H. Navigational Aid

Norwich •

Cambridge •

London •

R1

Release Point

Dortmund
•
Essen •
•
Dusseldorf

R2

Determination of position by
measuring range from two beacons

of the bombing. On return it was considered the bombs may have overshot the aiming point, but one large explosion was observed, which produced a column of dense black smoke. Flak was encountered in the le Touquet area, where PD262 HA-G was slightly damaged, but all of the crews landed safely back at Methwold.

August had been a busy and satisfying month for the squadron, characterised by a smooth transition to the Lancaster. 218 Squadron was back at the forefront of operations, and once more taking the war to the German homeland. It was also the first in the Command to be fully equipped with G-H, 514 Squadron, who had pioneered G-H back in 1943 had almost two flights equipped, while 149 was in the process of fitting out a flight. Daylight operations were now being undertaken regularly, some of them complex in nature, but they would soon become a matter of course for 218 Squadron and the group. Over 357 tons of bombs had been dropped, eighty-nine operational sorties had been carried out, and none of these were mining.

September

September would be devoted largely to returning to Allied control the three French ports still occupied by the enemy. 218 Squadron had reason to celebrate on the 1st, as the new communal sites were finally completed and the first official party was given in the officers mess. The following day, and a million miles from the destruction being wrought over Germany, the squadron held the finals of the base gardening competition. The judge was the respected Mr J Young, Air Ministry Horticultural Advisor, who presided over a keenly fought contest, and, after considerable debate, declared the winners to be Station Police, Main Guard Room, while second place went to 149 Armoury, and the SHQ Photographic Section, Hut 124, came third.

1 and 3 Groups opened the campaign against enemy positions around Le Havre on the 5th, when 218 Squadron provided fifteen Lancasters to an overall force of more than 340. Accurate bombing took place in good visibility, and the operation was concluded without loss. 218 Squadron supported the next visit with fourteen Lancasters on the 6th, and sent ten to the same destination on the 8th. This time the intention was to attack in two waves, each assigned to its own aiming point, and the 218 Squadron aircraft bombed from between 3,000 and 5,000 feet on instructions from the Master Bomber. In view of the proximity of Allied troops and the general uncertainty of the situation, two-thirds of the crews brought their bombs home after the Master Bomber called a halt to the proceedings. Four Stirlings from 149 Squadron took part, and carried out the type's final bombing sorties under Bomber Command. Over 250 aircraft went back on the 9th, but this time all were sent home with their bombs because of poor visibility. The squadron lost the services of two experienced crews on the 9th and 12th, when F/L John McAllister and F/L Robert Chaplin were posted to 1653 Conversion Unit for instructional duties on completion of their tours. Each would receive a well-earned DFC within weeks. The operation was rescheduled for the following day, when fifteen 218 Squadron Lancasters participated in a particularly concentrated attack in excellent weather conditions. All the crews bombed on a concentration of red TIs as instructed by the Master Bomber, and opposition was non-existent. The final operation was mounted on the 11th, and a few hours afterwards the German garrison surrendered to British forces.

Also on this day 370 aircraft carried out attacks on synthetic oil refineries at Kamen, Castrop-Rauxel and Gelsenkirchen under a heavy fighter escort. 218 Squadron supported the first-mentioned, which produced accurate bombing in conditions of good visibility. On the night of the 12th 3 Group participated in the final heavy raid of the war on Frankfurt. Among the aiming points was the marshalling yards, to which S/Ldr Brentnall led fifteen 218 Squadron Lancasters. German night fighters were active early in the proceedings, and a clear sky gave them an advantage, which they exploited. Heavy flak and searchlight activity in the target area was not considered by returning crews to have been unduly troublesome, but night fighters were, and NF911 HA-F was shot down at 23.25hrs soon after leaving the target, the possible victim of Ofw Kurt Karsten of I/NJG6. The Lancaster crashed near Nastatten, and there were no survivors from the crew of F/O Frank Smith, who had been with the squadron since July, and were on their fourth operation together. NF906 HA-B crashed near Bad Homburg, approximately six miles north of Frankfurt, and there were no survivors from the crew of twenty-five year old F/O John Corliss RAAF. The circumstances surrounding the loss of this crew are unclear, but there is every chance that they met their end after an encounter with a night fighter. The crew had arrived on the squadron from 1657 CU on May 3rd, and were on their eleventh operation. The third loss was that of F/L Howard Seller and crew, who were on their twenty-sixth operation. It is believed that PD262 HA-G collided with Lancaster ME854 of 576 Squadron over Germany at approximately 23.00hrs, before crashing one mile south of Eppelsheim. This was an experienced crew, some members of which had been with the squadron since late in 1943. An eighth member of the crew, flying as second pilot, was twenty-year-old F/O Winston Leichardt RAAF. Leichardt had already completed two operations as captain since his arrival on the squadron on September 1st from 31 Base.

Cornish born Squadron Leader Nigel MacFarlane arrived on the 14th from 31 Base to command A Flight on the departure of S/Ldr John Overton DFC. Weather prevented the squadron from operating again until September 17th, when Bomber Command dispatched 762 aircraft in daylight against the German positions around Boulogne in preparation for an attack by Canadian ground forces. Ten 218 Squadron Lancasters were involved, one of them flown by S/Ldr McFarlane, while W/Cdr Fenwick-Wilson flew with F/O H Hibberd. The Master Bomber instructed crews to bomb from below cloud, which in the case of 218 Squadron, was as low as 2,000 feet, and returning crews reported an accurate attack. This one operation delivered three thousand tons of bombs, and that was sufficient to demonstrate to the occupiers of Boulogne that their situation was untenable, and they surrendered a little over a week later. This left only Calais to be liberated, and moves to bring this about began on the 20th. Over six hundred aircraft took part, including eleven from 218 Squadron. Take off was late in the afternoon, and the force carried out a successful attack from 2,000 to 3,000 feet, meeting no opposition from the Calais defences.

By mid-September 1944 218 Squadron was at its peak, having an abundance of experienced crews within it ranks. Squadron Leader MacFarlane's A Flight had thirteen operational crews, of which the senior captains had between them a wealth of operational experience. Flight Lieutenant Lock RNZAF had completed thirty-four operations, F/L Gillies RAAF twenty-seven, F/L Coram RAAF also twenty-seven, F/L Stirling RAAF twenty-six, F/L Scammell twenty-three, F/L Ecclestone twenty-two and F/L Young RAAF twenty-one. Across the tarmac B Flight was equally experienced, and among its fifteen crews F/L Funnell had completed thirty operations, F/L Webster RAAF twenty-nine and F/L Arbury twenty, while F/Ls Walker, Rycroft and Field each had eighteen to their name. This was without the operational record of S/Ldr Brentnall, the former B Flight commander, who was now awaiting posting on completion of his operational tour of thirty operations. Operational experience was not just confined to the pilots of course, and F/Sgt Boon, a gunner in F/L Lock's crew, had completed thirty-seven operations, while P/O Gordon, a gunner in F/L Funnell's crew, had completed an equally impressive thirty-six. The squadron section leaders were all similarly experienced, F/L Glover, navigation leader having completed thirty-three operations, the signals leader, F/L Taylor thirty-five, F/L Russell, bombing leader, thirty-three, and the engineering leader, F/L Phillips, twenty-eight. The most experience airman on the squadron at the time was the gunnery leader, F/L Piper DFC, who had flown on sixty-four operations over three operational tours. Flight Lieutenant O'Brien arrived on the squadron from 31 Base on the 18th, having completed his conversion to the Lancaster at 3 LFS at Feltwell. Over the succeeding months he would become one of the squadron's most experienced and respected captains.

1, 3 and 4 Groups provided the main force for a heavy raid on Neuss on the 23/24th, when fifteen Lancasters represented 218 Squadron. Returning crews were not enthusiastic about the marking, and F/L Coram reported having to bomb on a reddish glow seen through the clouds. Contrary to the crews' opinions, however, the raid was a success, with the bombing concentrated in the docks and industrial areas, where a reported 617 houses and fourteen public buildings were destroyed and numerous others were damaged. Later on the 24th the second raid

The crew of Flight Lieutenant John O'Brian seen here at RAF Methwold. A vastly experienced pilot John worked tirelessly as flight commander, however his concerns about crew inexperience resulted in his posting.

was mounted against enemy positions around Calais. 218 Squadron sat this one out, but fourteen Lancasters left Methwold in marginal weather conditions on the afternoon of the 25th, and headed towards Calais as part of a force of 870 aircraft. Complete cloud cover in the target area resulted in the operation being abandon by the Master Bomber after less than three hundred bomb loads had been delivered. On the following day S/Ldr MacFarlane led ten 218 Squadron Lancasters back to Calais as part of a force of more than seven hundred aircraft. They found the Pathfinder markers to be initially scattered, and this caused a number of bomb loads to explode on the beach. The Master Bomber responded by instructing an overshoot of two seconds, which resulted in bombs falling beyond the aiming point. A timely intervention by the Deputy Master Bomber brought the attack back on track, and all aiming points were accurately targeted.

The last raid of the month took place on the 28th, and would prove to be the final one of the series against Calais. Ten 218 Squadron Lancasters were again led by S/Ldr MacFarlane, and they were part of a force of almost five hundred aircraft. Four enemy strong points were attacked, along with six coastal batteries at Cap Gris Nez, although the operation was curtailed after cloud intervened. The

Flight Sergeant Trevor Knapman RNZAF and crew seen here at the start of their tour in October 1943. Twenty-year-old Knapman carried out an impressive 37 operations with the squadron before he was screened. Seated in front is the crews original mid upper gunner, American Staff Sergeant George Furste.

job was done, however, and the German garrison surrendered to Canadian forces within days. Thus ended September, another busy month in which the squadron carried out 120 operational sorties, and delivered 762 tons of bombs in the process. However, the loss of three crews was a timely reminder to all on the squadron that the war was far from over. Two experienced captains and their crews completed their tours in September and were awaiting posting, F/L Ian Lock RNZAF had completed thirty-four operations and was posted to 1651 CU, while fellow New Zealander, F/L Trevor Knapman, had completed an impressive first tour of thirty seven sorties. Both officers would be awarded the Distinguished Flying Cross within a matter of weeks.

October

October would see the start of a new Ruhr offensive, and the heaviest attacks of the war on the German homeland. Rain and low cloud prevented any operations from taking place until the 3rd, when ten 218 Squadron Lancasters took off at lunch time to attack the sea wall at Westkapelle on the island of Walcheren. 250 Lancasters represented the heavy brigade, and they were to attack in sections of thirty aircraft under an escort of fighters from 11 Group. 218 Squadron contributed to the third wave, and bombed in excellent visibility from between 3,500 and 4,500 feet. Flight Lieutenant Stirling reported seeing his cookie hit the wall of the dyke, as did fellow Australian F/L Young and crew. The Master Bomber was clearly heard by all the crews, and they were enthusiastic about the outcome of the raid. On leaving the target water was seen to be flooding through the breaks in the wall and spreading

Wing Commander Fenwick Wilson AFC leads the cheers at the presentation of the honours board. The Honourable H Herman Hodge High Commissioner of the Gold Coast is in attendance.

inland. It was actually during the fifth wave that a breach occurred, and it was widened by those following behind. The squadron was now fully equipped and trained with G-H, as was 149 Squadron across the airfield. 514 Squadron had just two of its flights equipped, and this was because of delays in production and delivery. In the whole of 3 Group only sixty G-H sets were available. The new Mk II G-H was making an early appearance, replacing the almost exhausted stocks of the old Mk I. The group's ability to mark and bomb its own targets allowed it from now on to operate independently of the Pathfinders. AVM R Harrison had long championed a specialist role for the group in Bomber Command, and believed that it should be allowed to carry out independent G-H blind bombing operations.

In response to a request from the American Third Army, the squadron contributed fourteen Lancasters to a force of more than five hundred from 1, 3 and 8 Groups to attack the town of Saarbrücken on the night of the 5/6th. The two phase operation began with an attack on the marshalling yards, to disrupt supply routes to the front. The 218 Squadron element took part in this phase, which did not proceed as planned after a disagreement arose between the Master Bomber and his deputy over the accuracy of the markers. Ultimately the Master Bomber abandoned the attack, by which time all but one of the 218 Squadron crews had bombed on a number of scattered markers. The attack on the town itself followed two hours later, and was highly destructive, destroying almost six thousand houses and damaging a further eleven hundred. Happily, the majority of the inhabitants had fled the town as the front drew closer, but even so, more than three hundred people lost their lives.

The Hon Harry B Hermon-Hodge, official representative of the Colonial Office, paid a visit to the station on the morning of the 6th to present the squadron with a Mahogany Honours Board on behalf of the Gold Coast. A number of crews were introduced, and a series of official photographs were taken. The second Ruhr campaign was opened on the night of the 6/7th by a force of more than five hundred aircraft from 3, 6 and 8 Groups. The target was Dortmund, where the usual extensive catalogue of damage resulted to industry and communications. Only five aircraft failed to return, and none was lost from the 218 Squadron contingent. In order to protect the exposed Allied right flank following the failure of Operation Market Garden, daylight attacks were carried out against the towns of Cleves and Emmerich on the 7th. The former, situated near the Dutch Border and straddling the Rhine, was assigned to 350 aircraft from 3, 4 and 8 Groups, including ten 218 Squadron Lancasters. Crews bombed visually on smoke markers under the control of a Master Bomber, and the attack was reported to be accurate and concentrated, although smoke obscured most of the target. Medium flak was experienced, but no crews reported damage. Flying on this operation was the A Flight crew of F/O Robbie Roberts RAAF, who were on their first operation. The bomb-aimer was F/O Richard "Dick" Perry RNZAF, who kept a war time diary of the crew's operations.

We took off at noon into a clear sky and climbed up to 14,000 feet to meet the bomber stream. Crossed the Dutch coast at The Hague with very little flak in evidence. As usual Gee was out and, being a clear day, map read our way in to the target for our final bombing run. The target was a railway marshalling yards and, still with little flak to trouble us, unloaded our bombs as a clear straddle across the tracks. Bomb load was 11x1000's plus 4x500's. A Halifax, right in front of us, had its wing shot off and crashed, not the best of sights for us on our first bombing sortie. Map read all the way back to base, again encountering very little flak at the Belgian coast. All of our aircraft returned safely.

A thick blanket of fog and low cloud settled over East Anglia, which caused the cancellation of an operation planned for the 8th. It would be almost a week before the weather would clear sufficiently for operations to resume, and this respite gave the hard pressed ground crews time to install a number of newly arrived Mk II G-H sets, and carry out some long overdue inspections and repairs. For the aircrews the temporary reprieve from operations was especially welcome. Flight Lieutenant Dunham returned to the squadron from 31 Base on October the 12th. Peter Dunham had previously been with the squadron back in 1941 as an observer, completing twenty-nine operations on Wellingtons, for which he was awarded a well deserved DFC. Prior to his first spell with 218 in 1941 he had completed fourteen operations as a gunner with 214 Squadron. Now in 1944, married and the father of a young son, he had returned to the squadron as a fully trained Lancaster pilot.

The crews enforced lay-off came to an end on the 14th, when the squadron took part in the first of a series of raids under the code name *"Hurricane I"*. This was a campaign directed against oil and communications specifically located in the Ruhr. The aim of the raids was to disrupt and disorganise Germany's industrial heartland. The raids would also demonstrate to the enemy the overwhelming superiority of the Allied air forces ranged against it. At first light on the 14th over a thousand aircraft took off for Duisburg, among them twenty Lancasters representing 218 Squadron, led by the A Flight commander, S/Ldr MacFarlane in NF934 HA-G. Time on target was set for 08.45hrs, and 218 Squadron was part of the third wave timed to be over the target some twenty minutes later. 3 Group was allotted to the northern aiming points and attacked from between 17,000 and 23,000 feet. The attack was an outstanding success, which delivered almost four and a half thousand tons of bombs, and caused severe damage, particularly in the docks area. Flying Officer D Perry wrote in his diary:

Daylight raid on Duisburg, trip #2. Off the ground at 7 am and climbed to 18,000 feet to meet the bomber stream and away out across the Channel for Belgium. Arrived over the target at 9am to find heavy flak and a master bomber yelling "FREEHAND". We took him at his word, picked a target, a bridge over the Rhine, and bombed visually straddling the west end with our bomb load, 11+1000's and 4x500's. We raced away from the target, throwing out "Window" as we went and headed northwest for home. Map read across Belgium and so to baseball. All of our aircraft returned safely.

To emphasize the point about air superiority, Bomber Command returned to Duisburg that same night, dispatching 1005 aircraft, among them a further twenty from 218 Squadron. This time no cloud was encountered over the target, and the crews bombed from between 18,000 and 20,500 feet on TIs. Fires were still burning in the docks area from the morning raid, and F/O Ellis reported that *"The whole dock area was ablaze"*, while F/O Lloyd reported that he *"could see the fires from 15 miles before the T.Is went down"*. In all the squadron had dropped 227 tons of bombs in less than twenty-four hours. Remarkably, this massive effort of despatching 2,018 sorties within less than a day was achieved without the support of 5 Group. F/O Perry wrote:

Night raid on Duisburg, trip #3. Briefed at 8 pm, took off at 10.15 and were over Reading at about midnight, making for the French coast. Over the target, bombed on markers and were away again before anything serious started coming up. Same bomb load as for the previous trip. Looking back one noted the evident destruction. Searchlights weaving about the sky, flack bursting around and behind us like balls of smoke, markers floating down to lie on the city like varicolored flowerbeds and the streets lighted up by fires burning all over the city. Uneventful flight back to base and the usual de-briefing and bacon and eggs. Big headlines in papers. 10,000 tons of bombs and incendiaries during the 24-hour period. Germany's greatest inland port demolished.

A heavy attack was carried out on Wilhelmshaven on the 15/16th, for which the squadron put up nine crews led by S/Ldr MacFarlane. As events were to prove, this was the final of fourteen heavy raids directed at this port since early 1941. Thick haze was encountered over the target, and this resulted in some scattered bombing. Returning crews reported that fires could be seen in the target area from up to fifty miles away. On the following day another experienced and respected pilot was unexpectedly posted. The B Flight commander, acting S/Ldr Philip Brentnall DFC, joined the newly formed 195 Squadron after completing thirty-one operations. Phil Brentnall's contribution to the success of the squadron was unequaled. Respected and liked by all ranks, he had brought with him a wealth of experience which he freely passed onto all the crews. By the time of his posting he had amassed over 1,353 flying hours. Such was his high regard, Wing Commander Fenwick-Wilson rated his flying ability as exceptional. Peter Dunham was promoted to acting squadron leader on the 18th, and was appointed to succeed him as B Flight commander.

A new role was beckoning for 3 Group as an independent group using the G-H device. In order to gauge its effectiveness in the hands of a largish force, an undamaged urban target was required so that there would be no old craters to cloud the issue. The virtually virgin target of Bonn was selected to host a raid on the 18th, for which around a third of the group's Lancasters were equipped with G-H to act as gaggle leaders. To aid identification their fins were painted with two prominent yellow horizontal bars. The system had been in use for some time, but not by large forces, and it was to be employed by day and night, whenever the target was cloud covered, and the cloud did not extend beyond 18,000 feet. Eight 218 Squadron Lancasters joined 120 others from the group for this operation, with four crews, those of F/L Stirling RAAF, F/L Coram RAAF, F/O H Knight

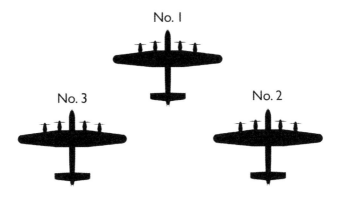

A standard Vic formation No. 1 was the G-H leader.

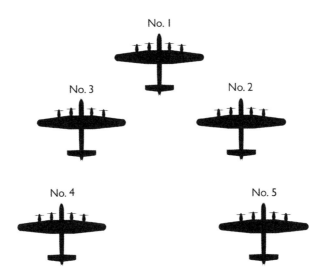

Formation of five aircraft, this formation often proved difficult to maintain. No. 1 is the G-H leader with No. 2 Deputy.

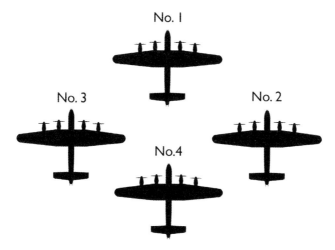

A four flight formation, again aircraft No.1 is the G-H leader.

and F/O D Cook RNZAF, selected as G-H leaders. The intention was for the formation to fly in sections of three, with a G-H aircraft leading. Forming up proved more difficult than expected, and the G-H leaders had four or possibly five followers, while some had no followers at all.

Eventually the gaggle set off, and met their fighter escort of seven Mustang squadrons east of Dunkirk, before proceeding south-east to the northern tip of Luxembourg, and then east-north-east to approach the target from the south. Seven squadrons of Spitfires also joined the formation from the River Meuse onwards. Contrary to expectations, the weather over the target was only three to five tenths, rather than the ten-tenths expected. With the gaggle of matt black painted Lancasters clearly visible against the clear blue sky, the city's flak defences were both heavy and accurate, and the formation was broken up and dispersed. To compound the problems, a fading G-H release pulse was experienced and many crews decided to bomb visually. Two 218 Squadron Lancasters were damaged by flak on the bomb run, and LM281 was extensively damaged after incendiaries hit the starboard-inner engine and caused a fire. Despite all of the difficulties, the attack was well concentrated in the centre of the city, where seven hundred buildings were destroyed. Evidence at debriefing demonstrated that the crews persevering with G-H had obtained good results.

The Group would still operate in tandem with others as required, and on the 19/20th it joined 1 and 6 groups in a two-phase assault on Stuttgart. 565 aircraft ultimately took off, the second phase four and a half hours after the first. F/O Perry.

Night raid on Stuttgart, trip #4. Briefed at 2 pm, took off at 5.00am. Same route to the French coast. Took over from Robbie for part of the trip out, which he found useful, as it allowed him to spend some time with the other members of the crew. Used H2S for the first time as a navigating aid and Frank, our Navigator, used it until we were some 20 miles from the target which was a marshalling yard. Bombed target visually in clear sky and very little flak. Bomb load was a 1x4000 (affectionately known as a cookie} and 6x1000's. On the way home we lost all of our navigational aids and had to rely on Frank's dead reckoning to bring us back to base. Proof of the pudding was that we were first to land.

This was the last operation to be presided over by the respected and admired W/Cdr Fenwick-Wilson AFC, who was posted to 31 Base Stradishall as Wing Commander Training (Plans) on the 21st. His contribution to the success of the squadron during 1944 cannot be overstated. Characteristically Canadian, he led from the front and oversaw a number of squadron transitions with a typical North American determination. He commanded the squadron during the conversion to the Lancaster, and was instrumental in the development and operational use of G-H, although, perhaps his most notable contribution to the war effort was his role as squadron commander during the training and application of Operation "Glimmer", which was never acknowledged. There were celebrations in the officers mess on the 19th, when the popular Aussie, F/L Jack Coram was screened from further operations, after he and his crew had completed their first tour of thirty-seven operations. He would be awarded a DFC in January 1945.

Squadron Leader W Smith arrived on the 21st of October from 115 Squadron, and he was promoted within days to assume command of the squadron. Thirty-one-year-old William John Smith had served with the Indian Army before joining the RAF in 1936. Prior to his period with 115 Squadron Smith had served the majority of the war in RAF Training Command, two years of which were in Canada, instructing on twin engine aircraft. Regrettably for the squadron, W/Cdr Smith brought with him the rather starched and authoritarian approach to commanding that was evident in Training Command, but was not appreciated on a front line squadron.

A daylight G-H raid was directed at Neuss on the 22nd, for which 218 Squadron contributed ten Lancasters. There was complete cloud cover with tops as high as 17,000 feet, but the G-H pulse was strong, and subsequent photographs showed that the bombing had been concentrated. Despite this, the operation caused the destruction of only around a hundred buildings. Wing Commander Smith's leadership style was demonstrated before this operation, as Australian F/O Lance Gregory, bomb-aimer to F/L Robert Stirling RAAF recalls:

Just before the departure of W/Cdr Fenwick Wilson he informed my crew that having completed 35 operations we were screened. However within days we were told that we were on op's again, not believing this we checked the "Battle Order" and at the top was F/L Stirling. The skipper went to see the Wing co and informed him what W/Cdr Fenwick Wilson had told the crew on completion of their 35th operation. The commanding officer was not happy having his decision questioned and replied "I am the commanding officer of 218 Squadron and if I say you fly tonight, you fly, how dare you question my orders." For his stand my skipper got sent on a course at RAF Cranwell. We went on to fly a further 3 op's bringing our tour up to 38 operations. It was not an auspicious start.

The Hurricane force moved on to Essen on the 23/24th, when 218 Squadron contributed twelve Lancasters led by S/Ldr MacFarlane. Seven of the squadron's crews were selected to bomb using G-H, and they were part of a record force of 1055 aircraft, which delivered 4,538 tons of bombs. A return to Essen was planned for the following day, but the weather closed in for the next twenty-four hours. A late afternoon take off by 770 aircraft on the 25th headed back to the Ruhr city, this time with eleven 218 Squadron Lancasters in support led by S/Ldr Dunham. Cloud over the target prevented the crews from identifying the aiming point, and the attack, therefore, proceeded on Pathfinder sky markers. Extensive damage was caused in the city and upon the Krupp Steelworks, and this once mighty armament producing giant now lay in ruins.

An all-3 Group attack on the chemical works at Leverkusen was undertaken on the 26th. The group dispatched 105 aircraft, ten of which represented 218 Squadron. Rendezvous was over Bury St Edmunds, where the squadrons formed up into their now familiar vic formations. The force made landfall near Ostende, and with their escort of four squadrons of RAF Mustangs swung due east towards Mönchengladbach. Predicted flak met the crews as they bombed on G-H over a cloud covered target, and a large column of black smoke was seen rising up through the clouds. News was received on the 27th that 149 Squadron was to expand to three flights, and would require the facilities at Methwold. Consequently, 218 Squadron was told to anticipate a move to Stradishall. Five of the squadron's Lancasters were dispatched against the heavy gun emplacements near Dishoek situated on the island of Walcheren on the morning of the 28th. Two large explosions were seen, and F/O Cook RNZAF reported that they appeared to be ammunition dumps. Just two crews represented the squadron in an operation against Cologne that evening, and the attack by over seven hundred

Wing Commander William Smith DFC last war-time commanding officer. His authoritarian style of command was not appreciated by the squadron crews. Group Captain Brotherhood station commander RAF Chedburgh recorded that Wing Commander Smith's inflexible resolve and insistence on the highest standards was the reason for the squadron's success.

aircraft appeared to be concentrated, with numerous fires reported in and around the aiming point.

Five 218 Squadron Lancasters took part in a daylight operation against Westkapelle on the 29th, led by S/Ldr MacFarlane. This was followed on the 30th by an attack on the oil refineries at Wesseling, near Cologne. This all-3 Group operation was carried out in conditions of total cloud cover, and for once, forming up and flying in formation went without a hitch. A total of 102 Lancasters carried out accurate bombing, despite an initial problem with a false G-H pulse. This was picked up by a number of crews, who, as a result, bombed some five miles from the aiming point. It was later established that the pulse had originated from a recently set-up ground testing station. The final assault on Walcheren was delivered by 5 Group on the 30th, before Canadian and British ground forces went in and secured the island after a week of heavy fighting. It would take a further month to clear the forty mile stretch of river of mines, and the first convoy would not arrive at Antwerp until the end of November.

It was back to Cologne on the evening of the 30th, when over nine hundred bombers inflicted further enormous damage. Marking was provided by Pathfinders, who dropped a number of accurate sky markers. The ninety-nine 3 Group Lancasters attacked in clear conditions using G-H. A full moon illuminated the aircraft, which were visible to each other for miles in the crisp freezing night air. Flak over the target was described as moderate but accurate. Returning crews reported a number of large fires in the target area, and one of them, slightly south-west of the aiming point, was particularly substantial. A number of fighters were seen, including a jet, but no encounters were recorded. F/O Perry:

Night raid on Cologne, trip #5. Took off into very bad weather and carried on to the target over 10/10ths cloud. Very pretty over target, very little flak, sky markers, bright moonlight and German fighters circling above us. Saw our first jet/rocket aircraft which went straight up through the bomber stream and started circling above us. Did not note that it accomplished anything. Bombed on sky markers, a cookie and 14 cans of incendiaries. Very uneventful trip and arrived back at base at 11.30 pm.

An all-3 Group daylight raid on a synthetic oil refinery at Bottrop was carried out by 102 Lancasters on the 31st. The target, to the north-west of Essen, was approached on an almost due south heading, and flak was reported as active. The aiming point was concealed under a complete cloud cover, and the G-H leaders consequently released sky markers. After bombing the crews turned to the north-west to pick up their fighter escort before heading back to the safety of the Allied front line. The last operation of the month was again directed at Cologne on the night of the 31st, when almost five hundred bombers attacked a cloud-covered target. The Pathfinders dropped a number of Oboe-assisted sky markers over the western suburbs of the city, and the six participating 218 Squadron crews successfully delivered their loads from between 18,000 and 20,000 feet. They encountered practically no flak, and below them the city still glowed from the previous night's raid. A familiar face met the crews at de-briefing, W/Cdr F Milligan AFC, the former commanding officer of 623 Squadron, spoke to the crews upon their return. Wing Commander Milligan was at the time serving at 3 Group HQ at Exning Hall.

October had been an extraordinary month for the squadron, and the busiest it had ever experienced. 206 operational sorties had been carried out during nineteen operations, eleven of which had been in daylight. A squadron record of 1,148 tons of bombs had been delivered, and all without loss. The month brought the one-thousandth sortie flown from Methwold since it became operational in May. The Group had beaten August's record of 1,341 sorties, by a considerable margin, and had, in fact almost doubled it with 2,676.

November

The squadron opened its November account on the 2nd, with a G-H raid on the Meerbeck synthetic oil plant at Homberg, just north-west of Duisburg. A new method of sky marking was employed for this attack, which involved the G-H leaders dropping green flares with their bomb loads, mimicking the Pathfinder technique known as the Wanganui method. Seventeen 218 Squadron Lancasters participated, and the force of 180 3 Group Lancasters was escorted by 109 Spitfires and forty-five RAF Mustangs. It was not until the formation was within five miles of the target that fairly accurate predicted flak was encountered, and this caused damage to sixty-two aircraft during the bomb run, including five from 218 Squadron. Flight Lieutenant "Wag" Walker was wounded by flak splinters in his shoulder while on the bomb run, as Sgt Aubrey Benns, the flight engineer, recalls:

> *We were over the target when we were hit, the skipper was hit in the shoulder and had to be helped from his seat to have his wound treated and to recover. I took over as pilot and boy o boy did I sweat. I reckon I lost ponds in the short time I was at the controls. My piloting experience up until then was two twenty minute periods on the link trainer! Somehow I managed to keep us in the air and out of danger. Thankfully "Wag" recovered enough to take over and bring us home"*

On his return F/L Walker was admitted to the SSQ were he remained for the next two days. Two large explosions were seen, and black smoke was rising up to 10,000 feet as the crews turned for home. At debriefing crews declared themselves unimpressed by the green markers, which had been difficult to pick out in daylight. They were, however, in agreement with the idea in principle, and that it was worth further trials. Lady luck was certainly with the group on this operation, as it was discovered later that over sixty enemy fighters had been dispatched to meet the force, but had been sent mistakenly towards Münster.

A 3 Group raid on the town of Solingen on the 4th involved 176 Lancasters, of which seventeen represented 218 Squadron. Sky marking was once again tried, but this time in the form of bundles of three red flares fixed together. There was nine-tenths cloud over the target with tops up to 8,000 feet, with limited defensive activity, all of the squadron's participants bombed on G-H. Bombing appeared concentrated, but this was a false impression, and the results on the ground were disappointing. F/O Dick Perry:

Day raid on Solingen, trip #6. Took off at 12 noon and proceeded to the target over 10/10 cloud. No flak evident and were able to bomb visually through a gap in the cloud cover. Target a marshalling yards and bomb load a cookie, 6/1000's and 6/500's. One unnerving experience, the aircraft next to us blew up for no explainable reason. Was it sabotage, who knows? Then to top things off, the Germans sent up two scarecrows, the first we'd seen. Very evident that they were not planes as there was no sign of any wreckage and we actually flew right through some of the debris. Flew back by way of the sunken island of Walcheren but could see no sign of activity even though it was a battlefield at the time. Map read back to base through clear skies and landed at 5.30 pm.

The group returned to Solingen on the 5th, when sixteen 218 Squadron Lancasters joined a further 159. The bombing proceeded in four waves with G-H leaders from the squadron at the head of three of them. There was complete cloud cover over the target as the attack began at 13.00hrs. Once again flares were dropped as the lead G-H crews bombed, and the group's experiments over the past few attacks had established the optimum frequency of marking required to achieve the necessary accuracy and concentration. The raid was an outstanding success, which left thirteen hundred houses and eighteen industrial properties destroyed, with over sixteen hundred other buildings severely damaged. Flight Lieutenant Gillies RAAF completed his tour of thirty-six operations on return from this raid, it had taken him almost a year. For some inexplicable reason twenty-six-year-old Leonard Scot Gillies did not receive any award in recognition of his operational tour. Dick Perry:

Back to Solingen, trip #7. Took off at 10.30 am and proceeded to the same target. My first experience with the Elsan, it was full up and liquid sloshing about. Used a perfectly good Mae West in order to clean myself up. This time we bombed over 10/10 cloud on sky markers. Also dropped some of our own markers for the following aircraft to bomb on. Same bomb load. Came home to pouring rain and had to virtually feel our way down to the runway. Advised that aircraft had been bombed by other aircraft on both of these days. Is it any wonder that we keep

Dennis, our mid-upper, searching the skies for aircraft above us with their bomb doors open.

The aerodrome was rocked by the explosion of a 500lb long delay bomb on the 6th. The bomb had been found to have a technical problem, and had been stored in the old sand pit for safety. Tragedy struck when it prematurely exploded, killing two members of the 2807 RAF Regiment from Feltwell. A civil inquiry was held by the local coroner on the 9th in the station sick quarters, and this was followed on the 10th by a Court of Inquiry to "allocate responsibility".

A raid on the town of Koblenz was detailed for the night of the 6th, for which seventeen crews had been briefed. However, the above-mentioned explosion in the bomb dump led to eight Lancasters being withdrawn because of delays in bombing up. This all-3 Group attack resulted in the destruction of 58% of the town's built-up area. Marking was carried out by G-H, and crews reported visibility over the target to be ideal, with the rivers Mosel and Rhine clearly evident, and the ground markers to be concentrated around the aiming point. The town offered practically no defence, and was blanketed in incendiaries, the glow of which was visible from Brussels on the way home. Bomber Command letter BC/S.25172/ORG arrived at Methwold on the 7th, advising the squadron of its move to Chedburgh, and not Stradishall as previously instructed and this was followed up on the 8th with Instruction No.44, confirming the move. Before this the Group had another crack at the Meerbeck synthetic oil plant at Homberg during the morning of the 8th. Fifteen Lancasters were away by 08.33hrs, and they joined up with over a hundred other 3 Group Lancasters at 10,000 feet over Bury St Edmunds in marginal weather. The cloud covered target was attacked from between 15,000 and 17,500 feet in the face of heavy and accurate flak, and sixty-five Lancasters sustained damage. Eight 218 Squadron aircraft were hit during the bomb run, and one was lost.

PD374 HA-C was in the first wave over the target, and was hit by flak in the starboard-inner engine immediately after bombing. The Lancaster was again bracketed by flak, which damaged the fuselage near the rear exit door, and set both port engines on fire. Twenty-six year-old F/O Leslie Hough RAAF instructed his crew to prepare to abandon the aircraft as he turned towards the west in an attempt to reach the safety of the Allied lines. With both port engines and the port fuel tank ablaze, it was obvious that the crew had to leave the aircraft without delay. As the wing dipped Les Hough shouted over the intercom *"Go – everybody out"*. The bomb-aimer, F/O John Barron, opened the front hatch and left, the flight engineer, W/O John Tales, secured the seat type parachute to his skipper and followed Barron out. Just before he left, Sgt Allen Clifford, the crews navigator exchanged a wave with his grim-faced skipper, before he too dropped head-first out of the hatch to leave the pilot alone in the forward section. At the rear of the aircraft, tail-gunner Sgt Stanley Lee made the short distance to the damaged exit, where he found the mid-upper gunner, Sgt J Lawson, and the wireless operator, Sgt H Burnside, seemingly unwilling to jump. Lee wasted no time and went out, leaving his two crewmates to their fate, and both were found dead in the wreckage.

Almost immediately after navigator F/Sgt Allen Clifford bailed out, the main spar folded and the aircraft disintegrated, taking with it the gallant young pilot. The main part of the Lancaster crashed at Krampf Farm near Horstgen. Flight Sergeant Clifford was shot at on his decent by the local Volkssturm, who put a number of rounds into his canopy. Such was the speed of his decent, that on hitting the tiled roof of a house, he smashed straight through and continued on until finally coming to rest in the attic. A local mob rushed into the house and found the winded navigator, whom they dragged down the stairs and out onto the road. He was immediately set upon by a group of hostile civilians who began to kick him to death, it was only the brave and timely intervention of a Luftwaffe Feldwebel that saved his life. It is believed that twenty-six-year-old W/O John Tales landed in a field owned by Herr Holland, he was also set upon by civilians at the instigation of Ortsgruppenleiter Kaumans, a local leader, who also took an active part in the beating. Soon afterwards a motor cycle combination arrived with two members of the SS aboard and another unidentified man. They drove off with the semi conscious Tales and headed towards Moers, where the defenceless young airman was cold-bloodedly murdered.

Having been saved by the Feldwebel, Allen was put into the German's side car and taken to a nearby police station. On the way the Feldwebel stopped in a quiet side street and told Allen in English that he would be safe as long as they avoided the SS. Eventually they arrived and Allen was placed in a cell, where he was later joined by a dishevelled and shocked Stan Lee. Allen takes up the story:

That afternoon we were paraded by armed soldiers through Duisburg. People were shouting Terrorfleiger" and throwing stones at us. We were marched through some badly damaged property and then put against a factory wall. A line of soldiers stood with their rifles against their shoulders. Stan said in a horrified voice "they are going to shoot us." I felt protective of Stan and said "For God's sake don't let them see you are frightened". He immediately pulled himself together. A soldier barked an order and we both waited terrified for the bullets, but then a fat old women appeared, shrieking, and placing herself between us and the execution squad. She ran in front of us screaming what sounded like propaganda at the soldiers. They shouted back but this brave woman stood her ground and saved our lives. The soldiers meekly shouldered arms and we were marched down the road, silently giving thanks to this one civilian in a vengeful city who had shown us mercy.

This ill-treatment of captured airmen would escalate as Germany's position declined, and it was a very bad time for crews to find themselves in enemy hands. In most such cases, and certainly in this one, the perpetrators underwent trial after the war, and were hanged. Leslie Hough had arrived on the squadron on August 10th from 31 Base, the crew had been on its fourteenth operation. There was some cause for celebration, as this was the last of thirty-five operations for F/O Jack Arbury and crew, who had joined the squadron in March 1944 from 1651 CU. It was now becoming a regular occurrence for crews to complete their operational tours, and it was, indeed, almost something of an expectation.

The oil plant at Castrop-Rauxel was visited by 117 Lancasters from 3 Group on the morning of the 11th, and among them were ten from 218 Squadron led by F/L R Scammell. The bombers tracked across a cloud-covered Ruhr, where the flak was initially ineffective, but this soon changed as the bombers began their bombing run from between 17,000 and 23,000 feet, and delivered what was believed to be an accurate attack. With the Group expansion programme in full swing the squadron received a telegram on the 12th informing it that the formation of a third flight would be imminent, and it would carry the code XH. The High Commissioner for New Zealand, Mr W.J Jodan, and Air Commodore E.G Olsen, Air Officer Commanding RNZAF, London, visited Methwold on the 14th and spoke to the New Zealand personnel. At the time the squadron had only five officers and just three NCOs, considerably less than the previous year, when it boasted a number of experienced Kiwi crewmembers.

The squadron operated against the synthetic oil plant in Dortmund on the 15th, when five recently-arrived pilots joined experienced crews for operational experience. Dick Perry:

Day raid on Dortmund, trip #8. Took off at 12.30 pm into 10/10 cloud and followed the main stream to the Belgian coast. This time we used Gee which was working for a change. We took an unorthodox course over Belgium and, as a result, arrived over the target before the bomber stream. We were leader to three other aircraft, AA-K, Y and B and they followed us faithfully, dropping their bombs when we dropped ours. Bomb load was a cookie and 14x500's. Target was a marshalling yards. There was very little flak although we heard, later, that it was much heavier when the main stream arrived. This was the first time that we had used G-H as the bombing device. Once again had scarecrows tossed up in front of us, two of them! Then our Gee caught fire and, fortunately, went out by itself. Back to map reading with the aid of H2S. Got back down at 5.30 pm with one aircraft, AA-K, still following us.

On the following day S/Ldr Dunham led thirteen Lancasters from the squadron to take part in the group's first daylight army support operation. 182 Lancasters attacked the town of Heinsberg in support of the US 1st and 9th Armies, and while orbiting the target directing proceedings, the Master Bomber, W/Cdr Watkins DSO DFC DFM of XV Squadron, was shot down by flak, and was the sole survivor from his crew. His demise was witnessed by 218 Squadron's F/O Cook and crew, who reported a Lancaster falling in the target area. Dick Perry:

Day raid on Heinsberg, trip #9. Army co-operation, breakthrough to Cologne. Took off at 1.30 pm in terrible weather which fortunately cleared up over the target. Ran up on G-H but were ordered to bomb the town visually rather than use either G-H or markers. That was the last we heard from the Master Bomber although we heard later that he had been shot down. Orbited around looking for a likely target and, then, dropped our bombs, a cookie, 6x1000's and 6x500's, in the town center. Very heavy light flak by this time so quickly exited from the area. Took over from Robbie as usual, and noted that this time he went up in the nose where he probably took a nap. He took over from me after we left the Belgian coast and proceeded to base. No brake pressure so was diverted to Woodbridge where we had a hairy landing using FIDO. Almost ran off the end of the runway before we came to a stop. Spent three of the worst days we have ever experienced, cold, and wet, nothing to do. Finally left for base again but were diverted to Newmarket. Eventually made it home on the 20th.

It was back to the Meerbeck synthetic oil plant at Homberg on the 20th, for which the squadron dispatched eleven Lancasters in mid-afternoon in foul weather. Conditions did not improve over the target, where crews encountered complete cloud cover reaching up to 24,000 feet. It created problems for the non G-H aircraft trying to maintain formation with their G-H leaders. F/O Dick Perry:

Flight Lieutenant Robbie Roberts RAAF and crew seen here on completion of their operational tour. Sitting 2nd left is Flying Officer Dick Perry.

Day raid on Homberg, trip #10. Really duff met, we hit cloud at the Belgian coast and it stayed with us, with few breaks, til we reached the target. Once again we bombed on G–H over 10/10 cloud and no flak. Carrying a cookie and 14x500's. In cloud all the way back till we were over the Channel when it cleared until we reached the English coast where it thickened up again. What a sight coming back. Hundreds of aircraft all leaving black vapor trails behind them and, at one stage, climbing up to 24.000 feet to get over the Cu–Nimbs. On this trip we actually saw three aircraft destroyed by bombs dropped from aircraft above them, and swerved away ourselves from beneath one that would have passed right over us with its bomb doors open. I'll always remember our mid-upper, Dennis, yelling out the instruction to swerve right.

With improved weather 3 Group sent 186 Lancasters back to Homburg to finish off what they had started on the previous day. Intensive accurate flak met them, and forty of the 160-strong force sustained damage. Among them was New Zealander F/O Cook's PD296 HA-B, which was hit in ten places, while F/O Stewart's PB291 HA-O was extensively damaged along the whole length of the fuselage, thankfully without crew casualties in either case. Bombing was considered scattered by returning crews, but those over the target later in the attack witnessed a vast sheet of yellow flame and black smoke rising to a great height. Dick Perry:

Return to Homberg, trip #11. Yesterday's effort was no good so back we go again, takeoff 12.30 pm. Bursts of cloud all the way back until we reached the target where it cleared so bombed visually on sky markers. No flak and great visibility, a perfect bombing run and bombs right on target. Once again, the target was a marshalling yards. We carried a cookie and 14x500's. Back to base and arrived home at 5 pm.

A Flight commander, S/Ldr Nigel MacFarlane, was posted to XV Squadron at Mildenhall on the 21st to succeed the above-mentioned W/Cdr Watkins as commanding officer. The experienced and highly respected F/L John O'Brien was promoted as his successor. The squadron dispatched twelve crews to the Nordstern oil plant at Gelsenkirchen on the 23rd, when G–H worked extremely well, and an accurate attack was carried out. An attack on the marshalling yards at Fulda on the 26th was unsuccessful, after the G–H pulse was found to be faint, and finally faded out over the target. This was at the maximum range of both B and C G–H slave stations. Without G–H guidance the crews bombed visually or on targets of opportunity, and to confuse matters more, a number of inaccurate flares were dropped and attracted some bomb loads. This was the deepest penetration into Germany to date by the group. F/O Perry:

Day raid to Fulda, trip #12. Takeoff at 8 am over 10/10 cloud, essentially to test the range of our G–H equipment. A very easy trip, no flak, no fighters and 10/10 cloud. The trip was unsuccessful as we were unable to pick up a signal at that range. Target was to be a marshalling yard. Returned to base, jettisoning our bombs over the Channel.

B Flight's F/O William "Shorty" Stewart RNZAF and crew were screened from further operations after completing their first tour of thirty-five operations on return from Fulda. It was another busy night in the mess, with the diminutive New Zealander, pint in hand, leading the charge at the bar.

The group dispatched 169 Lancasters on the 27th for a two wave attack on the Kalk railway yards at Cologne. Fourteen 218 Squadron aircraft were led away by S/Ldr Dunham as part of the first wave. A navigational error by the lead 75(NZ) crew took the first wave through most of the Ruhr defences before reaching the aiming point, and this resulted in the two formations converging on the target from different directions. Flak over the target was heavy and accurate, and a total of seventy-nine Lancasters sustained damage, five of them from 218 Squadron. The bombing was described by returning crews as fairly concentrated, and a dense column of brown smoke was seen rising up through 5,000 feet as the force withdrew. Dick Perry:

Day raid to Cologne, trip #13. Takeoff at 1 pm in clear skies. Everything went fine until we reached the target and the flak started coming up at us. I have never seen so many shell bursts at one time. We picked our target, marshalling yards, and went in on our bombing run. Everyone was yelling. "Drop those bombs and get out of here." We pressed on, dropped the bombs, a cookie and 14x500's, and raced for home. It's hard to describe the sheer terror and beauty that accompanied a raid like this one. 500 odd bombers above us, beneath us and around us, flak bursts like myriads of balls of cotton wool, aircraft spiraling down to crash into the holocaust below and tail gunner, Harry, shouting "Weave" as the predicted flak crept up behind us. My comment, I note, was that I hoped we would never again have to fly over Cologne in broad daylight with no cloud cover. We were one of the few aircraft that returned without any damage, our lucky day.

A G-H operation was carried out against the town of Neuss on the 29th by 145 Lancasters, including nine from 218 Squadron. A number of recently posted-in pilots were sent on this raid to gain first-hand experience of a night raid over Germany. There was complete cloud cover over the target, and results could not be assessed, although a glow was seen through the cloud and one large explosion was observed. Only slight flak was encountered and no fighters were reported during an otherwise quiet operation. Dick Perry:

Night raid Neuss, trip #14. A marshalling yards and an uneventful trip over 10/10 cloud. Off the ground at 2.30 pm, very little flak over the target, bombing on G-H and, for a change, equipment was operational. We ran up on the target, dropped our bombs, a cookie, 6x1000's and 6x500's, and headed for home to arrive back at 7.30 pm.

The final operation of the month was flown on the 30th, two separate targets in the Ruhr would be attacked, each by sixty Lancaster's. The attack on a coking plant at Bottrop included four aircraft from 218 Squadron, while the second element targeted an oil plant at Osterfeld. The two objectives were less than two miles apart, and situated west of Essen. Both formations attacked downwind from the direction of Cleve at lunchtime, and two aircraft from the latter failed to return. Group Captain Brotherhood, the Station Commander of Chedburgh paid a visit to Methwold on the 30th, together with W/Cdr Smith and Methwold's Station Commander G/C Yarde. They discussed the squadron's impending move to Chedburgh, where G/C Brotherhood had only taken command on the 27th, on the departure of G/C Bale to command North Luffenham.

Indifferent weather during the month resulted in the squadron carrying out just 166 sorties, 148 by day and eighteen by night, dropping in the process just over 960 tons of bombs for the loss of one crew. With the group undertaking principally daylight G-H raids, the need for tight formation flying was now essential. A number of telegrams from 11 Group HQ to 3 Group HQ raised concerns about the ability of the escort to shepherd and protect the Lancasters. On two operations during the month flak had scattered the formations and on almost every other occasion the gaggle of lumbering Lancasters had become too strung out, particularly on the way home, to allow the escorts to do their job effectively.

December

The expected moved to Chedburgh began on December the 2nd when the non-flying sections of the squadron took up residence. Operations for the new month began for 3 Group with a G-H raid on the Hansa benzol plant at Dortmund on the 3rd. A relatively small force of ninety-three Lancasters was escorted by six squadrons of Mustangs and four of Spitfires. The bombing took place over a cloud covered target in the face of spasmodic to moderate flak, and ten aircraft sustained damage, but all returned home. Once again the fighter escort expressed concerns that the bomber formation had become dispersed after the attack, and was consequently harder to protect. On a positive note, this was the first operation since October in which every G-H set had worked. This was a fine achievement from the manipulation of the sets by the crews to the servicing of the temperamental "George Henry" by the Radar Sections.

The town of Oberhausen was successfully attacked by 160 Lancasters on the 4th, despite complete cloud cover, and all thirteen 218 Squadron Lancasters bombed the target and returned safely. This proved to be the final operation by the squadron from Methwold, and it was also the last operation for F/L "Wag"

Walker and his crew, who had now completed their first tour of thirty-three sorties. F/O Perry:

> *Day raid on Oberhausen, trip #15. Took off at 12 noon over 10/10 cloud for an uneventful trip. Target was a marshalling yards, we bombed on G-H, a cookie and 14x500's, and headed back to base and were on the ground again at 5 pm.*

On the following day Chedburgh was declared serviceable following runway repairs, and eighteen Lancasters had arrived and been dispersed by mid afternoon. The move also signalled the squadron's upgrading to three flights. The squadron was not required to operate on the 6th and 7th, and the old hands of the squadron set about inspecting the new airfield and the local pubs. Chedburgh was part of 31 Base, originally planned as a subsidiary station serving Stradishall. It was built on farmland directly south of the village of that name, six miles from Bury St Edmunds. Major construction work was carried out by John Laing & Son Ltd during the early part of 1942, followed by an official opening of the station in 3 Group on September 7th of that year. The first resident was 214 Squadron with its Stirlings. Built to Class A standard, the airfield had three concrete runways, one of two thousand yards and two of fourteen hundred. Dotted along the concrete perimeter track were thirty-four pans and two loop hard standings. Prior to the squadron's arrival it had been home to 1653 CU since November 1943.

The squadron's first operation from its new home was undertaken on the 8th, when thirteen Lancasters were sent to attack Duisburg marshalling yards in daylight. Thick cloud up to 25,000 feet made forming up almost impossible, and the conditions remained the same all the way to the target. Surprisingly, individual crews or small gaggles managed to navigate to the target, where they emerged from the cloud in a surprisingly compact stream. The Lancasters of 31 Base were the first over the target between 11.03hrs and 11.06hrs, with two further waves close on their heels. Twenty-three of the 163 participating Lancasters sustained flak damage, but all returned home. Wing Commander Smith was taken ill on the 10th and was removed to Ely Hospital, whereupon command of the squadron passed temporarily to the B Flight commander, S/Ldr Dunham DFC.

The group was required to attack two targets at Osterfeld on the 11th, the marshalling yards and the coking plant. The 218 Squadron element was assigned to the former, which it attacked from around 20,000 feet, but heavy cloud prevented most of the crews from visually identifying the target and assessing the accuracy of the bombing. The raid on Osterfeld would witness the first operation undertaken by the recently arrived F/L George Allardyce and crew, who had been posted in from 3 LFS at Feltwell. Twenty-six old Allardyce had joined the RAF in 1939, having previously served with the 16th London Regiment, at Buckingham Palace Gate. The crew had followed the customary route to the squadron by training at 16 OTU Upper Heyford on Wellingtons, before moving on to the Stirling-equipped 1653 CU and finally to Chedburgh having converted to the Lancaster. Prior to this Allardyce had spent eighteen months in Winnipeg, Canada as an instructor. George would ultimately be promoted to squadron leader and take command of C Flight.

The marshalling yards at Witten came next on the target list on the 12th, when the 218 Squadron element was part of a force of 140 Lancasters. Heavy cloud outbound led to the 31 Base participants ending up seven miles ahead of the stream in what was a three wave operation. The bulk of the escorting fighters were operating with the main formation, while 31 Base and the 149 Squadron Lancasters out of Methwold had the escort of a single squadron of RAF Mustangs. The forward formation had been engaged by flak at Castrop-Rauxel, just north of the target, and now settling into their bomb run, they were attacked by over forty Bf109s and FW190s of JG3 and JG27. Flying Officer Les Harlow's Lancaster, which was the lead G-H aircraft of 31 Base, was attacked by a Bf109, while two others latched on to the two other Lancasters in the vic. Harlow's gunners had the satisfaction of watching their assailant take to his parachute, but his colleagues shot down the two 195 Squadron Lancasters, and only one rear gunner survived from the fourteen occupants.

Squadron Leader George "Ron" Allardyce "C" Flight Commander strikes a classic pose. Known as "Straight ahead Allardyce" he was a highly experienced pilot even before his arrival on the squadron.

Four more Lancasters were shot down from this forward formation, another from 195 Squadron and two from 149 Squadron, along with 218 Squadron's PB674, piloted by twenty-two-year-old P/O Robert Roberts RAAF. The Lancaster was seen to explode over the target, and there were no survivors from the crew, which was operating for the eighth time. It was the timely intervention of the Mustangs that prevented further losses from the formation. PB766 HA-C was hit by flak over the target, and both port fuel tanks were holed. Flight Lieutenant Harry Warwick decided to first nurse the Lancaster back to the Allied lines, and then decide if they could make it back to base. The Lancaster slowly lost height as it crossed the North Sea, and got to within fifty miles of Felixstowe before a ditching became inevitable. The force of the impact broke the Lancaster in two, but the entire crew managed to clamber out and gathered on the wing of the forward section, which remained afloat for forty-five minutes.

Flight Lieutenant Harry Warwick DFC and crew pose beside Avro Lancaster ME454 XH-L "lovely Lou".

When that sank, they climbed aboard the dinghy and bobbed around in the freezing and choppy sea awaiting rescue. A fighter from their escort had been circling above, and within eighty minutes an Air Sea Rescue Walrus flying boat appeared overhead. The Walrus remained until a launch arrived with an escort of two Spitfires, and the crew was taken aboard.

After a number of cancelled operations through unfavourable weather conditions, nine 218 Squadron Lancasters joined over a hundred other aircraft from the group on the 21st to attack the railway yards at Trier, a target which had hosted a small 3 Group G-H raid two days earlier. The crews arrived over the target to find it covered in a thick blanket of cloud, forcing them to drop their bomb loads on G-H from between 16,000 and 18,000 feet. A number of crews experienced hang-ups because of icing, and were forced to jettison their bombs on the way home. A column of brown smoke was observed to slowly emerge through the clouds at 12,000 feet. Dick Perry recorded the raid in his dairy:

> Day raid on Trier, trip #16. *The weather was so bad that 7 trips in a row were scrubbed. We took off at 12.30 pm over 10/10 cloud and proceeded to the target. Very little flak but, for the first time, our bombs hung up. Very disappointing. Came back over the Channel and jettisoned our bomb load and were on the ground again at 5 pm.*

After being discharged from hospital on the 22nd, W/Cdr Smith arrived back at the squadron in time to preside over a third operation to Trier on the 23rd. 153 Lancasters attacked the snow-covered target in good visibility under the control of S/Ldr Scott of 90 Squadron. The southern part of the town was enveloped in smoke as a succession of bomb loads struck home. It was difficult to assess the results, but the local authorities confirmed later that it was the town's worst experience of the war. The attacks on Trier were vitally important in slowing down the movement of the Wehrmacht in support of their Ardennes offensive. Flying Officer Perry:

Back to Trier, trip #17. Off at 12.30 pm into a beautiful clear sky. Target, the town of Trier, stood out like a sore thumb. A classic bombing run and all of our bombs, a cookie and 14x500's, right down on the target. Very little flak to contend with. Congratulations received from Bomber Harris. Two of us got direct hits on the target which was a tank concentration in the middle of the town. Back home at 5 pm.

A night G-H raid on the Bonn Hangelar airfield was carried out on Christmas Eve by 104 Lancasters, including twenty from 218 Squadron. By the time the Chedburgh gang reached the target, it was already covered by smoke, and numerous explosions were observed. Crews reported that the bombing appeared to be divided between two main groups of red TIs half a mile apart. German fighters were active, and a number of inconclusive encounters took place involving 218 Squadron aircraft, but all returned home. Dick Perry:

Night raid on Bonn Airfield, trip #18. A clear night, off the ground at 3.30 pm. Once again we were supposed to bomb on G-H but could not get any signal. Bombed visually on the aiming point, the airfield runways, and got a direct hit. Bomb load 11x1000s and 4x500s. Very little flak and were back at base at 8.30 pm.

The sixth Christmas Day of the war arrived, and as tradition dictated, it was celebrated in the customary RAF fashion. With the weather improving over the Ardennes, all groups were required to provide aircraft for operations in support of ground forces around St Vith on Boxing Day. 3 Group managed to send forty-six Lancasters, fourteen of which were from 218 Squadron. There was no cloud over the target and visibility was excellent, which enabled the crews to identify the target visually before a series of red TIs were dropped. Dick Perry:

Day raid on St. Vith, trip #19. Off the ground at 1.30 and clear skies all the way to the target. This was another tank concentration and, again, a classic bombing run with very little light flak. A cookie and 14x500s. The German tanks were clearly visible and, once again, a direct hit on the target. Back to base to land at 5pm.

The marshalling yards at Rheydt was the target selected for the afternoon of the 27th, and after a change of plans, just five 218 Squadron Lancasters were called upon to make up a force of ninety-one, which made landfall over France just south of le Touquet-Paris-Plage. 1 Group was to be first on target, followed by 3 Group and finally 5 Group. Visibility over the target was perfect, and bombing was carried out on Pathfinder TIs. Bombing was concentrated in spite of the defences, which became increasingly active towards the end of the attack. Bombs were seen exploding all over the marshalling yards, and plumes of smoke covered the aiming point as the bombers turned for home. It was the turn of Cologne Gremberg marshalling yards to face an all-3 Group attack on the 28th. Nineteen 218 Squadron Lancasters joined 168 others to form up over Brentwood, north London, before heading for the target. On leaving the English Coast the formation headed out over the Channel, before making landfall over le Touquet-Paris-Plage. Leading the squadron as Deputy Base Leader was the recently promoted S/Ldr O'Brian in PD256 HA-J. John had also taken over the running of A Flight on the departure of S/Ldr MacFarlane. H–Hour over target was scheduled for 15.00hrs, but one group of five Lancasters bombed 2½ minutes early. G-H leader F/L Spiers in PD278 HA-V, released his payload on the wrong release pulse, and the bombs fell harmlessly into fields. Flying Officer K McKenzie's aircraft was hit by flak from Bonn, which rendered the port-outer engine unserviceable, and they came home on three. Flying Officer Eyles' PD288 XH-F was struck on the port wing leading edge by a packet of Window. All of the crews were confident that the marshalling yards had been plastered, and described dense columns of smoke drifting up to 4,000 feet and more as they departed.

There were no losses, and returning crews were confident that the marshalling yards had been plastered, after seeing dense columns of smoke drifting up through 5,000 feet as they turned for home. F/O Dick Perry on his twenty-first birthday recorded:

> *Day raid on our "favorite", Cologne, trip #20. Off the ground at 11.30 pm over 10/10 cloud. Target was a marshalling yard to the south of the city. Bombed on G-H, a cookie and 14x500s. Noted smoke going up to about 8,000 feet so presumed that the target was hit. Very little flak to contend with, this time. Back to base to land at 5 pm.*

The last operation of the month was mounted on the 31st, and was another G-H daylight raid on the German transportation system, this time the Vohwinkel marshalling yards at Wuppertal. Seventeen 218 Squadron Lancasters lifted off shortly after 11.00hrs, and they joined up with 138 others from the group to make landfall over Boulogne, and pick up an escort of eight squadrons of Mustangs and nine squadrons of Spitfires. Weather conditions were marginal during the outward flight, with heavy cloud and stronger than forecast winds. Followers had difficulty in forming up and finding their G-H Leaders, and the stream became strung-out

A studio photo of Robert Kench RAAF with his recently presented pilot wings. The crew arrived on the squadron December 11th 1944 via 73 Base. The young Aussie completed two operations before his death, the first was a 2nd Dickie trip on Christmas Eve to Bonn Hangelar airfield with F/O Knight. On the 28th, he took his crew to the Gremburg Marshalling Yards.

as it headed across France. The three mile long marshalling yards were identified visually, and crews bombed on a number of red TIs dropped by the G-H leaders. Just after leaving the target two 218 Squadron Lancasters were involved in a suspected collision, after which NG330 HA-M crashed at Solingen, killing twenty-year-old F/O Robert Kench RAAF and his crew who were on only their second operation together.

The other Lancaster, C Flight's NF926 XH-X, contained the crew of F/O Roy Woodrow, and this crashed into a workshop also in Solingen. The twenty-three-year-old pilot and his navigator, Sgt William Watson, were found badly injured in the wreckage, the pilot still strapped into his seat in the cockpit, and asking for help. Sadly he was murdered by a local SA Policeman, Fritz Schulze, who then shot the navigator in the head. In October 1945 Schulze was arrested and interviewed by Major S Arnold, an investigator examiner for the Missing Research Enquiry Service. He was tried for the murder of the two airmen before the British Military Court at Hamburg between 8th and 17th July 1947, was found guilty and was hanged. The only survivor from this crew was the rear gunner Sgt V Wellbourne, who became a PoW. The crew had arrived on the squadron from 31 Base on August 12th 1944, and had flown twenty-six operations. There was one other collision, thankfully without fatalities, involving PB856 from 195 Squadron and XH-B from 218. Flying Officer G Armstrong RAAF, the skipper of the 195 Squadron aircraft, reported on his return that Lancaster XH-B collided with their Lancaster over the target rendering the rear turret unserviceable, but without injury to Sgt Norman, the rear gunner. The pilot of XH-B was F/L C Warwick, there is no mention of this incident in 218 Squadron records, one must assume that he was either unaware of the incident or decided to remain stumm!

So ended 1944, a year in which the group completed a total of 2,009 bombing and mining sorties. The group undertook fifteen G-H daylight attacks and two by night during the month. 218 Squadron dispatched 167 sorties, of which 145

Map showing routes (3) taken by 31, 32 & 33 Bases to formate and meet over Stowmarket leaving as one stream via Orfordness

Fakenham

King's Lynn

32 Base

Norwich

Watton

March

Methwold

Mepal

Witchford

Mildenhall

Waterbeach

Tuddenham

Newmarket

Bury St.Edmunds

Stowmarket

Cambridge

Chedburgh

Wratting Common

Stradishall
(31 Base HQ)

33 Base

Haverhill

Clare

Sudbury

Ipswich

Saffron Walden

Orfordness

31 Base

Colchester

It seems that: 33 Base Squadrons joined over Clare
(presumably timed to miss 186, 195 & 218!)
32 Base Squadrons joined over Newmarket
31 Base squadrons joined over Sudbury

A simplified diagram showing how all three No.3 Group bases formed up into their allotted positions before departure over the English coast, January 1945.

were successful, dropping in the process over seven hundred tons of bombs. The squadron's ranking had slipped to last place for sorties dispatched, but this was not surprising, as it had been among the last to introduce a third flight. The scent of victory was wafting over from the Continent, but the end was still some way off, and much remained to be done before the proud and tenacious enemy finally laid down his arms.

Chapter Eight

1945:
The Final Months

January

The New Year began with a bang, as the Luftwaffe launched its ill-conceived and ill-fated Operation Bodenplatte (Baseplate) at first light on the 1st. The intention was to destroy the Allied air forces on the ground at the recently liberated airfields in France, Belgium and Holland, and this was only modestly achieved. It cost the enemy around 150 pilots, killed, wounded or captured, and it was a setback from which the Luftwaffe would never recover. A legacy of the operation was itchy fingers among American anti-aircraft gunners, and a number of RAF bombers would suffer the consequences in the immediate aftermath. For 3 Group the year began as the old one had ended, with a raid on the railway yards at Vohwinkel in the early evening of the 1st. 218 Squadron despatched seventeen aircraft, one of which, PB768 XH-B, was hit by flak over the target damaging fuel lines to the port-inner engine, which was quickly feathered. Over Namur, homeward bound at 11,000 feet, the Lancaster was hit by American anti-aircraft fire, emanating from the 184th Gun Battalion, which held a defensive position along the River Meuse, and had seen considerable action during the recent Battle of the Bulge. Unbeknown to F/O Grivell, a minimum height order was in force over the area during the hours of darkness because of the importance of the rail and road bridges across the Meuse, the whole area was hotly defended.

Grievously hit, the entire port side of the Lancaster caught fire, and realising that the flames were spreading, the pilot gave the order to bail out. Almost immediately the aircraft was hit again, and went into a violent spin. The Canadian bomb aimer, F/O George Ingram, was thrown forward onto the bombsight, where the centrifugal force wedged him against the Perspex nose. Gripped by desperation, he kicked his way through and vacated the Lancaster at 2,000 feet, leaving the flight engineer, Sgt L Peckett, trapped in the forward section without his parachute. On landing, and believing he was still in occupied Belgium, Ingram spent a day and night wandering the countryside, exhausted and wounded, until finally giving himself up to a number of soldiers, who turned out to be American. He was the sole survivor from the crew, which had been on its fifth operation, the pilot on his seventh. Dick Perry:

Day raid on Vohwinkel, trip #21. Off the ground at 3.30 pm into clear skies. Bombed visually on target indicators, a cookie and 14/500s. Target was, again, a marshalling yard, and was clearly visible. Masses of searchlights criss-crossing the sky and every now and then, holding an aircraft in their beam. Masses of fighter planes, both coming in and going out which kept Robbie and our rear gunner, Harry, very busy. Our first experience with flash less flak, impossible to see where it is bursting. Escaped, unscathed, and were back at base at 10 pm.

3 Group dispatched two forces in daylight on the 3rd, to attack oil production plants at Castrop-Rauxel and Dortmund using G-H. 218 Squadron's seventeen participants were assigned to the former, which they found to be cloud-covered. The bombing appeared to be accurate and concentrated in the face of moderate predicted flak, and five Lancasters were hit. As the force turned for home white smoke was seen to be rising through the clouds, and all the crews were safely back at base by 15.42hrs. Dick Perry:

Day raid on Castrop Rauxel, trip #22. A daylight raid. Again a marshalling yard over 10/10 cloud. We were leading the group and got all the predicted stuff on our run in to the target. Bombed on G-H, a cookie and 14x500s. This was the first time that we'd been hit and, on landing, we counted 27 holes of various sizes and a piece taken half way through an elevator control rod!!!! Thankful for no injuries. Back on deck at 3.30 pm.

Before operations could begin on the 5th everyone, including W/Cdr Smith, was out clearing snow from the runways to enable the squadron to join an attack on the marshalling yards at Ludwigshafen. Ten Lancasters left Chedburgh after 11.00hrs and joined a further 150 from the group. Three of the 218 Squadron contingent turned back early along with five others from the group, but the remainder pressed on into southern Germany. A navigation error brought the force over Worms and Mannheim, and over 50% of the aircraft were damaged by flak. A number of enemy fighters appeared, but they were dealt with by the escorting Mustangs. Visibility over the target was excellent, and crews bombed from between 19,000 and 20,000 feet. Numerous explosions were seen across the marshalling yards, and other loads were seen to detonate in the town itself, some of them hitting the I.G Farben works and causing a vivid explosion.

1 and 3 Groups joined forces on the night of 6/7th to attack the marshalling yards at Neuss. Ten 218 Squadron Lancasters took part, one of which returned early. The initial marking was reported as concentrated, but a number of flares were rather less accurate, and bombing was reported to be rather scattered. Even so, more than seventeen hundred houses and nineteen industrial premises were destroyed or seriously damaged. Approaching the target at 19,000 feet LM187 XH-B was tossed about violently, possibly the result of a slipstream, the Lancaster

was almost flipped it onto its back. Flying Officer David Banton managed to bring the Lancaster back onto an even keel, but the port-outer propeller started to run away and could not be feathered. The aircraft became uncontrollable and began to lose height, and even the dumping of the cookie had no effect. As it passed through 14,000 feet the remaining bombs were jettisoned and the operation was abandoned. They were turning for home when the port-outer caught fire, and as the flames showed no signs of responding to attempts to quell them, fuel to both port engines was cut off, and the port-inner feathered. The power to the starboard engines was increased, but the trim had been lost, and it now became a battle to retain control. When twenty miles south-east of Brussels and down to 4,500 feet the pilot gave the order to abandon the aircraft. The flight engineer, Sgt Simms, accidentally deployed his parachute inside the aircraft, and was unwilling to risk using it. He asked the wireless operator, Sgt Longley, to allow him to cling to his back in a joint descent, and realising the extent of his colleague's predicament, Sgt Longley readily agreed, despite the risk to himself. As always seemed to happen in these desperate cases, when the parachute jerked open the flight engineer fell to his death. Sergeant Longley came down into trees and was badly injured, but survived the experience, and was awarded the coveted CGM for his selfless act.

Having satisfied himself that he was alone in the aircraft, the pilot made his way forward to the escape hatch, whereupon the now pilotless Lancaster went into a spin. He scrambled back to the cockpit, and managed by some miracle to regain control and bring the Lancaster back onto an even keel. At 1,200 feet he finally managed to bail out, but his harness slipped, and he found himself hanging only by the right foot. He immediately put a scissor lock on to his harness in a desperate attempt to stop himself falling to his death. Upside down and disorientated, Banton curled himself up as best as he could, and landed uninjured in deep snow on the side of a hill. On getting to his feet he could see a clearing at the bottom of the hill. Wading through the snow Banton manage to walk to Chateau de Savenel, where he found help and shelter. All the survivors were well cared for, the navigator F/O Lillis remaining in the 8th Military Hospital in Brussels, while Sgt Longley was kept for a few days in 101 Hospital Louvan. The remaining crew members were back with the squadron by the 10th and immediately sent on leave. The crew had been on its fifth operation, and Banton on his sixth. Dick Perry:

Night raid on Neuss, trip #23. Off the ground at 4 pm into 10/10 cloud. Another marshalling yard and bombed on G-H, a cookie and 14x500s. Very little flak. Used window on the way out from the target, very messy as the bundles tend to break up and the strips get jammed everywhere. On crossing the Channel we were told to divert to Mildenhall where we spent the night. Back to base on the 6th.

Another night operation was laid on for the 7/8th, which involved 645 Lancasters from 1, 3, 5, 6 and 8 Groups attacking Munich. It was a disappointing night for

218 Squadron, with four early returns out of the twelve Lancasters dispatched. Wing Commander Smith, commonly referred to as the "Vicar", was not happy with some of the decisions to abort. One of the reasons for the recent spate of early returns was attributed to the age and condition of some of the war-weary Lancasters recently taken on charge to form C Flight. In an effort to create the additional flight quickly the squadron had received a number of aircraft from other squadrons within the group, and they had taken the opportunity to offload their hacks!! The squadron did not operate for the next three days, after heavy snow and fog descended upon Chedburgh.

The 11th brought a return to daylight operations with an attack on the Uerdingen marshalling yards at Krefeld. Fifteen of the 3 Group force of 152 Lancasters were provided by 218 Squadron, and after forming up they headed towards France in solid cloud. An escort of seven squadrons of RAF Mustangs joined the gaggle as it crossed into Germany, and with cloud tops up to 23,000 feet, the followers struggled to keep their G-H leaders in sight. This led to a strung-out formation and some scattered bombing, but the defences were, fortunately, barely active. Operating with A Flight's Commander, S/Ldr O'Brian, who was tasked as deputy base leader, was G/C W Brotherhood, who was operating in the role of second pilot aboard PD323. This was strictly against all the rules, and was actively discouraged not only by group but also by Bomber Command HQ. However, to the members of the squadron it meant a tremendous amount, and went a long way to increase morale. One isolated Bf109 carried out an attack on a Lancaster in the rear of the formation, but it was quickly seen off by the Mustangs. The weather once again intervened on the 12th, this time in the form of continuous sleet, turning into rain, with a cloud base down to 300 feet. The first consignment of the new Frazer Nash FN121 turrets arrived at 31 Base on this date, but installation was delayed because of the failure at the factory to fit the appropriate gun sight. It would take a further two weeks for the squadron to receive a training turret and to equip two of the Lancasters.

The marshalling yards at Saarbrücken were attacked on the 13th, with 218 Squadron represented by sixteen Lancasters. An overall 3 Group force of over 150 aircraft was shepherded to the target by RAF Mustangs, and carried out a concentrated attack in fair visibility under the protection of US 9th Air Force fighters, which saw the bombers safely home. There was no opposition from the enemy, and the operation was described as almost a "milk run". The squadron bade farewell to S/Ldr Peter Dunham DFC on the 15th, on his posting to Tuddenham to command 90 Squadron. He had operated twenty-nine times with 218 Squadron as an observer in 1941, and since his return in October 1944 as a qualified pilot, he had added a further ten operations.

The new name of Erkenschwick appeared on the battle order on the 15th, a small town close to Recklinghausen and Gelsenkirchen in the Ruhr. Eighty-two Lancasters from 31 and 32 Bases were given its Benzol Plant to attack in mid afternoon, when green and blue smoke puff markers were used for the first time. Squadron Leader John O'Brien was again given the deputy base leader role, to which he and his crew were becoming accustomed. Frustratingly the stream was reported to be poor and strung out, and returning crews complained that bombing took considerably longer than intended, but still appeared to be concentrated. Flak was encountered on this occasion, and a quarter of the participating Lancasters sustained damage. A Benzol plant at Wanne-Eickel was the group's target on the night of the 16/17th, and twelve 218 Squadron Lancasters lined up for take-off at Chedburgh. Eight got away successfully, before one strayed off the perimeter track and shorted out the lights. This Lancaster was scrubbed, along with three waiting behind, and another was forced to return early with engine problems. 130 Lancasters ultimately converged on the target to find it completely cloud-covered, to the extent that even search lights were unable to penetrate it. Some crews reported a large red glow through the clouds with a number of sky markers directly above it, and the explosions of the cookies could clearly be seen. Intense flak was encountered, but none of the squadron's aircraft was damaged.

After a succession of cancelled operations, Bomber Command dispatched 286 crews to attack the benzol plants at Bruckhausen, Duisburg on the night of the 22/23rd. 3 Group's contribution of 130 Lancasters came from 31, 32 and 33 Bases. 218 Squadron was represented by fifteen led by Australian F/L Linder RAAF. The target was identified by red and green TIs dropped by the Pathfinders, and in the moonlight conditions, bombing was concentrated. Returning crews were enthusiastic about the outcome, and F/Sgt Connell's crew reported "*huge fires and a big pall of smoke over the aiming point*". Flak was moderate to intense, and PD229 XH-D, flown by F/O R Welsh RAAF, lost its starboard-outer, while another from the squadron suffered a large hole in the windscreen and port clear vision panel. Thankfully neither crew received any injuries.

After another four days of inactivity 3 Group dispatched 153 Lancasters on a daylight operation to the Gremberg marshalling yards at Cologne on the morning of the 28th. 218 Squadron contributed twenty Lancasters led by W/Cdr Smith, the crews arrived over the target at around 20,000 feet shortly after 14.00hrs to face accurate heavy flak. Wing Commander Smith's PD256 HA-J was repeatedly hit, sustaining in the process damage to the front turret and the airscrew lever quadrant, and the trim control next to the pilot's seat was also smashed. Undeterred, Smith, operating in the role of deputy base leader, continued on his bomb run. Two Lancasters in his formation were seen to be badly hit, and this dispersed the spearhead of the formation, causing the bombing by the lead section to be scattered and fall mainly to starboard of the planned aiming point. This was quickly corrected, and the following stream carried out accurate bombing on G-H, numerous bomb loads were seen to fall across the target. Crews were critical of the lead formation, and reported some bombs falling ten miles short of the aiming point. Flak accounted for two 218 Squadron Lancasters from W/Cdr Smith's gaggle, each containing an experienced crew. LM281 HA-E was hit just before bombing, and was seen to be losing height with both port engines feathered. Flight Lieutenant Hodnett and his crew all managed to take to their parachutes, and arrived safely on the ground to begin a short term in captivity. It had been the crew's seventh operation and F/L Hodnett's tenth. Tragically the other loss involved thirty-five-year-old W/O Gilbert Evers, who was on his thirtieth operation. PD296 HA-B was seen by W/Cdr Smith to be still apparently under control and in the stream just after leaving the target area, but soon afterwards it went into a dive. At 10,000 feet Evers managed to regain some control, but the Lancaster was hit again by flak and crashed near Bergisch-Gladbach about fourteen miles east-north-east of the target, killing all but one of the eight occupants. Operating as group leader for the squadrons of 31 Base, the crew contained an additional navigator, F/O F Norton, who survived in enemy hands. Evers had a reputation within the squadron of being an exceptional pilot, having been a pre-war regular, who left the RAF to join Imperial Airways. When war was declared he re-joined the RAF with something like four thousand hours in his log book. Apparently he had refused a commission, but there was absolutely no doubt that he was a very senior pilot on the squadron, and was known in the mess as "Pop" Evers. Dick Perry:

Cologne again, trip #25. Took off at 10 am over 10/10 cloud. The southern marshalling yards again and bombing on G-H. Very impersonal. We follow the track on the screen until we see a blip, enter the wind speed data and start counting, open the bomb bay doors and, after the required time interval, drop the bombs. Often wondered how many of these bombs actually landed on target, sight unseen. Back to base and landed at 3 pm. This was the trip that saw Evers and crew shot down on the last trip of their tour. Too bad but it happens.

On the way home W/Cdr Smith's flight engineer, W/O Williams, carried out urgently needed repairs to both the trim control and airscrew lever quadrant, but the temporary repairs still demanded a careful landing. Wing Commander Smith and his engineer, W/O David Williams, would be awarded a DFC for their actions on this operation. The last operation of the month was a return to the Uerdingen marshalling yards north east of Krefeld on the 29th. 3 Group dispatched a force of 148 Lancasters to destroy rolling stock and disrupt railway movement at this vital hub, half-way between Duisburg and Mönchengladbach. Twenty-one 218 Squadron crews were aloft from Chedburgh by 10.39hrs, and just one returned early. The entire outward flight was characterised by solid cloud, and the crews never once caught sight of the ground. The fighter escort made rendezvous on schedule and shepherded the formation to the target, where light flak was encountered. The bombing appeared to be concentrated, but was later found to have been scattered. Even so, a number of rails were cut and a bridge suffered the collapse of two spans, sixty-six craters were counted within the marshalling yards. Dick Perry:

Day raid on Krefeld, trip #26. Up at 12 noon into clear skies. We saw very little flak but others told us that they were faced with heavy stuff. Bombed on G-H, a cookie and 14x500s, and headed for home where we arrived at 3.30.

Heavy snow and low stratus covered much of East Anglia on the 30th preventing any operations, and this weather would continue over to the 31st. On the last day of the month, 3 Lancaster Finishing School at Feltwell was disbanded. Those crews still requiring training were sent to C Flight of 90 Squadron for completion of their programme. It had been a busy but frustrating month for the squadron, in which the weather had rendered fifteen days unfit for operations. Seven daylight and six night operations had been carried out, resulting in 187 sorties flown, which put the squadron fourth on the 3 Group sortie ladder. The squadron had dropped a total of 744 tons of bombs for the loss of two crews, and had provided the lead aircraft for the group on several occasions.

February

An inconclusive operation to the marshalling yards at Mönchengladbach took place on the 1st, when twenty-one 218 Squadron Lancasters contributed to the 160-strong force dispatched by the group. They attacked a cloud-covered target, at which the marker flares were scattered, and this allowed much of the bombing to fall starboard of the marshalling yards. There was very little resistance from the enemy defences, only some ineffective spasmodic flak, and there were no reports of damage. Dick Perry:

Day raid on Mönchengladbach trip #27. Up over 10/10 cloud at 10 am. Again bombing on G-H and no flak, a cookie and 14x500lbs. Arrived back at base at 3 pm. Uneventful!!

This was followed on the night of the 2/3rd by the launching of seventeen Lancasters for an attack on Wiesbaden. Situated on the right bank of the Rhine this relatively untouched city was the target for 495 Lancasters and twelve Mosquitos of 1, 3, 6 and 8 Groups. Flying with F/Lt L Harlow DFC as second pilot, and again flaunting regulations, was the station commander, G/C Brotherhood. One aircraft returned early, but the remainder pressed on to find the target obscured by a thick blanket of cloud. Five selected crews bombed on G-H, while the remainder aimed at the glow of fires beneath the clouds. The city's defences were described as negligible, but night fighters were evident. Useful damage was caused to a number of important factories and buildings, including the main railway station, which was an important connection to Cologne, Mannheim and Hanover. Dick Perry:

Senior Officers Chedburgh 1945. Left to right W/Cdr Smith, F/L Hunter GH specialist, S/Ldr Mayle RAAF station navigation leader, S/Ldr Jell DFC flight commander, F/Lt H Russell, bombing leader, Group Captain Brotherhood, station commander and Air Commodore Sylvester, Base Commander RAF Stradishall.

Night raid on Wiesbaden, trip #28. Off the ground at 8 pm over 10/10 cloud. Again bombing on G-H and no flak. Usual load. Had to climb up to 22,000 feet on the way home to clear the CuNims. Back to base and landed at 1.30 am.

On the late afternoon of the 3rd fifteen 218 Squadron Lancasters took off for the Hansa Coking Plant at Dortmund. Wing Commander Smith returned with engine trouble after three hours, but the remainder, along with around 130 other Lancasters from the group, attacked the target in clear skies, but conditions of ground haze made visual identification difficult. Marking was undertaken by selected G-H crews from each squadron in the face of a rare and spirited searchlight, flak and fighter defence, seven crews reported combats, including 218 Squadron's F/L Harlow and Nixon, both of whom had encounters with twin engine fighters. Whether or not this was responsible, the bombing missed the mark. Dick Perry's dairy records the tension:

Night raid on Dortmund, trip #29. A very shaky trip. Took off at 5 pm to arrive over the target just after dark. Hundreds of searchlights everywhere, and flak bursts all over the sky. G-H again went out and we bombed visually, on sky markers. Dozens of fighters around us but managed to get out without a scratch. Robbie and Harry again very busy. Back to base and landed 10 pm.

The squadron was stood down on the following three days before an operation to the synthetic oil plant at Wanne-Eickel was mounted on the 7th. One hundred Lancasters from 31 and 32 Bases were dispatched, and they were met by solid cloud, which persisted all the way to the target, making it difficult for crews to follow their allotted G-H leaders. As the formation approached Aachen the stream started to break up into individual vics and small formations, and by the time it passed between Cologne and Düsseldorf the stream had become elongated. The cloud continued to cause a number of problems, with visibility at times down to less than two hundred yards. Flying Officer Wilson RAAF stated, "*complete shambles, just lucky we saw a leader*". With the stream strung out the window coverage was greatly reduced, and this allowed the Rhine/Ruhr defences to put up an effective and accurate barrage. Flying Officer Charlton and crew had luck on their side, as a flak shell passed through the port wing's main spar of PB291 HA-O without exploding while they were on the bomb run. A number of crews had problems obtaining a G-H pulse, after the failure of a heavy mobile G-H station, and a light mobile G-H station was operating at extreme range. As a result bombing accuracy was poor. Dick Perry:

Day raid on Wanne-Eickel, trip #30. Off the ground at 10 am and fine weather until we hit the French coast. Took the aircraft up to 25,000 feet to clear the CuNims and stayed there until we reached the target. Dropped to 22,000 to unload bombs on G-H, the usual load, and back up again right after. Predicted flak followed us all the way in and out. Much weaving to avoid the predictors. We ended up being the only aircraft on the station that got the G-H signal. Back at base at 3 pm.

A tragic accident involving F/O William Perry occurred on station on the evening of the 7th. Flying Officer Jim Griffin, bomb aimer in the crew of F/O D Banton recalls:

On the afternoon of February 7th both Bill and I went into Bury to go to the cinema, that night there was an auction of cakes and other goodies being held during the interval. This was to raise money for a "Salute to the Soldier week". Both Bill and I paid £2.10.0d, quite a some in those days for the cakes. When we come out the cinema I suggested we go back to base by bus, but Bill said "Let's go to the cafe and have a cup of tea and we will catch the station wagon at the rail station." Off we marched with our cakes for a cuppa. We caught the wagon back which was as usual very full resulting in us having to stand at the back. When we got back to Chedburgh the wagon stopped at the Guard room, Bill jumped out over the tail gate and just as he did so the driver went into reverse knocking Bill over and reversed over him, killing him almost instantly. I was struck numb, only hours before he was laughing and full of life. I threw the cakes over the hedge and walked towards the officer's mess. I was so traumatised I did not tell anyone that I had been with Bill, not even when his parents came to collect his body, I just could not meet them.

Krefeld's main railway station at Hohenbudberg was the target for 151 Lancasters from 3 Group in the early hours of the 9th. Seventeen 218 Squadron aircraft took off with a time over target of 05.30hrs. Most of the sky marking was well concentrated, and the bomb loads fell directly beneath them. For the first time in months the returning crews reported a number of "Scarecrows" over the target, and one Lancaster was seen to explode at 06.18hrs. Despite the positive reports of returning crews, post raid reconnaissance showed that the majority of the bombing had fallen north-west of the aiming point. This was the last operation undertaken by F/L "Robbie" Robertson RAAF and crew, who had now completed their tour of thirty-one operations, although Robbie had completed one more. Dick Perry:

Night raid on Hohenberg, trip #31 – OUR LAST. Briefed at 12.45pm and take-off into clear sky at 4 am. A few scattered searchlights over the target and very little flak. One of aircraft in front of us blew up, again for some unexplained reason. Target was a marshalling yards and, again, bombed on G-H. Back to base and landed at about 8 am. Congratulated all round on finishing our operational tour.

The group was not required to operate again until the night of February 13th, when the target was the city of Dresden. This was the first in a series of heavy raids to be conducted against Germany's eastern cities under the codename THUNDERCLAP, ostensibly in support of the advancing Russian forces. A group record of 168 Lancasters was available for the operation, and twenty of these were to be provided by 218 Squadron. It would be the first and last visit to the Saxon capital, which was Germany's seventh-largest city, and, according to the RAF at the time, the largest remaining un-bombed built-up area in Germany. Although this operation would become a political hot potato later on, for the crews at Chedburgh it was just another raid, and a long one to boot. It took just over an hour to get the squadron airborne, and four returned early, thus sparing Dresden 27,000lbs of bombs. The main force of more than five hundred Lancasters from 1, 3, 6 and 8 Groups was following in the wake of a 5 Groups opening assault carried out three hours earlier. The fires started by 5 Group acted as a beacon to the second wave, and in clear skies they delivered over 1,700 tons of high explosives and incendiaries to add to the eight hundred tons dropped earlier. Returning crews were for once unanimous in their assessment of the raid as successful. Flying Officer Wilson RAAF reported, *"Exceptionally good attack"*, while C Flight's S/Ldr G Allardyce stated, *"Magnificent attack, whole town ablaze"*. Flight Lieutenant Spiers confirmed that, *"Patten of streets could be seen by light of incendiaries, fires seen at least 250 miles from target area "*. A firestorm developed within the city, and initial estimates of the death toll reached 250,000. This was due in part to the large number of refugees swarming in from the east ahead of the Russians, and no one knew just how many people were in the city. It is now accepted that the true death toll is nearer 25,000, which puts it second only to Hamburg.

Operation Thunderclap continued on the following night, when over seven hundred Lancasters and Halifaxes targeted Chemnitz, the third largest city in Saxony. Such was the city's war production capability, which included the important Astra-Werk AG oil plant, that this industrial centre was often referred to as the "Saxon Manchester". The operation followed the pattern of the previous night, with two forces bombing three hours apart, 4 and 6 Groups taking the first shift and 1 and 3 Groups the second. Fifteen 218 Squadron Lancasters departed Chedburgh as part of a 31 Base effort of fifty-one Lancasters, which were part of the third and final wave on target, scheduled to bomb during a four minute slot, eight minutes after the opening of the second attack. Small fires had already taken hold as they arrived in the target area at around 20,000 feet, and in the cloudy conditions the Pathfinder backers-up were employing sky markers. A few isolated fires visible below the cloud attracted a number of bomb loads, but the 218 Squadron crews allowed themselves to be guided by the Master Bomber, call sign "Falstaff". It was difficult to assess the results, and crews had mixed impressions of the bombing. Flying Officer Hill reported, *"tactics alright, but Pathfinders missing"*, while F/L Spiers recounted *"bombing appeared scattered"*. Flight Lieutenant Guinane thought that the city was *"a big mass of flame with incendiaries burning over a large area."* The Guinane crew became involved in an encounter with a twin engine fighter fitted with an orange light in the nose. It was seen at 23.29hrs at 17,000 feet at a range of 1,000 yards. The fighter reappeared at 600 yards with the nose light switched off, and the order to "corkscrew port" was given at the same time. Both gunners opened fire, the fighter was lost momentarily, only to reappear on the starboard beam dropping tracking flares. Thereafter it was not seen again, and there was no injuries to the crew or damage to Lancaster LM577 HA-Q. Post raid photo-reconnaissance established that the main weight of the bombing had fallen into open countryside.

A series of devastating attacks on what was now the frontier town of Wesel opened on the 16th, when a hundred 3 Group Lancasters carried out an accurate and punishing daylight raid. A follow-up on the 17th by 247 Halifaxes and twenty-seven Lancasters was aborted as soon as it began in the face of complete cloud cover. 218 Squadron took part in the third raid on the 18th, which was another 3 Group affair. 162 Lancasters were involved, of which twenty-one represented 218 Squadron. The twenty-two squadrons of Spitfires and Mustangs joined the bombers just south of the Belgian town of Mechelen, and shepherded them to Wesel, which sat on the confluence of the Rhine and Lippe Rivers. It served as a vital transportation centre with a number of semi intact bridges and important railway yards within it. With a planned major offensive by the Canadian First

Army it fell to the bombers to block the arrival of German reinforcements. Time over target was planned for between 14.00hrs and 14.07hrs, but weather conditions outbound were not ideal, with cloud tops up to 12,000 feet, and this resulted in the group becoming strung out. 31 Base provided seventeen G-H leaders, six of them from 218 Squadron, the crews bombed on a number of green smoke puffs from between 17,000 and 19,000 feet. Bombing was reported as concentrated, and one crew observed a direct hit on a bridge and the collapse of a span.

The assault continued on the 19th, when 169 Lancasters were dispatched in late afternoon sunshine, among them eighteen from 218 Squadron. Spitfires and Mustangs of 11 Group provided protection, but the formation encountered no opposition until reaching the Rhine at Emmerich, where heavy flak was thrown up. There was a thin layer of cloud in the target area with tops up to 6,000 feet, and the crews were able to pick out some ground detail. The bombing was reported as concentrated, and explosions were observed in the town and in the marshalling yards with smoke slowly rising. The tragic news that W/Cdr Peter Dunham DFC, now commanding officer of 90 Squadron, had been lost on the operation began to filter through to his former colleagues at 218 Squadron on the 20th, and even the cynical and hardened veterans on the squadron felt the loss of this former flight commander. Peter Dunham, with his bristling whiskers, was gone. The thirty-two-year-old father of one epitomised the bravery and courage of his generation and the men of Bomber Command. His flight had been taken over by veteran air gunner, S/Ldr R Jell. Ronald Jell's operational career had started in 1940 with 9 Squadron, with which he had completed his first tour. There followed various postings as an instructor, he took part in two of the Thousand Bomber raids in 1942 when temporally attached to 7 Squadron. In January 1945 he returned to operations joining the crew of F/O Phil Dyson DFC at 3 LFS. Phillip Dyson had previously completed an operational tour with 196 Squadron in 1943, they arrived at 218 Squadron at the end of January.

An area raid on the city of Dortmund was undertaken on the night of 20/21st by 514 Lancasters of 1, 3, 6 and 8 Groups. The squadron sent fourteen Lancasters as part of a 3 Group force of 111. The squadron was part of the third wave over the target, and crews reported the city's flak defences as moderate to intense. Night fighters were active, and several were seen in the target area, but there were no conclusive combats involving 218 Squadron aircraft. The impression was of a highly destructive raid, and some returning crews reported the glow of fires still visible eighty miles into the homeward leg. The group was split into two forces for daylight operations on the 22nd, eighty-six Lancasters of 31 and 32 Bases assigned to the Benzol Distillation plant and Coke Ovens at Scholven-Buer, while Lancasters of 33 Base joined others from Methwold to attack a similar target at Osterfeld. Weather outbound was clear but freezing, both formations met heavy flak as they penetrated the Ruhr. This was particularly so for the Scholven force, which encountered intense accurate flak on the approach to bomb. The

Squadron Leader Ron Jell DFC (centre) and his crew skippered by F/Lt Phillip Dyson DFC. Both had completed operational tours before joining the squadron.

218 Squadron element was given the Hibernia AG Coking works to attack, and what had been a reasonably compact formation soon began to break up as flak punctured the sky and damaged six of the 218 Squadron contingent.

Twenty-one-year-old F/O John Muschamp was skippering his crew on their first operation together, and they were unable to locate their allotted G-H leader in the confusion. The freshman crew managed to latch on to the vic of G-H leader F/L Spiers as the aiming point approached. The crew of Don Spier's watched helplessly as NG450 XH-B was bracketed by flak, dense smoke soon started to pour from the fuselage. Flight Sergeant J Yates was at the controls of PD439 XH-J, and heard another crew calling *"B Can I help you"*? B was not heard to reply. The bomb-aimer aboard NG450 XH-B was Sgt J Halsall, he recalls:

Our aircraft was hit around 15.30 while at 18,000 feet. We were over the target area with our bomb doors open when we were first hit immediately behind the mid upper turret. It must have been some type of incendiary as the aircraft was immediately consumed by flames. I grabbed a fire extinguisher and went back to fight the fire, but there was virtually no hope. It become apparent that the controls had severed as the pilot had virtually lost all control, and he ordered the crew to bail out. The pilot gave the command EMERGENCY-JUMP-EMERGENCY JUMP JUMP JUMP followed by the words GOOD LUCK CHAPS. We were then hit again in the port wing just after I left the aircraft which was in a steep dive. From the moment of the first hit I heard nothing from the two gunners, but the Wop/Ag said that the mid upper gunner was first behind him when the aircraft blew up. My chute was slow to open and although I was the second out I was the first on the ground. I landed in a field when some Germans from the local flak battery found me. They were elated at getting me and I was initially treated well. I had received some facial burns, broken ribs and a broken ankle from the heavy landing. Later, when we were all rounded up, we were knocked about a bit by a Gestapo Officer. We were then transferred to a local police cell, where another German officer showed us the ID discs of our pilot and two gunners. After a couple of days in the cells in Gelsenkirchen (we met up with a B24 Liberator crew shot down the same day) we were transferred to Dortmund where we were housed in a bombed out cellar of a Luftwaffe barrack block. We stayed here for about a fortnight before we were re housed in a sweet-box in the interrogation centre at Frankfurt. After a fortnight's solitary we were transferred to Weltzler Transit Camp. As the Allies were getting nearer we were again transferred, this time to Stalag XIID near Nuremburg, and after a fortnight we were moved again to Stalag VIIA Moosburg. While on route we were strafed by Yank fighters and bombed by the RAF. We were just at the point of moving to the Berchtesgaden camp when we were liberated by General Patton's 3rd Army on Tuesday 29th April. I have nothing but admiration for Johnny Muschamp our skipper, for he must have known there was little or no chance of getting out himself, and he tried his utmost to hold the plane while we bailed out.

Flying Officer John Muschamp was the son of Group Captain George Muschamp. The brave young pilot and his two twenty-year-old gunners, Sgts George Hogg and Thomas Darragh, now lie in the Reichswald Forest War Cemetery. In all forty-nine Lancasters were damaged by flak from the eighty-six dispatched by 31 and 32 Bases, the Osterfeld force was hit equally hard with forty-six Lancasters sustaining damage. Over at Mildenhall it was reported that every Lancaster dispatched by XV and 622 Squadrons sustained flak damage!

It was back to Gelsenkirchen and Osterfeld in the cauldron of the Ruhr on the following day, when 133 aircraft were given the Alma Pluto benzol plant as their primary target. Fifteen 218 Squadron Lancasters lifted off from Chedburgh and met thick cloud as they climbed over the coast. The formation remained fairly concentrated, despite solid cloud reaching up to 19,000 feet with horizontal visibility down to less than two hundred yards at times. The thirty-eight Lancasters of 31 Base had fallen behind the rest of the formation as they crossed into Germany, the escort of six squadrons of Mustangs and Spitfires was already stretched as the groups turned south below Düsseldorf, and attracted accurate predicted flak from the city. In contrast to the previous day the flak over the target was light, and lead aircraft reported a strong G-H pulse. They were confident that bombing was accurate, although no results could be seen through the complete cloud cover.

Mist and fog kept the group on the ground on the following day, and the main activity at Chedburgh involved the gradual return of Lancasters diverted on return from the previous day's operation. Thirteen crews were briefed to attack the Benzol oil plant at Kamen on the 25th, and they took off into the early morning overcast to rendezvous with the rest of the group at 9,000 feet over Tonbridge. One crew returned early with engine failure, while the remainder pressed on assisted by a strong tail wind that pushed them towards the target. Accurate predicted flak found them as they passed west of the Ruhr at Krefeld, but there was little opposition over the target itself. Bombing took place on a number of well placed G-H blue puff sky markers, the target was ablaze as the group turned for home. The return leg took the formation close to the Wuppertal and Leverkusen area just north of Cologne, were it was again engaged by accurate predicted flak, thirty-three Lancasters returned with various degrees of damage. A cloud-covered Hoesch Benzin oil Plant at Dortmund was attacked by 150 Lancasters of 3 Group on the 26th. Flak was negligible, and the shells that were fired burst well below the height of the bombers. Fourteen 218 Squadron aircraft attacked the target in the early afternoon, but the formation was somewhat chaotic in its timings with some sections bombing out of the planned sequence. The crews were critical of the discipline of some groups, which failed to obey the timing over target. Australian F/O R Welsh RAAF reported; *"Wave briefed to be behind us got in front of us and bombed in that position"*, whilst F/L K McKenzie RNZAF reported *"Stream and formation went to pieces "*.

There was no respite from operations for the squadron, which was briefed for a return visit to Gelsenkirchen on the 27th. Fifteen Lancasters were airborne by late morning to join 134 others from the group heading for yet another crack at the Alma Pluto Coking Plant. Flight Lieutenant Blenkin and crew operated as group leader on this operation. On approaching the target the stream separated into two formations with a five mile gap between, and, had enemy fighters attacked, the seven squadrons of escorting Spitfires would have been hard-pressed to ward them off. The squadron bombed a series of blue puff markers over a completely cloud-covered target, and the attack appeared to be concentrated around the markers.

For the fourth day in succession the squadron was called upon to operate, this time the target was the Nordstern Benzol and Coke plant in Gelsenkirchen. 3 Group dispatched 157 Lancasters on what would be the final raid of the month, and 218 Squadron provided nineteen of them. The squadron was given the honour of leading the group for this operation, which again suffered from visibility problems in the cloudy conditions, resulting in some crews finding it extremely difficult to formate on their allotted G-H leaders. This resulted in the formation being rather strung out as the cloud persisted into the Ruhr. Flak over the target was of the moderate predicted variety, and three Lancasters were hit. On leaving the target area crews reported thick black and green smoke coming up through the clouds, suggesting that the operation had been successful.

February had been a busy time for everyone on the squadron, 272 sorties had been launched on sixteen operations for the loss of one crew. This magnificent recorded kept the squadron in 4th place on the group operational ladder. 31 Group's 195 Squadron pipped 218 with 286 sorties, while 33 Base's 75(NZ) Squadron took second place with 294. 115 Squadron topped the listing with a remarkable 305 sorties flown, which is all the more significant given that it was a twenty-eight-day month, and weather intervened on four occasions. The entire group dropped over 10,387 tons of bombs, of which 218 Squadron's contribution was a respectful 1,023 tons, a total that had only once been exceeded. The installation of the new FN121 turret with the gyro gun sight and VHF R/T equipment was completed during the month. Among four DFCs gazetted were one each to F/L Ronald "Taffy" Ecclestone, who had flown thirty-six operations, and F/L Charles Young RAAF, who had completed thirty-eight in November 1944. Both these pilots were destined to die young, the latter not living to see the peace he had so bravely fought for. Charles Young was killed on July 2nd 1945, when his C-47 crashed in the Milne Bay area off New Guinea, while on a special flight to the Admiralty Islands carrying Royal Navy freight. "Taffy" Ecclestone was to become the first RAF pilot to break the sound barrier in 1951, when flying the North American Sabre jet fighter. On leaving the RAF he joined Handley Page as deputy chief test pilot, he was tragically killed on July 14th 1954 while testing the prototype Victor bomber on its penultimate flight before going into production.

March

Germany's oil plants remained the priority for 3 Group as the new month began, on the 1st a large force drawn from 1, 4 and 8 Groups carried out the final raid of the war on Mannheim. The 3 Group target was the oil plant at Kamen, for which 150 Lancasters were dispatched from 31, 32 and 33 Bases and Methwold. Ninety-one Mustangs picked up the bombers over the Channel, and they were joined by seventy-eight Spitfires of 11 Group over Belgium. Heavy cloud over the Continent made formation-keeping extremely difficult, causing the formation to split into two gaggles. Twelve aircraft of the leading formation overshot the turning point, resulting in the aircraft having to complete a half orbit at the target. All seventeen 218 Squadron aircraft reached and bombed the target experiencing negligible opposition before returning safely to base.

The cathedral city of Cologne was the intended target for a two phase attack on the 2nd, the first to be carried out by 698 aircraft of 1, 4, 6 and 8 Groups. This opening phase proceeded as planned, and inflicted considerable further damage to this already wrecked city. The afternoon attack by 151 Lancasters of 3 Group, of which an initial twenty-one represented 218 Squadron, was not as successful. A technical failure with the G-H releasing station resulted in most of the force returning with its bombs. The squadron had two aircraft return early, but the remainder reached the target under the umbrella of a Mustang and Spitfire escort in ideal weather conditions. Five crews were able to bomb before the operation was abandoned. Thus was Cologne spared what would have been its final few hundred tons of bombs, and it would fall within four days to the American 3rd Armoured Division.

The squadron did not operate on the 3rd, but provided twenty-one Lancasters on the following day for an attack on the Wanne-Eickel marshalling yards. They were part of a force of 128 sent to put even more pressure on the beleaguered Wehrmacht. It was believed that the Germans were using the marshallings yards to transport much needed equipment and reinforcements to the front. The formation crossed the coast over Belgium, and made for the Allied-occupied area around Cleves with its escort of ninety Mustangs in tow. The group leaders once again overshot the last turning point before reaching the target, and this initially caused some confusion. Thankfully matters had been rectified by the time the aiming point was reached, and the bombing appeared to be concentrated, although cloud prevented any assessment. The largest group effort of the month took place on the 5th, when 170 Lancasters were dispatched to the Schalke Coking Plant at Gelsenkirchen. Weather conditions were far from ideal, with considerable cloud up to 19,000 feet, poor visibility, and condensation trails forming in the freezing air. The escorting fighters found it difficult to keep their charges in sight as they flew through towering clouds and changing winds. The formation was reported to be confused as it made its way to the target, but thankfully by the time it arrived, the foreword formation at least had become compact, while the rearward formation was still spread out. The results of the bombing could not be assessed because of the cloud.

The Wintershall oil refinery at Salzbergen was the briefed target for 118 Lancasters on the 6th. Situated on the river Ems, it was the oldest oil refinery in the world, an honour that would ultimately bring death and destruction to the local town. Nineteen 218 Squadron Lancasters took off in the morning in fair weather, and joined a hundred others from the group to make their way over Belgium, where the fighter escort picked them up. The 218 Squadron element bombed between 12.13hrs and 12.19hrs from 18,000 feet on a number of well-grouped blue puff markers. Cloud once more prevented any assessment of the results, but returning crews were enthusiastic. Flight Lieutenant Spiers reported, *"Bombing was concentrated and a mushroom of black smoke was beginning to rise through the clouds as we left"*. Two 218 Squadron Lancasters were part of a small force of thirty-nine from 31, 32 and 33 Bases dispatched on a close support operation at Wesel in the early evening on the 6th. With the German Army in full retreat towards the east bank of the Rhine, a further raid was undertaken within a few hours. Six 218 Squadron Lancasters were aloft by 02.47hrs, with a time on target of 05.30hrs.

The crews were instructed to bomb on G-H, and all reported a concentration of explosions and fires below the cloud.

A new name appeared on the operations board on the early evening on the 7th. Dessau sat on the junction of the Mulde and Elbe Rivers, and was famous for the Bauhaus college of architecture, and producing a number of noted artists and lecturers. Thus far the war had largely passed it by. The group dispatched 127 Lancasters, including seventeen from 218 Squadron, which were part of the first wave detailed to be over the target in a four-minute slot from 22.00hrs. Patchy cloud over the target allowed the crews sight of the town and river below, and a number of well-placed Pathfinder markers resulted in some concentrated bombing in the face of moderate flak, but no searchlights. Crews reported black smoke rising from the target as they turned for home. Flight Lieutenant Warwick's Lancaster was attacked by a JU88 while homebound, and after a spirited response from the rear turret, the assailant was seen to roll over and dive vertically. A brilliant flash was observed, and the night fighter was claimed as destroyed. Flight Sergeant Cullen was attacked by a Me410 minutes after leaving the target area, but both gunners opened fire simultaneously when the fighter was within four hundred yards, and it was last seen diving to port. PD278 HA-V was shot down at 22.45hrs by Fw Helmut Burkhard of 1/NJG5, and crashed into a dense wood near Marisfeld. There were no survivors from the crew of F/L Kenneth McKenzie RNZAF, who were on their twenty-first operation together.

It was back to daylight operations on the 9th, when the squadron dispatched eighteen crews to attack the Emscher Lippe Benzol Plants at Datteln in the Ruhr. The force of 159 Lancasters was divided into two formations, each with its own target, the 218 Squadron element being assigned to target B along with others from 31 and 33 Bases. Once past Wesel the force headed towards Datteln, located ten miles north-west of Dortmund, where a number of well-placed and compact blue puff markers resulted in some concentrated bombing from 18,000 to 20,000 feet. There was one moment of danger, when an unidentified Lancaster of 195 Squadron flew across and above a formation of five 218 Squadron aircraft. It dropped its bombs perilously close to the G-H leader, and forced the followers to bomb visually. This was the third occasion in as many weeks that a crew from 195 had caused the squadron problems during the bomb run. Bombing was accurate, especially at target B regardless of 195 Squadron best intentions!

Germany's dwindling oil supplies were once again targeted on the 10th, when 155 Lancasters took off for a daylight attack on the Scholven-Buer Oil Plant. Seventeen 218 Squadron aircraft participated, and S/Ldr O'Brien was finally given the role of base leader, after operating in the role of deputy on no less than six previous occasions. On reaching the Continent the groups again found heavy cloud, and as always in such conditions, formation keeping was a problem. Large gaps began to appear between the first formation of 32 Base and the third formation of 31 Base. Such was the level of confusion that the 31 Base aircraft of

186, 195 and 218 Squadrons somehow found themselves in the second wave. The G-H leaders reported a strong signal, and a number of accurate blue puff markers were dropped, which resulted in some concentrated and precise bombing.

The operation on the 10th brought the twenty-eighth and final operation with 218 Squadron for S/Ldr John O'Brien and crew, and within days they were posted to 622 Squadron at Mildenhall. A disagreement between John and W/Cdr Smith regarding the inexperience of some of the recently posted-in crews resulted in John and his crew being posted off the squadron at a time when it could ill afford to lose such a fine officer. John had been A Flight commander for five months, and during that time he had proven himself to be an outstanding and courageous pilot, respected by all ranks. John's years of experience in Training Command and his professionalism, along with his obvious concerns over the welfare of those under his charge, were apparently not appreciated by the "Vicar". The circumstances surrounding the crews posting did not help the already fragile relationship between the senior crews and their commanding officer. Twenty-eight year old O'Brien relinquished the rank of squadron leader at 622 Squadron, he subsequently completed his tour of thirty-four operations against Potsdam on April 14th. John survived the war with a staggering 1,897 flying hours recorded in his log book. On May 18th he married his fiancée, Joyce, in his home town of Solihull.

The final raid of the war on Essen set an all-time record, when 1,079 aircraft took off during the late morning of March 11th. Fourteen Lancasters were dispatched by 218 Squadron, but F/O E Connell had to make an emergency landing at Juvincourt while outbound, after an engine fire developed. The remaining crews flew above a blanket of cloud, and picked up a fighter escort over the Continent. 3 Group took a slightly different route because of G-H signal issues, its 144 Lancasters were scheduled to be the final wave over the target. Masses of black and brown smoke welcomed the group, and all crews were confident that the raid was a success. The city was left in a state of paralysis, and it would be taken by American forces within a few short weeks. This was the final operation for F/L George "Dig" Klenner RAAF and crew, who had started their operational tour on October 14th against Duisburg. The crew was unique within the group, in that it completed a staggering forty-two operations on its first tour, against some of the most heavily defended targets in Germany.

A new record force of 1,108 aircraft took off for Dortmund in the early afternoon of the 12th to attack troop and communications targets at the behest of SHAEF. Sixteen 218 Squadron Lancasters took part, and once again 3 Group was scheduled to be last over the target either side of 17.00hrs. Aboard PD439 XH-J and alongside the Australian pilot, F/O Welch, was 31 Base commander G/C Brotherhood, flying yet another unauthorised operation. As usual bombing was by G-H, and a series of compact red and green smoke puffs dropped by the G-H leaders gave their followers an ideal target. A new record of 4,851 tons of bombs was delivered, and a dense billowing mass of black smoke was seen rising from the devastated city as the force turned for home.

Flying Officer James Yates and crew in front of "C" Flights PD229 XH-D. Note the 70 bomb symbols, PD229 arrived on the squadron December 7th 1944 via 622 Squadron.

No operations were carried out by the group on the 13th, but the 14th brought two targets, the Emscher Lippe Coking Plant at Datteln, and the Heinrich Hütte Benzol plant at Hattingen near Bochum. 218 Squadron was assigned to the former as part of a force of seventy-nine Lancasters from 31 and 32 Bases. The formation flew south of Calais and north of Arras in excellent weather, and under the protection of a Mustang and Spitfire escort. The Ruhr flak defences were active, and four of 218 Squadron's seventeen aircraft sustained some degree of damage. Such was the intensity of flak that the already ragged formation was broken up even more, and this resulted in some rather scattered bombing. Thirty year old S/Ldr Christopher Martindale arrived on the squadron from 1653 Heavy Conversion Unit on this date to take command of A Flight.

The crews had a two day respite from operations thereafter, mainly because of fog and low cloud, before another dual operation was undertaken on the 17th. The target for 31 and 33 Bases was the Augusta Viktoria Coking Plant at Hüls, while another element from the group went for the Gneisenau Coking Plant at Dortmund. All of the 218 Squadron Lancasters attacked the target, and experienced very little opposition from flak. A Flight's new commander, S/Ldr Martindale, joined the crew of C Flight's S/Ldr Allardyce on this operation to gain experience. This was his first operational sortie, having accumulated a massive amount of flying experience during the previous five years flying with various training schools in the UK and Rhodesia.

The practice of dividing the group to attack two separate targets continued on the 18th, when the squadron was dispatched to attack the Heinrichshütte Benzol plant at Hattingen. The fifteen 218 Squadron Lancasters joined a further thirty-five from 31 and 32 Bases, while fifty others from 33 Base targeted the coking and benzol plant at Bruchstrasse. Taking off at lunchtime, S/Ldr Martindale was captaining his own crew for the first time, and they like the rest of the squadron encountered eight-tenths strato-cumulus cloud with tops up to 8,000 feet. This persisted all the way to the target, where the crews reported the formation and stream to be good, except for the aircraft of 33 Base, which had closed up too much on the 31 Base formation. Flying Officer Mears of PD277 HA-A complained bitterly about the erratic flying of 514 Squadron Lancaster JI-J, which was out of formation and approached Mears' vic several times in an erratic fashion, and forced a number of minor course alterations. Crews bombed on a number of red puff markers, which were grouped closely together, and the attack appeared to be accurate in the face of slight to moderate flak. Taking part in this operation was the special flight of 514 Squadron, with its new GH/H2S Mk III equipment.

There was yet another visit to Gelsenkirchen on the 19th, when seventy-nine aircraft from 31 and 32 Bases were given the important Consolidated Benzol Plant to attack. Low cloud on take-off and at the rendezvous point created problems for the forming up process, and as a result the stream was strung out and rather unwieldy as it neared enemy territory. In fact an alarming twelve minute gap had developed between the two base formations, and this was exacerbated near Brussels, when 32 Base in the rear inexplicably decided to make an orbit. The scattered stream was engaged by accurate flak from the Rhine onwards, with a particularly heavy and accurate barrage south-east of Düsseldorf. Flight Lieutenant Hall and crew reported, *"stream rather a hopeless mix up"*, while W/O McDonald stated that *"Forming up was hopeless"*. Flight Sergeant Yates simply said *"Stream did not exist"*, and the experienced S/Ldr Allardyce, affectionately known on the squadron as *"straight on Allardyce"*, was equally critical, reporting that, *"stream was split up into little groups and the formations were rather confused and scattered"*.

The target area was clear of cloud, and this provided the crews with the opportunity to assess for the first time in weeks the accuracy of their bombing. Black oily smoke soon covered the aiming point as a concentrated raid developed, it was not all one sided accurate flak hit ME303 XH-F and LM577 HA-Q. The latter's rear turret was damaged, and the rear gunner picked up an eye injury. A further five aircraft were hit, including RA532 HA-V, which sustained damage to the port-inner and starboard-outer engines. Pilot Officer Johnson knew almost immediately that they would not reach Chedburgh, and with the undercarriage inoperable in the retracted position, he set course for Brussels Evere. Johnson, who was operating for the fifteenth time, made a successful crash-landing at

17.30hrs. The following day the crew was flown back from Neuville by Dakota to Down Ampney, where they were picked up by F/L Blenkin and transported back to Chedburgh. RA532 was a Metropolitan Vickers-built Mk.I, which had arrived on the squadron direct from A.V Roe on February 21st, and such was the damage that it was struck off charge on April 5th. A replacement Lancaster was available over at Wratting Common, the home of 195 Squadron. Flying Officer Ham flew P/O Johnson over to Wratting Common to collect ME545 A4-N, and on return to Chedburgh the aircraft was re-coded XH-L, and given the name "Lovely Lou". It would become the regular mount of F/L Warwick and crew, and it was this aircraft that featured in the final squadron photograph.

The squadrons of 31 Base were given a well-earned day off on the 20th, but they were back in action on the following morning for an attack on the railway yards and nearby railway viaduct at Münster. Sixteen 218 Squadron Lancasters joined twenty-eight others from 186 and 195 Squadrons and sixty-one from 32 Base. In clear skies the squadron attacked from between 18,500 and 20,000 feet on a number of blue puff markers, experiencing a moderate but accurate flak barrage. The G-H co-ordinates for the two aiming points somehow had been reversed, and this caused the main weight of bombs to fall south of the smaller of the two aiming points. A devastating attack on troop concentrations and their supplies in Bocholt was carried out on the 22nd. The operation, which involved thirteen 218 Squadron Lancasters, took place in ideal weather conditions, and the centre of the town became a mass of flames. On the following night the 21st Army Group entered the town, and a message was received by the C-in-C Bomber Command from Field Marshal Montgomery in appreciation of the vital role played by it in the campaign to cross the Rhine. The penultimate raid on the unfortunate town of Wesel took place on the 23rd in preparation for the Rhine crossing. The group detailed eighty Lancasters in the close support role, the aim of which was to target the German defensive positions on the opposite bank. In clear skies seven 218 Squadron Lancasters joined a further seventy-three from all three Bases, they left the shattered town of Wessel under a vast pall of smoke and flames.

The squadron was not required to operate again until the 29th, which gave everyone on the station a well earned respite. Wing Commander Smith proceeded on leave on the 28th, and command of the squadron passed temporarily to S/Ldr R Jell. The last raid of the month was directed against the Herman Göring Benzol Plant and Coke Ovens at Salzgitter near Brunswick. Twenty 218 Squadron Lancasters represented 31 Base, and together with 110 others from the group they headed in heavy cloud towards the east. With cloud tops up to 22,000 feet, visibility was a problem, and resulted in the formation splitting up into a rather disjointed stream. A navigational error by the group leader resulted in the squadrons encountering heavy accurate flak north of the Ruhr, and this had the effect of dispersing the stream even more. The G-H tracking pulse was strong, but not so the release pulse, and bombing was consequently rather scattered.

It was a disappointing end to a monumental month, in which 303 of the squadron's aircraft had attacked their primary target, and this magnificent record put the squadron in joint second place with 115 Squadron on the group sortie ladder. The Kiwis of 75 Squadron topped the ladder with 344 sorties. The squadron completed twenty of twenty-three operations, and delivered in the process 1,367 tons of bombs. The group as a whole had dispatched 2,791 sorties of which 2,739 were successful, and this was a record number for any month since the outbreak of war. The squadrons of 31 Base had been busy continuously throughout the month, and the ground crews should take credit for their efforts in all weathers, as should the WAAF and back room boys who kept the squadron operational behind the scenes. Four DFCs and a Conspicuous Gallantry Medal were announced at the end of the month. "Shorty" Stewart RNZAF who had completed his tour of thirty-five operations was one of the DFC recipients.

April

The new month began with low cloud and showers, and it was not until the 4th that the squadron was called into action. Twenty-one crews were briefed to attack the partly destroyed synthetic oil plant at Merseburg near Leuna. This was one of the largest synthetic oil producers in Germany, and was reported to be the most heavily defended. An unprecedented number of twelve new pilots would join experienced crews as second pilots on this night. The Pathfinders were to mark the target for the 3 and 6 Group force, but eight-tenths cloud obscured their ground markers. The first of two waves reported that the initial marking was scattered, and, being used to marking their own targets, 218 Squadron were somewhat critical. Flying Officer Cooper remarked, *"Trip would have been much better if the PFF had been on time, sky markers very late"*, while F/O Mears stated that, *"Marking on target very confused, Master Bomber hard to pick up"*. The experienced F/L E Blenkin was equally unimpressed, stating, *"T.I flares scattered, Master Bomber not heard"*. The bombing took place on a number of red and green TIs, and on leaving the target area the crews reported that a glow was visible beneath the clouds. The only incident of an otherwise routine operation involved PD323 HA-K, which ran into the rear of ME860 XH-G on the runway at 03.12hrs, no injuries were reported. PD323 required extensive repair, while ME860 although receiving less damage required the attention of 54 Maintenance Unit. Neither would be available for operations before war's end.

The next operation was another night raid on the 9th, when the squadron dispatched twenty-seven Lancasters to Kiel as part of a group record of 253 aircraft. The operation by a 1 and 3 Group contingent involved almost six hundred aircraft, and they found the weather over the target to be clear, and for once the squadron crews were enthusiastic about the marking. A large crimson explosion was witnessed at 22.40hrs, and crews reported a concentration of explosions and numerous fires around the aiming point. Such was the accuracy of the raid that the German pocket battleship *Admiral Scheer* capsized, and the Admiral Hipper and the Emden were both badly damaged, as was the docks area. This operation concluded the tour of F/O Douglas McClellan RNZAF and crew. Twenty-six year old McClellan had begun his operational tour on December 8th against Duisburg, and completed a further thirty-seven operations. He was awarded a well deserved DFC in September 1945. Flying Officer Boome and crew were posted to 7 Squadron of the Pathfinders on the 10th, the first crew from the squadron to join the Pathfinders since 1943.

The squadron had a two day break before it was once again required for operations. The target for the night of the 13/14th was again Kiel Harbour with the submarine yards as the primary aiming point. Twenty 218 Squadron Lancasters took off and headed north-east out over the North Sea towards Denmark, having joined up with 350 other aircraft from 3 and 6 Groups. The Pathfinders had already begun to mark when the 198 Lancasters from 3 Group approached the target, illuminating flares revealed the glow of red TIs in the cloud below. The raid was only partially successful, and the majority of the bombing fell almost two miles from the port area and largely into the suburb of Elmschenhagen. Fighters were active over the target area, F/L Warwick had a sharp encounter with a JU88, while the relatively inexperienced crew of P/O Yates fought off two separate attacks by a JU88 and a Bf109.

A new target was chalked up on the operations board on the 14/15th. Potsdam was situated amongst a series of inter-connecting lakes on the banks of the river Havel, and only fifteen miles south west of Berlin. This was the first incursion into the Berlin defence zone by RAF heavy bombers for more than a year. Twenty-four 218 Squadron Lancasters made up a force of five hundred of the type from 1, 3 and 8 Groups, which were tasked with the destruction of the local railway facilities and the former Old German Guards Regiment barracks used to house military and Nazis personnel. The target area was free of cloud as the bombing began at 23.07hrs on a number of red TIs dropped with precision over the aiming point. The Master Bomber, call sign "Zipfast", gave clear instructions to the crews, but there was constant interference from another aircraft giving a running commentary on proceedings. Flight Sergeant Bishop, skipper of PD440, recalled that, *"Master Bomber received OK but one aircraft interfering constantly, A CANADIAN crew "*. Squadron Leader Martindale reported, *"Huge explosions with high sheets of flames just leaving the target, Master Bomber continual interference from another aircraft"*. A number of JU88s were reported just before the bomb run, but none from the squadron were involved in combats. Accurate heavy flak worked in conjunction with numerous searchlights as Berlin lived up to its reputation as a "hot target", but Potsdam was left a mass of flames, smoke was rising over the whole target area as the force turned south.

Twenty-seven crews were briefed to attack naval guns and military installations on the island of Heligoland on the afternoon of the 18th. 3 Group put up a respectable 255 aircraft, 31 Base sending seventy-one Lancasters, 32 Base a creditable 102, while 33 Base added a further eighty-two. They were to be part of a force of over 950 aircraft from all groups, which had three aiming points to target, one at the north end, one at the southern end, and the main island. There was no cloud during the outward flight, the vast armada crossed the North Sea at 5,000 feet, before the force climbed to 15,000 feet for the attack. Watching over the enormous armada was an escort of twenty-two squadrons of Mustangs and Spitfires. The island was to be attacked over six waves, with 3 Group scheduled for the fourth wave, and timed to be on target between 13.05hrs and 13.15hrs. Only the north-western tip of the island could be visually identified as the group began its bombing run, as the remainder of the island was covered in thick smoke from the previous waves. Bombing was extremely concentrated, except for twelve sticks which were seen to explode in the sea short of the aiming point. The quick reaction of F/Sgt Talbot, the bomb aimer aboard W/Cdr Smith's Lancaster prevented a tragic accident over the target. With the Pathfinder markers lined up in his bombsight, an unidentified Lancaster flew directly across their track, a mere seventy feet below. Talbot delayed his bombing by just a fraction of a second, and this saved the lives of both crews. The island was shrouded in dense black smoke rising from the various aiming points, the islands facilities were almost completely destroyed, such was the concentration and weight of bombing the island was reminiscent of the Somme.

A daylight G-H raid on the 19th called for a modest fifty Lancasters, the target was the railway transformer station at Munich (Pasing). Ten of the aircraft were provided by 218 Squadron, and they found weather conditions to be far from ideal during the outward flight, with six to nine-tenths cloud and tops up to 10,000 feet. As always this impeded the forming up process, and the ability of the crews to maintain formation once established. This was a constant headache also for the escort of 138 Mustangs from 11 Group. As the formation approached the target area the crews could see the railway lines west of the aiming point, G-H reception was reported to be good as the bombing run commenced. The attack appeared to be concentrated, but no one hung around to find out, knowing that the photo reconnaissance boys would do that for them, and the photographic evidence would be pinned up on the notice board.

The final attack on an oil target was carried out by a hundred 3 Group Lancasters on the 20th. The Rhenania-Ossag Mineralölwerke A.G. oil plant was located in distant Regensburg in south-eastern Germany, and at the time was supplying the German armies in the south. The stream, which once again became strung out, approached the target from the liberated zone east of Frankfurt. Fourteen 218 Squadron Lancasters were involved, and were part of the final wave over the target. Visibility was perfect as the crews began their bombing runs. There

Lancaster's of 218 Squadron taxying out for the operation against Bremen on April 22nd 1945. The squadron dispatched 21 crew including F/Lt Spiers who crashed near RAF Chedburgh on their return.

was little opposition from the ground, and the operation was completed for the loss of a single 622 Squadron Lancaster. On return from this operation two of 218 Squadron's most respected captains were screened, F/Ls Les Harlow and Frank Blenkin having completed thirty-three and thirty operations respectively. The customary end of tour piss up followed, and the usual haunt, the Marquis Cornwallis, was used to celebrate the momentous occasion for two of the squadron's most popular crews. This was in marked contrast to the experience of W/O Bernard Aves after he completed his tour of thirty-three operations. Aves was instructed to make himself available at W/Cdr Smith's office, where he was told that he was to be screened with immediate effect, but that the "Vicar" wanted him to carry out one last operation that night. Bernard informed his C/O that he would go if ordered, but he would not volunteer. Bernard recalled that the "Vicar's" face turned red with anger, and he ordered the bemused Bernard to get off his station and go on leave forthwith!

Following its earlier success at Wesel, the army requested the help of Bomber Command on the 22nd to attack enemy strong points on the outskirts of Bremen, ahead of the advancing British XXX Corps. During the late afternoon over seven hundred aircraft set out for what was to be a four wave operation, with the squadrons of 3 Group allocated to the second wave. 1 and 3 Groups crossed the Zuider Zee and turned north-east to Wilhelmshaven, where the flak was particularly accurate, although not unduly heavy. From Wilhelmshaven to the target there was considerable opposition, and more than a third of the group's 195 aircraft sustained flak damage. The 3 Group element was given a factory strong point as its primary target, while 1 and 8 Groups had as their objective a number of fortified defensive positions, and 6 Group a hutted camp and barracks. The 218 Squadron contingent bombed on G-H between 18.32hrs and 18.35½hrs, and the crews described the bombing as concentrated and accurate.

Flight Lieutenant Spiers radioed that he was returning to base with engine trouble, he managed to nurse NF994 HA-N back to within a few miles of the Chedburgh circuit. Nine minutes later the Lancaster crashed on the airfield's outer circuit, killing all but the two gunners, and narrowly missing a local bus in the process. The driver and a passenger leapt from the bus, and with total disregard for their own safety, rushed to the blazing Lancaster and helped pull out two crew members who were trapped under the forward section. Despite the obvious dangers both continued to aid the injured airman until RAF help arrived. Miss Jean Herring, a member of the Women's Land Army, and Mr Claude Palfrey, the bus driver remained at the scene until no longer needed. Jean Herring was later found to be suffering from shock. For such an act of unselfish bravery, both were subsequently awarded the British Empire Medal (Civil). Sadly, the mid-upper gunner succumbed to his injuries the following day. Don Spiers had completed twenty-seven operations before his tragic death, nine of them at the controls of NF994. He was a local Suffolk lad from Haverhill, situated less than ten miles from Chedburgh.

Twenty-two of the squadron's crews were briefed for a daylight G-H attack on the marshalling yards at Bad Oldesloe on the 24th. Only 31 and 33 Bases were involved, putting up between them 111 Lancasters. The nineteenth Lancaster to line up on the main runway was piloted by Australian F/O Robert Jenyns RAAF. With all four engines through the gate the Lancaster struggled into the air, at which point the port-outer began to splutter, and then inexplicably cut at a hundred feet. Robert fought to keep the aircraft aloft and on an even keel, but with its speed falling off, the Lancaster staggered across the airfield, narrowly missing the control tower. The port wing slowly dropped and the Lancaster stalled and crashed into a hedgerow between a row of houses and the WAAF living site. It immediately burst into flames, and the twenty-eight-year-old from Western Australia died instantly along with his crew. A few minutes later a 500lb bomb exploded, followed soon after by another, and the station commander ordered the evacuation of the WAAF site, No.2 Living site and the entire village. This proved to be a prudent precaution, as a one thousand pounder went up twenty-five minutes after the crash. NF955 HA-H "How" had developed a reputation as a "Jinx" aircraft. Taken on charge by the squadron on August 18th it had maintained a relatively clean record until the attack on St Vith on December 26th, when the port-inner failed. On February 14th the port-outer engine failed while attacking Dortmund, and on the 20th the Fishpond apparatus caught fire. By 218 Squadron standards it was something of a veteran with fifty-six operations to its credit. Flying Officer Jenyns and crew had carried out twenty-five operations.

The remainder of the force headed north-east over the North Sea towards Northern Germany in excellent visibility. Six squadrons of RAF Mustangs provided the escort, and again reported the formation to be strung out over thirty miles, making it difficult to provide cover. Bombs began to fall at 10.37hrs on a number of 250lb blue sky markers from between 16,600 and 19,000 feet. As the group turned away large fires could be seen blazing all over the aiming point, dense smoke slowly obscured the target to prevent any further observation.

The squadron was not required to operate on the following day, the 25th, which proved to be the last day of strategic bombing. 1 and 5 Groups provided the main force for an all-Lancaster attack on the SS barracks at Hitler's Eaglesnest retreat at Berchtesgaden in the morning, before 4 and 6 Groups targeted heavy guns on the island of Wangerooge in the afternoon. Heavy rain and low cloud prevented any further flying until the 29th, when a new name appeared on the operations board. Operation Manna was an attempt to bring food to the starving Dutch people still under occupation. The German Army in Holland had put an embargo on all food transport to western Holland, after the country's railway system went on strike following an appeal from the exiled Dutch Government for the railways to help the Allied Liberation soon after Arnhem. The embargo was partially lifted in November, allowing only water-transported food to be distributed to the desperately hungry population. With the onset of winter, however, the canals froze over and made movement impossible, the already limited food stocks rapidly ran out. In an effort to relieve the famine negotiations took place with the Germans for a coordinated food drop. Instead of targets the bombers were given dropping zones, and the Germans agreed on a number of corridors of safe passage to and from the various zones. On April 29th the BBC broadcast a message to the Netherlands.

> *"Bombers of the Royal Air Force have just taken off from their bases in England to drop food supplies to the Dutch population in enemy-occupied territory"*

218 Squadron supplied ten Lancasters, each carrying four packages of urgently needed supplies. The operation was planned in four waves, the first three made up almost entirely of 1 Group, with thirty-one Lancasters of 33 Base making up part of the third wave, while the fourth wave consisted exclusively of aircraft from 31 and 32 Bases. They flew low over the flat, featureless and still potentially hostile Holland, it was an exhilarating experience for crews accustomed to flying at 18,000 feet and above. With Rotterdam on the horizon the sections dropped down to five hundred feet, whereupon a number of aircraft were hit by rifle fire. The sacks containing flour, sugar, tea, potatoes and cigarettes had been attached to modified panniers, and were dropped in good concentration in the briefed area. Hundreds of Dutch civilians were seen running onto the drop zone to collect up the packs, such was the haste

to reach the packages the civilians were seen to enter the drop zone impervious to the potential danger of failing panniers. The routes were thronged with flag-waving people, who made gestures of thanks to the low flying crews.

April had been somewhat of an anti climax for 218 Squadron after the record activity of March, with only nine operations undertaken, four at night and five in daylight. One welcome piece of news was the squadron's position finally at the top of the sortie ladder. The squadron's contribution to the final month of the bombing war amounted to 730 tons, plus 65½ tons of supplies to the starving Dutch. With conditions in occupied Holland described as critical, two more urgently needed supply drops were undertaken on May 1st and May 2nd, both to The Hague. The squadron dispatched twenty-one Lancasters on both drops, and in the process delivered 161 packages. Disappointingly, thirty-seven were brought back as a result of hang-ups. The crews supplemented the packages with their own sweet rations, which were dropped with great joy to the hundreds of children lining the routes. The excitement of the crews was matched by the joy among the Dutch, who once again waved madly with anything they could get their hands on. Both Dutch and Union flags were in evidence, which they must have hidden from the occupying Germans. Drops were carried out on each subsequent day, except for the 6th, until the end of hostilities on the 8th.

On May 8th the squadron dispatched eight crews once again to The Hague, thirty-six packs were successfully delivered to the drop zone identified by a number of red TIs. One pack was dropped directly above the 218 Squadron formation, necessitating a violent steep turn to starboard. The base commander sent a Special Order of the Day to the squadrons of 31 Base, and in response the station commander, G/C W Brotherhood, addressed the returning crews and assembled personnel, and informed them that Germany had surrendered unconditionally, and that the war in Europe was finally over. The squadron went wild, and everyone cheered, kissed and hugged regardless of rank. The joy on the station was infectious, and a party was quickly organised and celebrated in the traditional manner!!!

To add to the general excitement a piece of welcome news arrived from group, which confirmed that for the last full month of the war 218 (Gold Coast) Squadron had finally topped the operational ladder with a magnificent 186 sorties, pipping its great rivals, 75 (NZ) Squadron into second place with 184 sorties and 115 Squadron into third place with 176 sorties. The joy was complete.

The squadron was not idle over the next few weeks, as "Manna" operations were followed by "Dodge" operations, and "Exodus" flights, the last-mentioned to bring home prisoners of war from the Continent. The first of these humanitarian operations to involve 218 Squadron took place on the 10th of May, when W/Cdr Smith led eleven aircraft to Juvincourt. Over the course of two days the squadron ferried home 238 former captives. At the end of May S/Ldr Martindale and fourteen crews of A Flight were dispatched to 31 Base Stradishall, where they were to undergo secret training for the new Tiger Force for operations against Japan.

August began with rain and drizzle, which reflected the mood on the squadron. On the 3rd six of the squadron's Lancasters were flown over to Mepal for disposal, while a further two went to Hullavington on the 4th to be followed by two more on the 7th. The news that everyone knew was coming finally arrived on August 10th 1945, whereupon the squadron diarist wrote:

ON THIS 10TH DAY OF AUGUST 1945, THE SQUADRON DISBANDED AT R.A.F CHEDBURGH, AFTER HAVING SEEN CONTINOUS SERVICE SINCE IT WAS REFORMED AT UPPER HEYFORD ON 16TH MARCH 1936. THE COMMANDING OFFICER, WING COMMANDER W.J SMITH HAS BEEN POSTED TO NO.3 GROUP HEADQUARTERS, AND THE SQUADRON ADJUTANT FLIGHT LIEUTENANT N.C MINOR HAS RECIEVED POSTING INSTRUCTIONS TO R.A.F STATION WOODBRIDGE, THE TWO FLIGHT COMMANDERS SQUADRON LEADER ALLARDYCE AND SQUADRON LEADER MARTINDALE ARE NOT YET POSTED. ALL THE OFFICERS AND N.C.O'S ARE STILL AWAITING DISPOSAL INSTRUCTIONS.

In early August the Australian airman began their long journey home, while the few New Zealanders joined 75 (NZ) Squadron.

The final entry in the operational records book was made by S/Ldr George Allardyce, who signed the monthly summary on behalf of the already departed commanding officer. Despite the fact that his time at the helm had been characterized by his overly authoritarian manner, "Smithy" was, never the less, intensely proud of the squadron, and had made sure that it remained a well-organized and effective operational unit. He was not a man who endeared himself to those around him, and was certainly not from the same mould as Saville or Fenwick-Wilson. Even so, a farewell party was arranged for him on the 18th. On August 25th all the secret papers, charts, files and maps were ceremoniously burnt, although a few found their way into private hands to prevent them from being lost forever. The squadron's activities at Chedburgh were brought to a fitting conclusion on August 27th, when the final two 218 Squadron Lancasters departed the station for the very last time. F/O Watson lifted "Q" off from the main runway over Clay Farm, and pointed the nose of the unladen Lancaster skyward, climbing steeply to port before shooting-up the runway at 100 feet at 11.09 hours. Two minutes later F/O Stanley repeated the performance in Lancaster "V", and ended by beating up the station at low level. It must have been an impressive and emotional sight for those still on the ground, to watch these harbingers of death and destruction now being flown for fun by two experienced pilots. It was a fitting tribute, and as the familiar sound of Rolls Royce Merlins slowly faded into the distance, the thoughts of many of the onlookers would have returned to those who were absent, those young fliers who had surrendered their lives in the name of freedom.

Appendix I

Stations, Commanding Officers, Aircraft Types, Operational Statistics

Stations

AUBERIVE-SUR-SUIPPES	02.09.39. to 15.05.40
MOSCOU FERME	15.05.40. to 16.05.40
RHEGES/ST LUCIEN FERME	16.05.40. to 21.05.40
NANTES/ST AIGNAN	21.05.40. to 13.06.40
MILDENHALL	13.06.40. to 18.07.40
OAKINGTON	18.07.40. to 25.11.40
MARHAM	25.11.40. to 07.07.42
DOWNHAM MARKET	07.07.42. to 07.03.44
WOOLFOX LODGE	07.03.44. to 04.08.44
METHWOLD	04.08.44. to 05.12.44
CHEDBURGH	05.12.44. to 10.08.45

Commanding Officers

Wing Commander Lewin Bowring DUGGAN	01.06.39. to 28.06.40
Wing Commander Andrew Nicholson COMBE	13.07.40. to 02.02.41
Wing Commander Geoffrey Noden AMISON AFC	02.02.41. to 22.04.41
Wing Commander Herbert James KIRKPATRICK DFC	22.04.41. to 31.12.41
Wing Commander Paul Davie HOLDER DSO DFC	01.01.42. to 30.07.42
Wing Commander Owen Aubrey MORRIS DSO	05.10.42. to 28.03.43
Wing Commander Donald Teale SAVILLE DSO DFC	28.03.43. to 24.07.43
Wing Commander William George OLDBURY DFC	25.07.43. to 09.03.44
Wing Commander Royd Martin FENWICK-WILSON AFC	09.03.44. to 21.10.44
Wing Commander William John SMITH DFC	21.10.44. to 10.08.45

Aircraft

BATTLE	01.38. to 06.40.
BLENHEIM IV	07.40. to 11.40.
WELLINGTON IC	11.40. to 02.42.
WELLINGTON II	03.41. to 12.41.
STIRLING I	01.42. to 04.43.
STIRLING III	04.43. to 08.44.
LANCASTER I/III	08.44. to 08.45.

Aircraft Histories

BATTLE: From January 1938 to June 1940

K9251		From 185 Sqn. Probably FTR bridges at Sedan or troop column on the Bouillon-Givonne road 14.5.40.
K9252		From 185 Sqn. Crashed in France during training 1.3.40.
K9254		From 185 Sqn. To 1 Salvage Section.
K9255		From 185 Sqn. To 6MU.
K9256		From 185 Sqn. To 2 Salvage Section.
K9273	HA–R	From 185 Sqn. Probably FTR bridges at Sedan or troop column on the Bouillon-Givonne road 14.5.40.
K9323		From 185 Sqn. To 150 Sqn.
K9324	HA–B	From 185 Sqn. To 10MU.
K9325	HA–D	From 185 Sqn. FTR St Vith 11.5.40.
K9326		From 185 Sqn. To AASF.
K9327		From 185 Sqn. Damaged on the ground at Auberive when struck by **K9329**. 23.1.40. Abandoned on withdrawal in May 1940.
K9329		From 185 Sqn. Collided with K9327 on the ground at Auberive on landing from a training sortie 23.1.40. To 2 Salvage Section.
K9353	HA–J	FTR Bouillon 12.5.40.
K9355		To 8MU.
K9356		Crashed during dive bombing practice in France 13.11.39.
K9357		Crashed in France while training 12.1.40.
K9447		From 185 Sqn. To 22MU.
L5192		From 88 Sqn via AASF. Probably FTR the bridges at Sedan or troop column on the Bouillon-Givonne road 14.5.40.
L5193		To 22MU.
L5194		To 22MU.
L5195		To 22MU.
L5196		To 22MU.
L5197		To 35 Sqn.
L5198		To 22MU.
L5199		To 22MU.
L5200		To 226 Sqn.
L5201		To 22MU.
L5202		To 35 Sqn.
L5203		To 35 Sqn.
L5232		From XV Sqn via AASF. FTR the bridges at Sedan or troop column on the Bouillon-Givonne road 14.5.40.
L5235		From 142 Sqn. FTR the bridges at Sedan or troop column on the Bouillon-Givonne road 14.5.40.
L5237		From XV Sqn. To 150 Sqn.
L5245		From 40 Sqn. To 1 Salvage Section.
L5402		From 27MU. Damaged during operation over Luxembourg 10.5.40 and abandoned in France on withdrawal.

L5422		From 88 Sqn. FTR the bridges at Sedan or troop column on the Bouillon-Givonne road 14.5.40.
L5514		From AASF. To 103 Sqn.
L5579		From AASF. To 150 Sqn.
P2183		From 150 Sqn via 1 Salvage Section. FTR Bouillon 12.5.40.
P2189		From 142 Sqn via AASF. Probably FTR the bridges at Sedan or troop column on the Bouillon-Givonne road 14.5.40.
P2192		From AASF. Probably FTR the bridges at Sedan or troop column on the Bouillon-Givonne road 14.5.40.
P2201		From AASF. FTR from reconnaissance sortie over Germany 20.4.40.
P2202		From 105 Sqn. To 88 Sqn.
P2203		From 63 Sqn via Abingdon. FTR St Vith 11.5.40.
P2249		From 105 Sqn via AASF. FTR St Vith 11.5.40.
P2324		From AASF via 6RSU. FTR the bridges at Sedan or troop column on the Bouillon-Givonne road 14.5.40.
P2326		From AASF. FTR St Vith 11.5.40.
P2360		FTR the bridges at Sedan or troop column on the Bouillon-Givonne road 14.5.40.

BLENHEIM: From July 1940 to November 1940

L1137		From 57 Sqn. To 13 OTU.
L8848	HA-J	From XV Sqn. FTR from reconnaissance sortie 8/9.9.40.
L9264		Crashed after mid-air collision with T1929 also of 218 Sqn during training 18.8.40.
L9298		From 2SAC. To 70 OTU.
L9306		From 107 Sqn. To 2 OTU.
L9327		From RAE. To Far East.
L9381		To 614 Sqn.
N3561		To 17 OTU.
N3562		To 3 OTU.
N3563		To 13 OTU.
N3573		To FPP.
N3585		To 2SAC.
N3594		From 82 Sqn. Returned to 82 Sqn.
N6183		From 107 Sqn. Returned to 107 Sqn.
P6959		To 17 OTU.
P6960		To Admiralty 22.5.44.
R3597		From 114 Sqn. Crashed in Bedfordshire while training 13.7.42.
R3666	HA-J	From 57 Sqn. To 18 Sqn.
R3673		From 139 Sqn. To 21 Sqn.
T1863		To 75 Wing.
T1864	HA-B	To 13 Gp AAC Flt.
T1865		To 51 OTU.
T1888		To Malta.
T1929		Crashed after mid-air collision with L9264 (218 Sqn) during training 18.8.40.

T1987		From 107 Sqn. To 203 Sqn.
T1988		From 107 Sqn. To 608 Sqn.
T1990	HA-J	FTR from attacks on Brugge airfield 23.8.40.
T1996	HA-S	To 18 Sqn.

WELLINGTON: From November 1940 to December 1941

L4234		From 38 Sqn via 20 OTU. Became ground instruction machine 10.41.
L4293		From 148 Sqn via 15 OTU. To 1505Flt.
L7797	HA-F	From XV Sqn. To 20 OTU.
L7798	HA-S	From 115 Sqn. FTR Brest 22/23.4.41.
N2844	HA-M	FTR Duisburg 18/19.8.41.
N2937		From 75 Sqn. SOC 1.5.41.
P9207		From 115 Sqn. Crashed in Norfolk during training 13.1.41.
P9291		From 115 Sqn. To 2METS.
P9296		From 115 Sqn. To 11 OTU.
P9299	HA-R	From 115 Sqn. To Czech OTU.
R1008	HA-A	FTR Hannover 14/15.8.41.
R1009	HA-L	Crash-landed in Norfolk on return from Düsseldorf 25.2.41.
R1025	HA-B/J	To 16 OTU.
R1135	HA-S/N	FTR Kiel 15/16.11.41.
R1183		To 18 OTU.
R1210	HA-C/D	Abandoned over Westmoreland on return from Bremen 12.2.41.
R1326	HA-G	FTR Bremen 12/13.3.41.
R1328		From 12 OTU.
R1339	HA-J	From 149 Sqn. FTR Kiel 20/21.6.41.
R1346	HA-B	To 16 OTU.
R1368	HA-F	Abandoned over Norfolk on return from Brest 23.4.41.
R1400	HA-L	To 22 OTU.
R1401		To 27 OTU.
R1436	HA-M	From XV Sqn. To 20 OTU.
R1442	HA-D	FTR Brest 10/11.4.41.
R1448	HA-L/S/N	To 20 OTU.
R1496	HA-O/R	Fate uncertain. SOC 19.11.44.
R1497		To 311 Sqn.
R1507	HA-V	FTR Kiel 25/26.4.41.
R1511	HA-L	FTR Bordeaux 10/11.10.41.
R1524	HA-S	To 149 Sqn.
R1536	HA-G	FTR Duisburg 15/16.7.41.
R1594		To 311 Sqn.
R1596	HA-D	From XV Sqn. SOC 1.7.44.
R1597		To 23 OTU.
R1601		To 1505BAT Flt.
R1713	HA-V	From 115 Sqn. FTR Kiel 20/21.6.41.
R1719		From 11 OTU. To 22 OTU.

R1726	HA-O	FTR Brest 24.7.41.
R3153		From 115 Sqn. Destroyed by fire on the ground at Marham 16.9.41.
T2739		From 99 Sqn. To 311 Sqn.
T2801	HA-E	To 15 OTU.
T2806	HA-T	From XV Sqn. FTR Bremen 29/30.6.41.
T2885	HA-D	Force-landed in Gloucestershire on return from Bremen 12.2.41.
T2887	HA-W	From 115 Sqn. To 22 OTU.
T2958	HA-T	Crashed in Norfolk while trying to land at Marham on return from Kiel 25.4.41.
W5400		To 99 Sqn.
W5434		To 57 Sqn.
W5445		To 9 Sqn.
W5447	HA-C	To 305 Sqn.
W5448	HA-Z	Crashed in Norfolk while training 18.5.41.
W5449	HA-Y	From XV Sqn. Crash-landed in Norfolk on return from Berlin 8.9.41.
W5457	HA-Z	FTR Duisburg 18/19.8.41.
W5526		From 115 Sqn. To 305 Sqn.
W5727	HA-V	From 40 Sqn. Crash-landed in Wiltshire after early return from Brest 11/12.12.41. Became ground instruction machine.
X3217		To 18 OTU.
X9663		To 115 Sqn and back via 149 Sqn. To 16 OTU.
X9670	HA-N	FTR Frankfurt 12/13.9.41.
X9672		To 115 Sqn.
X9674	HA-H	To 99 Sqn.
X9677	HA-V	From 115 Sqn. Ditched in Channel on return from Bordeaux 11.10.41.
X9678	HA-F	To 22 OTU.
X9679	HA-D	From 149 Sqn. To 99 Sqn.
X9745		From 57 Sqn. To 311 Sqn.
X9747	HA-E	Abandoned over Norfolk when bound for Hanover 3.8.41.
X9751		From 115 Sqn. To 304 Sqn.
X9753	HA-G	FTR Hanover 14/15.8.41.
X9755		From 115 Sqn. To 25 OTU.
X9757		From 419 Sqn. To 20 OTU.
X9785	HA-X/O	From 40 Sqn. Crash-landed in Dorset on return from Brest 15/16.12.41.
X9787	HA-S	To 99 Sqn.
X9788		To 25 OTU.
X9810	HA-K	FTR Ostend 2/3.9.41.
X9833	HA-A	Force-landed in Norfolk while training 29.10.41.
X9871		To 115 Sqn.
X9875		From 115 Sqn. Returned to 115 Sqn.
Z1069	HA-J	From 115 Sqn. FTR Berlin 7/8.11.41.
Z1070		From 115 Sqn. To 311 Sqn.
Z1101		To A&AEE.
Z1103	HA-A	Ditched off Norfolk coast on return from Emden 26/27.11.41.
Z8375	HA-Z	From 115 Sqn. To 405 Sqn.

Z8399		To 305 Sqn.
Z8431	HA-J	To 405 Sqn.
Z8437	HA-X	To 405 Sqn.
Z8781	HA-S	FTR Hanover 3/4.8.41.
Z8853	HA-H	From 115 Sqn. Force-landed in Yorkshire on return from Kiel 15/16.11.41.
Z8865	HA-O	Crashed on approach to Marham following early return from Nuremberg 15.10.41.
Z8894		From 40 Sqn. To 99 Sqn.
Z8910	HA-F	Damaged beyond repair on landing at Marham on return from Nuremberg 13.10.41.
Z8957	HA-L	Abandoned over Norfolk after early return from Duisburg 16/17.10.41.
Z8965	HA-L	From 57 Sqn. To 214 Sqn.
Z8970		To 214 Sqn.
Z8982		To 214 Sqn.

STIRLING: From January 1942 to August 1944.

N3700	HA-O	From 7 Sqn. To 1657CU via 218CF.
N3706		To 7 Sqn.
N3708		To 7 Sqn.
N3709		To 7 Sqn.
N3710		To 7 Sqn.
N3712	HA-Y	Destroyed by exploding bomb on landing at Marham on return from Billancourt 3.3.42.
N3713		Crashed on landing at Lakenheath while training 13.2.42.
N3714	HA-Q	FTR Saarbrücken 1/2.9.42.
N3715		Crashed on landing at Marham while training 27.2.42.
N3717	HA-S	Collided with parked aircraft on landing at Marham on return from Nuremberg 29.8.42.
N3718	HA-C	FTR Bremen 2/3.7.42.
N3720	HA-B	From 7 Sqn. To 1651CU.
N3721	HA-C/S/P	To 1651CU.
N3722	HA-E	To 1657CU via 218CF.
N3725	HA-D	Crashed in Norfolk on return from Wilhelmshaven 15.9.42.
N3753	HA-U	Crash-landed at Marham after early return from Essen 2.6.42.
N3763	HA-Q	FTR Lübeck 1/2.10.42.
N6049		From 26CF. To 1651CU.
N6070	HA-A	FTR Pilsen 4/5.5.42.
N6071	HA-G	FTR from mining sortie 17/18.5.42.
N6072	HA-F/J/P	FTR Duisburg 6/7.8.42.
N6076		To XV Sqn.
N6077	HA-V	FTR from mining sortie 27/28.1.43.
N6078	HA-P	FTR Emden 22/23.6.42.
N6089	HA-L	From 26CF. To 1657CU.

N6104		From 1651CU. To 1657CU via 218CF.
N6126		To 149 Sqn.
N6127	HA-T	To 149 Sqn.
N6128	HA-T	From 26CF. To 1427CU via 218CF.
N6129	HA-X	From 7 Sqn. To 218CF. FTR Hamburg 28/29.7.42.
R9159		To 1651CU.
R9160	HA-G	FTR Kassel 27/28.8.42.
R9184	HA-U	FTR Genoa 23/24.10.42
R9185	HA-Y	FTR from mining sortie 6/7.11.42.
R9187	HA-A	FTR Vegesack 23/24.9.42.
R9189	HA-K	Crashed on take-off from Downham Market when bound for St Nazaire 28.2.43.
R9190	HA-E	FTR from mining sortie 11/12.10.42.
R9196	HA-G	To 1651CU.
R9203	HA-D	From 149 Sqn. To 214 Sqn.
R9241	HA-L	From 7 Sqn CF. Broke-up over Suffolk and crashed when bound for Milan 24.10.42.
R9244	HA-W	To 1651CU.
R9287		From 149 Sqn. To 1651CU.
R9297		To 7 Sqn.
R9298		To 7 Sqn.
R9303		From 101CF. Conversion Flt only.
R9311	HA-L	From 15 Sqn. Belly-landed at Marham on return from Cologne 31.5.42.
R9313	HA-Q	From 15 Sqn. Victim of friendly fire, crashing in Sussex on return from leafleting sortie to Laon 5.5.42.
R9332	HA-G	To 218CF. Crashed at Marham 31.7.42.
R9333	HA-Y	FTR Essen 5/6.3.43.
R9349		To 90 Sqn.
R9354	HA-N	Crashed on landing at Downham Market on return from Hamburg 27.7.42.
R9357	HA-E	To 218CF. FTR Düsseldorf 10/11.9.42.
W7449		From 214 Sqn via 214CF. To 1657CU.
W7451		From 7CF. Conversion Flt only. To 1657CU.
W7454		From 26CF. To 1657CU via 218CF.
W7459		From 26CF. To 214 Sqn via 1651.
W7464	HA-Z	From XV Sqn. To 218CF. FTR Hamburg 28/29.7.42.
W7466		To 7 Sqn.
W7467		To 7 Sqn.
W7468		To 7 Sqn.
W7469	HA-M	To 149 Sqn.
W7473	HA-F	Crashed in Norfolk when bound for Rostock 23.4.42.
W7474	HA-K	FTR Bremen 3/4.6.42.
W7475	HA-H	FTR Hamburg 9/10.11.42.
W7502	HA-N	FTR Cologne 30/31.5.42.
W7503	HA-B/R	FTR Bremen 25/26.6.42.
W7506	HA-K	FTR Pilsen 25/26.4.42.

W7507	HA-P	Damaged beyond repair during operation to Lübeck 28.3.42.
W7521	HA-U	Crash-landed in Norfolk on return from Stuttgart 5.5.42.
W7530	HA-Q	From 149 Sqn. FTR Emden 20/21.6.42.
W7535	HA-C	FTR Gennevilliers 29/30.5.42.
W7562	HA-R	FTR Frankfurt 24/25.8.42.
W7568	HA-D	Crashed in Suffolk when bound for Mainz 11.8.42.
W7571		From 1427Flt. Conversion Flt only. To 1427Flt.
W7573	HA-U	FTR from mining sortie 20/21.8.42.
W7575		To 214 Sqn.
W7612	HA-T	Crashed while trying to land at Tangmere on return from a leafleting sortie to France 9.11.42.
W7613	HA-N	FTR Lübeck 1/2.10.42.
W7614	HA-J	FTR Fallersleben 17/18.12.42.
W7615	HA-M	FTR from mining sortie 20/21.8.42.
W7618	HA-V	FTR Flensburg 18/19.8.42.
W7622	HA-B	To 1657CU.
W7636	HA-L	Crashed on take-off from Downham Market when bound for Krefeld 2.10.42.
BF309	HA-M	FTR Hamburg 28/29.7.42.
BF315	HA-F	FTR Kassel 27/28.8.42.
BF319	HA-C	FTR from mining sortie 20/21.8.42.
BF322	HA-F	Crashed in Suffolk when bound for Aachen 5.10.42.
BF338	HA-Q	FTR from mining sortie 20/21.8.42.
BF343	HA-M	FTR Stuttgart 11/12.3.43.
BF346	HA-S	To 90 Sqn.
BF349		From 149 Sqn. To 1651CU.
BF351	HA-C	FTR Düsseldorf 10/11.9.42.
BF375	HA-O	To 214 Sqn.
BF385		To 1651CU.
BF395	HA-Z	To 1651CU.
BF401	HA-N	Crashed on landing at Downham Market on return from Frankfurt 2.12.42.
BF403	HA-R	FTR Fallersleben 17/18.12.42.
BF404		To 90 Sqn.
BF405	HA-U	FTR from mining sortie 27/28.5.43.
BF406	HA-Q/E	FTR Hamburg 3/4.2.43.
BF408	HA-T	FTR Hamburg 3/4.2.43.
BF413	HA-H	To 1651CU.
BF416	HA-T	From 149 Sqn. To 1651CU.
BF440	HA-U/T	Crash-landed at Downham Market on return from Remscheid 30/31.7.43.
BF446	HA-B/H	To 1665CU.
BF447	HA-F	FTR from mining sortie 28/29.4.43.
BF450	HA-X	FTR Nuremberg 25/26.2.43.
BF452	HA-V	To 1657CU.
BF468	HA-K	To 1657CU.

BF472	HA–D	FTR Hanover 27/28.9.43.
BF473		To 90 Sqn.
BF480	HA–I	Crashed on landing at Downham Market on return from Bochum 14.5.43.
BF501	HA–N	From 7 Sqn. FTR Wuppertal 24/25.6.43.
BF502	HA–P	FTR Duisburg 8/9.4.43.
BF505	HA–Z	FTR Dortmund 4/5.5.43.
BF514	HA–X	FTR Mannheim 16/17.4.43.
BF515	HA–N	FTR from mining sortie 28/29.4.43.
BF519	HA–E	FTR Remscheid 30/31.7.43.
BF522	HA–N	FTR Berlin 23/24.8.43.
BF565	HA–H	From 214 Sqn. FTR Wuppertal 29/30.5.43.
BF567	HA–P	FTR Hamburg 24/25.7.43.
BF568	HA–B	To 623 Sqn.
BF572	HA–K	FTR Mülheim 22/23.6.43.
BF578	HA–A	FTR Hamburg 29/30.7.43.
BK596	HA–B	FTR Rostock 20/21.4.43.
BK597		From 149 Sqn. To 1651CU.
BK606	HA–N	Crashed in Cambridgeshire on return from Genoa 8.11.42.
BK607	HA–X	Crashed on landing at Downham Market after early return from Turin 28/29.11.42.
BK650	HA–L/T	FTR Mönchengladbach 30/31.8.43.
BK666	HA–Q	Crashed in Norfolk on return from Berlin 2.3.43.
BK687	HA–R	FTR Bremen 8/9.10.43.
BK688	HA–A	FTR Wuppertal 29/30.5.43.
BK689		From 214 Sqn. To 1657CU.
BK700	HA–W/L	FTR Hanover 22/23.9.43.
BK702	HA–O	FTR Berlin 29/30.3.43.
BK705	HA–K	FTR Duisburg 12/13.5.43.
BK706	HA–Y	FTR Dortmund 23/24.5.43.
BK712	HA–D	FTR Krefeld 21/22.6.43.
BK716	HA–J	FTR Berlin 29/30.3.43.
BK722	HA–G	FTR Krefeld 21/22.6.43.
BK727		To 623 Sqn.
BK761		From 7 Sqn. To 1661CU.
BK803	HA–D	To 623 Sqn.
DJ974	HA–T	FTR Bremen 27/28.6.42.
DJ976	HA–A	To 1657CU.
DJ977	HA–F	FTR Mannheim 19/20.5.42.
EE884	HA–X/B	FTR Mannheim/Ludwigshaven 18/19.11.43.
EE885	HA–G	FTR Nuremberg 10/11.8.43.
EE888	HA–H/K	FTR from mining sortie 16/17.12.43.
EE895	HA–S	FTR Hamburg 29/30.7.43.
EE903	HA–Q	FTR Mönchengladbach 30/31.8.43.
EE909	HA–H	To 623 Sqn.

EE937	HA-S/A	FTR Hanover 27/28.9.43.
EE941		To 199 Sqn.
EE943		To 199 Sqn.
EE944	HA-O/H	Crashed while trying to land at Tempsford on return from SOE sortie 5.3.44.
EE949		To 623 Sqn.
EE966		To 623 Sqn.
EF124		To 149 Sqn.
EF133	HA-A	From 15 Sqn. To 149 Sqn.
EF139	HA-B	From 623 Sqn. FTR Hanover 22/23.9.43.
EF141	HA-H/N	To 1654CU.
EF180	HA-D	FTR Berlin 22/23.11.43.
EF181	HA-J	From 75 Sqn. Crashed on take-off from Woolfox Lodge when bound for mining sortie 12.6.44.
EF184	HA-L/V/I	Crash-landed at Woodbridge on return from Chambly 2.5.44.
EF185	HA-L	To 149 Sqn.
EF207	HA-F	From 75 Sqn. To 149 Sqn.
EF233		From 75 Sqn. To 149 Sqn.
EF249	HA-H	Crashed on landing at Woolfox Lodge on return from mining sortie 9.5.44.
EF259	HA-G	FTR Chambly 1/2.5.44.
EF291	HA-C	From 214 Sqn. To 1653CU.
EF299	HA-Z	From 1657CU. Crashed on landing at Woolfox Lodge on return from mining sortie 13.6.44.
EF340		To 149 Sqn.
EF346		To 90 Sqn.
EF349		To 90 Sqn.
EF352	HA-Q	To 1657CU.
EF353	HA-O	To 1657CU.
EF356	HA-O	FTR from mining sortie 28/29.4.43.
EF365	HA-G/U	Crash-landed in Norfolk during air-test 31.5.43.
EF367	HA-G	Crashed at Chedburgh on return from Bochum 13/14.5.43.
EF410	HA-Z	To 1653CU.
EF413		To 1654CU.
EF425	HA-C	Crashed on take-off at Downham Market for air-test 15.9.43.
EF430	HA-W	FTR Gelsenkirchen 25/26.6.43.
EF448	HA-P	FTR Nuremberg 27/28.8.43.
EF449	HA-J/D	To 1660CU.
EF452	HA-V/O	Crash-landed in Algeria after being shot-up by another Stirling during Turin operation 13.8.43. Posthumous VC awarded to F/Sgt Aaron.
EF462		From 75 Sqn. To 1653CU.
EF489		To 623 Sqn.
EF504	HA-P	FTR Chambly 1/2.5.44.
EH878	HA-I	To 623 Sqn.

EH884	HA-X	FTR Turin 16/17.8.43.
EH887	HA-Z	FTR Düsseldorf 25/26.5.43.
EH892	HA-U	FTR Wuppertal 24/25.6.43.
EH898	HA-G	FTR Gelsenkirchen 25/26.6.43.
EH923	HA-W/E	To 1654CU.
EH925		3. 7.43. To 623 Sqn.
EH926		To 199 Sqn.
EH940		From 15 Sqn. To 1661CU.
EH942	HA-M	FTR Laon 22/23.4.44.
EH982		From 90 Sqn. To 149 Sqn.
EH984	HA-C	FTR Kassel 3/4.10.43.
EH986	HA-X	FTR Berlin 23/24.8.43.
EH988		To 1661CU.
EJ104	HA-G	FTR Mannheim 23/24.9.43.
EJ105	HA-N	Crashed in Suffolk on return from Hanover 22/23.9.43.
EJ112	HA-Q	To 1651CU.
EJ125	HA-J	FTR from mining sortie 21/22.2.44.
LJ446		To 1653CU.
LJ447	HA-F	To 149 Sqn.
LJ448	HA-D	FTR Chambly 20/21.4.44.
LJ449	HA-E	To 149 Sqn.
LJ452	HA-S	To 1651CU.
LJ472	HA-K	To 149 Sqn.
LJ481	HA-B	To 149 Sqn.
LJ506		From 90 Sqn. To 1657CU.
LJ517	HA-U	From 214 Sqn. To 1657CU.
LJ521	HA-W	From 214 Sqn. To 1657CU.
LJ522	HA-N	To 149 Sqn.
LJ568		To 149 Sqn.
LJ625		From 90 Sqn. To 149 Sqn.
LJ632		To 149 Sqn.
LK396	HA-M	From 75 Sqn. To 149 Sqn.
LK401	HA-I	To 149 Sqn.
LK568	HA-O	From 90 Sqn. To 149 Sqn.
MZ263	HA-B	Crash-landed at St Eval on return from mining sortie 17.12.43.

LANCASTER: From August 1944

LM187	XH-H	From 90 Sqn. Crashed in Belgium while returning from Neuss 7.1.45.
LM257	HA-P	
LM258		From 514 Sqn. FTR Vincly 25.8.44.
LM281	HA-F/T/E	FTR Cologne 28.1.45.
LM282	XH-C	From 622 Sqn. To 138 Sqn.
LM577	HA-Q	From 622 Sqn.

LM753	XH–B	From 195 Sqn.
ME303	XH–K	From 622 Sqn.
ME350	HA–L	To 138 Sqn
ME352		To 149 Sqn.
ME428		To 550 Sqn.
ME438	HA–H/ XH–H	
ME545	XH–L	
ME842	HA–G/R	From 514 Sqn.
ME860	XH–G	From 90 Sqn.
NF906	HA–B	FTR Frankfurt 12/13.9.44.
NF911	HA–F	FTR Frankfurt 12/13.9.44.
NF916		To XV Sqn.
NF926	HA–X	FTR Vohwinkel 31.12.44.
NF934		FTR Witten 12.12.44.
NF955	HA–H	Crashed on take-off from Chedburgh when bound for Bad Oldesloe 24.4.45.
NF956	HA–E	
NF994	HA–N	Crashed while trying to land at Chedburgh following early return from Bremen 22.4.45.
NG187	HA–J	From 195 Sqn. To 138 Sqn.
NG330	HA–M	FTR Vohwinkel 31.12.44.
NG335		To 149 Sqn
NG362		To 149 Sqn.
NG450	XH–B/ HA–B	From 195 Sqn. FTR Gelsenkirchen 22.2.45.
NG462	HA–B	
NG463	HA–F/ XH–F	
NN704	HA–S	From XV Sqn. To 514 Sqn.
NN706	HA–A	To 115 Sqn.
NN716	XH–A/Y	
PB259	HA–A	From 514 Sqn. To XV Sqn.
PB291	HA–O/C	From 514 Sqn.
PB352		From 460 Sqn.
PB674	HA–Q	From XV Sqn. FTR Witten 12.12.44.
PB721		To 115 Sqn.
PB766	XH–C	Ditched off Felixstowe on return from Witten 12.12.44.
PB768	XH–B	FTR Vohwinkel. Shot down by US flak 2.1.45.
PB837		To 195 Sqn.
PD223	HA–U	
PD229	XH–D	From 622 Sqn.
PD234		To 15 Sqn.
PD252	HA–D	FTR Rüsselsheim 12/13.8.44.
PD256	HA– B/J/X	To 514 Sqn.

PD262	HA-G	FTR Frankfurt 12/13.9.44.
PD277	HA-A	To 115 Sqn.
PD278	HA-V	FTR Dessau 7/8.3.45.
PD279	HA-W	
PD288	HA-H/	To 514 Sqn.
	XH-F	
PD296	HA-B	FTR Cologne 28.1.45.
PD323	HA-K	
PD364	HA-R/T	To 149 Sqn.
PD374	HA-C	FTR Homburg 8.11.44.
PD426		To 195 Sqn.
PD439	XH-J	To 514 Sqn.
PD440		To 90 Sqn.
RA522	HA-V	From 186 Sqn.
RA532	HA-L/	Emergency landing at Brussels-Evere on return from Gelsenkirchen.
	XH-L	19.3.45. Damaged beyond repair.
RF133	HA-M	
SW269	HA-R	

HEAVIEST SINGLE LOSS
14.05.40. Troop column on the Bouillon-Givonne road. 7 Battles FTR.

218 Squadron Roll of Honour

AARON	F/Sgt	Arthur Louis	Pilot	RAFVR	13.08.1943
ABBERTON	P/O	John	Pilot	RAFVR	11.08.1942
ABBISS	F/Lt	Leslie William	Air Gunner	RAFVR	30.05.1943
AGAR	F/O	George Brian Shelton	Pilot	RAF	25.04.1941
ALLAN	P/O	Stanley Gordon	Pilot	RAAF	29.05.1943
ALLEN	F/Sgt	Donald Charles	Bomb Aimer	RAFVR	28.01.1945
ALLEN	Sgt	Thomas Harold	Wireless Op	RAFVR	31.05.1942
ANDERSON	F/Sgt	Robert Edward	Observer	RCAF	10.04.1941
ANDERSON	F/Sgt	Richard John	Observer	RCAF	02.07.1942
ANDERSON	Sgt	Alexander Ian Pryce	Wireless Op	RAFVR	15.08.1941
ANDREWS	F/Sgt	Clifford William	Observer	RAF	25.04.1941
ARMSTRONG	Sgt	Frederick	Flt Engineer	RAFVR	30.05.1942
ARMSTRONG	Sgt	Frederick	Flt Engineer	RAFVR	30.05.1942
ARMSTRONG	Sgt	John	Wireless Op	RAFVR	28.06.1942
ASHBY PECKHAM	F/Sgt	Douglas Joseph	Wireless Op	RNZAF	22.06.1943
ASHWORTH	S/Ldr	Harold John Vincent	Pilot	RAFVR	20.06.1942
ASHWORTH	Sgt	Victor Edwin	Wireless Op	RAFVR	25.04.1941
ASTROSKY	F/O	Peter Clyde	Pilot	RAFVR	03.02.1943
BACHELDER	W/O II	Allen Leland	Wireless Op	RCAF	07.08.1942
BAGULEY	Sgt	Peter	Flt Engineer	RAFVR	13.09.1944
BAGULEY	LAC	Herbert	Wireless Op	RAF	10.05.1940
BAILEY	AC.1	Albert	Wireless Op	RAF	20.04.1940
BAIRD	Sgt	William John	Wireless Op	RAF	21.06.1941
BALDING	F/Lt	Keith Todd	Pilot	RAAF	27.09.1943
BALDWIN	Sgt	William Albert John	Air Gunner	RAFVR	22.11.1943
BALL	P/O	Brian Francis	Pilot	RAF	26.06.1942
BANKS	Sgt	George Leslie	Wireless Op	RAFVR	27.01.1943
BANTING	P/O	John Albert Stokes	Observer	RAFVR	26.04.1942
BARNARD	Sgt	William Arthur	Air Gunner	RAFVR	07.08.1942
BARNES	Sgt	Edwin Charles Albert	Air Gunner	RAFVR	31.07.1941
BARNFATHER	F/O	Eliot Ralph	Observer	RAAF	17.05.1942
BARRADELL	Sgt	Edward Bertram	Air Gunner	RAF (Aux)	28.01.1945

BARRETT	P/O	Harold Brisco	Observer	RAF	25.06.1943
BARROW	F/Sgt	Colin Hervey	Wireless Op	RAFVR	21.08.1942
BARROWDALE	F/Sgt	Joseph Lewthwaite	Observer	RAFVR	31.05.1942
BARTLETT	Sgt	Edward Albert	Wireless Op	RAFVR	31.07.1943
BARTON	Sgt	Percy	Flt Engineer	RAFVR	09.10.1943
BARTON	Sgt	John	Navigator	RAFVR	31.12.1944
BARTON	Sgt	Allan Ernest Ross	Pilot	RAAF	29.06.1941
BARTON	Sgt	Herbert Ronald	Wireless Op	RAF	24.07.1941
BARTON	Sgt	Ronald James	Wireless Op	RAFVR	29.04.1943
BASTEN	F/O	John	Bomb Aimer	RAFVR	23.08.1943
BATES	Sgt	James Dennis	Wireless Op	RAFVR	17.08.1943
BAXTER	Sgt	John Frederick	Wireless Op	RAFVR	22.06.1942
BAYLY	Sgt	George Lee Morris	Wireless Op	RAFVR	18.05.1941
BAZALGETTE	P/O	Frederick Sidney	Pilot	RAF	12.05.1940
BEALES	Sgt	Robert Walter	Flt Engineer	RAF	24.08.1942
BEAUREGARD	Sgt	Joseph George Wilfred	Air Gunner	RCAF	05.10.1942
BEAVIS	F/Sgt	Hugh Walter	Pilot	RNZAF	25.07.1943
BECK	S/Ldr	Anthony	Pilot	RAF	25.06.1943
BELL	W/OII	Murray Richard	Air Gunner	RCAF	02.05.1944
BELL	Sgt	Charles Armstrong	Bomb Aimer	RAFVR	29.03.1943
BELL	Sgt	Alfred Ronald	Wireless Op	RAFVR	15.08.1941
BELLMAN	F/O	George Charles	Navigator	RAFVR	03.02.1943
BELLWOOD	F/Sgt	Lawrence	Wireless Op	RAFVR	22.04.1945
BENDING	Sgt	Henry William	Flt Engineer	RAFVR	09.11.1942
BENNETT	Sgt	Stanley George	Pilot	RAFVR	31.08.1943
BENNETT	F/Sgt	Fred	Wireless Op	RAAF	31.12.1944
BENNETT	Sgt	Kenneth	Wireless Op	RAFVR	01.01.1945
BERRIDGE	F/Lt	Gordon Frederick	Pilot	RAF	28.04.1943
BILTON	Sgt	John Norman	Wireless Op	RAFVR	18.08.1940
BIRBECK	F/Lt	John Lancelot	Air Gunner	RAFVR	25.07.1943
BIRCH	Sgt	Frank	Air Gunner	RAFVR	02.09.1942
BIRD	F/Sgt	Joseph Ronald	Air Gunner	RAFVR	27.08.1942
BIRD	F/O	Kenneth Sidney	Navigator	RAFVR	17.04.1943
BIRD	Sgt	Thomas Cunningham	Pilot	RAFVR	26.04.1942
BIRD	Sgt	David Holley	Wireless Op	RAFVR	26.04.1942
BISHOP	Sgt	Cecil Thomas	Flt Engineer	RAFVR	20.04.1944
BLACK	P/O	Clarence Alwin	Air Gunner	RAAF	2.09.1944
BLACKLOCK	P/O	Henry Wales	Bomb Aimer	RAFVR	12.09.1944
BLAIR	P/O	Charles Edward	Air Gunner	RAFVR	25.04.1941
BLANCHARD	F/O	Cyril Francis	Navigator	RNZAF	26.05.1943
BLISS	W/O	Harry	Air Gunner	RAFVR	30.03.1945

BLYTH	Sgt	Jack Samuel	Wireless Op	RAFVR	24.08.1943
BOLTON	Sgt	John Albert	Air Gunner	RAFVR	28.04.1943
BOREHAM	Sgt	Lawrence Frederick	Wireless Op	RAF	24.08.1942
BOSTOCK	Sgt	James Trueman	Air Gunner	RAFVR	03.02.1943
BOSWELL	Sgt	Roy Gerald	Pilot	RAFVR	19.08.1941
BOWCOCK	F/Sgt	Frederick Hamilton	Air Gunner	RCAF	29.07.1943
BOWKER	F/Sgt	Thomas Layton	Pilot	RNZAF	23.10.1942
BOWLER	Sgt	Reginald William	Air Gunner	RAFVR	10.09.1942
BOXALL	Sgt	George Lascelles	Air Gunner	RAFVR	24.08.1942
BRACE	F/O	Adrian Colebrook	Pilot	RAFVR	23.09.1943
BRAMBLE	Sgt	James Alfred	Air Gunner	RAFVR	30.05.1943
BRANDISH	Sgt	Russell Stanley	Air Gunner	RCAF	29.07.1942
BRASINGTON	F/Sgt	George Charles	Air Gunner	RAAF	22.02.1944
BRAY	Sgt	William Richard	Air Gunner	RAFVR	27.09.1943
BRAY	F/Sgt	Earl Clarence	Air Gunner	RCAF	30.07.1943
BRENNAN	W/O II	Cornelius Alfred	Navigator	RCAF	12.08.1943
BRICK	F/Sgt	Eric David	Bomb Aimer	RAFVR	12.12.1944
BRIDEWELL	F/Sgt	Terrance Alfred Evelyn	Wireless Op	RAFVR	04.08.1941
BRIGHTON	P/O	William Job	Navigator	RAFVR	25.07.1943
BROADBENT	F/Sgt	Harold Cyril Frederick	Wireless Op	RAFVR	04.06.1942
BROOKS	Sgt	Arthur Leslie	Wireless Op	RAFVR	26.06.1942
BROWN	P/O	Stanley	Air Gunner	RAFVR	30.05.1942
BROWN	Sgt	Arthur	Air Gunner	RAFVR	23.10.1942
BROWN	P/O	Denis James	Pilot	RAFVR	29.04.1943
BROWN	Sgt	John Donald	Pilot	RAFVR	10.04.1941
BROWN	F/Sgt	William	Wireless Op	RAFVR	21.08.1943
BRYANT	Sgt	Charles Edward	Air Gunner	RAFVR	23.05.1943
BRYANT	P/O	Francis Egerton	Pilot	RAFVR	29.06.1941
BULLOCK	Sgt	Philip Harold	Flt Engineer	RAF	26.04.1942
BULLOCK	F/O	Derek Vaughan	Pilot	RNZAF	21.08.1942
BURKITT	Sgt	Albert Edward	Air Gunner	RAFVR	20.08.1942
BURNSIDE	Sgt	Henry Charles	Wireless Op	RAFVR	08.11.1944
BURR	Sgt	Ronald Henry	Pilot	RAFVR	21.06.1941
BURROWS	Sgt	Stanley Herbert	Wireless Op	RAFVR	22.06.1943
BUTLER	Sgt	Robert	Air Gunner	RAFVR	23.09.1942
BUTLER	Sgt	Harold	Wireless Op	RAFVR	31.08.1943
BUTTERY	F/O	Robert Thomas Lothian	Pilot	RAF	14.05.1940
BUTTRUM-GARDINER	Sgt	Edward Percival	Air Gunner	RAFVR	01.01.1945
CALVERT	F/O	Arthur James	Air Gunner	RAF	23.09.1942
CALWAY	Sgt	Frederick George	Wireless Op	RAFVR	09.10.1943

CAMPBELL	Sgt	Kenneth Munro	Air Gunner	RAF	30.05.1943
CAMPBELL	F/Sgt	Colin James	Air Gunner	RNZAF	12.03.1943
CAMPBELL	Sgt	Thomas McCord	Wireless Op	RAFVR	02.09.1942
CAMPBELL	Sgt	Hugh	Wireless Op	RAFVR	17.12.1943
CAMPBELL	F/O	John Michael	Wireless Op	RAFVR	29.03.1943
CARROLL	F/Sgt	Richard Francis	Observer	RAFVR	26.06.1942
CARTWRIGHT	LAC	Charles Henry	Airman	RAFVR	18.01.1943
CARVER	Sgt	Joseph	Air Gunner	RAFVR	31.12.1944
CASSIDY	F/Sgt	James	Wireless Op	RAFVR	24.08.1943
CATELY	Sgt	Basil MacCormack	Air Gunner	RAFVR	13.09.1944
CAVANAGH	Sgt	George Clayton	Wireless Op	RAFVR	07.08.1942
CHAMBERLAN	Sgt	William James	Wireless Op	RAF	12.03.1941
CHANDLER	F/Lt	George Neville	Pilot	RAF	31.12.1944
CHANDLER	F/O	Dennis Raymond	RAF	30.04.1947	
CHAPMAN	Sgt	Richard James	Navigator	RAFVR	29.07.1943
CHARLTON	Sgt	John Thomas	Air Gunner	RAFVR	05.03.1943
CHEW	F/Sgt	Alan David	Navigator	RAFVR	13.08.1944
CHUDZIK	P/O	Stanley Frank	Pilot	RCAF	16.08.1943
CLAGUE	F/O	William Henry	Pilot	RAFVR	31.08.1943
CLAPPERTON	Sgt	Robert White	Observer	RAF	18.08.1940
CLARK	Sgt	James	Pilot	RAFVR	29.07.1943
CLARKE	P/O	Donald Wallace	Navigator	RCAF	12.09.1944
CLARKE	P/O	Henry	Wireless Op	RAFVR	12.09.1944
CLAYTON	Sgt	Gerald Lawrence	Pilot	RAFVR	08.09.1940
CLAYTON	Sgt	Samuel Joseph	Wireless Op	RAFVR	02.05.1944
CLEMENTS	F/Sgt	Hugh	Navigator	RCAF	01.01.1945
CLEVELAND	Sgt	Scott Grover	Air Gunner	RCAF	14.05.1943
COADE	Sgt	Charles Frederick	Wireless Op	RAFVR	29.07.1943
COATES	Sgt	Kenneth Wilson	Pilot	RAFVR	18.05.1941
COGGIN	F/Sgt	Stanley Alfred	Pilot	RAFVR	19.05.1942
COISH	Sgt	Frederick Charles	Observer	RAF	08.09.1940
COLLINGWOOD	Sgt	Peter Edward	Pilot	RAFVR	24.06.1943
COLLINS	Sgt	Norman Sidney	Pilot	RAFVR	26.05.1943
COLLINS	Sgt	Dennis	Wireless Op	RAFVR	12.03.1943
COLLINS	Sgt	Charles Lloyd Allan	Wireless Op	RAFVR	16.11.1941
COLLOPY	Sgt	John Henry	Observer	RAF	12.03.1941
COLQUHOUN	F/O	Carman Mackenzie	Pilot	RCAF	22.09.1943
COOK	Sgt	William James	Air Gunner	RAF	23.04.1942
COOK	Sgt	Alan	Pilot	RAAF	15.11.1941
COOPER	Sgt	Kenneth John	Bomb Aimer	RAFVR	01.10.1942
COOPER	Sgt	William Reuben	RAFVR	12.06.1942	
COPLEY	Sgt	Dennis	Wireless Op	RAFVR	22...02.1944
COPPLESTONE	Sgt	Alan Frank	Air Gunner	RAFVR	17.12.1944

CORLIS	F/O	John Edwin	Pilot	RAAF	12.09.1944
CORNES	Sgt	Howard Melville	Flt Engineer	RAFVR	31.07.1943
COTTINGHAM	Sgt	James Charles	Pilot	RAFVR	15.08.1941
COULT	Sgt	Ernest Joseph	Air Gunner	RAF	12.03.1941
COVELL	Sgt	George	Air Gunner	RAFVR	25.08.1944
COWEN	Sgt	James	Air Gunner	RAFVR	29.07.1942
COX	Sgt	Godfrey Denis	Flt Engineer	RAF	31.08.1943
CRABB	P/O	George James	Pilot	RAFVR	03.08.1941
CRAGG	F/O	William Philip	Navigator	RAFVR	22.02.1944
CRAIG	Sgt	Angus	Air Gunner	RAFVR	25.08.1944
CRAMM	Sgt	Reginald Harrison	Navigator	RAFVR	23.06.1943
CRANE	F/O	John Frederick Ryder	Pilot	RAF	14.05.1940
CRAWFORD	F/Sgt	George Morris	Bomb Aimer	RAFVR	29.07.1943
CRAWSHAW	Sgt	Luther	Wireless Op	RAF	18.05.1941
CROOKS	Sgt	Malcom Bruce	Observer	RNZAF	22.04.1941
CROSSE	F/O	William Peter	Pilot	RAF	12.03.1941
CUMMING	F/Sgt	Alistair Godfrey	Navigator	RCAF	06.11.1942
CURLE	Sgt	Joseph	Bomb Aimer	RAFVR	11.10.1942
CURRAN	F/Sgt	John	Air Gunner	RAFVR	23.08.1943
CURSON	Sgt	John	Bomb Aimer	RAFVR	28.08.1943
DABINETTE	Sgt	Tahu William	Air Gunner	RNZAF	10.04.1941
DACRE	Sgt	Desmond Aubrey	Observer	RNZAF	21.06.1941
DARRAGH	Sgt	Thomas Foster	Air Gunner	RAFVR	22.02.1945
DAVEY	Sgt	Edward Victor	Air Gunner	RAFVR	22.06.1942
DAVIDGE	Sgt	Shirley Vincent	Pilot	RAFVR	23.04.1942
DAVIDSON	Sgt	Thomas Raymond	Air Gunner	RAFVR	08.04.1943
DAVIDSON	Sgt	John Thomson	Wireless Op	RAF	29.07.1942
DAVIES	Sgt	John	Bomb Aimer	RAFVR	13.05.1943
DAVIES	Sgt	Douglas Graham	Wireless Op	RAFVR	05.03.1944
DAVIS	Sgt	Hiley Rhys	Air Gunner	RAF	20.08.1942
DAVIS	Sgt	John William	Air Gunner	RAFVR	30.05.1942
DAVIS	Sgt	Wyndham Henry	Bomb Aimer	RAFVR	23.06.1943
DAVIS	F/O	Gerald Mayelle	Bomb Aimer	RAFVR	22.04.1945
DAVIS	F/Sgt	John Richard	Observer	RAFVR	28.08.1942
DAVIS	F/Sgt	Noel Michael	Pilot	RAAF	27.08.1943
DAVIS	F/Sgt	William Arthur Mathias	Pilot	RAAF	30.05.1943
DAVIS	P/O	Arthur Wilfred	Pilot	RAFVR	31.05.1942
DAVIS	LAC	Leslie Douglas	Wireless Op	RAF	12.05.1940
DAVIS	Sgt	William Albert James	Wireless Op	RAFVR	21.06.1941
DAVISON	Sgt	Edward	Observer	RAFVR	20.04.1940
DAWSON	Sgt	John William	Flt Engineer	RAFVR	01.10.1942
DE BOTTE	F/Sgt	Leo	Navigator	RAFVR	24.06.1943
DE SILVA	W/O II	Desmond Michael	Air Gunner	RCAF	24.08.1943

DEADMAN	Sgt	Kenneth David	Pilot	RAFVR	16.11.1941
DEANS	Sgt	Donald	Flt Engineer	RAFVR	17.08.1943
DE'ATH	F/O	Leslie James	Bomb Aimer	RAFVR	24.08.1943
DENNESS	F/O	Bernard	Navigator	RAFVR	05.03.1944
DENNIS	Sgt	David Wesley	Observer	RAFVR	18.08.1940
DENZY	Sgt	Albert Ronald	Wireless Op	RAFVR	14.05.1943
DETMOLD	Sgt	Percy George	Flt Engineer	RAFVR	26.04.1942
DEWAR	Sgt	Frank	Pilot	RAF	01.03.1940
DICK	Sgt	Frederick	Air Gunner	RAFVR	27.06.1942
DIXON	Sgt	Benjamin Robert	Air Gunner	RAF	24.08.1942
DIXON	Sgt	Thomas Wilkinson	Navigator	RAFVR	30.05.1943
DIXON	F/Sgt	Calvin Daniel	Wireless Op	RAFVR	21.08.1942
DOCKRILL	Sgt	Charles James Ernest	Pilot	RAF	11.05.1940
DODD	Sgt	Leslie Joseph	Pilot	RAFVR	03.02.1943
DODD	Sgt	Frank Craighton	Pilot	RAFVR	04.08.1941
DONALD	Sgt	John Abbott	Pilot	RAFVR	21.06.1941
DOOLAN	F/Lt	Gregory McGowen	Pilot	RAAF	20.04.1944
DORMER	Sgt	Percival Frank	Observer	RAF	11.05.1940
DOUGLAS	Sgt	Edward Reed	Flt Engineer	RAF	26.06.1942
DRABBLE	Sgt	Maurice Louis Seth	Flt Engineer	RAFVR	23.05.1943
DRAKE	F/O	John Randal	Flt Engineer	RAFVR	01.10.1942
DRISCOLL	P/O	Stanley Albert	Air Gunner	RCAF	09.10.1943
DRURY	Sgt	Jack Burton	Observer	RAFVR	16.11.1941
DU TOIT	F/Lt	Johannes Christiaan	Pilot	RAFVR	01.10.1942
DUCKWORTH	F/Sgt	Derek Dinshaw	Wireless Op	RAFVR	08.03.1945
DUFFY	Sgt	T	Air Gunner	RAFVR	02.10.1942
DUFFY	P/O	Rodney Ernest	Pilot	RAAF	23.09.1943
DYER	Sgt	David Patrick Henry	Air Gunner	RNZAF	16.07.1941
DYER	Sgt	William Augustus	Navigator	RAF	25.08.1944
EBERLE	P/O	Raymond Frederick	Air Gunner	RCAF	22.09.1943
EDEN	Sgt	Charles	Flt Engineer	RAFVR	29.07.1943
EDGOOSE	Sgt	Raymond Lynn	Bomb Aimer	RAFVR	24.06.1943
EDWARDS	P/O	Elwyn Hinto	Pilot	RAFVR	05.03.1944
EGGLETON	Sgt	Dennis Louis Noke	Flt Engineer	RAF	08.04.1943
EHRHART	Sgt	Loring Charles	Bomb Aimer	RAFVR	27.01.1943
ELDRIDGE	P/O	Roger Charles	Observer	RAFVR	29.07.1942
ELLIS	F/Sgt	Thomas Douglas	Navigator	RAAF	23.09.1943
ELLNER	P/O	Ernest Edward	Observer	RAFVR	29.06.1941
EMENY	F/Sgt	Dick	Wireless Op	RAFVR	10.09.1942

ENGLAND	Sgt	Kenneth William	Air Gunner	RAFVR	31.05.1942
ENGLAND	Sgt	Reginald Charles		RAFVR	29.10.1941
ERNE	Sgt	Kenneth Frank	Flt Engineer	RAF	28.04.1943
ERNE	Sgt	Arthur William	Wireless Op	RAFVR	24.06.1943
EVANS	Sgt	Edward Joseph	Wireless Op	RAF	28.11.1940
EVERS	P/O	Gilbert Davey	Pilot	RAFVR	28.01.1945
EXLEY	Sgt	Harry	Navigator	RAFVR	27.09.1943
FAIRGRIEVE	P/O	Thomas Darling	Flt Engineer	RAFVR	25.07.1943
FAIRHURST	Sgt	Norman Louis	Navigator	RAFVR	20.04.1943
FARLEY	F/Sgt	Leo Louis Joseph	Wireless Op	RCAF	04.06.1942
FARQUHARSON	P/O	Colin MacQueen	Pilot	RAFVR	29.07.1942
FARRIMOND	F/Sgt	John	Wireless Op	RAFVR	21.08.1942
FARRINGTON	F/O	Harry Gregory	Navigator	RCAF	29.03.1943
FAULCONBRIDGE	Sgt	Kenneth Richard	Bomb Aimer	RAFVR	20.04.1943
FAWCETT	Sgt	John Randall	Flt Engineer	RAFVR	12.09.1944
FERGUSON	Sgt	John	Navigator	RAFVR	31.07.1943
FERRIS	Sgt	Wilfred John	Air Gunner	RAFVR	24.10.1942
FILLMORE	F/Lt	Stuart Reginald	Pilot	RCAF	11.08.1943
FINCH	Sgt	Raymond Edward	Pilot	RAFVR	22.04.1941
FINCHAM	Sgt	Arthur William	Flt Engineer	RAF	26.05.1942
FITTON	Sgt	Jeffrey	Wireless Op	RAFVR	13.05.1943
FITZGERALD	F/O	William Vincent	Navigator	RNZAF	27.05.1943
FITZPATRICK	Sgt	Arthur Allan	Air Gunner	RAF	28.04.1943
FLETCHER	W/Cdr	John Lionel Howe	Pilot	RAF	04.08.1941
FLISHER	Sgt	Leonard Charles	Observer	RAF	12.05.1940
FLYNN	F/O	Leslie George	Wireless Op	RAFVR	25.06.1943
FOLLETT	Sgt	Ronald William	Air Gunner	RAFVR	09.11.1942
FORD	Sgt	Alfred James	Air Gunner	RAFVR	13.09.1944
FOREMAN	Sgt	George Henry	Air Gunner	RAFVR	22.02.1944
FORREST	Sgt	James	Air Gunner	RAF	08.04.1943
FORSHAW	Sgt	Harold	Flt Engineer	RAFVR	27.08.1942
FORTH	Sgt	William Norman	Air Gunner	RAFVR	04.05.1943
FORWARD	Sgt	Edward John	Flt Engineer	RAF	27.01.1943
FRANCIS	Sgt	Ernest Noel James	Flt Engineer	RAFVR	28.01.1945
FRANKCOMBE	F/O	John Clarence	Pilot	RAAF	14.09.1942
FRASER	F/Sgt	John Hugh	Air Gunner	RCAF	29.03.1943
FRASER	Sgt	Mason John	Pilot	RNZAF	21.06.1941
FRIEND	Sgt	Ian Ignatius	Observer	RNZAF	09.11.1942
FULTON	Sgt	Douglas Bloom	Air Gunner	RCAF	09.10.1943
GALES	F/O	Philip Frank	Observer	RAFVR	23.09.1942
GALLAGHER	Sgt	John	Bomb Aimer	RAFVR	03.02.1943
GALLOWAY	Sgt	Ernest Norman	Air Gunner	RAFVR	18.08.1942
GARAL	F/O	Earle Stanley	Bomb Aimer	RAFVR	30.05.1943
GARDINER	Sgt	Harold Phillip	Flt Engineer	RAFVR	07.08.1942
GARMAN	F/Sgt	Keith Lavon	Air Gunner	RCAF	13.05.1943
GARROD	F/Sgt	Ralph Frederick	Air Gunner	RAFVR	24.06.1943

GARSCADDEN	P/O	James	Pilot	RAFVR	04.06.1942
GARTLAND	Sgt	John Aloysius	Flt Engineer	RAFVR	22.11.1943
GEHRIG	F/Sgt	Roy Lawrence	Air Gunner	RAAF	23.09.1943
GEORGE	Sgt	Lothian Julyan	Wireless Op	RCAF	18.08.1941
GLENNY	F/Sgt	Robert Edmund	Air Gunner	RAFVR	16.11.1941
GLOVER	Sgt	Albert	Wireless Op	RAFVR	16.07.1941
GOODENOUGH	Sgt	Nigel Rodney	Observer	RAFVR	21.06.1941
GOODRUM	F/Sgt	William Heriot	Air Gunner	RAFVR	19.05.1942
GOSSELIN	W/O II	Joseph Simon	Observer	RCAF	22.06.1942
GOUGH	P/O	Arthur Edward	Pilot	RAFVR	27.01.1943
GOW	Sgt	George Anderson	Wireless Op	RAFVR	28.06.1942
GOWARD	Sgt	Raymond Percy	Flt Engineer	RAFVR	22.06.1943
GRAHAM	Sgt	Raymond Edgar	Flt Engineer	RNZAF	10.09.1942
GRAIL	F/Sgt	Frank	Air Gunner	RAFVR	04.08.1941
GRANT	Sgt	George Alan Ashley	Flt Engineer	RAFVR	30.05.1943
GRANTHAM	Sgt	John Raymond	Air Gunner	RAFVR	02.05.1944
GREEN	W/O	Edward Arthur	Air Gunner	RAFVR	21.04.1945
GREEN	Sgt	Arthur	Flt Engineer	RAF	05.10.1942
GREGG	F/Sgt	William Humphreys	Pilot	RAFVR	05.05.1942
GREGORY	AC.1	Kenneth George	Wireless Op	RAF	11.05.1940
GREGORY	Sgt	William Ronald	Wireless Op	RAFVR	03.03.1942
GRIEVE	Sgt	Bertram	Observer	RAFVR	02.10.1942
GRIFFITHS	Sgt	Maldwyn	Pilot	RAFVR	02.10.1042
GRIVELL	F/O	Robert Garfield	Pilot	RAAF	01.01.1945
GRUBER	P/O	John Anthony	Pilot	RAFVR	28.08.1942
GUDGEON	F/Sgt	Allan Harry	Air Gunner	RCAF	22.06.1942
GUEST	Sgt	Donald Charles	Wireless Op	RAFVR	08.04.1943
GUNTRIP	Sgt	Ronald Joseph	Pilot	RAFVR	31.05.1942
GURNEY	Sgt	Arthur Edwin	Air Gunner	RAFVR	22.06.1943
HADIKEN	F/Sgt	Alexander Alan	Air Gunner	RCAF	24.08.1943
HAGGIS	F/Lt	Douglas Charles	Pilot	RAFVR	25.08.1944
HAILEY	P/O	Kenneth Sidney	Pilot	RAFVR	29.04.1943
HALL	Sgt	Frederick Cecil	Flt Engineer	RAFVR	23.10.1942
HALL	F/Sgt	Philip Louis	Pilot	RAFVR	05.10.1942
HAMILTON	F/O	William Norman	Wireless Op	RCAF	27.09.1943
HANISH	F/Sgt	Frederick Nelson	Air Gunner	RAFVR	19.05.1942
HANNAM	Sgt	Robert Ville	Wireless Op	RAFVR	16.11.1941
HANSELL	P/O	Horace James	Air Gunner	RAFVR	22.11.1943
HARDY	F/Sgt	Harry	Wireless Op	RAFVR	12.09.1944
HARGEST	Sgt	James Phillip	Navigator	RAFVR	14.05.1943
HARGREAVES	Sgt	Ronald	Flt Engineer	RAFVR	03.02.1943
HARP	F/Sgt	Thomas Allen	Wireless Op	RCAF	29.07.1942
HARPER	F/Sgt	Harold Keith	Air Gunner	RAFVR	24.04.1945
HARRIS	Sgt	Stanley James	Air Gunner	RAFVR	27.09.1943

HARRIS	F/O	John Frederick	Pilot	RAFVR	29.03.1943
HARRISON	Sgt	James	Air Gunner	RAFVR	12.09.1944
HARRISON	A.C.1	Robert Hawley	F/Mech	RAFVR	18.08.1940
HARRISON	Sgt	Dennis Higham	Wireless Op	RAFVR	21.06.1941
HART	Sgt	Edgar Desmond	Air Gunner	RAFVR	22.06.1943
HART	Sgt	William Arthur	Navigator	RAFVR	22.09.1943
HARTLEY	Sgt	John	Observer	RAFVR	22.04.1942
HARTLEY	F/Sgt	Leonard	Pilot	RAFVR	21.08.1942
HARVEY	Sgt	Kenneth Bertram	Wireless Op	RAFVR	03.03.1942
HASSETT	F/Sgt	Graham Arthur	Navigator	RAFVR	02.05.1944
HAWKINS	F/O	Edward George	Flt Engineer	RAFVR	02.05.1944
HAWKINS	Sgt	Leo Henry	Observer	RAFVR	05.10.1942
HAWWORTH	Sgt	Kenneth	Flt Engineer	RAF	29.07.1942
HAXTON	Sgt	Andrew Scott	Flt Engineer	RAFVR	27.09.1943
HEAD	Sgt	James Alfred	Air Gunner	RAFVR	29.04.1943
HEAP	P/O	Joseph Ogden	Pilot	RAF	05.05.1942
HEARN	Sgt	John William	Air Gunner	RAFVR	26.02.1943
HEATH	Sgt	Denis Graham	Air Gunner	RAFVR	03.02.1943
HEATH	Sgt	Reginald Baron	Flt Engineer	RAFVR	12.03.1943
HEATH	Sgt	John Kingston	Flt Engineer	RAFVR	28.06.1942
HELVARD	F/O	Arne Rhoar	Pilot	RAFVR	22.06.1943
HELYER	Sgt	Rodney Kenneth	Flt Engineer	RAFVR	29.07.1942
HEMING	F/Sgt	Keith Ronald	Navigator	RAAF	05.03.1943
HENDERSON	Sgt	Norman	Observer	RAFVR	02.10.1942
HENDERSON	Sgt	David Francis	Wireless Op	RAFVR	10.04.1941
HENDERSON	Sgt	William Frederick	Wireless Op	RAFVR	29.05.1943
HENSHAW	Sgt	Douglas Bernard	Air Gunner	RCAF	29.07.1942
HERRIOT	Sgt	Norman Basil	Observer	RAF	14.05.1940
HEWITSON	F/Sgt	Kenneth	Wireless Op	RAFVR	22.09.1943
HICKLING	S/Ldr	Peter Frank	Pilot	RAFVR	09.11.1943
HICKS	Sgt	Norman	Air Gunner	RAFVR	08.03.1945
HICKS	Sgt	Harold James	Wireless Op	RAFVR	22.09.1943
HIGGINS	Sgt	Raymond Tom	Flt Engineer	RAFVR	21.08.1942
HIGGOTT	F/Sgt	Frederick Rex	Pilot	RNZAF	24.10.1942
HILES	S/Ldr	Waldo Harry Bentley	Pilot	RAFVR	23.08.1943
HILL	A.C.II	Lionel Peter	Fitter	RAF	30.08.1941
HINE	P/O	Alan	Pilot	RAFVR	18.11.1943
HINSHELWOOD	F/Sgt	George Allan	Air Gunner	RAF	04.05.1943
HOAR	F/O	William George	Pilot	RCAF	29.03.1943
HOEY	W/O	James William	Pilot	RAF	24.06.1943
HOGG	Sgt	George	Air Gunner	RAFVR	22.02.1945
HOLDEN	Sgt	Cecil Charles	Air Gunner	RAF	31.08.1943
HOLDEN	Sgt	Matthew Bean	Flt Engineer	RAF	03.02.1943
HOLLAND	F/Sgt	Eric	Wireless Op	RAFVR	28.01.1945
HOLLIMAN	F/O	Sidney Michael	Bomb Aimer	RAFVR	29.04.1943

HOLLOWAY	P/O	Frederick Charles	Bomb Aimer	RAFVR	29.07.1942
HOLMES	Sgt	Francis Bernard	Navigator	RAFVR	13.05.1943
HOLMES	Sgt	Stanley	Navigator	RNZAF	17.12.1942
HOOPER	Sgt	Harold Francis	Air Gunner	RAFVR	24.08.1943
HORDER	Sgt	Ronald Douglas	Wireless Op	RAFVR	28.07.1942
HORNER	F/Sgt	John Bland	Pilot	RAF	12.05.1940
HORNIDGE	W/O II	Joseph Noel Charles	Wireless Op	RCAF	17.12.1942
HORROCKS	Sgt	Thomas Bruce	Air Gunner	RAFVR	13.08.1944
HOUGH	F/O	Leslie Markland	Pilot	RAAF	08.11.1944
HOUSE	S/Ldr	Charles Constantine	Pilot	RAF	23.08.1940
HOWARD	Sgt	John Salisbury	Air Gunner	RAFVR	14.05.1943
HOWARD	Sgt	Ernest Thomas	Wireless Op	RAFVR	29.03.1943
HOWAT	F/Sgt	Adam Black Seaton	Air Gunner	RAFVR	25.07.1943
HOWE	Sgt	Vivian	Air Gunner	RAFVR	09.11.1942
HOWES	Sgt	John Frederick	Air Gunner	RAF	26.06.1942
HOWES	Sgt	Dennis Vincent	Air Gunner	RAFVR	26.06.1942
HOWES	Sgt	William Robert	Bomb Aimer	RAFVR	30.05.1943
HOWLETT	P/O	David Frederick	Pilot	RAFVR	17.04.1943
HUBBARD	Sgt	Henry Thomas	Wireless Op	RAFVR	27.05.1943
HUFFINLEY	Sgt	Jack	Wireless Op	RAF	13.03.1941
HUGHES	Sgt	Albert Frederick	Air Gunner	RAFVR	17.12.1943
HUGHES	P/O	Eric Charles	Pilot	RAFVR	16.06.1943
HUMPHREY	Sgt	Jack Ward	Observer	RAFVR	10.09.1942
HUMPREY	P/O	Vernon Leicester	Pilot	RAAF	12.08.1944
HURL	Sgt	William Thomas	Air Gunner	RAF	05.03.1943
HURST	F/O	George Gerard	Bomb Aimer	RCAF	27.09.1943
HUTCHINSON	Sgt	Harry	Air Gunner	RAFVR	21.06.1941
INNES	Sgt	Douglas Alexander	Observer	RAFVR	11.09.1942
INSCH	P/O	John Douglas	Observer	RAF	04.06.1942
IRELAND	Sgt	Eric William	Air Gunner	RAFVR	11.10.1941
JACKSON	Sgt	Norman Vincent	Wireless Op	RAFVR	29.07.1942
JACOB	F/O	Herbert Robert	Navigator	RAFVR	22.04.1945
JACQUES	Sgt	George Ronald	Bomb Aimer	RAFVR	16.06.1943
JAMES	Sgt	Francis John	Air Gunner	RNZAF	21.08.1942
JAMES	F/Sgt	Cyril Henry Robert	Bomb Aimer	RAFVR	31.12.1944
JAMIESON	Sgt	Thomas Arthur	Wireless Op	RAFVR	14.05.1943
JEARY	P/O	Geoffrey George	Pilot	RAFVR	02.07.1942
JEFFREE	Sgt	William John Roy	Flt Engineer	RAFVR	12.12.1944
JEFFREY	Sgt	Cyril Edward	Air Gunner	RAFVR	02.10.943
JEFFREY	Sgt	John Haggan	Flt Engineer	RAFVR	11.08.1942
JEFFREYS	Sgt	Ronald Eric	Navigator	RAFVR	29.03.1943

JENNINGS	Sgt	Cederic Maurice	Observer	RAF	11.05.1940
JENNINGS	Sgt	Bernard Arthur	Wireless Op	RAFVR	16.06.1943
JENYNS	F/Lt	Robert Lance	Pilot	RAAF	24.04.1945
JILLETT	Sgt	Gordon Grant	Pilot	RNZAF	21.06.1941
JOBLING	Sgt	Phillip Percy	Navigator	RAFVR	12.03.1943
JOHNSON	F/O	Philip Robert	Bomb Aimer	RAFVR	31.07.1943
JOHNSON	F/O	Raymond James	Pilot	RAFVR	25.06.1943
JOHNSON	Sgt	John Lawton	Pilot	RAFVR	29.07.1942
JOLLY	P/O	Clifford	Air Gunner	RAFVR	24.04.1945
JOLLY	P/O	Morrison	Pilot	RNZAF	24.07.1941
JONES	A.C.II	Alfred	Airman	RAFVR	17.06.1941
JONES	Sgt	William Trevor	Bomb Aimer	RAFVR	29.04.1943
JONES	Sgt	John Thomas	Observer	RAFVR	02.10.1942
JONES	F/Lt	Arthur Wyn Idwal	Pilot	RAFVR	30.05.1942
JONES	F/Lt	Arthur Ieuan	Pilot	RAFVR	02.05.1944
JONES	Sgt	Kenneth	Wireless Op	RAFVR	12.12.1944
JONES	Sgt	Louis Arthur	Wireless Op	RNZAF	27.08.1942
JONES	Sgt	George		RAFVR	12.06.1942
JOPLING	Sgt	Thomas	Pilot	RAF	20.04.1943
JORDAN	Sgt	John Johnstone	Wireless Op	RAFVR	29.06.1941
JUDGE	Sgt	Horace Hill	Observer	RAFVR	11.10.1942
KEDWARD	Sgt	Douglas	Air Gunner	RAFVR	12.09.1944
KEEL	Sgt	Royston Elvin	Air Gunner	RAFVR	01.01.1945
KEHL	Sgt	Edward Carl	Bomb Aimer	RCAF	06.11.1942
KELLIE	Sgt	Stuart Alan Bain	Air Gunner	RAFVR	26.04.1942
KELLY	Sgt	Leonard Anthony	Bomb Aimer	RAFVR	23.09.1942
KENCH	F/O	Robert Harold	Pilot	RAAF	31.12.1944
KENNEDY	Sgt	Ronald	Flt Engineer	RAFVR	29.03.1943
KENNINGTON	Sgt	George Thomas	Air Gunner	RAFVR	03.02.1943
KERMODE	Sgt	Brian	Bomb Aimer	RAF	22.06.1943
KERSHAW	Sgt	John Bailey	Wireless Op	RAFVR	23.08.1942
KETLEY-ROLPH	F/Sgt	Reginald John	Navigator	RAF	12.12.1944
KILPATRICK	F/Sgt	George	Wireless Op	RAAF	24.04.1945
KILSBY	F/Sgt	Peter Henry	Bomb Aimer	RAFVR	05.03.1944
KING	F/Sgt	George McGowen	Navigator	RAFVR	22.09.1943
KIRBY	Sgt	William George	Wireless Op	RAFVR	23.05.1943
KNEESHAW	Sgt	John	Pilot	RAFVR	30.05.1942
KNIGHT	Sgt	Frederick Joseph	Air Gunner	RAFVR	17.04.1943
KNIGHT	P/O	William Francis Cyril	Pilot	RAFVR	27.09.1943
KOLITZ	P/O	Louis Phillip	Air Gunner	RAFVR	24.07.1941
LABIUK	F/Sgt	George	Air Gunner	RCAF	23.06.1943
LAMBERT	F/Sgt	Frederick Walter	Air Gunner	RAFVR	23.04.1944
LAMOND	F/Sgt	James Crawford	Air Gunner	RCAF	26.05.1943
LANCASTER	Sgt	Harold	Flt Engineer	RAFVR	14.05.1943
LAURIE	Sgt	James Hunter		RAFVR	12.06.1942

LAVELLE	Sgt	Michael William	Flt Engineer	RAFVR	17.12.1942
LAVERS	Sgt	Alan John Claude	Bomb Aimer	RAFVR	17.12.1942
LAWLER	F/Sgt	Leonard John	Wireless Op	RAF	28.08.1942
LAWRENSON	P/O	George Ashley	Navigator	RAFVR	27.09.1943
LAWSON	Sgt	John	Air Gunner	RAFVR	08.11.1944
LAYLEY	P/O	Geoffrey Charles	Observer	RAFVR	27.01.1943
LEADBEATER	Sgt	Gordon Bruce	Air Gunner	RCAF	24.05.1943
LEDBURY	Sgt	William James	Navigator	RAFVR	26.05.1943
LEE	Sgt	Thomas William	Flt Engineer	RAFVR	22.04.1945
LEFEVRE	Sgt	Percy Thomas	Observer	RAF	23.08.1940
LEIBHARDT	F/O	Winston Leslie	Pilot	RAAF	12.09.1944
LENNOCK	Sgt	Rowland	Air Gunner	RAFVR	05.05.1942
LEWIS	F/Sgt	Kenneth Francis	Air Gunner	RAF	15.08.1941
LLOYD	Sgt	Thomas Evan	Air Gunner	RAFVR	24.06.1943
LLOYD	Sgt	Victor Marshall	Wireless Op	RAFVR	22.04.1941
LODGE	Sgt	Roy Edward	Flt Engineer	RAFVR	02.05.1944
LONGSTAFF	F/Sgt	Emmett Jay	Air Gunner	RCAF	17.04.1943
LOVELL	F/Sgt	Eric James	Navigator	RAFVR	23.11.1943
LOWE	Sgt	Evan Robert	Navigator	RAF	24.08.1943
LUCAS	Sgt	Frederick John	Air Gunner	RAFVR	31.08.1943
LUNN	Sgt	Thomas Reginald	Bomb Aimer	RAFVR	22.06.1943
LYMBERY	P/O	Brian Edward	Pilot	RAFVR	18.05.1941
LYNCH	F/Sgt	John	Air Gunner	RAAF	30.08.1943
LYNN	W/O	Robert John Thomas	Bomb Aimer	RCAF	03.02.1943
LYON	W/O	Abraham Thomson	Wireless Op	RAFVR	13.08.1944
MACFARLANE	Sgt	Thomas	Wireless Op	RAFVR	26.04.1942
MACKENZIE	F/Lt	Kenneth James	Pilot	RNZAF	08.03.1945
MACLAREN	F/O	Phillip Frederick	Pilot	RAF	15.01.1941
MAGLADRY	F/Sgt	Harold Ernest	Air Gunner	RCAF	02.07.1942
MAGUIRE	Sgt	Sydney Arthur	Wireless Op	RAFVR	18.08.1941
MAHONEY	Sgt	Alan	Observer	RAFVR	24.10.1942
MAINWARING	Sgt	Jack	Flt Engineer	RAF	02.07.1942
MALCOLM	Sgt	James Berkley	Air Gunner	RAFVR	22.09.1943
MALPASS	Sgt	David Vincent	Observer	RAF	13.07.1940
MARKE	LAC	James Sylvester	Airman	RAFVR	29.06.1941
MARSHALL	F/Sgt	Thomas Robson	Wireless Op	RAF	29.06.1941
MARTIN	P/O	William	Pilot	RCAF	24.08.1943
MATHEWS	W/O II	George	Observer	RCAF	26.02.1943
MATHIAS	F/Sgt	Geoffrey Alan	Bomb Aimer	RNZAF	27.05.1943
MATHIAS	F/O	Glyn Davies	Flt Engineer	RAF	25.08.1944
MATTHEWS	Sgt	Charles James	Wireless Op	RAFVR	15.08.1941
MAXWELL	P/O	John Arthur	Pilot	RCAF	03.07.1941
MAYCOCK	Sgt	Dennis Walter	Air Gunner	RAFVR	31.12.1944
MAYER	F/Sgt	Leonard Aspinall	Navigator	RAFVR	05.05.1942

MAYNARD	Sgt	Derek Charles	Air Gunner	RAFVR	26.05.1943
McARDLE	Sgt	Patrick Desmond	Navigator	RAFVR	22.06.1943
McARTHUR	Sgt	George Arthur	Air Gunner	RAF	24.08.1943
McAULEY	P/O	George	Pilot	RAFVR	20.08.1942
McCALLUM	Sgt	Douglas Izett	Navigator	RAFVR	18.11.1943
McCANN	F/O	Charles Curtiss Merrill	Observer	RCAF	17.12.1942
McCARTHY	P/O	William Ronald	Pilot	RAF	27.08.1942
McCAW	F/Sgt	John Francis James	Air Gunner	RAF	29.03.1943
McDONAGH	Sgt	Thomas	Wireless Op	RAF	19.05.1942
McDONALD	W/O	John Swan	Air Gunner	RCAF	19.03.1945
McGANN	F/Sgt	John Claude	Wireless Op	RAF	24.08.1942
McGOVERN	Sgt	John	Air Gunner	RAFVR	09.11.1942
McKINNELL	Sgt	Robert Smith	Wireless Op	RAFVR	19.08.1941
McSHANE	F/O	James Vincent	Bomb Aimer	RAFVR	08.03.1945
MEARS	Sgt	Ronald Albert	Bomb Aimer	RAF	29.03.1943
MEDHURST	Sgt	Gordon Francis	Air Gunner	RAFVR	27.08.1942
MEDUS	P/O	Richard William	Pilot	RAFVR	22.06.1942
MEES	Sgt	Bernard Joseph	Wireless Op	RAFVR	21.06.1941
MELVILLE	Sgt	David Henry	Bomb Aimer	RAFVR	05.03.1943
MENARD	F/Sgt	Joseph Donat	Air Gunner	RCAF	01.10.1942
MERRITT	Sgt	Dennis Edward	Observer	RAFVR	29.07.1942
MEW	Sgt	Ronald George	Air Gunner	RAF	20.05.1941
MIDDLETON	W/O	Franklin	Bomb Aimer	RCAF	31.8.1943
MILLICHAMP	P/O	Harold Reuben	Pilot	RCAF	26.04.1942
MILLIGAN	W/O II	Geoffrey Eaton	Pilot	RCAF	10.09.1942
MILLS	F/Sgt	William David	Pilot	RAF	27.05.1943
MILLWARD	P/O	Joseph	Navigator	RAFVR	12.03.1943
MINNS	Sgt	Cederic Roland	Wireless Op	RAFVR	23.06.1943
MITCHELL	F/O	Arthur Page	Pilot	RAF	15.08.1941
MOLYNEAUX	Sgt	Geoffrey	Wireless Op	RAFVR	22.04.1941
MONEY	Sgt	Kenneth Gerald	Air Gunner	RAF	13.05.1943
MOORE	Sgt	Stanley	Air Gunner	RAFVR	27.05.1943
MORGAN	F/Sgt	James Auld	Pilot	RNZAF	24.08.1942
MORGAN	F/Sgt	Arthur Henry John	Wireless Op	RNZAF	23.09.1943
MORGAN	Sgt	William Wynne	Wireless Op	RNZAF	09.11.1942
MORLEY	Sgt	Roy	Air Gunner	RAFVR	31.12.1944
MORRIS	Sgt	Derek	Flt Engineer	RAFVR	31.12.1944
MORRIS	P/O	Frederick Anthony	Flt Engineer	RAFVR	24.04.1945
MORRIS	F/Sgt	Anthony	Navigator	RAFVR	28.01.1945
MOSLEY	F/O	Harold Edwin	Bomb Aimer	RAFVR	23.09.1943
MOSS	Sgt	Anthony Cade	Pilot	RAFVR	24.07.1942
MULLEN	Sgt	Daniel Joseph	Navigator	RCAF	28.08.1943
MUNRO	Sgt	Gordon Alexander	Observer	RAFVR	15.08.1941

MURRAY	Sgt	Thomas Edward	Wireless Op	RAFVR	30.05.1942
MURREY	F/Sgt	Ernest George	Wireless Op	RAF	25.08.1944
MUSCHAMP	F/O	John Edward George	Pilot	RAF	22.02.1945
MYERS	F/O	Douglas Vernon	Navigator	RAFVR	08.03.1945
NAULT	W/O II	Joseph.B	Bomb Aimer	RCAF	17.12.1942
NEALE	Sgt	George Leonard	Flt Engineer	RAF	20.08.1942
NETTLETON	Sgt	Eric	Wireless Op	RAFVR	20.08.1942
NEWELL	P/O	Isaac Charles	Bomb Aimer	RAFVR	21.08.1942
NEWTON	F/Lt	George Edward	Pilot	RAF	18.08.1940
NEWTON	F/O	Terence	Pilot	RAF	13.07.1940
NICHOLLS	W/O	Peter Maurice	Bomb Aimer	RAFVR	24.04.1945
NOCKELS	Sgt	Leslie	Wireless Op	RAFVR	24.10.1942
NORTHCOTE	Sgt	John Richard	Air Gunner	RAFVR	31.10.1941
NOTON	F/Sgt	Reginald Frederick	Wireless Op	RCAF	02.07.1942
O'CALLAGHAN	Sgt	Charles	Flt Engineer	RAFVR	02.10.1942
ORME	Sgt	Alexander Colin	Flt Engineer	RAF	17.12.1943
OSBORNE	F/Sgt	Ronald Henderson	Bomb Aimer	RAAF	02.05.1944
OSBORNE	F/Sgt	Ronald Henderson	Bomb Aimer	RAAF	02.05.1944
O'SULLIVAN	Sgt	Denis Graham	Flt Engineer	RAF	16.06.1943
OTTER	Sgt	Eric	Flt Engineer	RAFVR	27.09.1943
OXENHAM	F/O	Charles Bryce	Bomb Aimer	RNZAF	25.08.1944
PAGETT	Sgt	Henry Samuel	Air Gunner	RAFVR	16.06.1943
PAMENTER	Sgt	George Arthur Francis	Bomb Aimer	RAFVR	23.10.1942
PARFITT	P/O	Leslie William	Pilot	RAFVR	16.07/1941
PARKER	Sgt	Robert Peter Melton	Pilot	RAF	19.05.1942
PARKINSON	P/O	Gerald Andrew	Pilot	RNZAF	12.03.1943
PARKINSON	Sgt	Alan Irwin	Wireless Op	RNZAF	01.10.1942
PARRY	Sgt	Edward William	Flt Engineer	RAFVR	22.09.1943
PARRY	F/Sgt	Thomas Campbell	Wireless Op	RAFVR	28.06.1942
PARSLOE	F/O	Cyril Vincent	Wireless Op	RAFVR	28.04.1943
PAUL	Sgt	Jamie Kitchener	Wireless Op	RAFVR	23.04.1942
PAVELEY	Sgt	Derek Arthur Frank	Bomb Aimer	RAFVR	23.05.1943
PEARCE	F/Sgt	Donald Ivor	Pilot	RAFVR	15.09.1942
PECKETT	Sgt	Leslie	Flt Engineer	RAFVR	01.01.1945
PELLOW	Sgt	Ernest Trevor	Bomb Aimer	RNZAF	14.09.1942
PERRY	Sgt	Wilfred Harry	Air Gunner	RCAF	18.11.1943
PERRY	F/O	William Neilson	Bomb Aimer	RAFVR	07.02.1945
PETRE	Sgt	Alfred Charles	Wireless Op	RAFVR	27.09.1943
PETTMAN	F/Sgt	William Henry	Flt Engineer	RAFVR	12.09.1944

Surname	Rank	First Names	Role	Service	Date
PHELPS-HOPKINS	P/O	Ronald Vivian	Bomb Aimer	RNZAF	25.06.1943
PHILLIPS	Sgt	Victor Thomas	Flt Engineer	RAFVR	31.12.1944
PHILLIPS	F/O	John	Pilot	RAFVR	24.05.1943
PICKARD	Sgt	Raymond Stuart	Pilot	RAFVR	30.07.1943
PICKEN	Sgt	Valentine	Flt Engineer	RAF	15.09.1942
PIKE	Sgt	Richard Cecil	Observer	RAF	13.11.1939
PITHERS	F/Sgt	Ronald Ernest	Wireless Op	RAFVR	02.07.1942
PITT	Sgt	James Andrew	Navigator	RAFVR	24.08.1943
PLEASS	Sgt	Henry Norman	Flt Engineer	RAFVR	23.09.1942
PLUMB	Sgt	Arthur George	Pilot	RAFVR	10.04.1941
POCKNEY	P/O	Ewart Duncan	Air Gunner	RAFVR	19.08.1941
POCOCK	Sgt	Henry Arthur Douglas	Wireless Op	RAFVR	05.10.1942
PODMORE	Sgt	Norman Vincent	Observer	RAFVR	21.08.1942
PORTREY	Sgt	Thomas Lloyd	Wireless Op	RAFVR	30.05.1943
POULTER	S/Ldr	Cecil Wardham	Pilot	RAFVR	23.04.1944
POWELL	S/Ldr	Gordon Allen	Pilot	RAF	29.07.1942
PRESTON	F/Sgt	Ronald John Craig	Air Gunner	RAF	29.07.1942
PRICE	Sgt	Stanley Victor	Air Gunner	RAFVR	23.10.1942
PRICE	Sgt	Glyn	Air Gunner	RAFVR	17.12.1942
PRIOR	S/Ldr	Garfield Wallace	Pilot	RAFVR	22.01.1944
PROSSER	Sgt	Peter	Wireless Op	RAFVR	15.08.1941
PRYCE-WILLIAMS F/O	Wilfred Selwyn	Bomb Aimer	RAFVR	23.09.1943	
PRYDE	Sgt	Francis George	Wireless Op	RAFVR	31.09.1943
PUGH	Sgt	James Douglas	Observer	RAFVR	11.10.1941
RADDALL	Sgt	Philip Smythe	Air Gunner	RAF	22.09.1943
RATCLIFFE	P/O	George Arthur	Pilot	RAFVR	05.03.1943
RAWLINGS	Sgt	Donald Peter Jack	Wireless Op	RAFVR	17.08.1943
RAYMOND	S/Ldr	Cuthbert	Pilot	RAF	23.09.1942
READ	W/Cdr	Montagu Francis	Pilot	RAF	01.10.1942
REDSTONE	P/O	Gilbert Peter Lewis	Pilot	RNZAF	25.04.1941
REEVE	Sgt	Fred Charles	Wireless Op	RAFVR	16.11.1941
REID	Sgt	George Ernest	Bomb Aimer	RNZAF	02.09.1942
REYNOLDS	P/O	Harry Churchill	Wireless Op	RAFVR	21.08.1942
RICH	Sgt	Thomas	Navigator	RAF	29.04.1943
RICH	Sgt	Royston Dudley	Observer	RAFVR	21.08.1942
RICH	P/O	Donald Robert	Pilot	RAAF	21.06.1943
RICHARDSON	Sgt	Arthur Edward	Observer	RAFVR	24.08.1942
RICHARDSON	AC.1	Vivian William Liddle	Wireless Op	RAF	13.09.1939
RIDDLE	Sgt	Hoskin Peter	Flt Engineer	RAFVR	15.03.1944
RIDGE	Sgt	Arthur George	Bomb Aimer	RAFVR	08.04.1943
RIETER	Sgt	Willem Joseph Gerard	Pilot	RAFVR	23.04.1942

ROBERTS	F/Sgt	David Eric	Bomb Aimer	RCAF	17.04.1943
ROBERTS	P/O	Robert Edward	Pilot	RAAF	12.12.1944
ROBERTS	F/Sgt	Brian Williams	Wireless Op	RAFVR	20.08.1942
ROBERTSON	Sgt	William Mitchell	Air Gunner	RAF	29.03.1943
ROBERTSON	F/Sgt	Donald	Navigator	RAFVR	12.09.1944
ROBINSON	Sgt	Frank Norman	Pilot	RAFVR	04.05.1943
ROBINSON	AC.1	William	Wireless Op	RAF	14.05.1940
ROBSON	Sgt	Keith	Flt Engineer	RAF	24.08.1943
ROBSON	Sgt	Joseph	Wireless Op	RAFVR	18.11.1943
ROGERS	P/O	Francis	Air Gunner	RAF	03.09.1942
ROGERS	P/O	Frederick William	Bomb Aimer	RAFVR	13.09.1944
ROGERS	F/Sgt	Eric	Pilot	RCAF	09.10.1943
ROGERS	P/O	Walter	Wireless Op	RAFVR	23.10.1942
ROGERS	Sgt	Kenneth George	Wireless Op	RAFVR	25.06.1942
ROLESTON	Sgt	Frederick Livingston	Wireless Op	RAFVR	02.10.1942
ROSE	Sgt	Gilbert Ernest	Flt Engineer	RAFVR	23.06.1943
ROSS	Sgt	James Hamilton	Air Gunner	RAFVR	12.03.1943
ROSS	Sgt	Douglas Alexander	Air Gunner	RCAF	28.08.1943
ROUGHAN	Sgt	John Patrick	Wireless Op	RAFVR	26.05.1943
ROUTLEDGE	Sgt	Joseph Newton	Observer	RAF	13.07.1940
RUSHTON	Sgt	Dennis John	Bomb Aimer	RAFVR	11.09.1942
RUSSELL	Sgt	Henry Millen	Pilot	RCAF	27.09.1942
RUTHERFORD	F/Sgt	Kenneth	Wireless Op	RCAF	23.09.1942
RYAN	F/Sgt	Keith Forbes	Pilot	RNZAF	02.09.1942
SANDERSON	F/O	Owen James	Pilot	RAAF	20.08.1942
SAVILLE	W/Cdr	Donald Teale	Pilot	RAFVR	25.07.1943
SAWKINGS	Sgt	Herbert Ward	Air Gunner	RAFVR	04.05.1943
SCANLAN	P/O	Thomas Patrick	Observer	RAFVR	27.08.1942
SCOTT	F/O	John Wardle	Bomb Aimer	RAFVR	29.04.1943
SCROWTHER	Sgt	Ronald	Air Gunner	RAFVR	08.13.945
SELBY	F/Sgt	Richard Charles	Observer	RAFVR	03.02.1943
SELLER	F/Lt	Howard Thomas	Pilot	RAFVR	12.09.1944
SHARPE	Sgt	John Arthur	Flt Engineer	RAF	21.08.1942
SHEARING	Sgt	Kenneth Charles	Pilot	RAFVR	18.08.1941
SHEPHERD	F/Sgt	Leonard Clarence	Pilot	RNZAF	17.12.1942
SHERWOOD	Sgt	Thomas Randall	Flt Engineer	RAF	05.05.1942
SHILLINGLAW	P/O	William Golder	Pilot	RAAF	22.06.1943
SHRUBSALL	Sgt	Leonard Richard	Air Gunner	RAFVR	29.03.1943
SIBLEY	Sgt	Norman Cyril	Air Gunner	RAFVR	04.06.1942
SIMMS	Sgt	Norman Holland	Air Gunner	RAFVR	24.10.1942
SIMMS	Sgt	William Edward	Flt Engineer	RAFVR	06.01.1945
SIMON	P/O	Horace Martin	Observer	RAFVR	28.06.1942
SINCLAIR	F/O	Graham Olaf Barratt	Navigator	RAFVR	12.09.1944

SINDREY	Sgt	Arthur George	Navigator	RAFVR	29.04.1943
SLATER	Sgt	Thomas	Flt Engineer	RAFVR	08.03.1945
SLATFORD	Sgt	Frederick Herbert	Observer	RAFVR	30.05.1942
SMALLBONE	Sgt	Donald Charles	Wireless Op	RAFVR	29.06.1941
SMALLEY	F/Sgt	Kenneth George	Navigator	RCAF	09.10.1943
SMITH	A.C.2	Alfred	Airman	RAFVR	17.06.1941
SMITH	Sgt	Leonard James	Flt Engineer	RAF	04.06.1942
SMITH	Sgt	Stanley	Flt Engineer	RAFVR	27.05.1943
SMITH	Sgt	Maurice James	Navigator	RAFVR	17.12.1943
SMITH	F/Sgt	James Brooks	Pilot	RAAF	22.06.1943
SMITH	Sgt	Keith Ernest	Pilot	RAFVR	15.08.1941
SMITH	F/O	Frank John	Pilot	RAFVR	13.09.1944
SMITH	Sgt	Colin Hervey	Wireless Op	RAFVR	21.08.1941
SMITH	W/O	Edmund	Wireless Op	RAFVR	13.09.1944
SMITH	Sgt	William Leslie	Wireless Op	RAFVR	18.08.1940
SNODDON	Sgt	George	Wireless Op	RAFVR	10.04.1941
SNOOK	Sgt	Alfred Arthur	Wireless Op	RAFVR	02.05.1944
SOUTAR	P/O	James Ronald	Observer	RCAF	18.08.1942
SPARKS	F/Sgt	John Adam	Air Gunner	RAFVR	20.08.1942
SPEED	Sgt	James	Air Gunner	RAFVR	01.10.1942
SPENCER	F/Sgt	Norman Vincent	Pilot	RCAF	22.09.1943
SPEPHENSON	Sgt	John Henry	Air Gunner	RAF	19.05.1942
SPIERS	F/Sgt	Kenneth Charles	Air Gunner	RAFVR	12.09.1944
SPIERS	F/Lt	Donald Seymour	Pilot	RAFVR	22.04.1945
SQUIRES	Sgt	Abson	Flt Engineer	RAF	23.04.1942
STAGG	F/Sgt	John Leslie	Wireless Op	RAAF	31.12.1944
STANLEY	Sgt	John Glynne	Air Gunner	RAF	31.03.1941
STANLEY	F/Lt	Thomas Albert	Wireless Op	RAFVR	25.07.1943
STELMAN	F/Sgt	Alexander Colin	Wireless Op	RCAF	22.06.1942
STEPHENSON	Sgt	John Henry	Air Gunner	RAF	19.05.1942
STEPHENSON	Sgt	Robert Worrall	Wireless Op	RAAF	10.10.1941
STEVENS	Sgt	Edward Arthur	Air Gunner	RAFVR	31.07.1943
STEVENS	F/Sgt	Stanley Edgar	Observer	RAFVR	20.08.1942
STEWART	F/Sgt	Frank Campbell	Air Gunner	RCAF	03.02.1943
STOKES	F/Lt	John	Pilot	RAF	16.07.1941
STONEY	Sgt	Francis Oliver	Bomb Aimer	RAFVR	22.11.1943
STOREY	Sgt	John Harold	Observer	RAFVR	16.07.1941
STREET	Sgt	Eric Thomas Charles	Air Gunner	RAFVR	29.07.1943
STRONG	Sgt	Donald Percy	Air Gunner	RNZAF	30.05.1943
STRUDWICK	Sgt	Percival George	Flt Engineer	RAFVR	18.08.1942
STUART	Sgt	Lloyd Lincoln	Bomb Aimer	RAFVR	26.02.1943
STUBBS	Sgt	Harry Gordon	Flt Engineer	RAFVR	21.08.1942
STUDD	F/O	Reginald Arthur	Pilot	RAF	23.10.1942
SURTEES	Sgt	Andrew George	Flt Engineer	RAFVR	29.04.1943
SUTTON	Sgt	George	Air Gunner	RAFVR	29.04.1943

SWAIN	Sgt	William Henry	Pilot	RNZAF	22.04.1941
TAIT	Sgt	John Robert	Navigator	RAFVR	08.04.1943
TALES	P/O	John Henry	Flt Engineer	RAFVR	08.11.1944
TATE	Sgt	Maurice	Bomb Aimer	RNZAF	10.09.1942
TAYLOR	Sgt	Herbert	Air Gunner	RAF	24.08.1943
TAYLOR	LAC	Alfred James	Air Gunner	RAF	14.05.1940
TAYLOR	Sgt	Charles Edward	Bomb Aimer	RAFVR	17.08.1943
TAYLOR	P/O	John Alexander	Bomb Aimer	RCAF	16.12.1943
TAYLOR	Sgt	Cyril Martin	Flt Engineer	RAFVR	17.12.1942
TAYLOR	F/Sgt	Robert Edward	Pilot	RAFVR	31.07.1943
TAYLOR	P/O	Kenneth	Pilot	RAFVR	27.01.1943
TAYLOR	Sgt	Gordon	Wireless Op	RAFVR	08.09.1940
TERRY	Sgt	George Louis	Flt Engineer	RAFVR	28.08.1943
THERIAULT	F/O	Henri Paul	Bomb Aimer	RCAF	22.02.1944
THOMAS	Sgt	A.	Flt Engineer	RAFVR	23.09.1943
THOMAS	Sgt	John Charles	Flt Engineer	RAFVR	29.05.1943
THOMPSON	Sgt	Gerald	Flt Engineer	RAFVR	23.08.1943
THOMPSON	Sgt	John Robert	Navigator	RAF	13.05.1943
THOMPSON	F/O	Walter	Pilot	RCAF	24.10.1942
THOMSON	Sgt	James	Flt Engineer	RAFVR	24.06.1943
THOMSON	Sgt	Adam Haddon	Wireless Op	RNZAF	09.11.1942
THORBURN	Sgt	Archibald John	Wireless Op	RAFVR	23.04.1942
THORNHILL	F/Sgt	Wilfred	Wireless Op	RAFVR	25.04.1941
THYNNE	A.C.1	Robert	Wireless Op	RAF	13.11.1939
TOMKINS	P/O	Douglas Arthur	Pilot	RAFVR	08.04.1943
TOMS	Sgt	Charles Cecil	Wireless Op	RAFVR	17.12.1943
TOWE	Sgt	Eric	Air Gunner	RAF	16.06.1943
TOWNS	W/O	John	Air Gunner	RAFVR	28.01.1945
TRAVER	F/Sgt	Howard William	Air Gunner	RCAF	03.02.1943
TRAYNOR	P/O	James Mellon	Navigator	RAFVR	28.04.1943
TREVES	F/Lt	Stanley Leonard	Pilot	RAF	03.02.1943
TROWBRIDGE	P/O	Vincent Charles	Wireless Op	RCAF	27.08.1942
TUDOR	P/O	Gerald Leslie	Observer	RAF	21.08.1942
TURNBULL	Sgt	James Edward	Flt Engineer	RAFVR	29.03.1943
TURNER	Sgt	Albert	Bomb Aimer	RAFVR	09.10.1943
TURNER	Sgt	James	Flt Engineer	RAF	05.03.1943
TURNER	F/Lt	Wilbur Lewis	Pilot	RCAF	04.05.1943
TWINING	F/O	Robert Ernest Samuel	Air Gunner	RAFVR	02.05.1944
TWYDELL	Sgt	Victor Leonard	Flt Engineer	RAFVR	22.02.1944
URE	F/O	Norman Vincent	Navigator	RAFVR	23.08.1943
VALLANCE	Sgt	Robert	Flt Engineer	RAFVR	10.09.1942
VAMPLOUGH	Sgt	Ernest	Flt Engineer	RAFVR	05.03.1944
VENN	Sgt	Alfred Gordon	Air Gunner	RAFVR	21.01.1941
VERNEY	F/O	Stanley John	Bomb Aimer	RAFVR	27.09.1943
VRAI	P/O	James Bernard	Air Gunner	RAF	27.05.1942

WADDINGTON	Sgt	William Edwin	Wireless Op	RAFVR	05.03.1943
WADE	Sgt	James Christopher	Flt Engineer	RAAF	25.02.1943
WADE	Sgt	Horton Neilson	Navigator	RNZAF	30.05.1943
WAKEFIELD	P/O	Ernest	Observer	RAFVR	15.08.1941
WALSHAW	Sgt	Kenneth	Flt Engineer	RAFVR	18.11.1943
WARD	F/O	Arthur William	Navigator	RCAF	23.09.1943
WARD	Sgt	Peter Hallam	Observer	RAFVR	19.05.1942
WARNES	F/Sgt	Jack	Wireless Op	RAFVR	20.04.1943
WATERS	Sgt	Ralph	Pilot	RAFVR	27.06.1942
WATERSON	A.C.II	William Coates	Air Gunner	RAF	14.05.1940
WATSON	Sgt	William Neil	Navigator	RAFVR	31.12.1944
WATSON	Sgt	Ernest	Observer	RAFVR	15.09.1942
WATSON	Sgt	Walter McDonald	Wireless Op	RAFVR	02.07.1942
WATT	Sgt	William Rebecca	Air Gunner	RAFVR	21.06.1942
WATTERWORTH	Sgt	Mack William	Wireless Op	RCAF	05.10.1942
WEBB	Sgt	John Henry	Air Gunner	RAFVR	21.08.1942
WEBBER	Sgt	Wilbur Frederick	Observer	RCAF	18.05.1941
WEBBER	P/O	John Richard	Pilot	RAFVR	04.06.1942
WERNER	Sgt	Harry Victor	Wireless Op	RAFVR	25.02.1943
WHEELER	Sgt	Kenneth	Wireless Op	RAFVR	05.05.1942
WHEELHOUSE	F/O	Thomas Charles	Bomb Aimer	RAFVR	28.04.1943
WHEELWRIGHT	P/O	William Brian	Pilot	RAF	18.08.1940
WHETTON	Sgt	Jack Adam	Flt Engineer	RAFVR	31.08.1943
WHITE	Sgt	Frederick Charles	Air Gunner	RAFVR	18.11.1943
WHITE	Sgt	Edwin James	Flt Engineer	RAF	31.05.1943
WHITE	Sgt	Raymond William	Pilot	RAFVR	26.02.1943
WHITEHEAD	Sgt	Norman Vincent	Bomb Aimer	RAFVR	27.01.1943
WHITEHEAD	Sgt	William Edwin	Wireless Op	RAFVR	20.06.1942
WHYTHE	P/O	Robert	Bomb Aimer	RAFVR	05.10.1944
WHYTHE	Sgt	Thomas	Wireless Op	RAFVR	05.05.1942
WIGHAM	Sgt	Robert	Flt Engineer	RAFVR	26.06.1942
WILDMAN	F/O	Stanley David	Pilot	RAFVR	14.06.1945
WILKES	Sgt	John Bennett	Flt Engineer	RAF	28.08.1942
WILKIN	Sgt	George William	Bomb Aimer	RAFVR	23.09.1943
WILLERTON	Sgt	George Ronald	Air Gunner	RAFVR	23.04.1945
WILLIAMS	Sgt	Harry Roy	Air Gunner	RAFVR	12.12.1944
WILLIAMS	Sgt	John	Air Gunner	RAFVR	12.12.1944
WILLIAMS	F/Sgt	Celt	Navigator	RAFVR	31.12.1944
WILLIAMS	F/Sgt	Henry Ronald	Navigator	RAFVR	24.04.1945
WILLIAMS	P/O	Walter Stanley	Pilot	RAFVR	24.08.1943
WILLIAMS	F/Sgt	Dennis	Pilot	RAFVR	17.12.1943
WILLS	Sgt	Stanley Archibald	Air Gunner	RAFVR	02.09.1941
WILSON	Sgt	Alexander MacGregor	Observer	RAAF	18.08.1941
WILSON	P/O	Winston Claude	Pilot	RAFVR	15.08.1941

WILTSHIRE	A.C.1	Robert Francis James	Wireless Op	RAF	01.03.1940
WINDERS	F/Sgt	Bruce Dean	Air Gunner	RCAF	27.09.1943
WINDLE	Sgt	Harold	Wireless Op	RAFVR	29.07.1942
WISEMAN	F/Lt	James Ian	Pilot	RAFVR	22.02.1944
WISHART	Sgt	George Sinclair	Navigator	RAFVR	23.05.1943
WOLSTENCROFT F/Sgt	Bertram Arthur	Wireless Op	RAF	28.08.1942	
WOOD	Sgt	Fred	Wireless Op	RAF	16.07.1941
WOODHOUSE	P/O	Robert Beck	Air Gunner	RAFVR	23.09.1943
WOODHOUSE	Sgt	Fred	Wireless Op	RAF	16.07.1941
WOODROW	F/O	Roy William	Pilot	RAFVR	31.12.1944
WORTHINGTON F/Sgt	Hugh Arthur	Observer	RAF	19.05.1942	
WREN	Sgt	George Ernest Smyth	Air Gunner	RAFVR	21.08.1942
WRIGHT	Sgt	George Arthur	Wireless Op	RAFVR	22.11.1943
WURR	Sgt	Donald	Flt Engineer	RAF	14.05.1943
WYLIE	W/O II	Douglas McKay	Bomb Aimer	RCAF	22.09.1943
YARDLEY	Sgt	Dennis George	Navigator	RAFVR	31.08.1943
YATES	F/Sgt	Robert	Pilot	RAFVR	24.08.1942
YEOMAN	F/O	John	Navigator	RAFVR	13.09.1944
YOUNG	Sgt	Ronald John Craig	Observer	RAFVR	30.05.1942
YOUNG	W/O II	Kenneth Ian	Observer	RCAF	26.02.1943
YOUNGMAN	F/O	Louis Rousseau	Navigator	RAFVR	23.10.1942
YOXALL	Sgt	Charles Henry	Wireless Op	RAFVR	03.02.1943
YULE	Sgt	James	Bomb Aimer	RAFVR	22.09.1943

Appendix III

Key to Abbreviations

A&AEE	Aeroplane and Armaments Experimental Establishment.
AA	Anti-Aircraft fire.
AACU	Anti-Aircraft Cooperation Unit.
AAS	Air Armament School.
AASF	Advance Air Striking Force.
AAU	Aircraft Assembly Unit.
ACM	Air Chief Marshal.
ACSEA	Air Command South-East Asia.
AFDU	Air Fighting Development Unit.
AFEE	Airborne Forces Experimental Unit.
AFTDU	Airborne Forces Tactical Development Unit.
AGS	Air Gunners School.
AMDP	Air Members for Development and Production.
AOC	Air Officer Commanding.
AOS	Air Observers School.
ASRTU	Air-Sea Rescue Training Unit.
ATTDU	Air Transport Tactical Development Unit.
AVM	Air Vice-Marshal.
BAT	Beam Approach Training.
BCBS	Bomber Command Bombing School.
BCDU	Bomber Command Development Unit.
BCFU	Bomber Command Film Unit.
BCIS	Bomber Command Instructors School.
BDU	Bombing Development Unit.
BSTU	Bomber Support Training Unit.
CF	Conversion Flight.
CFS	Central Flying School.
CGS	Central Gunnery School.
C-in-C	Commander in Chief.
CNS	Central Navigation School.
CO	Commanding Officer.
CRD	Controller of Research and Development.
CU	Conversion Unit.
DGRD	Director General for Research and Development.
EAAS	Empire Air Armament School.
EANS	Empire Air Navigation School.
ECDU	Electronic Countermeasures Development Unit.
ECFS	Empire Central Flying School.
ETPS	Empire Test Pilots School.
F/L	Flight Lieutenant.

Flt	Flight.
F/O	Flying Officer.
FPP	Ferry Pilots School.
F/Sgt	Flight Sgt.
FTR	Failed to Return.
FTU	Ferry Training Unit.
G/C	Group Captain.
Gp	Group.
HCU	Heavy Conversion Unit.
HGCU	Heavy Glider Conversion Unit.
LFS	Lancaster Finishing School.
MAC	Mediterranean Air Command.
MTU	Mosquito Training Unit.
MU	Maintenance Unit.
NTU	Navigation Training Unit.
OADU	Overseas Aircraft Delivery Unit.
OAPU	Overseas Aircraft Preparation Unit.
OTU	Operational Training Unit.
P/O	Pilot Officer.
PTS	Parachute Training School.
RAE	Royal Aircraft Establishment.
SGR	School of General Reconnaissance.
Sgt	Sgt.
SHAEF	Supreme Headquarters Allied Expeditionary Force.
SIU	Signals Intelligence Unit.
S/Ldr	S/Ldr.
SOC	Struck off Charge.
SOE	Special Operations Executive.
Sqn	Squadron.
TF	Training Flight.
TFU	Telecommunications Flying Unit.
W/Cdr	Wing Commander.
Wg	Wing.
WIDU	Wireless Intelligence Development Unit.
W/O	Warrant Officer.

A Representative List of Aircraft Used by 218 Squadron 1938–1945

Fairey Battle Mk.I

K7647	17.01.1938 To No.185 Sqdn, 10.10.1938
K7651	20.01.1938 To No.185 Sqdn, 10.10.1938
K7652	20.01.1938 Engine cut, Belly landed, Upper Hayford, 29.03.1938,
K7653	21.01.1938 To No.185 Sqdn, 10.10.1938
K7654 HA-O	24.01.1938 To No.185 Sqdn 12.10.1938
K7655 HA-F	26.01.1938 To No.185 Sqdn 10.10.1938
K7656	26.01.1938 To No.185 Sqdn 12.10.1938
K7657	27.01.1938 U/C failed to lock on landing, Boscombe Down
K7658 HA-J	31.01.1938 To No.185 Sqdn 10.10.1938
K7659	31.01.1938 To No.185 Sdn 11.10.1938
K7660 HA-L	31.01.1938 To No.185 Sqdn 10.10.1938
K7661	03.02.1938 U/C jammed, bellylanded Boscombe Down
K7663 HA-N	10.02.1938 To No.185 Sqdn, 10.10.1938
K7664 HA-O	10.02.1938 To No.185 Sqdn, 11.10.1938
K7665 HA-P	10.02.1938 To No.185 Sqdn, 10.10.1938
K7666 HA-Q	10.02.1938 To No.185 Sqdn 10.10.1938
K9251	10.10.1938 Presumed abandoned France June 1940 Via No.185 Sqdn
K9252	11.10.1938 Ran into bad weather on navex, crashed 40 miles N Dijon
K9253	11.10.1938 Belly landed in error, Boscombe Down, 15.08.1939
K9254	11.10.1938 No.1 Salvage Section 17.01.1940. Via No.185 Sqdn
K9255	11.10.1938 To No.6 MU, 05.03.1940 Via No.185 Sqdn
K9256	11.10.1938 No.2 Salvage Section, 07.03.1940 Via No.185 Sqdn
K9260	11.10.1938 Overshot landing at night, Boscombe Down, 11.04.1939 K9273
SV-R	11.10.1938 Presumed lost in France May 1940. HA-T-R Via No.185 Sqdn
K9323	10.10.1938 To No.150 Sqdn Via No.185 Sqdn
K9324 HA-B	10.10.1938 To No.10 MU, 07.03.1940 Via No.185 Sqdn
K9325 HA-D	10.10.1938 Via No.185 Sqdn. Shot Down 11th May 1940
K9326	10.10.1938 To No.6 MU, 12.04.1940 Via No.185 Sqdn
K9327	10.10.1938 Damaged in force landing, Monchy, 10.01.1940
K9328	10.10.1938 Hit pylon during low-level practice, crashed Carlton, 11.08.1939
K9329	10.10.1938 Collided with K9327 on landing due to flap failure, Auberive,
K9353 HA-J	20.10.1938 Hit by Flak, crashed near Sensenruth 12th May 1940.
K9354	24.10.1938 To No.98 Sqdn, 30.11.1939
K9355	24.10.1938 To 8 MU, 02.03.1940
K9356	26.10.1938 Lost wing during dive. Crashed near Auberive, 13.11.1939
K9357	26.10.1938 Crashed during forced landing, 3m WNW of Soissons, Aisne
K9384	17.11.1938 Linton-on-Ouse, 27.09.1940

L5192 HA-P	11.03.1940 Presumed lost in France May 1940. Via No.88 Sqdn
L5193	05.07.1939 To 22 MU 14.09.1939, No.301 Sqdn 30.08.1940
L5194	03.07.1939 To 22 MU 18.09.1940, 47 MU 09.11.1940
L5195	03.07.1939 To 22 MU, 14.09.1939, to 19 MU 28.05.1941
L5196	05.07.1939 To 22 MU 19.09.1939
L5197	03.07.1939 To No.35 Sqdn, 24.10.1939
L5198	12.07.1939 To 22 MU 14.09.1939
L5199	03.07.1939 To 22 MU 14.09.1939
L5200	14.07.1939 Abington, 30.11.1939
L5201	10.07.1939 To 22 MU, 17.09.1939
L5202	03.07.1939 To No.35 Sqdn, 24.10.1939
L5203	12.07.1939 To No.35 Sqdn 24.10.1939
L5232	04.03.1940 Via No.15 Sqdn. Shot Down 14th May 1940
L5235 HA-W	Unknown Via No.15 Sqdn. Shot Down 14th May 1940
L5237	30.11.1939 To No.150 Sqdn, 21.05.1940
L5245	03.05.1940 To 1 Salvage Section, 19.04.1940 Via No.40 Sqdn
L5402	05,1940 Damaged by ground fire near Luxembourg, 10th May 1940
L5422	Via No.88 Sqdn. Shot Down 14th May 1940
L5514	15.05.1940 To No.103 Sqdn, 18.05.1940
L5579	13.05.1940 To No.150 Sqdn, 14.05.1940 Via A.A.S.F
P2183	30.11.1939 Damaged ground fire and crashed, Nouvion-sur-Meuse, 12th May
P2189	05.03.1940 Presumed lost in France June 1940 Via A.A.S.F
P2192 HA-E	12.03.1940 Presumed lost France, June 1940.
P2201	06.03.1940 Via A.A.S.F. Shot Down 20th April 1940
P2202	10.10.1939 To No.88 Sqdn, 11.10.1939 Via No.105 Sqdn
P2203	17.01.1940 Via Abington, 30.11.1939. Shot Down 11th May 1940
P2249 HA-U	26.01.1940 S.O.C 31st May 1940 Via A.A.S.F. Shot Down May 11th 1940
P2315	18.05.1940 To No.103 Sqdn, 21.05.1940 Via A.A.S.F
P2324	20.04.1940 Via 6 RSU. Shot Down 14th May 1940
P2326	19.04.1940 Via 6 RSU. Shot Down 11 May 1940. Abandoned
P2360	13.05.1940 Via A.A.S.F. Shot Down 14th May 1940

Bristol Blenheim Mk.I & Mk.IV

L1137	Delivered via No.57 Squadron – 218 Squadron-No.13 O.T.U (used by the squadron as a duel trainer)
P6959	218 Squadron – 17 OTU dived into ground 03.01.1942
P6960	218 Squadron – To Admiralty 22.05.1944
L8848 HA-J	Delivered via No.15 Squadron
L9264	Delivered via No.4 M.U 05.07.1940
L9298	Delivered via No.70 Squadron – O.T.U
L9306	Delivered via No.107 Squadron-218 Squadron-No.2 O.T.U
L9308	No details
L9327	To Abbotsinch/FE
L9381 HA-T	To No.614 Squadron
N3561	To No.17 O.T.U
N3562	To No.3 O.T.U
N3563	To No.13 O.T.U
N3573	To F.P.P

N3594	To No.82 Squadron
N3625	To No.13 O.T.U
N6183	delivered via No.107 Squadron–218 Squadron–No.107 Squadron
T1863	218/75 Wg/
T1864 HA-B	218 to 13 Grp
T1888	218/82 ditched off Malta returning from shipping sweep 19.6.41
T1929	218 collided with L9264 on training flight and crashed 18.8.40
T1987	107/218/203
T1988	107/218/608/203
T1990 HA-J	218 crashed at Guines, Pas-de-Calais, after raid on Bruges 23.8.40
T1996 HA-S	218/18/105 to Turkish AF 27.3.42
R3597	Via 10 M.U 28.06.1940. Hit Tree 13.07.1940
R3666	No Details. First Blenheim to be exchanged for the Vickers Wellington
R3673	Via No.139 Squadron. To No.21 Squadron